Peace Culture and Society

Published in Cooperation with the
International Peace Research Association

Peace Culture and Society

Transnational Research and Dialogue

EDITED BY

Elise Boulding, Clovis Brigagao, and Kevin Clements

Westview Press

BOULDER • SAN FRANCISCO • OXFORD

This Westview softcover edition is printed on acid-free paper and bound in library-quality, coated covers that carry the highest rating of the National Association of State Textbook Administrators, in consultation with the Association of American Publishers and the Book Manufacturers' Institute.

Published in 1991 in the United States of America by Westview Press, Inc., 5500 Central Avenue, Boulder, Colorado 80301, and in the United Kingdom by Westview Press, 36 Lonsdale Road, Summertown, Oxford OX2 7EW

Library of Congress Cataloging-in-Publication Data
Peace culture and society : transnational research and dialogue /
  edited by Elise Boulding, Clovis Brigagao, Kevin Clements.
    p. cm.
  ISBN 0-8133-1218-3
  1. Peace—Research—Developing countries. I. Boulding, Elise.
II. Brigagao, Clovis. III. Clements, Kevin.
JX1904.5.P393 1991
327.1′72′07201724—dc20   90-26353
                                                                  CIP

Printed and bound in the United States of America

The paper used in this publication meets the requirements
of the American National Standard for Permanence of Paper
for Printed Library Materials Z39.48-1984.

10   9   8   7   6   5   4   3   2   1

Contents

Preface
Kevin Clements   vii

Acknowledgments   xiii

INTRODUCTION
1. Introduction to the Book, *Elise Boulding*   3
2. A Challenge from Latin America,
    Adolfo Perez Esquivel   11

PART ONE   Common Security: General and Regional Approaches
Introduction to Part One, *Elise Boulding*   15
3. The Path to Common Security,
    Peri Pamir   17
4. The European Experience and Its Meaning for
    Central America, *Lothar Brock*   30
5. Zone of Peace or U.S. Strategic Primacy?
    The Politics of Security in the Caribbean,
    Dion E. Phillips   42
6. Peace Initiatives in Africa: Prospects and Realities,
    Peter Bushel Okoh   54
7. Common Security: Three Conflicts in the Middle East,
    Sanaa Osseiran   62
8. Common Security in the Asia-Pacific Region,
    Kevin Clements   77
9. Stable Peace Among Nations: A Learning Process,
    Kenneth E. Boulding   108

PART TWO   Cultures of Peace: From Violence to Nonviolence
Introduction to Part Two, *Elise Boulding*   117
10. Ten Bases for a Culture of Peace,
    Vicenc Fisas Armengol   119
11. From Violent to Nonviolent Discourse,
    Chaiwat Satha-Anand   124
12. The Earth as Peace Teacher,
    Patricia M. Mische   133

13. Conflict and Values: A Study of Grassroots
    Conflicts in India. *Ranjit Chaudhuri*   147
14. Citizenship and Rural Social Conflicts in Brazil,
    Alfredo Wagner Berno de Almeida   156
15. The Role of Social Conditioning in Male Violence,
    Ian M. Harris   166

PART THREE   Cultures of Peace: Voices from the Periphery
Introduction to Part Three, *Elise Boulding*   179
16. Human and Peoples' Rights in the Banjul Charter,
    Amechi Uchegbu   181
17. Development Through the Eyes of a Child,
    Georg Sorensen   196
18. Underdevelopment and the Oppression of Women: A
    Feminist Perspective, *Birgit Brock-Utne*   212
19. Women Under Dictatorship and Military Regime:
    The Case of Chile, *Maria Elena Valenzuela*   229

PART FOUR   The Agents of Peace Cultures
Introduction to Part Four, *Elise Boulding*   241
20. Creating Global Visions for Peace Movements,
    Chadwick F. Alger   243
21. A Paradigm for the New Peace Movements
    in Western Europe, *Katsuya Kodama*   261
22. Mass Communicators for Peace: Another Way,
    Kusum Singh   278
23. Research Network on the Churches' Role
    in Peace and Development Project Outline,
    Roger Williamson   293

Appendix on the International Peace Research Association   303
About the Editors and Contributors   304

Preface

At certain moments history turns on a hinge of new ideas.

E.P. Thompson[1]

1989 certainly represents one of those moments, yet, when IPRA held its 12th General Conference in August 1988, few of the participants imagined that within the space of 13 months popular social movements would topple socialist regimes in Poland, Czechoslovakia, Hungary and the German Democratic Republic.

Nobody imagined the Berlin wall or the wire fence between Hungary and Austria being dismantled. Even fewer contemplated the overthrow of the Ceaucescu regime in Rumania, pluralistic politics in Bulgaria, a single German economy or a reunited Germany.

No one knew much about the growing democracy movement in China, or if they did, they would have been unable to foresee its tragic denouement. The idea of the Baltic and other Soviet Republics withdrawing from the USSR would have seemed fanciful in 1988, and the political situation in Central America looked bleak. Namibia had not attained independence; Nelson Mandela was still in a South African prison and the bloody Iran-Iraq war was still in progress.

While there were signs of a slight thaw in the old cold war, there was continuing anxiety about the modernisation and deployment of medium-range nuclear missiles in Europe.

In 1988 it would have been considered quite surreal for a gathering of peace researchers to suggest that an imprisoned playwright would become president of Czechoslovakia, a musician prime minister of the German Democratic Republic and a dissident writer president of Hungary.

Yet, if something profound happened between 1988 and 1989, and history did turn on a hinge of new ideas, the ground had been prepared at least in part by the peace research community. The slow undramatic work of peace researchers, a sample of which appears in this book, has been an important element in new thinking about the cultural and political conditions necessary for stable peace, alternative means of achieving security, the catalytic role of popular movements in political and social transformation and the necessity to connect struggles for peace and justice. While excitement about events in Europe has drawn attention away from North-South issues, the peace research community has paid attention to such issues and will continue to do so.

The first year of the 1990s presents dangers, as well as opportunities. There are nationality conflicts in Eastern Europe, bloody and corrosive conflicts in the Middle East, apartheid splutters along; long suppressed ethnic and nationality disputes are emerging throughout the Soviet Union and in South and East Asia; seemingly intractable development problems continue to afflict Africa, Central and South America and the whole world is confronted with profound challenges to the global biosphere.

It is absolutely premature, therefore, to announce the "end of history." On the contrary, the current easing of East-West tension simply provides an opportunity to highlight issues that have long been obscured by superpower rivalry and the cold war. It provides a moment for the relatively wealthy European nations of the world (both East and West) to direct attention and energy towards North-South issues: the satisfaction of basic needs, the quest for social and economic justice - within and between nations - and the development of a new global security regime. While most political and economic attention is currently directed towards Europe, this focus will certainly not result in stable peace, justice or security unless there is an equal commitment to listen and respond to the Third World and to heal the damaged planet.

As these pages show, a number of peace researchers were, at least in part, imagining alternative futures and not just reviewing the past. Had even more attention been given to best case scenarios, it is possible that more of the unexpected events might have been envisaged in Rio in 1988. Peace researchers, along with other social scientists, have been challenged by events to develop analytic frameworks sufficiently large and flexible to encompass political surprises and currently implausible events. The often questioned element of idealism and utopianism in peace research, an element clearly present in the chapters dealing with the development of a peace culture, has been more than justified by recent events.

In fact, while few people in 1988 had the imagination and vision to see the specific events that took place in 1989, many of the ideas that constituted the "new hinge" had been articulated by peace researchers for many years.

The 1980 Palme Commission Report on Common Security, for example, long foreshadowed by the work of peace researchers, has become the basis of a new paradigm for international affairs. Although the Palme formulation was rather cautious and stressed disarmament and confidence building measures, the underlying principles gave considerable legitimation to the CSCE process in Stockholm and underpinned the discussions on conventional force reduction in Europe. In Moscow, Kremlin foreign policy advisors not only paying lip service to Common Security, but are making serious efforts to ensure that future

Soviet defense and security policies do not generate feelings of insecurity or actual insecurity for neighbors or potential adversaries. And in smaller more insignificant countries, Common Security assumptions legitimate the co-operative principles which size and vulnerability have long dictated as the most pragmatically sensible. It would not have been possible for these ideas to have gained currency, however, without peace researchers addressing the realities of the 1980s and devising both pragmatic and visionary alternatives.

The continued contact and collaborative activity among peace researchers of East and West Europe, begun at the very founding of IPRA in 1964, laid some of the fundamental groundwork for the dissolution of the old cold war. The iron curtain never isolated peace researchers from each other, any more than it isolated peace movements from each other. These continuing contacts resulted in the negotiation of a new consensus about appropriate ways of organising relations between different political and economic systems. This consensus is manifesting itself in the current discussions abut peace and security in the "new" Europe.

While East-West questions received less attention at Rio than at many earlier IPRA conferences, this was not because they were seen as unimportant but because of the Latin American setting and a desire to focus on Latin American and Third World issues. In discussion about these, a number of European participants were very concerned to work out what features of the new paradigm underlying East-West relations (e.g., how to promote confidence building, the development of stable security regimes, etc.) might be applicable to the Latin American, Asian and African contexts. Conversely there was a desire to work out how North-South issues might affect progress towards the generation of more creative East-West relations.

It is sometimes difficult for those who participate in conferences of peace researchers to gauge their effectiveness. The promise of peace research is ambitious. It is a scientific endeavour that tries to understand how to restore wholeness to fragmented and destructive relationships; to substitute nonviolent for violent resolution of dispute; to contemplate how nonsentimental love/care might be restored to relationships where these qualities have been driven out by fear and hatred; to move societies from reliance on threat and coercion (and a thriving weapons culture) to consensus and persuasion; and how to move from a militarised to a demilitarised world. It is concerned with which cultural, educational and political systems are conducive to these ends and whether any of these things are possible as long as the world is so radically divided into rich and poor. In all of this endeavour, peace researchers are dominated by the need to be analytic, visionary and realistic; to begin with the real world but not become mired in it.

There is always a tension within peace research between those who see their work in "purely" academic terms and those who desire to combine their academic work with prescription, policy formation and political action. This is a healthy tension because it forces the "pure" researcher to test the validity of her conclusions in relation to those who are involved in the difficult business of determining the applied implications of research. Conversely, wise policy makers or peace activists should explore the more abstracted pure research to determine what application it has for their own particular policy or movement dilemmas. The important point is to maintain a creative tension between both emphases because the particular demands of the 1990s are going to require peace researchers who have an ability to move between pure and applied research, between the ivy covered halls of academe and the concrete and glass of the economy and polity.

It was appropriate that the 1988 IPRA conference was held in Brazil since that is the country which reflects most of the major developmental, ecological and military dilemmas facing Third World countries. Being there highlighted many of the limitations of applying "Western" paradigms to Latin America's problems; but more importantly underlined the extent to which 'abstracted' peace research is only minimally helpful to those grappling with the quest for internal justice and the achievement of a peaceful role regionally and internationally. It was relatively easy for Western participants to fly to Brazil bringing conventional Western wisdom about world order, peaceful transformation, modernisation and the international economic order. It was much more difficult seeing how this might help Brazilian academics make sense of their own political economy; what significance it might have for religious and non-religious change agents in the slums of Sao Paulo, Rio de Janiero or Recife and whether anything that was said about weapons technology would make that much difference to the Brazilian armaments industry.

And yet, surely it meant something that people from all around the world gathered in Brazil to discuss such matters? What did it mean and how does it help the new hinge of ideas to take root in places remote from where many of them have been articulated?

First, meeting in a country that is experimenting with new ways to meet old problems of resource depletion, violence and poverty offers new insights to participants from other countries and continents. What do First World researchers have to learn from these experiences? A great deal.

Second, confronting unfamiliar realities provides an important mirror for determining whether any society is able to resist the global pressures which contradict the normative assumptions of peace research and which undermine the conditions that produce reasonably peaceful domestic environments. For those from other Third World countries, meeting in such places provides an opportunity for determining what it is that unites the poor peoples and poor nations of the world in their quest for peace and justice.

Third, meeting in Third World countries raises some important questions about global responsibility and the extent to which scholars individually and collectively have an obligation to ensure that what they do in their own milieux (academic, personal and political) has a positive rather than negative effect elsewhere. To what extent is the scholarly common discourse really common? Or, is it simply a reflection of broader economic, cultural and military dominance which is arrogantly assumed to be a common/consensually reached analytic framework?

Fourth, such gatherings raise fundamental questions about the extent to which issues of gender, class and ethnicity transcend national divisions and provide quite different analytic lenses for making sense of violence, nonviolence, violability, inviolability, security, insecurity, peaceful and unpeaceful processes.

Fifth, they are a salutary reminder of ways in which different national processes contradict global processes; which groups global communications serve and which remain unserved; which peoples are touched and which untouched by international non-governmental movements, and what connects grass roots movements in the periphery and the centre.

It is a challenge to peace researchers to see whether they might be able to engage in some best-case imaging of ways in which Europe, the Americas, Africa and Asia might benefit from the rapid changes that are occurring on each continent. It would be a terrible irony if the major consequence of the 1989 revolutions would be the economic and political transformation of certain parts of the world and relative stagnation elsewhere.

While it was not possible in 1988 to imagine some of the unique opportunities that exist in 1990, the contents of this book do provide new conceptual frameworks for peace research and specific examples of ways in which governments and peoples are building and might build on peaceable processes in different parts of the world. Whether these tendencies manifest themselves in a heightened stress on peace education or a renewed commitment to negotiations aimed at regional confidence building and disarmament, they are all having an impact on the development of cultures that stress nonviolence rather than violence and which provide spaces for diverse voices and new movements from the periphery to emerge.

Who knows exactly what "new hinge of ideas" will coalesce in the 1990s? One thing is clear, however, the need for peace research and peace researchers will not recede or diminish in importance. On the contrary, the relatively simple revolutions of Europe in 1989 have revealed much more fundamental problems that will require all the imagination, creativity and energy that the researchers can muster. The transnational dialogue that this book addresses is a beginning, not an end. Transnational dialogue involves a willingness on the part of all participants to listen deeply and attend to the deepest intellectual and social needs of those involved. It also requires a commitment to continue the dialogue in whatever ways seem appropriate. Peace researchers have a special responsibility to ensure that such processes never end because they lie at the heart of creative peacemaking.

Kevin Clements

Notes

1.   E.P. Thompson "History Turns on a New Hinge," *The Nation*, January 29, 1990, p. 120.

Acknowledgments

We are grateful to Luciane Souza Cesar and Joao Luiz P. Neves for their work in making the initial compilation of papers from the Rio conference from which the papers in this book were selected.

We are grateful to Lois Muller and Deborah Hailey for their careful reading and editing of this manuscript and to Ellen Wild and DeLinda Wunder for their painstaking work at the computer to produce camera-ready pages and to Marty Gonzales for patiently overseeing the massive task of moving from a loose collection of papers to the finished book.

The Editors
Elise Boulding
Clovis Brigagao
Kevin Clements

INTRODUCTION

1

Introduction to the Book

Elise Boulding

The International Peace Research Association is a community of peace researchers in 75 countries. The scholars included in this book of papers presented at IPRA's Twelfth Biennial Conference, held in Rio de Janeiro August 14-19, 1988, represent only 16 of these countries. Nevertheless, the diversity of perspectives from Latin America and the Caribbean, North America, Europe, Africa, Asia and the Middle East are all included here, as is the diversity of work in the field of peace research. As this book clearly demonstrates, peace researchers work in many arenas. Most obvious to the observer from outside the field is the work on security--which for the peace researcher has always been *common security*, well before the Palme Report popularized that term. Less obvious is the cluster of arenas that are here labeled "cultures of peace". This term has not been widely used in the peace research community, although many scholars have studied and taught about peace culture using other terminology. It has therefore been one of the special contributions to the field made by my predecessor as Secretary General of IPRA, Clovis Brigago of Brazil, to utilize the concepts of culture and communication as the main themes of the 12th General Conference. As you the reader progress through this book, you will discover how many of the processes, structures, perceptions and values associated with conflict, violence and peace development can be subsumed under the concept of culture.

Culture is about patterns: behavior patterns, imaging and perception patterns, structural and institutional patterns. Discovering the patterns liberates us from entrapment in them. It does this both by opening up the possibility of creative repatterning in the face of injustice and oppression and by renewing appreciation of those traditional patterns that have served the human species well. Awareness of the diversity of patterns also enriches our understanding of the many approaches to peace-building. The Rio conference was in a sense part of the inauguration of the UN World Decade for Cultural Development,

1988-1997. This Decade offers the First World an opportunity to look at, and learn from, the resources for cultural development in the Third World. Cultural development is the neglected underside of human and social development. Having devalued that underside in the course of industrialization, it is now time for us to go back and look at social patterning in a more thoughtful way.

While many of the articles that follow are about conflict, violence and oppression, central topics for the peace scholar, they are also about the development of creative lifeways that make violence and oppression obsolete. Conflict itself will never be obsolete, arising as it does from the basic individuality of human beings, and the uniqueness of individual perceptions, wants and needs that stem from the fact that no two human beings are alike. The practice of dealing with conflict by force, domination and oppression can however become obsolete. It is the primary goal of peace research to hasten that obsolescence. It is therefore appropriate that the book begins with the anguished reminder given at the opening plenary of the conference by Adolfo Perez Esquivel, Nobel Peace Prize Laureate and IPRA member, that the 1980s have been a lost decade, characterized by the predominance of force over reason. Rather than giving way to despair, Perez calls for defeating the culture of fear with human effort fueled by love. Peace researchers have something to say about how to do this, and that is what this book is about.

The book's four parts reflect the work of different IPRA Study Groups and Commissions. Part I, Common Security, includes papers given by members of the Weapons Technology and Disarmament Study Group, one of IPRA's most active Study Groups. Part II, Cultures of Peace: From Violence to Nonviolence, includes papers prepared by members of the Study Group on Nonviolence, Women and Militarism, and the Peace Education Commission. Part III, Cultures of Peace: Voices from the Periphery, includes papers by members of the Study Group on Human Rights and Development as well as from the Women and Militarism Study Group. Part IV, Agents of Peace Culture, includes papers by members of the Peace Movements Study Group, the Communications Study Group, and the new Religion and Conflict Study Group. The papers selected are representative of ongoing collaborative work among Study Group members. This collaborative activity represents the core of IPRA activity between biennial conferences. Some groups publish their own books, notably the Weapons Technology and Disarmament, and the Peace Movements groups.

Space limitations permit only a sampling of the work of each Study Group, and none of the lively discussions taking place around the papers can be reproduced here. However, the Editors hope that the nature and range of peace research inquiry as a transnational enterprise in the late 1980s--its theories, its normative orientation, its empirical research, its policy orientations and action concerns--are illuminated here.

Common Security

Reading what the authors in this section have to say about common security in the light of post-1988 events in Europe, one realizes that the basic problems remain the same. Peace has not broken out in Europe or anywhere else, but the signaling process has changed, and the value set on negotiation has probably increased. In Pamir's opening examination of security there is a very practical focus on elimination of the nuclear threat in order to achieve more long-run goals of common security. This focus serves to highlight the very serious problem that states are unwilling to depart from the traditional goal of dealing from positions of strength, and from the habit of defining power as brute force rather than as the capacity to act on the basis of the merits of the situation. She suggests ways to move from an adversary to a partner model in international relations, and ways to break the "deterrence habit".

The next three papers deal with common security in Latin America and the Caribbean. Brock draws on the experience of the European Conference on Security and Cooperation and the Helsinki Act to show how stable security arrangements are possible between states with different social systems. If regional pluralism can work in Europe, it should be able to work in Central America as well. The establishment of a Central American CSC could be a symbolic problem-solving act opening the door for concrete actions, and serve as a complement, not an alternative, to the OAS. Brock's paper needs to be kept in mind in reading Phillip's more pessimistic assessment of the proposal to create a zone of peace in the Caribbean put forward at CARICOM in 1979. Trends toward increased use of force in the area point away from such a development.

Turning to African security issues, Okoh points out that Africa has been helping fund the First World arms race through its costly debt payments, and is beginning to reconsider defense policies on the continent that increase vulnerability through increasing economic insecurity. In the years since the OAU tabled a resolution to make Africa a nuclear free zone in 1966, there have been a series of conferences from Nairobi and Lomé to Dar es Salaam, each of which has opened up significant initiatives for cooperation among African states. With confidence in the continued slow growth of these initiatives, Okoh sees an African Treaty of Tlatelolco as emerging in the future.

Three Middle Eastern conflicts: Israel-Palestinian, the Lebanese civil war, and the Iran-Iraq war, are considered by Osseiren in terms of the disastrous exacerbation of each conflict through superpower intervention. This intervention seriously hinders the necessary process of bringing all parties in each conflict into negotiations. Quoting the Chinese maxim, "Everyone in the land under heaven serving the public interest," she suggests a new way to think about public interest in this conflict-ridden part of the world.

Clements' analysis of complex trends in the Asia Pacific Region points both to the positive (integrating) and negative (environmentally exploitative) effect of market forces on common security. The theme of the distorting effects of great power intervention, and the need to pay attention to indigenous zone of peace initiatives, relates this analysis to the analysis of the Central American and African regions. The concluding paper in this section by Kenneth Boulding treats common security and stable peace as learning processes. For peace researchers the challenge is to identify the conditions under which such learning takes place.

What emerges strikingly from these papers is the contrast between the assumptions of the central significance of the "great powers" anywhere on the globe, with an accompanying reliance on force and short-term perspectives with regard to security, and the regional realities of creative initiatives that depend on the possibility of long-term evolution of structures of cooperative problem solving rather than the use of threat.

Cultures of Peace: From Violence to Nonviolence

Implicit in the previous section was the dependence of stable common security on a supportive cultural milieu. This section picks up on the processes involved in the evolution of these long-term structures of cooperation. Armengol begins by outlining the elements required for a peace culture in terms of human needs, education for change, new ways to perceive and respond to threat, and a recovery of understanding the significance of the local, the small-scale, and the individual. Satha-Anand moves on to discuss how our conception of problems and openness to alternative solutions are limited to the way in which we talk about our problems. Thus, the hegemony of violent discourse, making violence seem like appropriate human behavior, normalizes the use of force interpersonally and internationally. Satha-Anand describes a counter-discourse on nonviolence, and the role of the peace researcher in developing that discourse. Following Satha-Anand, Mische points the way to a shift from the *pax romana* to the *pax gaia* by utilizing the earth itself as teacher. The principles on which this approach to peace education are based include a deeper understanding of the processes of differentiation, and the inner workings of life--what Mische calls interiority--linked to community-building and creative problemsolving. Mische's approach to peace education provides valuable additional insight into the nature of the counter-discourse proposed by Satha-Anand.

Moving form the general to the specific, Chaudhuri and De Almeida describe the extremes of violence experienced at the grassroots level in rural India and Brazil. Chaudhuri shows how inter-caste conflict has intensified with the introduction of human rights and democratization values in villages, as competition for leadership upsets traditional panchayat practices. In the very different settings of rural Brazil, a similar derailing of programs for democratization has taken place. In this case a state land reform program has led to intensified violence, the reassertion of power by the old elite of landowners, and a breakdown of traditional violence-controlling social codes. The recommendations made by Chaudhuri and De Almeida for a long-run conscientization process, including training in negotiation, empowerment of weaker parties and a general raising of the level of social interaction skills, suggest some very specific hands-on applications of the principles and educational practices enunciated by Armengol, Satha-Anand and Mische. Both Chaudhuri and De Almeida are able to see signs of hope in otherwise grim situations.

The final paper in this section by Harris moves to the basic theme of male violence, and asks the interesting question, why are not *all* men violent, given that they are all socialized in cultures of male dominance? While his research is based on a U.S. male population, his findings have implications for every culture. Because men are socialized by female as well as male family and community figures, they carry far more complex and conflicting messages inside their heads while growing up than is generally realized. One can infer that a small shift in male socialization practices could have very large consequences. Taken together, the five papers in this section offer a theory and practice of cultural movement from violence to nonviolence with important policy implications for education, development and security planning.

Cultures of Peace: Voices from the Periphery

One of the most important findings from the past three decades of peace research relates to the power of the powerless. The reconceptualization of power itself as power *to* rather than power *over* has led to an examination of the kinds of competencies and skills to be found in the world's social, economic and political peripheries. The resources for social transformation lie as much in the peripheries as in the centers of the contemporary world. The four papers in this section provide exemplars of power as competence, building on the previous section to show how excluded populations can move a society from violence to nonviolence.

Uchegbu's paper reminds us that human rights were first defined in the context of Western traditions, and describes the struggle to redefine human rights in a way that authentically roots them in African traditions. The Banjul

Charter is the fruit of continuing efforts to make this adaptation from 1963 when the OAU was born to 1986, when the Charter came into force. The Charter refers to human and *peoples* rights, and enjoins the upholding of traditional values and of the family as the basis of society. Conflicts between African and Western concepts and laws continue, and some of them will puzzle readers from the West with no grounding in the traditions under discussion. Yet, as indicated by the Indian and Brazilian experience of the intensification of village conflict along with democratization described in the previous section, creative development of human rights thinking in each cultural context is necessary to achieve a peace characterized by justice and social integrity.

In power terms, children are the periphery of all peripheries, the ultimate in excluded populations, on all continents. Yet all human and social development depends on the health, education and welfare of the world's children, and Sorensen proposes a Treatment of Children Index (TCI) to measure that critical aspect of each society's well being. Sorenson's emphasis is on placing children on the development planners' agenda. However, the fact of children's critical economic role in the Third World (and more in the First World than most people realize), and the fact that children comprise a substantial part of many Third World armies, makes them a resource and repository of knowledge and skills that should be taken account of in the same way that other peripheries should be taken account of. Here is clearly a field to which peace researchers must pay more attention.

Women come a close second to children in terms of peripheralization, and indeed there are still societies in which they have the status of children, in law. The parallel to the TCI index offered by Sorenson would be the TWI--the Treatment of Women Index. But as Brock-Utne points out, the problem of the relations of women and men in society runs much deeper than measures of equality. It has to do with the very nature of human interdependence, with the falsity of dominance relations, with the liberation of the full range of human potentials into the social order. In the world of the future, center-periphery relations will be replaced by partnership--partnership of women and men, children and adults, partnership of all kinds of identity groups. Paternalism as a role model for human relations can only hold back human and social development.

Valenzuela's analysis of how the female periphery took on its own life during military dictatorship in Chile is a fine case study of the development of competence in problem solving under extraordinarily limiting conditions. Women used their forced peripheralization into traditional family roles (counter to earlier trends of increased labor force and social participation) as a springboard to political action from the very sphere that was to remove them from politics. The economic crises they faced as women heads of household generated thousands of popular survival organizations and led to the development of a significant political voice for women.

The significance of these voices from the periphery--the periphery of the South, the periphery of childhood, the periphery of womenkind, lies in the fact that each set of voices arises from marginalized cultures that have generated strengths, skills, imagination and capacity for action that are critical to the social transformation of societies from violence to peaceableness.

The Agents of Peace Culture

The voices from the periphery described in the previous section are of course in their own way agents of peace culture. In terms of specific identifiable contributions to this new nonviolent culture, however, it is important to look, as we do in this section, at social movements, at the mass media and at the more specific elements in communities of faith. Alger looks at peace movements as part of the larger phenomenon of social movements, and finds that the broader definition of peace, inclusive of institutions, structures, lifestyles and values, has given a visioning quality to peace movements without sacrificing the commitment to local action for global ends. The sense of a common foe--the old patriarchal, competitive, anti-environmental order, the "Dominant Social Paradigm"--animates a great variety of movement groups united by their practical idealism in opting for "micro practice, macro thinking."

While Alger's observations can fit a number of different cultural settings, Kodama offers a study of a specific Western European paradigm for peace movements anchored in a specific middle class group composed largely of women and students (with higher status men in the prime of life notably absent). The clarity of self-identity as Europeans rather than as citizens of particular states that characterize these peace activists of the mid-1980's gives us clues about the groundwork that was being laid for the emerging Europe of 1990. Kodama is describing a silent revolution of values towards post-materialism. Declaring a pox on both European houses, capitalist and communist, these activists define themselves as world citizens committed to a "green" lifestyle, to a feminist, localist, participation-oriented peace culture. They represent only a small part of the larger peace movement described by Alger, but a highly educated, highly articulate part.

Peace movements generally think of the media as a set of powerful forces representing major obstacles to change by their refusal to report movement activities. Singh, a communications scholar, offers a surprising analysis that turns such views upside down. She suggests that the media are not as powerful as we think, and that movements on the other hand are much more powerful than we give them credit for. By emphasizing the importance of face-to-face contact and local networking, whether it is Gandhi walking across India, political campaigners going from door to door in an election campaign, or underground networks in repressed areas from occupied Norway during World War II to the Druze in the Golan Heights today, Singh reminds us that human interaction can achieve what the media can never achieve. Challenging peace researchers to look at all forms of communication, not just the media, she herself chooses to focus on what she calls "bottom-sideways" communication at all levels, not just up-down information flows.

Churches of all denominations, and communities of faith from all religious traditions, have nurtured and served as agents for two contrasting cultures throughout history: that of the warrior, and that of the peacemaker. The closing decades of the twentieth century are seeing a new mobilization of communities of faith in the face of mounting dangers to the survival of the human species, in order to recover and update the teachings and practices of the peace culture. Williamson, convener of IPRA's new Study Group on Religion and Conflict, began at Rio the process of creating a global network of religious activists to do just this. The closing piece in this section, part of a longer memorandum prepared for the Rio meeting, is included as an example of how a new world network starts. The process of establishing partner relations, developing a common discourse and shared theoretical understandings, establishing a research agenda, and providing for carrying it out, are challenging tasks that face peace researchers in every field of endeavor.

The papers included in this book, representing the work of a number of IPRA's Study Groups and Commissions, are but a small part of the total number of papers given at Rio. They represent the craft of the peace researcher working in the fields of disarmament and security studies, peace education, conflict resolution, communication, nonviolence, human rights, feminist theory, ecological security and social movements. By the choice of papers focussing on common security and the relationship between peace culture and security, we hope to have shown how peace research moves from theory to the study of process to practice. Violence moves fast, peace evolves slowly. By examining some of the most difficult and violent aspects of twentieth century reality on five continents, the scholars represented in this book have uncovered peace potentials in the most unlikely situations. While indicating the need for further research, as scholars must always do, they have also shown new ways to approach the task of peace building, and provided the basis for renewed confidence in the human capacity to develop a more humane and peaceful world order.

A Challenge from Latin America

Adolfo Perez Esquivel

The challenges that the battle for peace poses for us are innumerable. Each day we discover new obstacles, yet the peoples of the world do not yield in their endeavors. For this reason we are assembled; to provide answers, hopefully many answers, to the sad reality in which we now survive.

I will refer especially to my continent, Latin America, and to its present situation--to the great problems that we now confront which force the peoples of this region of the world to swing between anguish and hope.

Hunger, alienation, the violation of human rights, military dictatorships, and conditioned democracies are without a doubt elements that, with their effects and causes, make more difficult the attainment of a stable peace on the continent. Foreign debt, with its burden of injustice and the movement of pillage to the First World, converts the impoverished Latin American countries into exporters of capital in exchange for indispensable resources, not for a comfortable life, but rather for mere subsistence. It is not possible to avoid relating this new form of slavery to the fortunes of millions of Latin Americans that cannot even satisfy their most basic necessities. This violence takes place daily in the region to which I am referring and not only to Latin America: foreign debt is an aggression against the entire Third World.

If we analyze how this debt has continued to accumulate in the accounts of the debtor nations, it is not difficult for us to recognize the relation of this debt to another factor that openly acts against the peace of the world, the arms race.

The billions of dollars spent on the purchase of armaments could alleviate the hunger of the Third World in a very short time. These billions in loans, received with the objective of supplying countries with lethal instruments, represent a good percentage of what today the people must pay to the creditors of the developed world.

Perhaps one way of solving both problems with one solution would be the compromise of the creditor nations to destine a growing percentage of their armament expenses to development programs for underdeveloped countries. This does not seem an absurd suggestion, when in Latin America thousands of children die every minute, some due to a lack of nourishment and others to the repression caused by militarized societies where the life of the people rapidly loses its value.

The decade now ending leaves us with an ominous balance in regards to life and peace. For many it is a lost decade with setbacks suffered by various people. The eighties were characterized by the predominance of force over reason, imposed by the military dictatorships. For me, and I consider myself a man of hope, these years have also been an education, at a horrific price. This has been a decade in which the peoples of the Latin American continent and those of us who work for peace have arrived at very serious conclusions.

The restricted democracies, a product of these years of terror, today condition the life of the people through legal and political mechanisms that look to maintain an order imposed by the dictatorships, and involve crimes against humanity. *Lese-humanity* today is law in many of the Latin American countries and a fact of life in those where it has not been legislated. Such an order abandons to oblivion all the damage, loss and terror lived by the peoples of the region in the past years.

In my mind, knowledge of the truth and the application of justice together are essential to achieve a true peace. I, like Pope Paul VI, consider Peace to be the fruit of Justice. Therefore, justice cannot be applied only to the few; it must also apply to those whose human rights have been violated. This, it seems to me, is presently of primary importance.

There are elements such as these that should incite us to struggle ever more decidedly to eradicate the violence, and its principle causes, that impede peace among peoples. We must struggle courageously to defeat the culture of fear, of violence and of injustice. It is an arduous task, to which we must give all the wealth of love required in order to construct a different history.

The peoples of the world have very diverse origins, cultures, languages and religions. Their problems and priorities are likewise diverse. Nevertheless, the clamor for Peace is unanimous, and in it coincide all or at least the majority of men and women of the planet who want to see their children grow up in a world not adverse to them where all enjoy a free and dignified life.

I leave you with a brotherly greeting of PEACE and WELL-BEING.

PART ONE

COMMON SECURITY:
GENERAL AND REGIONAL APPROACHES

Introduction to Part One

Elise Boulding

Although "common security" is a phrase widely used, as a concept it remains difficult to understand. Pamir highlights these difficulties for us by pointing out the contrast between the intellectual understanding of security, as global and indivisible, and the highly charged preoccupation of nation states with nuclear-based national security. By distinguishing between power as brute force (the use of which is a sign of weakness) and power as skill, confidence and the capacity to act, Pamir shifts the security argument from threat to confidence-building, from bluster to competence. Her emphasis on competence, patience, and the willingness to ride with ups and downs and take risks for peace instead of for war, sets the theme for this section.

Brock, in his application of the Palme Commission Report on Common Security and of the European experience in confidence-building to Central America, makes it very clear that there are many ups and downs in such processes. He likens the current deteriorating situation in Central America to an earlier deterioration in East-West relations in Europe. He also points out that patience, tactical adjustments during setbacks and the slow development of new competencies gradually drew the European process from purely symbolic to substantive problem-solving. Regionalization is the key, Brock believes. He sees the same process happening region by region around the world, however slowly.

When Phillips describes the same process for the Caribbean, the tone is more somber, the awareness of the downs after the ups and the role of the intervention-prone U.S. in those downs more intense. The concept of the zone of peace only seems viable on the basis of a longer time perspective than Phillips is dealing with. Okoh, looking at the struggles of the Organization of African Unity to declare Africa a Zone of Peace, inclines to Phillips' view that regional efforts are at the mercy of outside intervention. Yet, Okoh also sees the slow development of increasing regional competence and autonomy in spite of the negative impact of the arms race on African development.

Osseiren, looking at the conflict-torn region of the Middle East, notes that most of the current developments are extremely negative; but that nevertheless, the resources for problem-solving are present in the traditional cultures of the region. The recovery of internal autonomy and competence in the face of outside pressures requires time, but will, Osseiren feels, eventually take place.

This theme of an underlying development of autonomy and competence in the face of violent ups and downs is documented by Clements with a detail that deserves careful reading, for the South West Pacific and South East and East Asia regions. The steady increase in problem-solving behavior over time takes place in spite of heavy interventions by the major powers. While there are many problems, and the integrative power of market forces brings its own dangers, the long-term future is promising.

Kenneth Boulding goes to the heart of the issue of how common security and its accompaniment, cooperative problem-solving behavior, develop, by asking: What are the conditions for social learning? While his examples are Eurocentric, his point that we need to study this kind of learning even as it is happening, in order to be able to extend that learning process, is an important message for peace researchers.

The Path to Common Security

Peri Pamir

Introduction

The concept of common security emerged in response to deepening anxiety over the perceived implications to world peace and security of continued reliance on the strategy of nuclear deterrence. The imperative for other forms of security[1] rests on the firm conviction that nuclear weapons have ceased to play any viable political or military role.[2] The so-called 'threat of mutual destruction' is regarded as having lost its 'credibility' as the ultimate guarantor of 'nuclear peace,' the main problem arising from the constant attempt to counter mutual vulnerability through offensive military build-ups suggesting first-strike postures. What these have done is to create a situation which has effectively moved *beyond* the generally presumed stage of a symmetric or stable balance of military power. Because of the mutually reinforcing link between the spiral of arms competition and the ensuing cycle of mutual insecurity, deterrence is increasingly being perceived by observers on both sides as an offensive and terrorizing strategy which poses inherent dangers of failure, instability and risk of predominantly inadvertent nuclear war. Magnified by the pace of technological military advancements, enhanced fear and mistrust, and a concomitant deterioration in political relations, these destabilizing elements have upset the delicate equilibrium of nuclear deterrence by rendering the attendant risk of mutual devastation unacceptably high.

There is also the obvious moral dimension associated with the policy of seeking security by resorting to nuclear terror. For peace and security, in their complete and desired sense, imply not only guarantees of permanent absence of conflict, but also freedom from the terror to which the constant threat of nuclear confrontation aspires, and on which nuclear deterrence is based. Given this aspiration, the threat to use nuclear weapons constitutes the purest form of terrorism. For in this case, not only does the nuclear menace hold *the entire world* hostage to the fear of total nuclear catastrophe, but it also denies people their fundamental right to choice in their future. Furthermore, in seeking to create fear by power and to coerce conduct by fear, which is tyranny, nuclear terrorism constitutes the most blatant instrument of the strategy of domination. A further liability is created by the dangerous precedent set for other countries in the world by the major powers' continued reliance on nuclear arms as an essential instrument of national security. The pursuit of nuclear deterrence and the arms race thus makes a mockery of attempts to forestall global nuclear proliferation, by strengthening the perception among other potential contenders that nuclear weapons constitute a necessary and legitimate device for safeguarding national security interests.

In view of the dilemmas, uncertainties and risks connected with the present system of security, national consensus on nuclear defense policies in many countries has broken down. Public dissatisfaction on this issue has been particularly manifest in densely militarized Europe. Such reactions suggest a progressive erosion of public faith in the hypothetical claim, oft-invoked by Western governments to justify continued reliance on nuclear strategy, that the maintenance of post-war peace is largely attributable to the existence of nuclear weapons. This argument--or myth--rests on the assumption that the mutual threat of war has enabled the big powers to exercise great caution in avoiding direct military confrontation. The emergence of important and increasingly more powerful peace movements attests to the growing view that far from assuring survival, nuclear weapons in fact constitute a fundamental threat to it. They also testify to the awareness that since nuclear war would not respect frontiers and would not be containable, questions of nuclear defense concern not only the nuclear powers or the governments, but *all* peoples. Domestic political pressure has consequently had an impact in obliging opposition parties and even elected governments in Europe and elsewhere to adopt postures favoring policies of nuclear disengagement. Even though the vision of a nuclear-free world is still a remote one, the manifestation of widespread international concern about peace and security has necessitated serious consideration of alternative approaches to defense which offer a more viable and sound basis for both national and global security. Any attempt to seek solutions to the present problem will, however, have to be preceded by a fundamental reassessment of what exactly constitutes security in the contemporary nuclear age.

In this vein, the advocates of a new mode of political thinking on security policy rightly argue that if the present danger is to be reversed, it is above all imperative for the nuclear power states--and especially the two superpowers--to recognize that security in the nuclear age has become indivisible; that it can no longer be gained unilaterally, or on the basis of a zero-sum ordering of military power. Since conflicts can no longer be resolved on the basis of military force, it is widely admitted that the only possible means to assure security--indeed, survival--is to move away from confrontational postures towards greater political accommodation.

The philosophy of common security embraces this logic. The full meaning of the term as used here describes both an *objective* and a *strategy*. Ultimately, it seeks to ensure those conditions whereby nuclear--and, eventually, any kind of war--will not be started, and consists of a process which aims in the first instance at addressing both the military and political sources of conflict and insecurity. In terms of strategy, the underlying objective of common security is to establish a process of mutual restraint and cooperation between states based on a common perception of their mutual dependence and shared interest in reducing the threat of nuclear war. Such an approach would flow from the mutual appreciation that the consequences of nuclear deterrence have ultimately overridden and overtaken any justification it may have had at the outset.

Eliminating the threat of nuclear war would, however, represent the *primary*, not the *ultimate* aspiration of common security. Its longer-term and more comprehensive version would presumably envisage a global order where the threat of all types of violence and conflicting has receded and been replaced by stability and cooperation. Although the two meanings will clearly overlap in certain instances, in this paper the term 'common security' will more frequently than not be equated with the 'primary' goal. This is based on the reasoning that in order to attain global security, states initially have to reach a realization of their common interests which, in the first instance, involves the reduction and eventual elimination of the nuclear peril.

Although this conception of security yields easily enough to moral approbation, the question of translating it into political reality is a different matter altogether. This paper will limit its scope to a preliminary analysis of what such a policy would mean and imply in political and perceptual terms. The discussion on common security will be preceded by a closer look at some aspects of the 'security dilemma' engendered by continued dependence on the strategy of nuclear deterrence. We will then proceed by identifying certain situations which either help or hinder the development of a common security process. Specific reference to the situation in Europe will be made where appropriate.

Security Dilemma

One of the major flaws of the doctrine of nuclear deterrence is that it still operates on the basis of traditional concepts of power. This is generally understood as the ability to deal from a position of strength. Quite apart from the fact that this definition is no longer tenable in the era of relative 'nuclear parity,' it is also, more significantly, riddled with inherent weaknesses. 'Power' that must constantly be struggled for and aggressively backed by military prowess is not power, but rather brute coercive force. To make this correlation is in fact a contradiction in terms. *Real* power derives from a sense of inner strength and confidence which endows the bearer with the capacity to act and implement on the basis of natural and proven merits. "Insofar as one's capacity to act must be supported by force, one is, to that degree, powerless, not powerful. One is relying on something other than power."[3] It is interesting to observe in this connection, that the 'macho image,' as characterized, for instance, by a sense of grandeur, arrogance, toughness or self-aggrandizement, whether in individual or nations, represents a conscious or unconscious response to the need to cover up or compensate for inner fears and insecurities through an inflated projection and assertion of self. Far from being a portrayal of strength or confidence therefore, such an attitude actually reflects a deep-rooted sense of impotence and a lack of self-confidence at a deeper level of consciousness.

Since myths generally tend to outlive reality, strength or power is still widely confused with force and offensive posturing. This is because we still live in an age where each state feels obliged to display its ability and willingness to wage war in defense of what it regards as its vital national interests. Military strength is seen as a symbol of this resolve, and lulls nations into a false sense of security. It also reflects the false premise that producing a consciousness of strength, the attempt to gain military advantage over the adversary creates a "consciousness of the strength of other nations and a sense of fear." Fear begets suspicion and distrust which, in turn, feed the rationale for more rearmament.[4] The psychological dynamics of the perceptual conflict which drives the arms race are thus nourished by reciprocal misperceptions of intent, which often lead to an overestimation of the other side's hostility (worst-case assessment). Since both sides respond to the same imperatives, attempts to assure one's own security by seeking damage-limiting or war-fighting capabilities for use 'if deterrence fails' thus becomes counterproductive and self-defeating mainly because the technological dimensions of the arms race heightens the dangers of a breakdown of deterrence. The end result is a constantly recurring cycle of self-induced insecurity, commonly known as the 'security dilemma,' and a dynamic arms race as states strive in vain to overcome their mutually perceived vulnerability.

Other consequences of the 'security dilemma' relevant to the discussion of a common security programme include the following:

1. The more the diversion of precious human and material sources from the urgent requirements of socio-economic development to military security, the more vulnerable a society becomes to threats of economic erosion and social disruption.[5]

2. An escalating arms race also changes the character of the societies within the participating countries. The emphasis placed on war preparations and high technology will have the effect of:
   - endowing the technological revolution with a strong military bias by curtailing non-military industries and diverting scientific and engineering talent to military applications;
   - increasing the power and influence of the military-industrial complex;
   - subordinating politics to the interests of militarism;
   - enhancing the power and authority of the state in matters related to defense and security, thereby inducing a corresponding reduction in the participation of the citizen in decisions affecting his/her destiny;
   - creating a military culture or a militarized society which threatens to undermine the bases of the democratic governing process as well as the more humanitarian aspects of social and cultural life.

3. The perpetuation of a constant state of tension and hostility towards the adversary, administered through a process known as 'de-humanization' (i.e., where the human characteristics of the enemy are denied) postpones any real commitment to solving basic problems "because it automatically eliminates the expectation, and thus the possibility, of their being seen as capable of positive human responses."[6] Negative images of the adversary kept alive through government propaganda, the media, and to varying degrees, also through the educational system, seek to justify and reinforce existing attitudes in the public and international mind, and thus "reduce...pressures to undertake the more complex tasks that would be required for real understanding and reconciliation."[7]

4. Another problem concerns the loss of sovereignty rights for allied states which shelter under the nuclear umbrella. The perception of having traded control over its own destiny to the vagaries of superpower politics, in exchange for so-called 'protection' at the risk of self-annihilation, has left Western Europe deeply divided and uncertain about its nuclear involvement.

Common Security

While all states agree on the imperative to avert nuclear holocaust, there is nevertheless disagreement on the policy that would best serve this purpose. What is lacking in other words is a common perceptual appreciation of the objective realities of the nuclear age, and a proper understanding of the changes in individual national attitudes and policies required if peace is to be placed on more stable foundations. The most essential factor in this scenario is the recognition that since the security and existence of the nations of the world are interdependent, the avoidance of war, and particularly nuclear conflict, becomes a common and international responsibility. As peace cannot be obtained through military rivalry, "it must be sought through a tireless process of negotiation, rapprochement and normalization with the goal of removing mutual suspicions and fear" between nation states.[8] Common security is thus seen as an attempt to transcend traditional concepts of security, generally confined to purely domestic considerations of national self-interest, to encompass a broader meaning where the principal threat to one's security is perceived as coming not so much directly or, only, from the enemy itself, but from the dynamics of the conflictual situation which both sides have helped to create.

Translating this into political reality would, in the first instance, require mutual recognition and acknowledgement that the imperative to prevent a nuclear war constitutes a *top* priority security objective for *all* the states concerned, and that its achievement requires a coordinated approach. The immediate problem arises, therefore, where perceptions differ with respect to effective strategy, which also inevitably affects the outcome. In the case of Europe, for instance, common approach becomes difficult when the Soviets advocate nuclear disarmament; NATO and the U.S. stubbornly cling to deterrence; while the Europeans generally call for a revival of detente as the most effective means for securing peace in the nuclear age. Presumably these discrepancies reflect something about individual threat perceptions. The Soviets argue that the main threat comes from nuclear weapons; for NATO and the U.S. it comes from the USSR; while for most of the Europeans, it comes from a combination of both these factors; which is why they see detente as the most effective strategy for neutralizing these dangers, as well as a means of lessening their security dependence on the U.S.

It is interesting to observe that out of the three positions, the NATO/U.S. one appears to provide the clearest case of a behaviour pattern known as 'cognitive dissonance.' Applicable to both individuals and nations, this theory refers to the psychological 'denial of reality,' whereby new evidence is automatically assimilated or forced to conform with a pre-existing perception. Theorists argue that any change in self-perceived reality (e.g., regarding a threat factor) is unlikely to occur unless there is overwhelming evidence to the contrary, or if there is a reassessment of priorities induced by these or other factors.[9] The Gorbachev arms control proposals might ultimately have precisely this effect on Western European consciousness, by eventually forcing a reappraisal of prevailing threat perceptions and, hence, of the military measures taken in response to them.

How Can Common Security Be Achieved: The Case of Europe

Striving for common security, as we have seen, means striving for security with and not against the potential enemy. The process, however, of accepting the transformation of a presumed adversary into an indispensable partner requires, a fundamental change in modes of thinking. It would involve an explicit acknowledgement of mutual dependency, and acceptance of the reality that national security can *only* be achieved to the extent the adversary is made to feel more, and not less, secure. It would follow therefore, that any unilateral steps exercised in recognition of this principle should be perceived as being in the fundamental interests of the side taking it, and not be regarded as a 'concession.' This attitude would in turn incorporate the understanding that any independent measures taken would reduce the danger equally for both sides.

Recognition that security cannot be obtained by assuming provocative confrontational postures also involves a commitment to establishing some form of balance or equilibrium between the major military blocs, which takes into consideration geographic, historic, strategic and other circumstances. In Europe, this would involve attempts aimed at alleviating NATO concerns related to real and perceived asymmetries in the geographic as well as conventional force characteristics of the two sides, as these provide the main justification for the Western Alliance's continued reliance on nuclear deterrence.

Given this objective, the concept of 'non-provocative defense' offers the most effective path to mutual security by creating the necessary prerequisites for it. Namely, it meets the two most essential requirements of national defense and security by integrating a credible conventional defense posture with a nonthreatening one. It thus offers a possibility for reversing present NATO perception that conventional forces alone are not adequate providers of security, and hence, the opportunity for ultimately removing the rationale for nuclear deterrence. Moreover, by proposing to reduce the confrontational and destabilizing aspects of conventional forces in Europe (i.e., to a level consistent with crisis stability), it also promises to diminish the chances of outbreak of conventional and, by extension, also nuclear war, at least within a European context.

Other complementary measures for reducing the nuclear threat and starting the common security process in Europe include the Palme Commission's recommendation for the establishment of a battlefield nuclear weapon-free zone (NWFZ) in central Europe, eventually extending to the northern and southern regions of the continent. Recognizing the interdependence between political and military factors, the Report maintained that "even the process of beginning to negotiate such limitations... would reduce political tension," and would thus pave the way for increased political collaboration.[10]

Since the roots of East-West confrontation are more deeply conditioned by political perceptions than they are by strictly military matters, a main ingredient to stabilizing the security situation in Europe would be through the undertaking of a systematic process of political confidence-building. Steps taken towards this end would need to address the political sources of individual as well as collective insecurity, stemming from prevailing threat perceptions, whether real or imaginary, since these provide the ultimate justification for existing defense doctrines and postures. The progressive elimination of fear, distrust and hostility between the two superpowers through these and other measures would no doubt constitute a major step in the right direction. Smaller countries in East and West could also play a valuable role by enhancing confidence and trust amongst themselves; Bulgaria and Turkey or Greece and Turkey, for instance, would be good candidates for such a task. The idea would be the cultivation of a political attitude that seeks to transcend Cold War (and in some cases, also historical) passions and divisions, fostered through the medium of increased political, diplomatic, economic, scientific, cultural and other exchanges which emphasize common values, concerns and interests. The ultimate aim might be the creation of a more integrated European political structure which allows the continent to exercise greater control over its own defense, and to have a more influential role as an entity on the world political scene.

Other basic guidelines for getting the common security process underway include the conclusion of a comprehensive test ban treaty, which constitutes a primary step towards minimizing the role of nuclear strategies. A similar intent would also be expressed by the universal renunciation of the threat of use of military force as an instrument for resolving disputes between nations--an obligation incorporated in the U.N. Charter. The main significance of a no-first-use declaration on the part of NATO would be to underscore the purely deterrent value of nuclear weapons in the service of an overall policy designed to maximize the prevention of nuclear war. By enabling NATO to abandon the nuclear crutch, such a step would also help to rectify the distortions which have occurred in conventional and nuclear force postures on the continent.

Finally, it is clear that given the technological and military potential of the major military powers, the main task and responsibility for initiating and sustaining efforts in this direction would have to be assumed by them. This need not, however, exclude the participation of allied and other neutral states in undertaking independent or joint initiatives which underscore their concern about the problem of nuclear war. The Five Continents Peace Initiative calling for a comprehensive test ban, and the bold actions taken by the New Zealand government on anti-nuclear policies would represent endeavors of this kind. European correlations of such actions would include the measures taken or attempted by governments in Greece, Spain, Portugal and Denmark towards policies of superpower/nuclear disengagement.

Other complementary processes necessary for the successful achievement of a common security policy include the following:

1. Moving away from patriarchal structures and statist definitions of power which associate security with military prowess, and power with instruments of high technology and violence.

2. Linked to the above, the power and role of the state in relation to the determination of military policies should be actively challenged and reduced, essentially by making it constitutionally more accountable and responsive to societal pressures. In fact, since the state is not likely to be the innovator in areas where the sources of its own power are concentrated, the most likely catalyst for change in the present military/security system will be the pressure that public and other interest groups will bring to bear on their respective governments. Such processes, which are already considerably under way, can be strengthened through a vast campaign of education, debate and public participation.

3. Insofar as the militarization of high technology is a symbol and expression of state prestige and power, it creates dangerous illusions of potency and a propensity for seeking technical solutions to political problems. The SDI is a perfect example of this tendency and, in this sense, can be said to represent an 'unconscious escape' on the part of the U.S. administration from its inability to formulate a rational approach to the challenge of nuclear war. It also reinforces the potentially hazardous illusion that safety in the nuclear age is more readily available through independent action than through cooperation. More importantly, however, the SDI pursuit threatens to escalate the arms race into a new and dangerous phase both in space and on Earth, thereby further distancing the prospects for alleviating the security problem in the nuclear age. What would be needed to reverse this process is a different technology culture whose objective is to harness available technology in the service of humanity, and not in the exaltation and pursuit of instruments of its possible destruction. The recent Chernobyl and Challenger disasters served as tragic reminders of the limits

and risks of high technology. A first step would entail purging high technology of its currently militaristic tendencies and using it towards the *achievement* of a common policy (e.g., increased technical cooperation in the field of mass communication and information services).

4. What common security implies in the human and societal sense is a global situation where diversity and difference are allowed to exist without invoking fear and resistance. The endeavor to try and rise above or, in another sense, to accept such differences would thus enable mankind to realize the full potential of its human richness and creativity, whose essence, in fact, lies in its diversity. On the national level, an attempt to give the enemy a human identity which people could relate to more easily would also remove one of the principal obstacles to the successful development of a common security policy.

5. Lastly, it is evident that the role of the media in shaping the above areas of social, political and perceptual change is an extremely crucial one. Its main responsibility in this sense lies not in relaying the language of power, but in providing the public with a critical and objective assessment of facts which will better enable it to grasp the complexities of reality.

Conclusion

The concern for alternative forms of security is easily understood when one considers that the deterrence doctrine is "a theory based on the interface between logical opposites. It connects war prevention with the capacity to fight wars."[11] Since nuclear deterrence and the arms race go hand in hand, the buildup of ever more sophisticated and dangerous weapons continues unabated, while prevention of their use is sustained at the risk of self-annihilation. Far from being a solution to the problem of threat of nuclear war, deterrence in fact exacerbates this danger by increasing military instability, political tension and, consequently, also mutual fear, hostility and mistrust.

It is clear that 'security' at such high cost cannot be maintained indefinitely. The highly destructive and inherently uncontainable power of modern nuclear weaponry has completely altered not only the scale of warfare, but the very concept of war itself, which has become unthinkable. While most governments which participate either directly or indirectly in the nuclear system continue to deny its inherent risks, a large part of the public in these and in other countries around the world have become conscious of the fact that times have changed. A security policy predicated on mutual threat and mutual fear of war is no longer perceived as being compatible with the goal of peace. Widespread international manifestation of such concerns have raised hopes that the political force of popular insight will provide the main driving force behind efforts to reverse the present concern, eventually forcing governments to come to terms with the nuclear reality.

It is therefore of greatest importance that the momentum of this period be maintained. If nations are to become party to a common security policy, a primary prerequisite would have to be the de-mystification or re-humanization of the enemy image at all levels of society and international exchange. There has, in recent years, been a tremendous flow of creative energy released by an almost explosive awakening of a hitherto dormant populace to the dangers of nuclear-based security, and the traditional authority of the state in making decisions which affect their lives. This prerogative is now being challenged as many feel that the state has shaken their faith and confidence in its own credibility by allowing the situation to reach the present critical level. The main dynamic for change comes from an inner conviction of the urgent need for citizens to take over responsibility for their own destinies from the state. It also arises from the awareness that their action could have an impact by eventually forcing governments to respond, and therefore, they have to act. It is in this source of popular rebellion and civic consciousness of a shared fate that lies the power to change the present situation. What is therefore crucial is to be able to harness the creative potential of these energies constructively, and to channel them towards the meeting of objectives that are in everyone's interest.

Common security offers a framework for this by providing the organizing principles for joint efforts to achieve common goals perceived as being in the common interest; namely, to reduce the risk of nuclear catastrophe by lowering the political tensions and the military/technological instabilities which make war more likely, and to alleviate the socio-economic burdens of the arms race. Most importantly, it recognizes that mutual susceptibility to the danger of nuclear war can be overcome *only* through coordinated action and the gradual cultivation of mutual trust. The possibilities of initiating such a policy and of finally moving towards a period of greater global peace and stability have unexpectedly been brought within reach by the bold proposals put forth in recent years by the Eastern bloc. Despite the prevailing sense of skepticism, there is also a distinct realization that if grasped, this opportunity could open the way to dramatic breakthroughs in arms reduction. A major part of the hesitation, as one political analyst has observed, derives from the fact that the "West [has] focussed on an exaggerated Soviet threat and its own vulnerabilities, thus blinding itself to the evidence that the Soviets have such serious interest in reducing nuclear arsenals that they are willing to make major concessions to reach an agreement."[12] All the same, the high level of expectation created by these developments in public and political circles around the world, testifies to the widespread aspiration to replace existing readiness to accept the risk of war, by a willingness to run risks for the sake of a more reliable peace. It is in the recognition of the far-reaching implications of this challenge, and in the determination to face up to it, that there lies a historic chance for mankind to finally transcend the nuclear peril and to ultimately seize control of its own destiny.

Notes

1. The term 'security,' as used in this paper, refers mainly to the requisites of *external* security policy whose top priority objective is defined as the prevention of nuclear war. Given this premise, the paper argues that due to changed global realities, security can no longer be assured by traditional military means. In today's world of growing global interdependencies, it has become a multidimensional concept encompassing both internal and external conditions which go far beyond the conventional confines of military politics.

2. As long as nuclear weapons exist, however, it is generally acknowledged that the only (military) role they could serve would be limited to that of preventing their possible use by someone else (minimum deterrence).

3. Wilma Scott Heide, cited in *IFDA Dosier*, 57/58, July/April 1987, p. 13.

4. Edward Grey, *Twenty-five Years*, Vol. 1 (London: Hodder & Staughton), cited in: Robert Jervis, *Perception and Misperception in International Politics* (Princeton University Press, 1976), p. 65.

5. Though the more severe examples of this are in the Third World, the industrialized nations are also beginning to feel the crunch of the opportunity costs involved. The loss, for instance, of U.S. economic pre-eminence in recent years, is also attributed to its huge military expenditures which have placed a heavy burden on its ability to compete in an increasingly competitive world. *International Herald Tribune*, 9/4/1987.

6. Barry Childers, "But What About Our Fears of the Russians?," Paper presented at the International Congress of Philosophy (Montreal, Canada, August 1983), p. 7. Hostility also enables each side to project its insecurities onto the other with impunity, and "helps preserve a sense of self-righteousness" about one's attitude. Ibid., pp. 3, 6.

7. Ibid., p. 6.

8. *Common Security, A Programme for Disarmament*, The Report of the Independent Commission on Disarmament and Security Issues (Pan Books London & Sidney, 1982), p. 12.

9. For further elaboration, see: Jervis, *op. cit.*, Chap. 4.

10. Palme Commission Report, *Common Security, A Programme for Disarmament, op. cit.*, p. x.

11. "The Concept of Common Security," in: *Arms and Disarmament, SIPRI Findings*, SIPRI (Oxford University Press, 1986), p. 207.

12. Michael MacGwire, Brookings Institution, Washington, D.C., USA; cited in George Perkovich, "Beyond the Cold War," *Nuclear Times*, January/February 1987; p. 15.

4

The European Experience and Its Meaning
for Central America

Lothar Brock

The Regionalization of Conflict Resolution
in Central America

The initiative of the Contadora countries to strengthen the role of regional Latin American interests and governments in coping with the Central American crisis grew out of frustrations over a long tradition of violence in Central America and an equally long tradition of external interference in Central American conflicts, first and foremost by the United States.

The history of inter-American relations as viewed from the Latin American side is a history of persistent attempts to attach strings to U.S. policy vis-a-vis Latin America. Thus, when the Organization of American States was founded in 1948, its charter contained an all-inclusive prohibition of intervention which applied to direct and indirect, military or non-military attempts to interfere with the internal affairs of another member of the organization. The crux of the matter is, however, that it was precisely this prohibition of intervention which allowed the United States to define interventionistic action on its part as being in accord with the right to individual or collective self-defense against the alleged intervention in the region by extra-continental powers, (i.e., the Soviet Union, "International Communism," or, since 1959, by Cuba).

Along this line, the 1983 intervention in Grenada was defined as serving not only the "restoration of the rule of law" and "respect for human rights of the people of Grenada," but also self-determination and sovereignty.[1]

The Grenada intervention added to the fears which had gradually built up during 1982 and all of 1983, that the United States might try to "clear things up" in Central America by a military invasion of Nicaragua. The Reagan administration proper followed a course of deliberate uncertainty: Politicians close to the administration served warnings that direct military action was possible while at the same time it was officially denied that any such action was imminent. But there could be no doubt that the Reagan administration had decided to bring military force to bear in its attempts to influence the Central American conflicts. On the one hand, it prepared for big military maneuvers, on the other, it supported the Duarte government in El Salvador militarily and helped the "Contras" to start their first offensive into Nicaragua from Honduran territory in March, 1983.

Not surprisingly, this action led to a dramatic worsening of relations between Nicaragua and Honduras in addition to the tensions already existing between El Salvador and Nicaragua.

The UN Security Council on May 19, 1983, called upon all states in the region to solve their conflicts peacefully (Resolution 530). But such an appeal necessitated decisive follow up action if it was to have any meaning at all. It was therefore important that the Contadora Initiative had come about a few months earlier.

The idea behind the initiative was to prevent a further escalation of existing tensions, especially between the three countries in the core area of Central America, and to enhance the chances for a political solution of the crisis. To this end, the Contadora group engaged in active crisis management and at the same time tried to get a dialogue started on the possibilities of reaching a broader agreement on some of the crucial issues (including a halt to the arms build-up, a recall of foreign military advisors as well as the protection of human rights and the stimulation of social reform and economic cooperation).

For the latter purpose, the Contadora group drafted a comprehensive "Act for Peace and Cooperation in Central America" which was ready for signature in June 1984. While Nicaragua as the first Central American country declared its willingness to sign, Costa Rica, Honduras and El Salvador refused to do so. This refusal was in line with the verdict of the Reagan administration that the Act was premature.

A year later, when the Contadora group presented a revised version of the Act which took into account the critique voiced by Costa Rica, Honduras and El Salvador on verification measures, it was Nicaragua which refused to sign. The Nicaraguan government argued that the Act did not commit Washington to cease aid to the "Contras" and that it linked Nicaragua's strength only to that of its neighbors when Nicaragua's main threat came from the United States.[2] In December of 1985, Nicaragua even requested the suspension of the Contadora process for a period of five months until the dust could have settled on the then forthcoming presidential changes in Guatemala, Honduras and Costa Rica.

This policy has to be seen against the background that the United States had suspended the bilateral negotiations with Nicaragua in January 1985 and later on had declared a trade embargo on Nicaragua after the latter had rejected a peace plan which Washington presented as an alternative to the Contadora Act and which was a reflection of U.S. security interests as defined by the Reagan administration. Nevertheless, Nicaragua's strategy of postponement, in the situation existing at the end of 1985, almost led to a break-down of the whole Contadora process. Since this was not in the interest of the country, it signaled its readiness for continued cooperation shortly before the Contadora meeting in January 1986 at Caraballeda, Venezuela. This way, the Contadora group was able to formulate a "Caraballeda Message for Central America's Peace, Security and Democracy," which was endorsed by the foreign ministers of the five Central American countries only two days later on the occasion of the inauguration of the new Guatemala president Vinicio Cerezo (the first civilian president of Guatemala since 1970).

In May 1986, the presidents of the five Central American countries met to reaffirm their support for the Contadora Initiative ("Esquipulas I"). They also agreed to install a Central American parliament, which is to be located in Guatemala. Despite this meeting, however, even a third version of the Contadora Act was not signed; instead, the tensions between Nicaragua on the one hand, Costa Rica and Honduras on the other, mounted again as Nicaragua took the two countries to the International Court of Justice at the Hague for carrying out illegal activities against Nicaragua.[3]

Despite the fact that the Contadora Initiative had found unequivocal backing in Latin America (as expressed through the formation of a support group consisting of the "new democracies," Brazil, Argentina, Uruguay and Peru) and also in Western Europe, by June 1986, it had become clear that the Peace Pact would not be signed. Thus, the Contadora Initiative to bring about a regional settlement of the Central American disputes seemed to end in the same frustrations which had given birth to it.

One of the most important aims of the Contadora Initiative was to bring together the five Central American states at the negotiating table. In February 1987, Oscar Arias, who had been elected president of Costa Rica a year earlier, presented his peace plan which finally led to an agreement of the five countries on August 7, 1987. This success had to do with the fact that the Arias approach to negotiated conflict solution was free of the "fraternal tutelage" which--in the eyes of the Central Americans--went along with the Contadora Initiative. On the other hand, the Esquipulas II agreement cannot be isolated from the preceding Contadora Initiative; it was not the fruit of an entirely new approach to the problem, it rather was a variation of the theme worked out by the Contadora group. After all, the foreign ministers of the Contadora countries and the countries of the support group are members of the International Control Commission which was constituted on August 23, 1987, as a consequence of the Esquipulas Agreement. But the Esquipulas variation of the Contadora theme, while progressing to a point where formal agreement between the five Central American states had become possible, quickly ran into difficulties, too, this time with respect to the implementation of the agreement.[4]

Relevancy and Persistency of the Regionalization Process

One can argue, of course, that the difficulties into which the regionalization process, both on the Contadora and on the Esquipulas levels, has encountered are a result of U.S. hegemony over the region. From this viewpoint it would seem that regionalization works, if the United States is in agreement with it and does not if the U.S. disagrees. One could then conclude that it makes much more sense to talk about U.S. policy in the area than about regionalization of conflict resolution through intra-Latin American initiatives.

Certainly, prospects for a negotiated settlement for the Central American crisis cannot be discussed without taking U.S. policy in the area into account. But the U.S., despite the military power and "structural force"[5] which it can bring to bear in its relations with other countries, cannot control political developments in other parts of the world *ad libitum* or impose its own solutions to any regional controversy. It cannot do so even in Central America. This is to say that U.S. foreign policy, like the foreign policy of any other country, has to adjust to the conditions existing in the various world regions and that these conditions certainly are being influenced by local forces. Therefore, discussion of the possibilities for the regionalization of conflict solving activities in Central America must take U.S. preponderance in the region into account. Doing this generates some regional possibilities for changing the conditions under which U.S. policy is being conducted.

We should realize that the most remarkable aspect about the process briefly sketched in the preceding chapter is not that it failed to bring peace to Central America, but rather that Latin American countries took the initiative for intra-Latin American conflict resolution outside the established international organization (United Nations, Organization of American States); that this initiative was kept alive over a period of four years despite differing interests and views of the Contadora countries (not to mention the five Central American republics); and that it was flexible enough to help prepare the road towards a formal agreement between the five Central American countries, even though the agreement finally reached *strictu sensu* came about outside the Contadora framework.

The Contadora Initiative was launched as a peace process. This was so, because it was clear from the very beginning, that agreement on the principles of a peaceful settlement of the Central American disputes and the implementation of such agreements could only be reached through a gradual build up of the willingness and ability of the conflicting parties to enter into some form of communication, negotiation and finally cooperation. If Central America has been in turmoil through almost all of its history, then it would be illusory to expect that sustainable solutions to present controversies, all of which are deeply rooted in Central American history, could be worked out and brought about through a solitary diplomatic act.

The Esquipulas agreement likewise is based on the notion of a peace *process* (and not simply a peace agreement). The setbacks which both processes suffered were to be expected. The question is, whether they are long term obstacles to an ongoing process of strengthening the Latin America role in regional conflict resolution or whether they mark the end of such a process for the time being.

In Central America's precarious political situation, regional attitudes or beliefs about the best way of dealing with the situation are of considerable importance in determining possible outcomes. General disappointment about the results of the peace process or failure to regard present developments under a broader historic perspective, may themselves become a source of discouragement. On the other hand, if the meaning of what has been understood by a peace process so far, could be extended so that setbacks are answered by tactical adjustment (instead of strategic resignation), then the chances for continuing the search for a negotiated settlement of Central American disputes may be enhanced. This is a conclusion to be drawn from experience with the Conference of Security and Cooperation in Europe. Therefore, the question arises whether it would make sense to apply some of the principles and procedures developed in the European context to the Central American situation.

The Approach: Regional Conferences
on Security and Cooperation

Proposals for the convocation of regional conferences on security and cooperation in the Third World have emanated from quite different sources.

The Palme Commission in its Report on Common Security, which was published in 1982, specifically referring to the European experience, suggested the development of regional security conferences (like the CSCE) in Asia, Africa and Latin America.[6]

Gorbachev, during his first year in office, took up an older Soviet proposal for an Asian regional security system and suggested making use of the European experience in establishing such a system. He also suggested combining the institutionalization of regional security with specific agreements between those states of the region which had strongly conflicting interests (India, People's Republic of China, ASEAN countries, Vietnam, Japan, Soviet Union).

This was quite in line with the CSCE approach, since the initial phase of the CSCE went along with specific negotiations between the former war-time Allies on the status of Berlin, bilateral agreements between the superpowers (Moscow Accord of 1972) as well as bilateral treaties between the FRG on the one hand, the Soviet Union, Poland, CSSR and the German Democratic Republic on the other.[7]

The President of the Interparliamentary Union, the German Christian Democrat Stercken, in the fall of 1987 suggested a global application of the CSCE rules and procedures. Stercken referred explicitly to the Gulf region and Central America as the two Third World regions in which application of CSCE rules seemed especially urgent.[8]

The organization of detente politics in Europe merits special attention with a view to regional conflict in the Third World since it demonstrates that a long-term perspective of cooperation can be developed out of a situation of acute conflict.[9]

The magnitude of this task in Europe can hardly be overstated. It involved overcoming mutual vilification, mistrust and even hate, and called for an entirely new thinking about the long-term perspective of East-West relations.

It demanded an unequivocal determination to come to an agreement on the future of Berlin, which was the place of the most intensive East-West confrontation, interim solutions to the German question including mutually acceptable forms of peaceful change in Central Europe, on methods for slowing down and possibly reversing the arms race and on increased economic cooperation and transnational communication across the East-West dividing line.

Responding to this challenge within a few years, the former war-time allies came to a consensus on Berlin: the two German states worked out agreements on their future relations, with the Federal Republic on the one hand, and the Soviet Union, Poland and Czechoslovakia on the other. They signed treaties on the denunciation of the use of force and the conditions of peaceful change with regard to the borderlines established in Central Europe in the wake of the Second World War. Finally, the thirty-five states assembled in the Conference on Security and Cooperation in Europe and established a broad consensus on the principles of peaceful East-West relations as embodied in the Final Act of Helsinki, signed in 1975.

The Final Act of Helsinki was not designed by any of the countries involved to do what could not have been done by any agreement; that is to end the East-West conflict. Its main task was rather to help mitigate the conflict and to prevent its eruption into a third (and last) world war. Furthermore, it was well understood that East-West detente could not be decreed by a multilateral agreement, nor could it come about through a single conference. Detente was

initiated as a long-term process because under a realistic assessment of the past
it would have been naive not to expect setbacks in the ensuing years. Such
setbacks promptly occurred.

After 1975, East-West relations quickly deteriorated again and to many
detente appeared to have been nothing but an episode. In the early eighties, fear
spread in Europe that East-West relations were not only moving back to the
days of the Cold War, but that we were actually getting closer to a hot one.
This fear was expressed by the peace-movement which gained tremendously in
momentum within the context of the stationing of medium-range missiles in
Central Europe. But detente was not lost entirely. Instead, under the surface of
the day-to-day power-play, a rudimentary process of detente was kept alive by
the Europeans in East and West. It guaranteed a certain degree of continuity of
inter-systemic communication, even at the height of the conflict over Afghanistan, Poland and the missile question, and it helped to pave the way for a return
of the super-powers to the negotiating table in Geneva. The new policy of
Gorbachev, to the extent that it was influenced by outside developments, was a
reflection of the ongoing normalization of political and economic East-West
relations in Europe, and not of the determination of some Westerners to out arm
the Soviet Union.

The important point is that detente in Europe turned out to be not only the
expression of a passing mood or of popular illusions prevailing in the early
seventies. Detente was the expression of the common understanding between
East and West that military security politics had created evermore insecurity
and that therefore, it would take more than military strength to prevent a worldwide holocaust. The means designed by the CSCE in the early seventies to this
end were complex. Instead of pushing a single line of action, the clue of the
CSCE approach to East-West relations was that it opened up chances for compromise through the agreement on a wide variety of activities under the roof of
the CSCE. These were lumped together in three "baskets": the first one on
principles of inter-state conduct (including human rights) and confidence-
building, the second one on cooperation in the field of economic relations,
science and technology as well as ecology, the third one on humanitarian
cooperation as well as transnational contacts and communication. A fourth
"basket" provided for follow-up conferences and prepared the way for an institutionalization of East-West conference diplomacy not necessarily in the form
of a new international organization or a permanent secretariat but, for the time
being, by opening up the perspective of continuing talks and negotiations. Such
a perspective, in principle, widens the margins for compromise, because one
can make concessions at one meeting counting, if necessary, on a better deal in
another.

This form of informal institutionalization of multilateral East-West conference diplomacy was put into practice and has led to three major follow-up conferences in Belgrade, Madrid and Vienna. The Madrid conference took place at the climax of renewed East-West tensions and lasted, with intermissions, from November 1980 until September 1983. In addition, there were numerous expert meetings and other specialized conferences, the most important being the Conference on Confidence Building and Disarmament in Stockholm, which was carried through in various rounds of negotiations between January 1984 and September 1986.

The various talks and negotiations did not lead to spectacular results. But, the participating states found it worthwhile to devote energy and patience to keep the CSCE process going. In this respect, the neutral non-aligned countries (Sweden, Switzerland, Austria, Finland, Yugoslavia) played a special role during the early eighties.[10]

Applicability to Central America

When we look at detente in Europe and its relevance for Central America, we are doing so against the background of vast discrepancies between the two regions in terms of geo-political factors, the distribution of military power and economic potentials and the history of regional relations. Nevertheless, some aspects of the European experience in dealing with international conflicts may be helpful for Central America as they may be helpful for the Far East. In general, the European experience suggests that viable security arrangements are feasible between states with different social systems. One of the special features of the CSCE was that it took up questions of the domestic order of the participating states by referring to certain human rights standards and calling for more transnational communication and contact. At the same time, however, the final Act of Helsinki did not question the legitimacy of the socio-economic and political order in the participating states. This way it provided for *regional pluralism* instead of one-sided change. Why should regional pluralism, understood as a concept of mutual concern without intervention and as an open-end process of self-determined change, not be possible in Central America?

Another general conclusion to be drawn from the European experience is that any attempt to institutionalize some form of constructive dialogue between countries with different political and social systems requires patience. There are bound to be disappointments, misunderstandings and setbacks which, however, are reasons not for reducing communication but, instead, for intensifying it. This argument refers to the early break-up of American aid to Nicaragua, the discontinuation of the bilateral talks between Nicaragua and the U.S. and the call by Nicaragua, in December 1985, for a halt to the Contadora mediation efforts.

A third general conclusion from European experience would be that it is important to have some sort of institutionalized multilateral conference diplomacy which opens up the perspective of *continuing* efforts to come to terms with each other. This would create a higher degree of crisis stability than would exist without the assurance that there will always be a mutually acceptable forum for "talking things over."

Along this line, it could be helpful to organize a Conference on Security and Cooperation in Central America and the Caribbean, which would

1. be conceptualized as a contribution to a long-term process of peaceful change in Central America,
2. provide for a multiplicity of activities covering security, economic relations and transnational communication and contacts and
3. provide for participation of all Central American and Caribbean countries and establish continuing consultation and cooperation with a support group consisting of the countries at the Northern and Southern fringe of the area (including, of course, the United States), as well as countries which are of crucial importance for the economic development of the region (Western Europe, Japan).

Such a conference would have to be non-discriminatory. No country would be excluded because of its political and economic system. To the contrary, this approach would be geared towards *regional pluralism*, instead of conformity of social order and political system.

As the CSCE experience demonstrates, such a system can only work if it is accompanied by bilateral negotiations between the parties to the various conflicts in the region (e.g., U.S. and Cuba). One could object, of course, that this is the point at which the whole idea crumbles since it was the United States, not Cuba, that stopped the process of normalization which made some headway during 1974. However, in this respect we should take into consideration the interrelationship between developments in various Third World regions. Since Cuba has now retreated from Angola, there may be better prospects for a normalization of relations with the United States.[11] As far as Nicaragua is concerned, the resumption of bilateral negotiations may be helped along by a broad regional framework for tension reduction and cooperation.

In combination with such bilateral negotiations, a Central American and possibly Caribbean Conference on Security and Cooperation should commit itself to the following tasks in addition to a cessation of fire and the other concrete points mentioned in the Esquipulas II agreement:

1. confidence building not only in the military field but also through extended transnational communication (e.g., within the proposed Central American Parliament),
2. revival or modification of instruments for the peaceful settlement of disputes within and outside the UN and the OAS,
3. sustainable arms control measures encompassing a cutback of the military presence of any extra-regional power including the United States,
4. in connection with the latter point an international guarantee for the security of sea-lanes in the Caribbean,
5. coordination of economic aid to the region at large, especially by the U.S., Western Europe and Japan, in connection with the promotion of new initiatives for intra-regional economic cooperation,
6. preparation of a program for coping with the foreign debt of the region by drafting regional guidelines for adjustment policies that would strengthen the position of the various countries in country by country negotiations with the International Monetary Fund on the specific terms of adjustment measures,
7. systematic and unbiased evaluation of the experience with land reform programs in different countries of the region,
8. concerted efforts of intra- and extra-regional research institutions to shed some more light on the relationship between peace, the protection of human rights and the chance for a sustainable development in the region,
9. working out of a regional resources plan which would identify possibilities of a sustainable exploitation and priorities for the protection of the natural resources of the region,
10. convocation of a group of eminent persons which would periodically evaluate the implementation of these tasks, taking into consideration both sides, the Latin American and the Caribbean countries of the region on the one hand, the policy of the industrialized countries towards the region on the other.

Conclusion

Needless to say, a Conference on Security and Cooperation in Central America and the Caribbean would produce no miracles. But on the other hand, what would a continuation of present developments have to offer? Endlessly protracted civil strife in El Salvador; and a reversal of the "civil" non-militarised development of Costa Rica as the only country in the hemisphere without

an army? And all this within the context of a severe economic crisis and strategic scenarios of "low intensity warfare" and an intensified war on drugs on the
part of the United States.[12] There is an utter need for conceptual alternatives to
"low intensity warfare." The idea of a comprehensive Conference on Security
and Cooperation in Central America and the Caribbean could serve this purpose.

For the time being, a Conference on Security and Cooperation in Central
America and the Caribbean would only be an instrument for creating new
confidence that political solutions are possible as long as the problems of the
region are the objects of continuing talks. Thus, the conference would constitute an act of symbolic problem-solving. Of course, symbolic problem-solving
cannot go on for long without any real progress along the road of peaceful
change. Such progress would call for a constructive dialogue between the
United States and all Central American States on problems and possibilities of a
demilitarization of the present struggle and of coping with the underlying social
and economic problems. The EC countries are interested in such a dialogue
because the mitigation of conflict in the Third World is vital for the continuation of detente in Europe. The EC therefore should be expected to commit
itself in a more substantial way to aiding economic and social progress in
Central America than it has been willing to do so far.

Western Europeans have experienced during the last ten or fifteen years,
that stepping up communication, commerce and cooperation across the East-
West dividing line has served neither side as a mere maneuver to gain tactical
advantages in the East-West struggle. Instead, multilateral East-West communication under the roof of the CSCE has begun to transform the long-term
perspective under which this struggle takes place. There is a growing confidence that war, which served the Western European countries as a regulating
device for so many centuries and which now has given room to integration, may
also be overcome as a regulating device among industrialized countries with
different social systems.

Such a hopeful development may call for an increased regionalization of
security politics. Trends pointing in this direction are visible not only in
Europe but also in Asia and even in the Middle East. Perhaps the Latin American and Caribbean states, too, have to think about a continually growing role in
providing for their security. Such a regionalization of security politics in the
southern part of the Western Hemisphere as such does not constitute an alternative to the Inter-American approach within the Organization of American
States. It could even help to revive the OAS on the basis of a more effective
dialogue between the Latin American and Caribbean state on the one hand and
the United States on the other.

Notes

1. Jeane Kirkpatrick, "The U.S. Action in Grenada: Its Context and its Meaning," in Walter F. Hahn (ed.), *Central America and the Reagan Doctrine* (University Press of America, 1987), p. 318. John Norton Moore, *Law and the Grenada Mission,* (Charlottesville Center for Law and National Security, 1984), p. 138.

2. "The Contadora Process--A Balance Sheet," Institute for European-Latin American Relations (IRELA), Dossier No. 1 (Madrid, January, 1986), p. 2.

3. "Central America Today: The Current Situation," IRELA, Dossier No. 7 (Madrid, November, annex 1, 1986).

4. For a detailed report on the Implementation of Esquipulas I cf. *FLACSO*, Csuca, Universidad Para La Paz, Informe blanco sobre los avances logrados en el proceso de cumpolimiento de acuerdo de Paz para Centroameri-co--"Esquipulas II"--a los noventa dias de haberse firmado, San Jose, November 1987. The same, Segundo informe blanco, segundo periodo: Nov. 6, 1987-ene. 16, San Jose, 1988. For an early evaluation of the Arias plan cf., "The Arias Plan, A Way Out for the Central American Peace Process?", IRELA, Dossier No. 10 (Madrid, May, 1987).

5. For an explanation of the concept of structural force see Susan Strange, "The Persistent Myth of Lost Hegemony," in *International Organization* (41/4, 1987), pp. 551-574.

6. Der Palme-Bericht, Common Security (Berlin, 1982), p. 185.

7. See the critical report by Gerhard Baumann, "Kollektive Sicherheit fur Asien. Moskaus Vorschlag fur eine asiatische Sicherheitskonferenz," in *Beitrage zur Konfliktforschung* (1, 1987), pp. 51-72.

8. *Frankfurter Allgemeine Zeitung* (October 6, 1987), p. 4.

9. See Mathias Jopp, "Zehn Jahre KSZE-Proze," in Jost Delbruck, Norbert Ropers, Gerda Zellentin (eds.), *Aus Politik und Zeitgeschichte* (Koln: Grunbuch zu den Folgewirkungen der KSZE, B 37/85, 1977), pp. 1-24.

10. Editor's Note: Recent events in Europe (1989-90) have given additional significance to the CSCE framework in the transition to a new security system in Europe.

11. Editor's Note: Except that the U.S. in 1990 seems committed afresh to the destabilisation of Castro.

12. Fred C. Ikle, Albert Wohlsteeter, et al., *Discriminate Deterrance. Report of the Commission on Integrated Long-Term Strategy* (Washington, D.C., January, 1988).

5

Zone of Peace or U.S. Strategic Primacy? The Politics of Security in the Caribbean

Dion E. Phillips

Introduction

The aim of this paper is to trace the course of events in the Commonwealth or English-speaking Caribbean since 1973, relative to the question of whether this subregion will ever be declared a zone of peace or will instead remain under the United States (U.S.) sphere of influence.[1] The objective of the "zone of peace" concept is to ensure that the Caribbean is free of all foreign military bases as well as foreign military maneuvers within the context of East-West politics. The continued U.S. sphere of influence approach, what the author refers to as "strategic primacy," involves the tendency to interpret Caribbean concerns in relation to East-West rivalry. A concomitant of this approach is the practice of intervention, direct or indirect, by the U.S. when deemed necessary.

I begin by tracing the history of intervention or "strategic primacy" in the wider Caribbean from 1898 to 1965 as an appropriate backdrop to the time period that is of primary concern here, namely 1973 to the present. Against the background of this cursory treatment of U.S. policy toward the Caribbean, I will address the following two major developments:

1. The behavior of the English-speaking Caribbean states relative to the zone of peace resolution.
2. The restructuring of U.S. foreign policy to the Caribbean begun in 1979 and the manner in which this has produced an unprecedented increase in military activity in the subregion.

The paper is predicated on the notion that the above mentioned patterns are adverse to the possibility of the region becoming a zone of peace. Finally, I conclude by offering a series of policy suggestions.

Strategic Primacy: U.S. "Special Relationship" with the Caribbean

The perception of the Caribbean by the U.S. as an area of strategic primacy is longstanding. It has led U.S. policy makers to forge a "special relationship" between the U.S. and the Caribbean. This "special relationship" in which the Caribbean is often regarded as "our sea" has, from Monroe to Reagan, worked against the Caribbean ever being regarded as a zone of peace.

It was in the Caribbean that the U.S. first asserted its hegemony and first wielded its "Big Stick." Intervention in the affairs of Caribbean nation states, militarily and otherwise, has been the tool most often used to maintain strategic primacy.[2]   The most recent example of this strategy took place in Grenada in October 1983. It has served as the cutting edge of the militarization of the English speaking Caribbean, a factor that works against the adoption of the zone of peace option for the subregion.

The cornerstone of U.S. foreign policy toward the Caribbean was set in 1823 with the proclamation of the Monroe Doctrine. This doctrine warned European powers to refrain from intervening in the Western Hemisphere and, in turn, promised that the U.S. would not intervene in European affairs.[3]

Intervention in the affairs of the Americas by any force was regarded as a threat to the "peace and safety" of the U.S. Although the doctrine was unenforceable at the time of its declaration, it became the justification for U.S. intervention in the Caribbean. However, the Spanish American War in 1898 was the watershed in United States-Caribbean relations. With the defeat of Spanish colonialism, U.S. predominance in the New World had begun.[4]

What followed was a series of U.S. interventions in the Caribbean under the guise of political "protection," through the use of economic pressure, financial control and military occupation.[5]   As a consequence of the war with Spain, the U.S. gained Puerto Rico. In 1901, it also constrained the Cuban government to adopt the Platt Amendment, giving the U.S. the right to intervene as was repeatedly the case, and the right to establish a naval base in Cuba, namely Guantanamo Base. It also signed the Hay Varilla Treaty with Panama in 1903 which led to years of U.S. intervention and Panamanian opposition.[6]

In 1904, President Theodore Roosevelt unveiled the "Corollary" to the Monroe Doctrine which established a kind of U.S. protectorate over the Caribbean. The objective was to prevent European interference in "our hemisphere."[7] In 1904, the Dominican Republic, after a number of crises, defaulted on its payments to a U.S. financial company. The result was that

Roosevelt ordered U.S. intervention. In so doing, he took over the customs house and assumed responsibility for collecting and distributing Dominican customs receipts as well as positioned the U.S. Navy off the Dominican coast.[8] A 1907 treaty prohibited the increase of Dominican debts until all foreign claims had been honored.[9]

A second U.S. military intervention of Cuba lasted from 1906 to 1909. When a crisis in Cuba threatened American property, Roosevelt sent William Howard Taft, his Secretary of War, to spearhead a commission which would confer with Cuban officials and arrive at a political agreement. The Cuban President and Cabinet resigned and Taft appointed himself as governor.[10]

In 1909, the U.S. also intervened in Nicaragua, supporting the establishment of a more pro-American government. In the face of imminent overthrow, the Nicaraguan government, in 1912, called for U.S. assistance. In response, President Taft dispatched more than 2,000 marines and eight U.S. warships. The marines were forced to remain until 1925 because the Conservative Party there could hardly remain in power without foreign military reinforcement.[11]

When a crisis in Haiti attracted European threats of intervention, President Wilson sent in U.S. troops, installed a new government and established a virtual U.S. protectorate over Haiti.[12] In spite of sustained Haitian opposition, the U.S. intervention remained in existence until 1934.[13]

In 1916, there was a second military intervention of the Dominican Republic instituted by Wilson under the guise of bringing stability to the island. U.S. Secretary of State William Jennings Bryan desired not only to supervise Dominican revenue collection but also to determine its distribution. The Dominican government balked at the idea, and U.S. warships again landed a force of marines who occupied the country until 1924.[14]

In 1917, the U.S. invoked the Platt Amendment and invaded Cuba for a third time. Early that year, there was a rash of disturbances in Cuba and the U.S. issued instructions that it would not countenance armed resistance. Between February and August of that year, detachments of marines were landed in Cuba as a show of support for the status quo. Finally, in August, a full regiment of marines was summoned to resolve the crisis.[15]

President Coolidge ordered a second military occupation of Nicaragua in 1927. After a Mexican supported revolution began, the U.S. protested "Mexican-fostered Bolshevik hegemony between the United States and the Panama Canal," and dispatched the marines. This time Nicaraguan opposition mushroomed into a liberation struggle led by General Augusto Sandino against both U.S. and Nicaraguan troops. After the 1932 elections, the marines were finally withdrawn.[16]

The "Good Neighbor Policy" of Franklin Roosevelt promised to be the converse of past U.S. policy toward the Caribbean. Roosevelt assured Latin America that "the definite policy of the United States from now on is one opposed to armed intervention."[17]   He stated that if intervention were expedient it would be a joint concern of the whole continent and not a unilateral U.S. action. However, the first test of U.S. resolve came on the heels of this enunciated policy. As opposition to the repressive Machado regime grew, the U.S. responded. Constrained from engaging in direct military action by his "Good Neighbor" promise, Roosevelt intervened politically by sending a U.S. ambassador to preside over the "restructuring" of the Cuban government.[18]

The U.S. contemplated intervention in the British Caribbean colonies but decided that the islands' domestic problems were too big a problem. Roosevelt instead gave Britain, under Prime Minister Winston Churchill, 50 destroyers in exchange for bases in Jamaica, Trinidad, Guyana (then British Guiana), Antigua and St. Lucia. The U.S. maintained these bases long after the war was over.[19]

The election of the Arbenz regime in Guatemala in 1954 brought cold war politics to the Caribbean. As alluded to by Milton Eisenhower, "when communism threatened to engulf Guatemala in 1954, the American people became uneasy. For the first time, we began to fear that the backyard could suddenly become a path for communist subversion. We breathed in relief when forces favoring democracy restored Guatemala to its normal place in the American family of nations..."[20] The "forces for democracy" pointed to by Eisenhower were nothing more than a "ragtag 'national' army hired by the CIA" to overthrow the reform-oriented, not communist, democratically elected government of Guatemala.[21]   It is believed by some that the Arbenz government was the first in the region to be victim of U.S. covert activity.

The cold war again manifested itself in 1959 with the Cuban revolution. The U.S. made several attempts to intervene in the internal affairs of Cuba. Though it was President Kennedy who ordered the eventual Bay of Pigs invasion, it was long approved by President Eisenhower in 1961. Subsequently, succeeding U.S. presidents have repeatedly attempted to topple the Cuban government. They have employed various methods ranging from threats and economic blockade to even attempted assassination.

Cold War politics first visited the English-speaking Caribbean in the country of British Guiana (now Guyana). In the early 1960s, U.S. covert activity assisted in the ouster of Cheddi Jagan. The American Institute for Free Labour Development (AIFLD) initiated a campaign to unseat Jagan by instigating a general strike. It is believed that the CIA may have paid more than $1 million in strike pay. Kennedy influenced the British Prime Minister to stymie British Guiana's independence plans until after the 1962 midterm American elections, so as to avoid the allegation that he was "soft on communism." Eventually, at U.S. bidding, the British government established an electoral system based on proportional representation which resulted in Jagan's defeat.[23]

Previous to the invasion of Grenada in 1983, the last exercise of strategic primacy in the Caribbean transpired in the Dominican Republic in 1965. Because the U.S. seemed fearful of the emergence of "another Cuba," President Johnson ordered the military occupation of that island. Seven months after the election of President Juan Bosch in 1963, he was deposed by the military. However, in order to counter the armed revolt which was being waged to return Bosch to power, Johnson ordered a military invasion.[24]

Throughout the period 1898 and 1965, during which time U.S. strategic primacy was strident in the Spanish-speaking Caribbean, the Commonwealth Caribbean, although under the influence of the U.S., was largely spared any direct military intervention. The U.S. covert activity which ejected Jagan from office was the only exception. However, many of the Commonwealth Caribbean countries accommodated U.S. bases up until the time of the attainment of sovereignty as was the case with Trinidad, while others like the Bahamas and Antigua currently permit U.S. naval facilities on their shores.

The Zone of Peace Resolution and the Behavior of the Caribbean States

The year 1979 held much significance for the Caribbean. In March, Maurice Bishop and the New Jewel Movement toppled the Gairy government in Grenada. In July, the Frente Sandinista de Liberacion National (FSLN) defeated the Somaza regime in Nicaragua. These two events in particular did not go unnoticed by the U.S. In fact, they resulted in an expansion of U.S. naval exercises in the region.[25]

This resurgence of U.S. military presence was deemed to be heightening tension in the Caribbean. It was, therefore, viewed as inimical to the peace and security of the Caribbean and prompted the call for the Caribbean to be regarded as a zone of peace.

In La Paz, Bolivia on October 31, 1979, the Organization of American States (GAS) at its twelfth session adopted a resolution, the thrust of which was to declare the Caribbean a zone of peace.[26] This resolution called upon all states to recognize the region as such and to devote all their efforts in appropriate regional and international fora to the advancement of the concept. More substantively, the OAS resolution, which was preceded by a similar one at the Non-Aligned summit conference in Lusaka, Zambia, in 1970, stated the importance of:

"...recognizing that it is within the exclusive competence of sovereign states to decide upon the path to be taken for the attainment of the goals of democracy, social justice and integral development for their people."

In regard to the Commonwealth Caribbean, the idea to declare the Caribbean as a zone of peace was first introduced at the July 1981 meeting in Grenada to the Standing Committee of CARICOM ministers responsible for Foreign Affairs. The proposal was strongly supported by Grenada under Maurice Bishop and Guyana headed by Forbes Burnham. A working group was appointed to pursue the proposal. However, it proved difficult to convene this working group. When it finally met in Belize in March 1982, there was a sharp conflict of views. Grenada and Guyana favored the adoption of the proposal, whereas the remaining CARICOM countries of Jamaica, Barbados, Bahamas, Belize, Trinidad and Tobago and the Eastern Caribbean countries indicated that their lack of enthusiasm took account of the existence of bases or installations within certain CARICOM territories from which the respective host states derived economic advantages. Belize, the Bahamas, Antigua and Barbua were the cases in point. With the reversal of the Grenada revolution and the emergence of conservative governments which opposed the resolution, it was quietly removed from the agenda of concerns of CARICOM Foreign Ministers. In fact, any chance of its adoption in the immediate future seemed to recede further into the horizon with time.

Hence, given the inability of Commonwealth Caribbean countries to reach a consensus on the issue of the Caribbean being declared a zone of peace, the U.S. is under little or no pressure to respond positively to the resolution than would otherwise be the case. In so doing, Caribbean countries strengthen (even legitimize) the enhanced presence of the U.S. in the affairs of Caribbean countries. As a consequence, U.S. strategic primacy is a fait accompli.

From Carter to Reagan: Restructuring of U.S. Military Policy

Between 1973 and 1979, there was a marked decline in U.S. military activities in the western hemisphere, including the Caribbean. This reduction was due in part to military readjustments on a global scale undertaken by the Pentagon as a result of the Vietnam War, the energy crisis and the Watergate affair. This hiatus was reflected in Carter's administration tentatively embracing ideological pluralism and a human rights policy in Latin America and the Caribbean.

During the initial years of Carter's term in office, the Caribbean region and Central America were perceived as relatively stable and without immediate threat to U.S. interests. Terrance Todman, Assistant Secretary of State for Inter-American Affairs explained that:

> "We no longer see the Caribbean in quite the same stack military security terms that we once viewed it. Rather, our security concerns in the Caribbean are increasingly political in nature."

This new perception of the region was demonstrated not only by efforts at rapprochement with Cuba but also by the increased diplomatic importance attributed to the Eastern Caribbean by the visits of Rosalyn Carter and Andrew Young. It was hoped by Washington that an effective utilization of non-military instruments of foreign policy would be adequate to diffuse any tensions in the region and serve to neutralize progressive and radical elements who would otherwise be hostile to U.S. interests.

Concomitant with this initial U.S. regional policy of the Carter administration was the belief that it was no longer necessary for the U.S. to maintain a military presence of the same magnitude as during the previous decade. Moreover, it should be noted that the rebellions that occurred in Jamaica in 1968, Anguilla in 1969, and Trinidad-Tobago in 1970, did not require the involvement of U.S. military forces. In Haiti, there was "an orderly transfer of power" from Francois to his son, Jean-Claude Duvalier, and a mutually agreeable political and diplomatic solution to Panama was arrived at between the U.S. and Panama.

Also, in the early Carter years, the U.S. had long abandoned the naval bases at Chaquaramas in Trinidad as well as those at St. Lucia, Jamaica and British Guiana (now Guyana) which Roosevelt had acquired from the British during World War II in exchange for destroyers. During this period, there seemed to be little or no effort on the part of the U.S. to restore and/or expand its infrastructure of bases and installations in the Caribbean. The only installation in CARICOM dating back to the World War II agreement which remained in U.S. hands was the air and naval installations of some importance on the island of Antigua. Moreover, even though the socialist-oriented government of Bishop and the New Jewel Movement had come to power on March 13, 1979 the U.S. still elected, as planned, to pull out of the naval facility it had maintained in neighboring Barbados since 1956 on March 31, 1979.

Beginning, however in 1979, there was a restructuring of U.S. policy in the region leading to a gradual integration of the countries of OECS, Barbados and Jamaica within the framework of that policy. This redefinition of U.S. policy was underscored by Admiral Wesley McDonald, Commander-in-Chief of U.S. Atlantic Forces who wrote:

"Until 1980, the major thrust of U.S. plans in the Atlantic arena focused on the North Atlantic Ocean and the Mediterranean Sea.... However, since that time the Soviet sponsored build-up in Cuba has obliged us to re-evaluate our position in the Caribbean.... I am persuaded that we must focus more clearly on both the strategy and the means to ensure a secure and stable Caribbean flank, particularly during an East-West crisis in Europe.... The area is now one of my major concerns."[27]

The origin of this new policy toward the Caribbean is traceable to October 1, 1979 when Carter, under pressure from National Security Advisor, Zbigniew Brzezinski, decided to get tough in a nationally televised speech and reassert traditional U.S. supremacy in the Caribbean. To do so, he blew out of proportion an already known fact that there was a brigade of 2,600 Soviet combat troops in Cuba. In this speech he announced the establishment of a new Caribbean Joint Task Force with headquarters at Key West, Florida. Also, in that month, the U.S., in a show of power, dispatched over 1,500 marines to the U.S. complex at Guantenamo Bay, Cuba, to engage in military manoeuvres. Sending troops to Cuba in this manner indicated that the political pendulum had swung away from the earlier Carter administration trend toward possible normalization of U.S.-Cuba relations. The recalling of Philips Habib, former diplomat, from retirement and sending him to the English-speaking Caribbean in August 1979, two months earlier, as well as, his meeting in London to plan joint U.S-British responses to Caribbean economic and security needs, pointed to a clear shift in U.S. policy.

The reorientation in U.S. regional policy was explained by Robert Pastor in the best possible cold war terms. He stated that:

"Changes in the region and the world in 1979 and 1980 made the Carter administration more sensitive to traditional military concerns. The coup in Grenada in March, 1979, and the collapse of the Somaza dynasty in July both brought new leaders to power, who tended to see Castro's Cuba as the answer... and the U.S. as the problem. ...simultaneously an economic decline in the region and a more aggressive Cuban posture--exemplified by the obstrusive role played by the Cuban ambassador in the 1980 Jamaican elections--further unsettled the region. This instability naturally was viewed in the U.S. in the context of more ominous international developments--the invasion of Afghanistan, hostages in Iran, uncertainty in the Persian Gulf, and

Soviet threat against Poland. The U.S. cooled the relationship (with Grenada) and sought to expand aid to Grenada's neighbors as a signal that only democracy would be rewarded in the region."[28]

Concrete evidence of this kind was exhibited in 1980 with the visit of U.S. warships to Caribbean ports spiraling to a high of 125 calls.[29] And so, as the 1980 U.S. elections approached, the halcyon days of Andrew Young and tolerance of ideological pluralism faded as the Carter administration became convinced that it faced the spectre of a hostile axis involving Cuba, Nicaragua and Grenada, not to mention Surinam where a left-wing military regime had seized power in February. Such a rapid succession of events in the late 1970s, undoubtedly ushered in the second cold war period in the Caribbean. Unlike the previous Carter posture, conflict and instability in the Caribbean were no longer perceived in North-South but East-West terms, a posture that was not only sustained but intensified by the Reagan administration.

However, U.S. strategic primacy, reminiscent of that which has long prevailed in the Spanish-speaking Caribbean was consummated in the Commonwealth Caribbean when the U.S., nominally supported by a token force of soldiers and police from four of the Organization of Eastern Caribbean States (OECS) [Antigua/Barbuda, Dominica, St. Lucia and St. Vincent/Grenadines] as well as Barbados and Jamaica, invaded Grenada on October 25, 1983. Such an action was a clear and resounding manifestation that, unlike the post-Vietnam era, the U.S. was again prepared to assert its strategic primacy. Not only did this action constitute the first time that the U.S. had directly and militarily intervened in a country since the Dominican Republic in 1965, but it represented the first and only U.S. intervention in a Commonwealth Caribbean country.

Another solid reminder of the consolidation of U.S. strategic primacy in the Commonwealth Caribbean is the staging of naval exercises or war games.

Prior to 1981, in spite of Cuba, the military was not a major actor in the English-speaking Caribbean. However, the militarization of the Caribbean to act as a "shield for democracy" accelerated swiftly after Reagan took office. In November 1981, the Pentagon reorganized and upgraded its regional defense network under a single umbrella called the U.S. Forces Caribbean Command. This command, one of three full-scale NATO Atlantic Commands, has shifted most of its routine Atlantic training to the Caribbean. In undertaking its responsibility of surveying the "waters and islands of the Caribbean, Gulf of Mexico and parts of the Pacific bordering Central America," this new U.S. strategic vision of the Caribbean has integrated the security forces of the Eastern Caribbean Regional Security System (RSS) and Jamaica, to whom it has provided aid and military training, into the U.S. global military policy.

An integral part of this strategic primacy is the frequent staging of naval exercises or war games to intimidate countries considered enemies and to serve as dress rehearsals for actual intervention. As shown in Table 1, between 1985 and 1988, there have been a series of multinational manoeuvers involving Commonwealth Caribbean forces and the U.S. and sometimes Britain and Canada. The first was conducted in St. Lucia and the most recent transpired in St. Kitts. This pattern which has served to integrate Commonwealth Caribbean countries into the U.S. regional policy, is uncompromisingly averse to the zone of peace concept.

Table 1

MAJOR U.S. MILITARY EXERCISES IN THE COMMONWEALTH CARIBBEAN, 1985-1988*

September 1985	Exotic Palm	St Lucia
May 1986	Ocean Venture	Grenada
April 1987	Operation Camille	Dominica Lava Flow
September 1987	Exercise Trade Winds	Jamaica
June-July 1988	Exercise Trade Winds	St.Kitts/Nevis

*Those do not constitute the totality of U.S. military exercises involving Commonwealth Caribbean countries. The region has witnessed small-scale exercises in involving U.S. forces and a given country.

Conclusion

In its early years, the Carter administration exhibited some openness and seem favorable toward ideological pluralism and a human rights policy for the Caribbean region. However, beginning in its latter phase and continuing under Reagan, there was a restructuring of U.S. regional policy which served to integrate the Commonwealth Caribbean countries into America's military strategy. The Regional Security System (RSS), under whose auspices military exercises involving the U.S. and select Commonwealth Caribbean security forces are held, provide the framework for this integration. Curiously, the same group of countries which comprise the RSS were the very ones that supported U.S. intervention in Grenada.

The increasing militarization of the Commonwealth Caribbean means that the new U.S. regional policy is more inclined toward a show of force and resolve rather than negotiation and restraint. Further, it also demonstrates that the unprecedented emphasis on defense and security by Commonwealth Caribbean governments themselves is closely linked to the strategic perception and behavior of the U.S. and its allies, Britain and Canada. The latter point is pertinent, since the inclination of the Caribbean states to cooperate (albeit for their own reasons) strengthens the strategic anchorage of the U.S. and undermines any semblance of the Caribbean becoming a zone of peace.

Thus, the pursuit of the zone of peace concept not only has little verbal support in the Commonwealth Caribbean but in practical terms, given the prevailing political landscape, is even less attainable because of the relentless disposition of the U.S. for strategic primacy. This reality renders the concept of the zone of peace an artifact in Caribbean realpolitik.

Notes

1. The term "Commonwealth Caribbean" is used to distinguished the English-speaking Caribbean countries from the other Dutch, French and Spanish speaking territories of the region.

2. Frederico C. Gill, *Latin American-United States Relations* (New York: Harcourt Brace Jovanovich, Inc., 1971), p. 71.

3. Ronald Steel, *Pax Americana* (New York: Viking Press, 1967), p. 194.

4. Gill, *op. cit.*, p. 70.

5. Gill, *ibid.*, p. 88.

6. John Bartlow Martin, *U.S. Policy in the Caribbean* (Boulder: Westview Press, 1978), p. 17.

7. Gill, *op. cit.*, p. 70.

8. Martin, *op. cit.*, p. 18, 19.

9. Gill, *op. cit.*, p. 95.

10. Robert F. Smith, *The United States and Cuba* (New Haven: College and University Press, 1960), p. 25.

11. Gill, *op. cit.*, p. 102, 103.

12. Martin, *op. cit.*, p. 22.

13. Gill, *op. cit.*, p. 99.

14. Martin, *op. cit.*, p. 22.

15. Smith, *op. cit.*, p. 8.

16. General Augusto Sandino was eventually murdered by Anastasio Somozo. The latter was installed in power in 1933 with the support of the U.S.

17. Gill, *op. cit.*, p. 156.

18. Smith, *op. cit.*, pp. 144-164.

19. Martin, *op. cit.*, pp. 28, 29.

20. Quoted in George Black and Judy Butler, "Reagan Interventionism - Old Wine in Its Original Bottle," *NAGLA, XVI*, No.1, (January-February 1982), p. 4.

21. Stephen Schlesinger and Stephen Knzer, *Better Fruit: The Untold Story of the American Coup in Guatemala* (Garden City, New York: Doubleday and Co., Inc., 1982).

22. Black and Butler, *ibid.* p. 4

23. Martin, *op. cit.*, p. 67, 68.

24. Gill, *op. cit.*, pp. 250-253.

25. Abraham F. Lowenthal, "The Insular Caribbean as a Crucial Test for U.S. Policy," in H. Michael Erisman, ed., *The Caribbean Challenge: U.S. Policy in a Volatile Region* (Boulder, Colorado: Westview Press, 1984), p. 184.

26. Lloyd Searwar, "The Small State in the Caribbean: Policy Options for Survival," a paper presented at the workshop on Peace and Development sponsored by the International Peace Research Association, University of the West Indies, and the Jamaica Peace Committee, Jamaica, W.I., May 16-18, 1988, p.14.

27. Admiral Wesley McDonald, "Atlantic Security: The Cuban Factor," *Jones Defense Weekly*, (December 22, 1984).

28. Robert Pastor, "U.S. Policy Toward the Caribbean," in Jack W. Hopkins, ed., *Latin America and Caribbean Contemporary Record*, Vol. 1, (New York and London: Holmes and Mecer, 1983), pp. 78-89.

29. Lowenthal, *op. cit.*, p. 184.

6

Peace Initiatives in Africa: Prospects and Realities

Peter Bushel Okoh

Never, since the 1960s, when most African countries became formally independent, has there been so much danger to their existence as sovereign states. Faced with the most crucial problems of foreign debts, ecological disasters and regional wars, most African states have been reduced to the status of semi-colonies with few sovereign rights. The proliferation of regional conflicts in Africa has complicated relations between states, undermined regional security, created economic hardships and seriously contributed to the erosion of collective resistance to new forms of subjugation to imperial interests. The Organization of African Unity, which has been the main body through which African governments have tried to resolve the continent's conflicts, needs complementary support at the grass roots level.

The Declaration of 1986 as International Year of Peace by the United Nations created a new awareness about world peace in Africa. Seminars, conferences and other events on peace have been organized in many African countries. A special conference on peace and disarmament in Maputo, Mozambique in June 1986 called for the peaceful resolution of the conflict in Western Sahara and the destruction of the apartheid system. It also called for increased support for the role of the Organization of African Unity and the United Nations in the maintenance of global peace. The Harare Conference of May 1986 on the role of the OAU and Peace specifically called for the establishment of a Pan-African special force under the OAU Chairman as an instrument of maintaining continental peace and security.

These various peace forums in Africa emphasize the linkage between development and peace on one hand, and the threat to world peace by apartheid on the other. The anti-war movements in Africa cannot ignore the fundamental fact that regional conflict can be eradicated only on the basis of collectivity through political means; and the recognition of people's rights to choose their own independent path of development. In the absence of this, the growing aggressiveness of neo-colonialists on the continent can lead to further armed interventions and aggravations of old conflicts.

In this paper some of the peace initiatives of the past decade will be discussed (both governmental and non-governmental), with an assessment of their potentials for contributing to the future security of Africa.

Movement for Nuclear-Free Zone in Africa

The aggravation of world tensions caused by imperialism in the 1980s did not bypass Africa. But, until a few years back, although approximately 30 African states had signed the Non-Proliferation Treaty, countries of the continent were showing little concern over the arms race. African countries felt that they had more urgent problems and, until recently, the nuclear threat seemed somewhat remote even though, according to the so-called "nuclear winter" theory, the ecological balance in Africa would be completely upset in the case of a nuclear war in the North. Therefore, if by chance no nuclear weapons were dropped onto the continent, its population would still perish in a "nuclear winter." Today, Africa is faced with a nuclear threat posed by the apartheid government in Pretoria and the growing militarization of the Mediterranean and the Indian Ocean.

South Africa's acquisition of nuclear capability and the consequent nuclear threat constitutes a serious breach of Africa's security and international peace. It also clearly runs counter to resolutions adopted at a summit Conference of the Heads of States and Governments of the Organization of African Unity (OAU) in Cairo. At this conference, the Heads of States solemnly declared their readiness to undertake, through an international agreement to be concluded under United Nations auspices, measures against manufacturing or controlling atomic weapons. They appealed to all peace loving powers to respect and adapt the declaration.

An important arena in which the peace movement in Africa can mobilize popular support is the movement for the declaration of Africa as a nuclear weapon-free zone. The movement for the creation of nuclear weapon-free zones constitutes a very important aspect of global effort aimed at the elimination of the risk of nuclear war. It is has been twenty-two years since this key aspect of African security was tabled by the Organization of African Unity (OAU) and little has been achieved in the struggle towards this goal. Now, considerable efforts are being made by Africans to further this movement. UN General Assembly sessions and the Conference on Disarmament in the past years demonstrated that the countries of the continent stick to an active position in matters of war and peace. African states have made substantial contributions to important UN decisions aimed at the prevention of the arms race in outer space, the freeze of nuclear weapons, the cessation of nuclear tests and the ban on chemical weapons.

The representative of Senegal, Sarre, in the First Committee at the Thirty-Eighth Session of the UN General Assembly, stated on behalf of the African countries that until efforts are being made to achieve disarmament and improve international relations, the peoples of the world are under constant threat of nuclear catastrophe and are helpless victims of the huge resources wasted on armaments which could be utilized to eradicate critical socio-economic problems facing Third World countries. Immediate attention should also be given to the more recent threat of severe environmental degradation and pollution in Third World countries, as a result of developing countries dumping nuclear waste.

Arms Race, Foreign Debt Crisis and Peace Movement

The arms race is a global problem since it affects the social activity of all nations, their economies, inter-nation ties, regional peace and international peace co-existence. According to a U.N. study, the growing sophistication of the weapons being purchased by the developing countries has made it more difficult now for those countries' military services to play the role they sometimes play as "school" for the nation (i.e., providing a rudimentary education to large numbers of conscripts) at the same time teaching them basic military skills. Modern weapons systems require skilled people to operate and maintain them. So, a buildup of a country's military forces inevitably siphons off, from the civilian and potentially productive factors, some of the most educated and skilled members of society.

It is evident that armamentism has greatly distorted the socio-economic situation in many African countries. It has created a general climate of insecurity, domestic violence, wars and regional conflicts. The arms race in its present form is particularly disastrous for African countries which constitute a subsystem of the global economy. Third World countries are experiencing serious economic crises compounded by the burden of heavy foreign debt. At the moment, this debt is estimated at one trillion U.S. dollars, which is just a little less than the present world annual defense spending. The foreign debt crisis has hit many developing countries and cannot be seen in isolation from the nightmare of the arms race.

Along with trying to keep up with the arms race, Third World countries must also think about educating their people. 178 million children in the age group 6-11 years will require primary education; 152 million, aged 12-17 years, will require secondary education; and 124 million, aged 18-23, will be in need of higher tertiary education in 2008. When the concept of militarization and development is applied to this social and economic crisis in Africa the picture becomes very bewildering.

Many African states spend one-third or half of their national budgets on armaments. Many of them have no domestic arms industries, so there are no advantages in terms of employment in armaments-based industries, nor foreign exchange earnings from arms export. Unlike the advanced countries, many African states have been locked in the vicious cycle of committing a sizable part of their meager foreign reserves to the purchase of weapons, most of which are either obsolete or too sophisticated for legitimate domestic defense requirements. Certainly, large budgets on armament, most of which end up being of no use to Third World countries receiving them, constitute a large drain of resources which could have been put to far more useful purposes in development. This realization has led peace movements to advocate peace and disarmament more actively at the United Nations and other international fora.

The unabated increase in defense spending of the 80s in the imperialist centers had dire repercussions for many African countries. To meet targeted increased military spending, the Western nations, who are the dominant economic and trading partners of most African states, raised bank rates, provoking capital flight from the country. In other words, African states have been pushed to a situation of financing the arms race in the imperialist centers through the payment of thousands of millions of dollars on foreign debt. About 250,000 million dollars is annually siphoned out of the developing countries.

The pressure put on developing countries because of foreign debt is enormous. The long-term objective of hand twisting tactics is to completely paralyze any form of sovereign or economic rights. Foreign debt has actually become a modern day form of colonial control over sovereign and independent states of many developing countries. President Alan Garcia of Peru, known for his steadfast resistance to blatant IMF dictates, has aptly described the IMF as a "colonial house."

The Third World nations really have no alternative but organized unity in their determination to rid themselves of the tag of under-development and exploitation. This unity has become more pressing if seen against the background of neo-conservative accession to power in the leading Western countries. These various right-wing governments are pursuing policies of increased defense spending, general arms race and organized anti-Third World policies.

A necessary condition for peace and social and economic development of all African countries is an end to the arms race. According to President Mugabe of Zimbabwe, 1988 Chairman of Non-Aligned Movement, "only one-fifth of the world's annual military spending would be enough to save Africa and other regions from the hard scourges of hunger up to the year 2,000." African experts have said that to raise the level of industrial production, farming, transport and communications, Africa will need nothing less than $150 billion, until the year 2000; this can be possible only if we put a stop to the arms race going on in Africa and the rest of the world.

For the past 20 years, African nations' military spending has grown much faster than other developing regions of the world. In 1970, they reached $8 billion, while in 1988, they rose to $20 billion. Most of these arms were purchased from the United States and other Western countries. According to Robe Ouko, the Kenyan Minister of Foreign Affairs, "Africa would never be able to cope with its economic problems if it keeps its military spending going at current fast rates, including those used to buy arms supplies. The disarmament process should go both globally and regionally."

Education for Peace

Education has a very important role to play in the development of peace processes in Africa. It has been said that war intentions and their preparations take place in people's minds. Peace educators have consequently argued that the fight against armamentism should begin with the mind. UNESCO has been steadfast on the role of education in the quest for peace, security and disarmament. It convenes conferences, seminars, special weeks and projects on this key aspect of the global disarmament campaign.

Organizations like the World Association for the Schools as an Instrument of Peace, the World Council for Curriculum and Instruction, the Association for World Education, the International Federation of Free Teachers Union, International Federation of Teacher's Association, the International Association of Universities and the World Federation of Scientific Workers are involved in efforts to make education an instrument for peace and disarmament.

In Africa, where public awareness about the dangers of the arms race and especially nuclear threat is still very limited, education programs involving scholars, students, teachers and their professional associations can constitute a strong foundation for the ultimate development and growth of peace initiatives on the continent. A seminar on "Peace Education" was organized in the fall of 1988 by the Nairobi based African Association for Literacy and Adult Education, the purpose of which was to define African perspectives and issues on peace and to lay the ground for a network of peace educators and NGO's in Africa. Many Nigerian and other African Universities now have Peace Studies in their curriculum.

African Peace Initiatives

The first African conference on security, disarmament and development in the history of Africa was held in Lome, Togo in 1985. The conference adopted a programme for peace, security and co-operation on the continent and appealed to permanent members of the UN Security Council to assume responsibility prescribed by the UN charter, for international security and to take effective steps to end the growing military and nuclear programmes.

The OAU, the largest African forum, plays a major role in the peace and disarmament movement in Africa. It is our hope that security and stability will be brought to the continent through, or with the help of, this forum. To a certain extent, this has been achieved. Some countries have restored diplomatic relations through the OAU, while others have settled border conflicts.

There are manifestations that the fight against forces of the arms race at the grass roots has intensified in recent years. The International Conference on Peace, Disarmament and Solidarity held in Brazzaville in September 1986 brought representatives of more than twenty African countries, the national liberation movements and international and regional organizations, who adopted the Brazzaville Declaration. This was a major stage in mobilizing popular support for disarmament in Africa. Significantly, this conference unanimously proclaimed Africa as a nuclear-free zone and called for establishment of national committees for peace and against the arms race.

Other activities such as peace marches are held all over Africa from time to time. In 1986, thousands of people took part in marches in Kenya, Mozambique, Zambia and Ethiopia. The then Chairman of the OAU, President of Zambia, Kenneth Kaunda, addressed the participants in the peace march in Lusaka in November of that year. He stressed the importance of the struggle for peace throughout the world, condemned the arms race and called for an end to the production of new types of deadly weapons.

A movement for averting nuclear war was formed in Zimbabwe in the Spring of 1985. It called for the mobilization of the Zimbabwean public in the struggle for peace and the prevention of nuclear catastrophe. The broad-based movement has scientists, physicians, teachers, students and workers. Among its plans, the movement is setting up branches in all major towns, establishing links with the media and getting involved in various anti-war activities. The University of Zimbabwe has set up a special disarmament group, made up of 70 members, to disseminate information and conduct public opinion polls on disarmament questions.

The Informal Meeting of Researchers and Scholars from Benin, Togo, Burkina Faso, Nigeria and Ghana from 24-31 October, 1987, was organized by the United Nations Regional Centre for Peace and Disarmament in Africa to discuss "the impact of the international arms race on peace and development in Africa. With special emphasis on its implication for the West African sub-region," the group issued a final statement touching many keen questions on peace, disarmament and development. Most importantly, it set up a commission on border crises in the sub-region, a youth exchange programme, Peace Trophy for a football competition and a body on Human Rights in Africa.

In Zaire, a Peace Research Institute has been set up with objectives to promote peace on the continent. The African Peace Research Institute, in Lagos, Nigeria, has held seminars and publishes a journal for the purpose of promoting peace and security and to find resolutions to local as well as global problems.

The Centre for Foreign Relations in Dar Es Salaam, Tanzania has for the past four years held international conferences to promote peace and stability in Southern Africa.

Peace initiatives will do well to focus around the objectives of the United Nations International Disarmament Fund for Development. The objectives of the fund are to correct the negative aspects of the present situation with regard to disarmament and development. It also suggests new initiatives for overcoming obstacles affecting both East-West relations and North-South dialogue; establishes institutional machinery to ensure that resources for armaments are reallocated to development; and establishes a disarmament fund for development.

African governments hold conferences and seminars regularly on how to solve the problem of external debt crisis, regional border conflicts and other problems.

The growing interest in peace initiatives on the part of African educators, scientists and nongovernmental associations can strengthen the efforts of the OAU to ease tensions regionally, achieve progress in disarmament and development, and seek support from the great powers for such efforts. For example, a convention establishing a nuclear-free zone in Africa should be recognized and safeguarded by the great powers, as was done concerning the Treaty of Tlatelolco declaring Latin America a nuclear-free zone.

Efforts should be made towards the removal of foreign bases from Africa, which constitute a possible threat to the security of the continent. At present, several African and other developing countries are planning to refuse to allow these bases on a permanent basis once their present lease has expired. African countries could for now ban storage of nuclear weapons at such bases and ban calls made by foreign ships carrying nuclear weapons.

Citizen's initiatives are concerned with the creation of justice and development and demands for cooperation, internationally. Global peace cannot be achieved if the issue of Third World development is not taken seriously. As President Nugabe of Zimbabwe said, "the largest number of international hotbeds of tension today exist mainly on the soil of non-aligned countries!" This assertion is supported by the findings of peace researchers that the number of wars is increasing "almost exclusively" in the Third World. That is not all. There is famine, drought, instability and regional conflicts and, of course, apartheid, smoldering in Africa.

The peace research community in Africa must invite the cooperation of the rest of the world in working together to achieve a world free from domination, injustices, inequality, exploitation and discrimination. Neither Africa, nor any other region, can do this alone, peace, security and human well-being are global tasks, to be achieved through local cooperation on a global scale.

7

Common Security:
Three Conflicts in the Middle East

Sanaa Osseiran

Security is understood to mean in general terms safety from danger and aggression. Similarly, a secure living denotes the ability to survive and fulfill basic human needs--those of shelter, food and human dignity. This concept of security evolved throughout history from guaranteeing that individual's needs be met to ensuring that community requirements be met as well. Nation-states have become the symbol of this security phenomenon. The notion of security became that of sovereignty, independence, and freedom, with the state ensuring the welfare of its citizens internally and externally.

At various times in history, communities and states shared a strong sense of common security. This was due either to their perception of a common danger, or by virtue of ideological and religious beliefs. It was then easy to identify common security because the values defended were shared by the different parties. It was an ambiguous sharing and permitted a sense of interdependence. In today's world, common security signifies for many the possibility of threatening another collective group. It implies defensive or strategic alliances that serve the economic and military interest of one group over another. Therefore, in order to view common security in a new light, we have to reconsider the ancient Chinese concept, "everybody in the land under heaven serving the public interest."

In the Middle East region today, the nations share a sense of common insecurity. This is due to the existence of three major conflicts in the area. The first and oldest conflict is that between a state and a nationalist movement aspiring to create its own statehood, the Palestinian-Israeli conflict; the second is the Lebanese conflict, a conflict within a state; and the third is the Iran-Iraq war, a conflict between two states.

The three conflicts are linked with each other by the following factors:

1. Impact of colonial history
2. Superpower rivalry and militarization of the area
3. Media power and propaganda

Impact of Colonial History

The Middle East region fell under British and French mandatory rule after the dismemberment of the Ottoman Empire. The allegiance of the majority of the population was transformed from that of an Islamic Uma, or community of believers, to that of modern nation-states based on Western models. Hence, the cohesive tie that formed these societies in which the state, religion and family ties were intermingled, were then transformed into Western models without the development the Western societies had undergone.

Different Arab states achieved their independence after mandatory rule, except for Palestine. The British Government made a promise to the Zionist movement that Palestine would be the homeland of the Jewish people. It was the first verbal aggression on Palestine that preceded demographic and military aggression. The Zionist movement was seen as a product of Western and colonial power. Arab Jews were not part of the movement until after 1948. Zionism expressed Eurocentric solidarity and personified what Samir Amin calls "the coloured fear of white danger manifested in a Eurocentric solidarity."[1] Zionism emerged as a result of European anti-Semitism culminating in the persecution of Jews under Nazi Germany. From that time onward, the activities of the movement were viewed as an expression of Judeo-Christian civilization and emphasized hierarchy of cultures, itself being the center. Neither the Palestinians nor the Arabs accepted this hierarchy or the implanting of a foreign body on their land. The Palestinians did not accept this sudden realization of the divine rights of Jews over Palestine. Furthermore, they did not judge these rights as morally and politically superior to their own rights over the territories they had inhabited for centuries. But, despite their protestation and revolt at different periods prior to the creation of the State of Israel, Palestine was partitioned by the United Nations in 1947. It is the only time in history that a nation was established by a resolution of this international body. At the time, the UN was dominated by the victorious Western powers and had only two Arab states as members, Egypt and Iraq. The Palestinians and Arabs refused the partition plan of a Jewish and Palestinian state. They could not accept this partition which allocated more of the surface of Palestine to the Jews than to the Palestinian Arabs.[2] The Arabs constituted 96% of the inhabitants of this territory, the Jews only 6%.

This perception of Western collusion with the newly established Jewish state became evident to Palestinians and Arabs over the past forty years, starting with the 1956 Tripartite aggression on Egypt by Israel, France and Great Britain. The subsequent attitude of the U.S. government towards Israel perpetuated this perception. Successive American governments joined with the Israelis in denying the legitimate rights of the Palestinians as expressed by the Palestine Liberation Organization. Violation of human rights, in particular the 4th Geneva Convention, by Israel in the occupied territories since 1967 was not condemned most of the time by the U.S. at the UN Security Council. There has been complete international indifference to what occurred to Palestinians living inside Israel as a result of the Israeli absentee law, massacres, and expropriation of Palestinian lands for security purposes. During its invasion of the Lebanon in June 1982, Israel used and experimented with American weapons on the Lebanese and Palestinian population. They used cluster bombs, concussion bombs and anti-personnel grenades.[3] Only recently, the Palestinians in the occupied territories witnessed more evidence of U.S. collaboration with Israel. The weapons used to suppress the uprising had the following inscriptions on the aluminum canisters: "MK II 560 CS, Long projectiles 150 year...Federal laboratories, Inc. Saltsburg, PA., 15681, U.S.A...FOR OUTDOOR ONLY...MUST NOT BE FIRED DIRECTLY AT PERSONS OR INDOORS AS DEATH OR INJURY MAY RESULT."[4] Many other examples can be cited. The Arab perception of American concordance with Israel can be explained in such actions as: the annexation of the Golan Heights in 1980 by Israel; the Israeli raid on the Iraqi nuclear reactors in June 1980; the Israeli attack on Tunisia in 1985 and the 1988 violation of the sovereignty of the Arab states. All of these violations took place after signing the peace treaty with Egypt in 1979.

Israel has engaged itself in four wars for defensive purposes, and used defense and security arguments whenever it judged fit to attack the Palestinians. Its invasion of Lebanon could not be justified by this defensive argument, especially since the PLO did not violate the cease fire agreement throughout 1981. In the Israeli-Palestinian conflict, there is no symmetry in the political or military dimension. The only language used by the Israelis is the language of power and force. Consequently, there is no possible agreement or feeling of the need for common security in such an unbalanced situation, and in a militarized society. The Israeli government lacks so far the human dimension which has characterized the Jewish people throughout their history. They remain prisoners of their past fears, and endeavour to transmit this ghetto mentality to another community and neighbouring country, Lebanon.

Lebanon

The modern state of Lebanon was established in 1920 when the French government added to Mount Lebanon parts of the Syrian province, coastal towns and southern Lebanon, to make Lebanon a viable state. Thus, seventeen religious communities formed the Lebanese society. At this time, the Maronite Christians felt a part of the Arab World, and contributed largely to secular Arab nationalism in the late 19th and 20th century. Events in neighbouring Palestine were to influence the Lebanese society. And, as the Lebanese writer and journalist Michel Chiha wrote June 15, 1944, "we have to recall that Palestine borders Lebanon in the south. Aren't these people, holders of the past, afraid to lose their highest virtues in this adventure, and that the second generation, or the third, will resemble Israel of the old times? We in Lebanon need all our lands, our last grain , as well as our last olive tree. Our country is over-populated, and its population will increase. Is it necessary to add that Lebanon wants to live, and it is absolutely determined to live?"[5] It was with this spirit that the Lebanese Christians and Muslims embarked upon building the Lebanese state, a state which would be part of the Arab World. Lebanese leaders signed the National Pact of 1943, which at the time permitted power-sharing of different communities, allocating key posts to the Maronites who formed the majority of the population at the time. However, this fragile balance was too weak to withstand the pressures and problems befalling Palestine. The creation of the state of Israel caused coup d'etats in Syria and Egypt, as well as popular revolts in the area. The defeat of Arab armies in 1948 was the main cause. Israeli leadership had its own designs on Lebanon. In fact, the Zionist movement asked the British government in 1919 to include in the Jewish homeland southern Lebanon to the Litani river, and the Golan Heights in Syria.[6] Ben-Gurion, Defense Minister, and Moshe Dayan, Israeli Prime Minister, wanted to establish a Maronite state in Lebanon as of 1952. They perceived that the Jews and the Maronites were two religious minorities surrounded by a hostile Muslim environment.[7] Ben-Gurion even wanted the partition of Lebanon in 1954.[8]

The flow of Palestinian refugees after 1948, 1967 and 1970 into Lebanon, and the alliance between the PLO and nationalistic forces in Lebanon militarized the Lebanese society. The 1969 Cairo Agreement permitted the PLO to carry out operations against Israel from southern Lebanon. This Agreement was signed by all Christian leaders except one. Israel used this as a justification to bombard Lebanese and Palestinian civilians regularly.

The brutal methods of Israel in the occupied territories, against Palestinians in the form of land expropriation, expulsion, collective punishments and imprisonment, reinforced Palestinian determination. Consequently, Lebanon became the center of Palestinian and Arab nationalistic activities against Israel.

This in turn aroused fear among the Maronite population, particularly the Phalange party. The attitude of the Palestinians and the Lebanese nationalists increased these fears. The Phalange estimated that the Palestinian presence and Arab nationalism would threaten their existence and power in Lebanon. As a result, the internal cohesion, which was being molded, eroded and the collective memory of the Lebanese citizens suddenly became associated with their religious affiliations. It should be noted that the short-lived civil war in 1958 was precisely due to Lebanon's policies favorable to Arab nationalism, and against any defense arrangements with the United States. The Phalangist capitalized on Maronite fears. By the same token, Maronite monks spared no effort in intensifying these apprehensions. The Lebanese Muslims and their Palestinian allies wanted the Phalange to join forces in their battle against Israel. However, the Phalange party collaborated openly with Israel alongside the Lebanese National Liberal Party, headed by the former Lebanese president, Camille Chamoun. This was despite Syrian intervention on their side against the Lebanese National movement and the Palestinians in 1976. The 1978 Israeli invasion of South Lebanon marked the concretization of Ben-Gurion's designs on Lebanon. During this invasion the Israelis committed acts violating the spirit of all UN conventions related to human rights, using its surrogate Lebanese general in southern Lebanon to implement its policies. Consequently, their invasion caused the militarization of the Shiite community against Israel. Ten years have elapsed since this invasion, and despite the presence of UNIFIL, Israel has yet to withdraw from southern Lebanon and the southern population became refugees in 1978 and in 1982.

The Iranian revolution in 1978 helped to radicalize the Shiite population further. Thus, it is not surprising that many of them joined the hezbollah party (Party of God). Consequently, the presence of Palestinians and Shiite refugees from the south provoked further imbalance in the Lebanese society, particularly in the capital. The U.S. government and Israel, along with the different militias undermined the sovereignty of the Lebanese state. The state was completely paralyzed, accused at different stages of serving the interests of one community, Israel and the West. The Iranian revolution, the Palestinian problem, the security problem for both Israel and Syria, exasperated the division among Arab states. These conflicts left their marks on the third conflict, the Iran-Iraq war.

Iran-Iraq Conflict

This conflict like the aforementioned conflicts has its roots in colonial history. Modern Iraq and Persia were both under British mandatory power. Their frontiers were set up in the Treaty of Erzeroum of May 1847 and the Treaty of Constantinople of 1913, guaranteed by Great Britain and Russia.

However, Reza Shah of Iran violated the Treaty in 1937 and took parts of Iraqi territory. On the whole, relations between Iran and Iraq were never normal because of their dispute over Chatt Al Arab or the Persian/Arabian Gulf. Both countries claimed dominance over this strategic area. Iraqi Arab nationalism was feared by both Iranians and Israelis alike. From the outset, Iraq supported Palestinian rights against Israel, and denounced British hegemony. It would have succeeded in its revolt of 1941, had it not been for British intervention in crushing the revolt. Consequently, the British government ensured the dominance of their protege, the Iraqi regent. The U.S. intervened in a covert operation, crushing the Moussadaq revolt in 1953 in Iran, and installed on the throne again the late Shah. Western intervention in both countries was most visible. Inevitably, it strengthened the control of pro-Western governments against popular will. The Shah and Israeli leaders found their 'common security' and interests overlapping. The Israelis sided with any power that was anti-Arab. Thus, it is not so surprising that they undermined the Iraqi regime with U.S. acquiescence throughout the 60s until 1975 by arming, financing and training the Iraqi Kurdish rebels. This situation forced the Iraqis to sign "The Algerian Agreement of 1975" in which it promised to share equally the Gulf waters with Iran. The Shah undertook to return territories, taken unlawfully by his father, to Arab sovereignty. Both countries agreed not to interfere in the internal affairs of their respective states. Henceforth all aid to the Kurdish rebels ended, and their revolt was suppressed.

The deteriorating situation in Iran throughout 1978 forced Iraq to demand that Khomeini leave Iraqi territories where he had lived in exile for the past fourteen years. The Shah blamed Iraq for Khomeini's subversive activities against his regime. He judged that the Iraqis were violating the Treaty of 1975. This act by the Iraqi regime against Khomeini caused the latter's personal antagonism towards Saddam Hussein, the Iraqi president. Consequently, Iran under Khomeini provoked Iraq by meddling in its internal affairs, inciting their co-religionist Shiites to overthrow the Iraqi president. Iran refused to abide by the Algerian Treaty of 1975, and refused to return territories to Arab sovereignty. Thus, Saddam Hussein canceled the Treaty, and made the tactical error of attacking Iran. In fact both leaders made errors in their judgment. The Iraqi president thought that he would gain a quick victory over Iran, and underestimated the depth of the Islamic revolution. Equally, he misjudged the mood or loyalty of Arabs living on Iranian territory to support his war. Similarly, Khomeini also miscalculated the attitude of his co-religionists, the Iraqi Shiites. The latter proved that their nationalistic loyalty overrode their religious affiliation. And, although Iraq expressed from the first week of the war its desire to make peace if the Algerian Treaty was respected, Khomeini had other plans for Iraq and the whole Middle East region, exporting his Islamic revolution.

Iran under Khomeini posed no threat to the Israelis, despite the former's rhetoric against Israel. Israelis believed that historical animosity between Iran and Iraq would reappear. Ouri Loubrani, the last Israeli ambassador to Iran under the Shah's regime said, "The Shah had two fears: the Soviet Union and the Arabs. The attitude of Israel towards Iran today is that of its certainty that historical Iran will appear."[9] In addition, the specialist on military questions in Haaretz, Mr. Zeev Schill wrote, "It is better for Israel that this war continues as long as possible. Our interest resides in the survival of Khomeini and Saddam Hussein."[10] This Israeli strategy proved to be advantageous for her security. It further divided the Arab world. The destabilization of the Gulf countries was feared, forcing these Middle East states to purchase more and more weapons, instead of concentrating on badly needed development for the entire region.

These three conflicts would not have lasted that long had it not been for superpower rivalry and their increased confrontation in this region of the world. The U.S. considers the Middle East as its exclusive zone of influence. Since the 1950s, its strategy has aimed at obstructing Soviet influence and encroachment in the region in order to insure the flow of oil to the Western world, and to guarantee its superiority in the Mediterranean and the Indian Ocean. This rivalry caused the nuclearization of the Middle East, the Gulf, the Mediterranean and the Indian Ocean. The U.S. and the Soviet Union have introduced nuclear weapons into the region on a continuing basis. Equally, both superpowers and Western countries have provided arms to all the belligerents.

American strategy in the area made it regard Israel as its staunchest ally. Israel had all the attributes that promoted this belief. It was a homogeneous society, capable of providing any technical assistance for the American raid deployment force. It shared similar cultural and moral values with the 'free world.' Most of all, American leaders admired Israel's military professionalism. Israel desired from the outset to forge this strategic alliance with the U.S. They conceived their 'common security' profitable to both. So the U.S. provides huge amounts of financial and military aid to Israel in order to enable its continued survival.

The Irangate and the Eurogate scandals permit us to say that Western powers have a vested interest in perpetuating these regional conflicts. The Irangate scandal could have escaped being known to the international public had it not been published in an insignificant Lebanese newspaper. It was organized by what Theodore Draper named as "The American Junta." In his article he conveys to us "how a group from the executive board of a country employs a large scale covert operation putting the American body politic at maximum risk."[11] How many covert actions have been undertaken by superpowers and other nations in the name of security or 'common security'? The Eurogate scandal awaits a similar public hearing as its American counterpart. According to Walter De Bock and Jean-Charles Deniau, in their book "Arms for Iran," all

European states supplied Iran with arms since 1980. They maintain that the global cost of the Iran-Iraq conflict was estimated in 1987 to reach 400 billion dollars.[12] We also know that the Arab oil producing countries gave Iraq 181 billion dollars to finance its war efforts.[13] Aside from arms, the Iranians have bought food products, chemical products and manufacturing equipment worth millions of dollars from Western countries. In 1984, total imports to Iran were estimated at 1,550 million, in 1985, 1,180 million and in 1986, were 1,037 million dollars.[14] In short, one may reason that the West has an interest in perpetuating this Iran-Iraq conflict. It revives their national economy, and heightens the relationship between arms production and regional conflicts. All Western countries declared their neutrality in this conflict. Yet, all these countries have been furnishing Iran with arms. Thus, it is not surprising that the authors of Eurogate call this scandal 'the voyage in hypocrisy.' The same could be said of Israel.

The indifference amidst Western public opinion to these conflicts stems partially from the media and from general Eurocentric attitude. The media has often played, directly or indirectly, the game of their governments. So often information is withheld from the public in the name of 'security;' even in societies that claim to be democratic. The Palestinian and Arab cases received, for the most part, a negative response from the media. This is more the case with respect to American media, than European. A case in point is the Hasbara project aimed at selling Israel to America. Robert I. Friedman wrote in *Mother Jones* how criticism of Israel is carefully avoided. He quotes Abraham Foxman, associated national director of the ADL (Anti-Defamation League of B'nai B'rith) as saying on behalf of his organization and the American Jewish Committee, as well as the American Jewish Congress, that "Public criticism is to be silent when Israel is concerned. Public criticism of Israeli government policies gives ammunition and greater credibility to the Arab position." Friedman ends his article maintaining that "objective reporting about Israel can only strengthen those democratic forces that are struggling to solve the fundamental problems that threaten the country's very existence, and to prospect for Middle East peace."[15] In retrospect his remarks tend to apply to the current situation and media coverage of the uprising in the occupied territories. It has shown to the world the solidarity and desire for peace, from a fraction of the Israeli public, to end the Palestinian-Israeli conflict and call for the creation of a Palestinian state. Likewise, it brought the message to those Arabs who witnessed these scenes on television, of the existence among the Israelis, of those who challenge their government's policy. This is the kind of positive solidarity that can eventually lead to an environment where "common security" is conceived by all.

Information and media reporting has to be symmetrical so as to be credible and conducive in building a 'secure' international environment. It should not be based on state 'interest.' An example is the way the media covers Islam and Muslim leaders. Khomeini's Islam is 'bad,' and the Moujahideen Afghan Islam is labeled that of 'freedom fighters,' when both are equally exclusive Muslim extremists. This double standard in reporting hinders people from relating to each other, and accentuates the difference between cultures. Another negative contribution by the media to 'common security' is feeding the public with false information. This was the case in the Libyan-American confrontation and in the accusations against Syria for the terrorist attack in London (the Hindawi case.)[16] This was in spite of the confirmation by the Germans and the French Prime Minister at the time (Jacque Chirac) to the contrary. By the same token the Israelis 'sold' the Lebanese forces (an offshoot of the Phalange party) and Bashir Gemyal, the assassinated Lebanese president, to the American public. Jonathan Randal wrote that "some Western media built Bashir Gemayal into a paragon of free world virtues." Geraldo Rivera, in April 1981 on ABC's 20/20, depicted Bashir as a latter day crusader doing battle against the Soviet cat's-paw of the PLO in the name of common Western values shared, of course, by the U.S. and Israel.[17] This image, of the relationship between the Soviet Union and the PLO, portrays the Palestinians and Arabs as terrorists or communists and dehumanizes them, which deepens the gap between these different people. Hence the rift between "us and "them" is underlined.

The Israeli authorities have relentlessly cultivated the image of the Palestinian and the Arab as an enemy. Since 1973, Israelis have portrayed the Arabs in their children's books as thieves, blood-suckers, peasants, tomb looters, workers, spies, gangster, etc.[18] Similarly, we learn from Amia Lieblikh, professor of psychology at Hebrew University, that the Israeli youth while carrying out their military service in Lebanon were taught to regard the Lebanese and the Palestinians as terrorists. The author maintains that these young soldiers are highly influenced by the omnipresence of the army in the Israeli society.[19] This is not so astonishing given the fact that Israel from its inception, and even before its de facto creation, depended on para-military organization. The Israeli society is a military society where every citizen is a reserve officer. Consequently, military options, force and power are the guidelines of its leadership.

In conclusion, the factors that hinder "common security" in the Middle East stem from Western intervention; indifference towards the culture and the dignity of the people in the region; division of interest and lack of vision among the Arabs; propagation of an exclusivist, nationalistic attitude favoring racism and intolerance; and an inequitable growth-oriented economic development.

The Chinese concept "everybody in the land under heaven serving public interest" should be again the guiding line to "common security." "The land under heaven" refers to the whole of human society, and all people regardless of their nationality, race, and religion. The public interest refers to the indispensable needs of everyone's existence and development. The plurality is assured by the different forms that cultures and people express themselves.[20]

Concrete Policies

The three conflicts in the Middle East have forced the states in the region to allocate a huge percentage of their national budget for defense purposes. They all share a common interest in putting an end to their conflicts, to concentrating on developing their human and material potential. In order to make this possible, several factors of a psychological nature have to precede the political settlement of each issue, without which 'common security' can never be obtained.

The first question to be asked is whether there is a possibility to progress in this direction, so that common security becomes an intrinsic value in the minds of people of the region. Recent events in the Occupied Territories lend hope that a popular strategy can be pursued in this direction. What are the conditions that will permit the end of these hostilities; and what is the process by which the political sources of the conflict can be solved, so that 'common security' may prevail?

Six fundamental requirements have to be ensured prior to any series of endeavours. The first is a genuine international commitment not to sell arms to any of the belligerent parties. The second is to follow a policy of non-intervention in the internal affairs of any state. The third is condemning any resort to military force to solve disputes. Fourthly, is the equal disapproval of human rights violation, denouncing discrimination and oppression. Fifthly, is rejecting the hierarchy of cultures and religion, and finally ensuring that economic interdependence does not hide economic hegemony of one group over the other.

The Palestinian-Israeli Conflict

There exist, among the Palestinians and Israelis, groups that strive for mutual recognition of both peoples in two separate states. In Israel, the Peace Now movement embodies this trend. A similar peace movement does not exist among Palestinians for the simple reason that they live in host Arab countries, where they do not have the freedom of such action. The same can be said of their fellow Arabs. However, many Palestinians in the Occupied Territories are aware of the necessity to guarantee the security of both people. M. Mohammed Awad, an American of Palestinian origin, has established 'The Center for

Nonviolence' in Jerusalem. Many Israelis have condemned the government's decision to expel Mr. Awad, and joint actions were undertaken. World solidarity and action should be taken against any Israeli measure of this kind.

The Peace Now movement should be encouraged to include Oriental Jews in their movement. This could be the starting point to bridging the gap between Palestinians and both Sephardic and Ashkanazi Israelis. One basic reason is that Sephardic Jews constitute the majority of the Likud party (right wing) in Israel. According to the late Sami Maari, professor at Haifa University, Oriental Jews have joined the Likud out of their need to establish themselves and make their voices heard within the Israeli society dominated by Ashkanazi or Western Jews. Recent opinion polls in Israel taken after the beginning of the uprising in the Occupied Territories, indicate the following: 69% of those interviewed wanted the Israeli government to take more repressive measures against the Palestinians. Only 30% disapproved of these measures. This 30% has to increase so as to create a popular movement in Israel, capable of dictating its terms to the government. All peace movements have to take concrete measures that consolidate the dialogue between Palestinians and Israelis. For example, Pax Christi in the Netherlands organized a conference between 14-15 February 1986 where Palestinian scholars in Israel and from the diaspora had dialogue with Israeli scholars on the Palestinian-Israeli conflict. This conference was made possible with the cooperation of a number of European and American peace movements. Such dialogues should be multiplied. Research institutes involved in peace studies could embark on a similar strategy. Such debates will not only help Israeli and Palestinian citizens to bridge the gap, but also bring out common human interests. They will view each other less as enemies. It would be most helpful if extremists were invited, or at least those who belong to the majority of the Israeli population. Furthermore, such dialogues will provide more opportunity for their Western colleagues to understand more deeply the cultural, political and religious dimension of the issue.

Another possibility of solidarity action is through the work of Palestinian and Israeli non-governmental organizations. While everyone is aware of the political limitation of NGO activities, the NGOs can be the spearhead for coordinating initiatives. For example, 600 Israeli university lecturers signed a petition in Israel during the month of January 1988. Likewise 400 artists and writers signed a petition in February 1988 demanding that Ishak Shamir, Israel's prime minister, hold negotiations with representatives of the Palestinian people.[21] These activities should be publicized to the world, as Israeli public opinion is sensitive to its image. Israelis should be made more aware of the consequences of their government policy so that no one can claim one day "we did not know."

Peace prize winners should to be asked to contribute their work and reputation to this issue. They should help analyse the concrete problems that cause the absence of 'common security.'

The Palestine Liberation Organization should not be marginalized. Peace groups and researchers, scholars and politicians should emphasize the positive peace responses from the PLO to end the conflict. Any attempt to exclude the PLO and try to solve the problem as though it were a concern of Israel and the Arab states alone, will not guarantee or enhance common security. The PLO's move toward peace has been going on since 1973. They have agreed to join the peace process and the Geneva conference. They have committed themselves in the 1974 session of the Palestinian National Council to a Palestinian state in any part of Palestine. The PLO responded favorably to the joint American-Soviet communique in 1977 and in 1981 to the Brezhnev plan which called for direct recognition of the state of Israel. The PLO endorsed the 1982 Arab Fez plan which recognized indirectly the state of Israel. Likewise, they accepted the French-Egyptian 1982 draft resolution on mutual and simultaneous recognition.

It should be noted that the famous United Nation Resolution 242 is unacceptable by itself to the Palestinians. This is because this resolution considers the Palestinians as refugees and has no reference to either their legitimate rights to exercise their self-determination or to establish their state. Other UN resolutions have to be included. If Israel was created by a UN resolution, why can't a Palestinian state have the same privilege now? It needs the approval and concord of the superpowers, and members of the Security Council. But both the U.S. and Israel maintain a 'no' attitude to such an eventuality. American public opinion should be more informed about Palestinian willingness to give up, to make this concession of recognizing the state of Israel, in return for peace and the establishment of its own state on the Occupied Territories and the Gaza strip.

The Arab Fez plan committed and engaged all Arab states including Syria in the peace process. It spoke of peace and security guarantees for all states in the region. It recognized Israel implicitly. This security issue for Israel can be endorsed by the superpowers and the international community. What more security guarantees can be given? Israel's military superiority is in itself a safeguard against any possible threat from a Palestinian state. If anyone examines the map of Israel/Palestine one can argue more forcefully that the security issue that Israel keeps evoking is existent in their minds. This issue underlines Israel's incapacity of thinking in terms of security except through force and military options.

The Zionist movement wanted to create a homeland for Jews in Palestine. Its religious and nationalistic desires can be satisfied within the limits of its 1967 border. Similarly, the Palestinians can achieve their identity and sovereignty by the establishment of their statehood. This state can be viable through the help of the Palestinian diaspora and the financial contribution of Arab states. All Arab money spent on arms would be diverted not only to help this new Palestinian state to develop, but also to develop their own potential. Israelis can, with Palestinian help, cultivate relations slowly with the different Arab states, and their people. Each can then appreciate the specificity of different Arabs and Jews, the only basis for achieving 'common security.'

Lastly the International Peace Research Association (IPRA) could contribute by emphasizing, through a research cultural project with UNESCO, the positive contributions of Arabs, Jews and Christians under Moorish Spain to world civilization. This unique peaceful coexistence should and can be revived. Such a project may pave the way to find shared positive experiences, and mutual human interest. Otherwise it will be as the Israeli poet, Yehuda Amihai, wrote "And everything is written in three languages: Hebrew, Arabic and death."

If so much space has been given to the Israeli-Palestinian conflict, it is because we view this conflict as the core of the other two conflicts, and the bases on which 'common security' can be achieved. If an international conference is held with all parties to the conflict involved, then the territorial sovereignty of Lebanon will be safeguarded. Neither Israel nor Syria can advance security pretexts for being in Lebanon. The Palestinians present will have their government representative in Lebanon, and their status will be finalized. The Lebanese state would and should be strengthened. And all the militias should be disarmed. One has to visualize the impact of the existence of a Palestinian State, and the end of war with Israel, in Lebanon.

The Iran-Iraq conflict will cease if Western states end their arms trade to both states. Undoubtedly an arms embargo will force Iran to accept the UN resolution and end the state of war. Throughout the eight year conflict, Iraq has accepted to make peace and return to the 1975 frontiers. The Iranian and Iraqi people share a common religious and cultural heritage. Therefore an end to the conflict will inevitably have an impact on Lebanon as well. Iran's leadership will be accountable for any subversive encouragement of its co-religionist elements in Lebanon and Iraq.

Weapons by themselves do not make wars, human beings do. In today's world, there are no more impermeable frontiers or communications. These three conflicts could degenerate to involve most nations. Boundaries can be a positive element if people endeavour together for a universal interdependent outlook, rich in its pluralistic expressions. It requires peaceful coexistence, awareness, conscientiousness and solidarity among people. This is the sine qua non to 'common security' in the Middle East and elsewhere.

Notes

1. Samir Amin, "Eurocentrism and Politics" *IFDA Dossier*, No. 65 (Nyon, Switzerland, May/June 1988).
2. The total surface of Palestine was 27 million dunum (1 dunum = 1,000 square meters). The Jews numbered 666,000 people at the time of the UN partition plan out of 2,011,000. The partition plan allocated 15 million dunum for the Jewish state and 12 million dunum for the Palestinian state. From Walid Khalidi, "Palestine, Several Propositions for the Future," *Revue d'Etude Palestinienne* (Winter 1984), p. 100.
3. For a detailed account of Israeli use of American weapons in Lebanon, see "Israel in the Lebanon," *The MacBride Commission Report* (Ithaca Press, London, 1983), pp. 223-236.
4. International Coordinating Committee on Palestine (NGO), *The Children of Stones*, document No.1 (May 10, 1988), p. 8.
5. Miche Chiha, *Palestine*, Editions du Trident, Beirut, reprinted 1980, pp. 12-13.
6. See H.F. Frischwasser-Ra'anan, *The Frontiers of a Nation*, (London: The Batchworth Press, 1955), pp. 101-109, 129. This source is taken from W. Khalidi, REP (Winter 1984), p. 98.
7. The diaries of Moshe-Sharret published in 1979 by his son. Excerpts of these designs are in Jonathan Randal, *The Tragedy of Lebanon* (London: The Hogarth Press, 1983), pp. 189-195.
8. *Davar* (October 29, 1971).
9. *Liberation* (Nov. 14, 1986).
10. Amnon Kapilouk, "Comment Israel tire parti d'une Guerre Prolongee," *Le Monde Diplomatique* (October 1987), p. 4.
11. Theodore Draper, "The American Junta," *The New York Review of Books* (October 22, 1987), p. 45. His articles in the November and December issues summarize well the whole Irangate scandal.
12. Water De Bock & Jean-Charles Deniau, *Des Armes pour l'Iran* (Gallimard, 1988), p. 15.
13. Ahmad Faroughy, "Linterminable dependance de l'Iran," *Le Monde Diplomatique* (April 1988), p. 9.
14. *Ibid*.
15. Robert I. Friedman, "The Hasbara Project Targets the U.S. Media," *Mother Jones* (Feb/March 1987), p. 52.
16. The interview given by Prime Minister Jacque Chirac to Arnold De Bochegrave, chief editor of the *Washington Times*.

17. Jonathan Randal, *The Tragedy of Lebanon: Christian Warlords, Israeli Adventures and American Bunglers* (London: The Hogarth Press, 1983), p. 141.

18. Mandler Nili, Haaretz (October 18, 1985), taken from the *Revue d'Etudes Palestiniennes* (Winter 1986), No. 18, p. 240.

19. Amia Lieblikh, "Au printemps de la vie," taken from the *Revue d'Etudes Palestiniennes* (Summer 1988), No. 28, p. 188.

20. Pei Xiaotong, "On Human Identity," paper submitted to workshop on World Project Models (November 1985), pp. 21, 23.

21. Israeli-Palestinian joint activities and addresses are published by the International Coordinating Commission on Palestine, Box 127, 1211 Geneva 2D, Switzerland. Information on Israeli solidarity action with the Palestinians is taken from I.C.C.P. document No. 1 (May 10th, 1988), p. 17.

8

Common Security in the Asia-Pacific Region

Kevin P. Clements

The leaders of the two nuclear superpowers are finally beginning to acknowledge the necessity for alternative security systems to those based on nuclear overkill, mutual threat and mistrust. In order that this summit momentum be maintained it is important that other peoples, political leaders, governments and regions work to consolidate the progress that has occurred between the superpowers while arguing for alternative security doctrines that will truly enhance peaceful relations within and between all nations.

To do this effectively in the late 1980s means extending and developing the defense, security and disarmament doctrines enunciated in Olaf Palme's Independent Commission on Disarmament and Security Issues. This is a critical starting point because the doctrine of common security which emerged from that Commission is now a legitimate concern of many defense and foreign affairs professionals and also embodies many of the deepest aspirations of peace movements around the world. Since common security links the concerns of officials and popular movements it provides a good basis for challenging the outdated dictates of "realpolitik" and for articulating plausible but imaginative security doctrines which might guarantee more peaceful relations between nations in the future.

This paper focuses on the Asia-Pacific region in order to determine the extent to which governments and peoples in this area are beginning to develop defense and security strategies consistent with the central goals of the Palme Commission.

For purposes of analysis the Asia-pacific region is divided into three subregions: the South-West Pacific region, which includes Australia, New Zealand and the diverse states of Polynesia and Melanesia; South East Asia, which includes the Association of South East Asian Nations as well as Indo-China (Vietnam, Kampuchea and Laos); and North East Asia, which includes China,

Japan, Korea, Taiwan, Hong Kong and Soviet Asia. It is not possible to assign hard and fast boundaries to these particular sub-regions since the region as a whole is a focus of intense transnational communications and economic activity. This activity (e.g., strong and expanding Japanese investment in North East and South East Asia, Australia and New Zealand) is resulting in strong moves towards regional integration and a tendency to blur national political divisions in pursuit of economic growth. Despite the tendencies towards higher levels of economic integration and cooperation within and between the sub-regions, however, in defense and security terms the boundaries between the sub-regions are more distinct and reflect their very specific geopolitical characteristics.

The central question for any analysis of common security in the region, therefore, is whether the pressures for economic and social integration will result in the development of more peaceable defense and common security doctrines or lead in a more nationalist, competitive direction, thereby counteracting the tendencies towards integration.

Irrespective of what one thinks of the negative social and environmental consequences of the capitalist development model it seems reasonable to hypothesize that pressures for economic integration within the Asia-Pacific region will continue into the 21st century. The region has been identified as an important new motor for the world economy. The rush to develop preferential trading arrangements with Japan and the other high-growth economies in the region confirms this assessment. Insofar as businessmen and politicians believe that a narrow preoccupation with national security and militarization is bad for business and higher rates of profit are achievable within a relatively tranquil demilitarized region (where relations between nations are based on trust rather than threat), there will be expanded demands for common rather than national security strategies.

If, on the other hand, current economic strategies turn sour and activate latent nationalist sentiments it is likely that demands for alternative security strategies will give way to an assertion of a narrower view of national security interest and renewed pressures for militarization. At the moment, however, the dominant trend suggests that economic growth and the development of more integrated markets requires security strategies consistent with those outlined by the Independent Commission on Disarmament and Security Issues.

If this assessment is correct it raises some interesting questions for those concerned about in the development of alternative security strategies and just, self-reliant, ecologically sustainable development policies. The integrative market hypothesis is that good business in the Asia-Pacific region is not helped by security strategies based on competition and threat. On the other hand, locally based, organically sustainable development processes do not require the same degree of transnational integration and cooperation and do not necessarily require fundamental changes to national defense strategies in the direction of common security although they are clearly not consistent with militaristic defense strategies which generate insecurity for others either). The dilemma thrown up by current developments in the Asia-Pacific region is that capitalist economic integration--with all its negative features--may result in more real pressure for alternative international security policies than economic develop-ment strategies consistent with a quest for social justice and ecological sustain-ability.

In the medium to long term, however, the market pressures forcing changes to Asia-Pacific security policies will probably result in more structural violence, national resistance to hegemonic economic tendencies and an unraveling of alternative security doctrines. The challenge confronting popular movements, therefore, is to ensure that current economic trends towards integration are accompanied by the entrenchment of common security policies in the Asia-Pacific region while simultaneously generating space for environmentally sus-tainable and socially just development strategies in the future. This challenge requires new sorts of strategic and tactical thinking on the parts of popular movements interested in promoting both peace and justice. This paper is pri-marily concerned with the question of building on existing pressures for economic integration in order to create space for common security doctrines in the Asia-Pacific region.

Common Security

When Olaf Palme's Independent Commission on Disarmament and Securi-ty Issues first coined the concept of common security in the relatively dark days of 1981-82, United States' defense expenditure was booming and relations between the superpowers were stagnant or deteriorating. (There was, for exam-ple, a 12%, real increase in United States' defense funding in 1981.)

This increased expenditure on defense, antagonistic "cold war" rhetoric, gloomy and unsubstantiable reports of a window of vulnerability[1] between the United States and the "Evil Empire" culminated in the announcement of the Strategic Defense Initiative (SDI) in 1983. All these factors presaged an awesome arms race between the Soviet Union and the United States in both nuclear and conventional weapons, and heightened international and regional tensions. Meeting in these crisis conditions the Palme Commission was very concerned that the bellicose lead given by the United States would generate considerable global insecurity and reinforce the dangerous illusion that defense and security dilemmas were capable of unilateral military solutions.[2]

It was in response to such bellicose (as opposed to peaceful) unilateralism that the Palme Commission suggested alternative ways of achieving security and disarmament through cooperation and negotiation rather than through coercive solutions. Although the report has been criticized for its reformist and incremental recommendations[3] and for not tackling military doctrines and the industrial and political complexes behind them, the Palme Report was the first "official" step away from an international system based on mutual threat to one based on common security and survival. Common security helped generate a vision of a world where defense and security would be pursued in collaboration with potential adversaries and not by generating insecurity for others. Implicit within the vision was transparent, nonaggressive defense policies; cooperative relations within and between blocs and maybe the eventual elimination or transcendence of blocs altogether. "A doctrine of common security must replace the present expedient of deterrence through armaments. International peace must rest on a commitment to joint survival rather than a threat of mutual destruction."[4]

These were and are noble aims but does common security, as a doctrine guiding national defense and security practice (rather than a holistic vision) really provide ways out of national security dilemmas (especially for states subject to external threat or coercion) and is it a doctrine that has global scope and applicability?

From the perspective of most states in the Asia-Pacific Region, common security both as a vision and as a doctrine guiding specific national defense policies seems very Eurocentric. The original action program, for example, heavily emphasized bilateral and European negotiations on strategic offensive forces, intermediate nuclear forces, parity, conventional forces, chemical weapon and battlefield nuclear weapon free zones, and confidence building in Europe, etc. The recommendations on the role of the United Nations in the promotion of common security were largely confined to improving the ability of the Security Council to promote global and regional collective security and trying to ensure that the UN secretariat could intervene more easily in Third World border disputes. Specific regional approaches to common security were confined to encouragement of regional conferences on security and cooperation, establishment of zones of peace and nuclear weapon free zones using the models provided by the European Conferences on Security and Cooperation (Helsinki and latterly Stockholm).[5] While there was a concern to develop an inclusive view of security that included economic as well as political dimensions there was little explanation of the specific nonpolitical dynamics propelling governments to adopt common security as a foreign policy and defense objective.

In most of the discussions of common security there is a strong assumption that if the superpowers and Europe can get their act together the rest of the world will automatically be safer, more secure and peaceful. European economic and political cooperation is expected to provide a powerful example of peace in action to other less secure or unstable regions.

Because of this concentration on European security problems, non-European regional moves towards common security, while adjudged useful, tend to be assigned a rather residual status in much of the literature on the subject. The few positive moves towards confidence building, disarmament or more peaceful relations in the Asia-Pacific, Middle East, Latin American and African regions, for example, (which is where most "hot" conflicts have occurred since 1945) are not generally considered as important as the bilateral and multilateral negotiations that take place in Helsinki, Stockholm, Geneva or Vienna. Like other examples of structural imperialism this Eurocentric approach to common security has resulted in the underdevelopment of regional common security initiatives and/or largely imitative responses (e.g., the various calls for a Stockholm-style conference in the Asia-Pacific region suggested by the Governments of Mongolia and the Soviet Union and different academics and peace movement activists).[6]

What is becoming increasingly clear is that the United States and the Soviet Union and their respective allies (despite the Soviet call for an Asian Stockholm-style conference) do not accord non-European or other multilateral initiatives towards common security and disarmament the same salience as specific bilateral or multilateral European negotiations.

While arms control, nuclear weapon free zones, reductions in conventional force levels and expanding trust between NATO and the Warsaw Pact are critical to European and by extension global security, the overwhelming primacy accorded to these processes by politicians, academics and even peace activists induces a largely passive observational role for the rest of the world. This in turn reduces the impetus for other regional moves towards common security.

If common security is to become a guiding global doctrine, capable of resolving the defense dilemmas of all nations, it is vital that more time and energy be directed towards the development and affirmation of distinctive non-European regional initiatives to supplement those that are occurring in the West. In particular it is important that people, movements, companies and states become active participants in the quest for cooperative regional and global solutions to security dilemmas rather than simply constituting a passive audience for discussions between the superpowers.

If this does not happen then important national and regional steps towards common security will be overlooked or relegated in importance by the major players. At the Third Special Session on Disarmament, for example, while many nations in the plenary heartily endorsed the thawing of relations between the Soviet Union and the United States and the successful conclusion of the INF Treaty, there was no particular acknowledgement of or encouragement for the successful implementation of the South Pacific Nuclear Weapon Free Zone and other positive initiatives in the Asia-Pacific Region. It was left to the countries that had been involved in these regional processes (prompted by nongovernmental organizations) to inform other countries of the small but regionally important initiatives that had taken place between the second and third special sessions on disarmament.

Until national leaders everywhere acknowledge the importance of such regional moves there will be no sense of a global movement towards common security. It is important that such an awareness emerges fast so that all nations and peoples can begin affirming the commonality, worthwhileness and centrality of common security principles and specific action plans.

For non-nuclear weapon states (such as New Zealand) which have explicitly rejected nuclear deterrence, the enthusiastic endorsement of common security as a concrete program of action raises additional questions about the compatibility of common security with the maintenance of minimal nuclear deterrence. There is considerable ambivalence about this question. On the one hand the Palme commission states "Nuclear deterrence cannot provide the *long term basis* for peace, stability and equity in international society. It must be replaced by the concept of common security."[7]

This formulation conveniently sidesteps the issue of how long is long term and indicates that in the short to medium term, nuclear deterrence will continue to determine relations between the nuclear powers and their allies. This means that nuclear threat will continue to be a spectre hanging over non-nuclear weapon states even if risk factors are reduced. It also places a question mark over the integrity of the non-proliferation regime. If nuclear deterrence is only something that is inappropriate in the long term why should threshold states not cross over in the short to medium term? Even R. Vayrynen in a well considered discussion of the connection between nuclear weapons and common security concludes that "In the nuclear realm common security should be equated with a search for a minimal nuclear deterrence."[8] He suggests that the objective of minimal deterrence is politically realistic and compatible with common security aspirations and objectives.

While the enunciation of minimal nuclear deterrence and an abandonment of first use or flexible response principles provide some realistic transitional objectives towards a safer world, declarations and concrete programs aimed at eliminating all nuclear, chemical and biological weapons fit the common security vision better. Such declarations, while no substitute for hard-headed negotiations and specific agreements, create a more congenial climate for confidence and trust building, arms control and disarmament negotiations, exercising restraint on defense and security issues, and development of institutional arrangements aimed at nonviolent resolution of conflicts and disputes. Unequivocal non-nuclear weapon states, like New Zealand, have a particular concern with the resolution of this dilemma. If common security is compatible with medium-to long-term nuclear deterrence where will the passion and impetus come from for disarmament, conflict and crisis management measures that will reduce the risk of nuclear war to zero? If minimal deterrence becomes the agreed goal will peoples and governments simply stop worrying about nuclear threat because arsenals are at lower more stable levels? What motivation would there be for sustained opposition to qualitative arms racing? Answers to these sorts of questions seem rather important for regional discussions of common security. Without a clear commitment to non-nuclear solutions at all times what is to prevent the Japanese government, for example, from taking an initiative to go nuclear in order to ensure regional balance in the North-East Pacific? What is to prevent the qualitative improvement of Chinese nuclear weapons?

For non-nuclear states such as New Zealand the success of common security nationally and regionally hinges on adhering unswervingly to a vision of a world beyond minimal nuclear deterrence. Irrespective of how current Soviet disarmament measures are evaluated, for example, my personal inclination is to be generous and optimistic--it is important to endorse the Soviet vision of a world without any nuclear weapons and express the desire that the United States adopt this as a long-term aim also. This would encourage further Soviet flexibility and hopefully contribute to an enhancement of cooperative rather than antagonistic strategies between the superpowers.[9] It would also maintain pressure on negotiators to decrease existing arsenals to minimal levels en route to total nuclear disarmament. (It is salutary to note, for example, that the levels of nuclear weaponry being mooted for "minimal deterrence" are at higher levels than those which precipitated the first waves of public protest against nuclear weapons in the early 1960s.)

The transformation of common security from a vision into a doctrine or concrete program of action applicable to states in the Asia-Pacific region requires: an affirmation on the part of the superpowers and European nations that other nations and regions have equal status and significance in relation to the negotiation of a truly global common security regime. (While most other countries are not nuclear players and therefore cannot participate as equals in international arms control and disarmament discussions they do have interests which are affected by the success or failure of such talks. It is appropriate, therefore, that the superpowers devote more time to hearing and incorporating these preferences into the discussions.) To this end all national and regional negotiations towards disarmament, trust and confidence and which help secure economic development and social justice should be acknowledged as important steps towards a global common security regime.

The concept of common security has created an important opportunity for a paradigmatic break with the past and the development of quite different political and security relations between nations. The precise form this revolution takes, however, will be dependent on specific national and regional contributions to the global processes. (In the Asian region a Chinese/Japanese Confucian perspective on security is likely to be very different from a European conception. Linguistically, for example, security in Chinese means peace, harmony, quietude, completeness and the characters for An Quan represent a woman under a roof. These conceptions of security are very different from many dominant occidental ones.) Such linguistic and cultural differences have to be incorporated into the new common security discourse which is beginning to emerge throughout the world.

Common security involves more than changes to military capabilities and intentions, it also raises questions about the best ways of preempting conflicts, dealing with historical enmities, and ensuring that socioeconomic development occurs so that conditions for conflict increasingly disappear. To pursue common security through nonmilitary means will require considerable knowledge of other languages, cultures and traditions.

While there is considerable dispute about the place of nuclear deterrence in the quest for common security most evidence suggests that nuclear deterrence-- even at minimal levels--can only be proven in a post hoc fashion and has negative and disturbing impacts on international relations. To transcend deterrence, therefore, and to reject the doctrines associated with it (extended deterrence, flexible response etc.) is a prerequisite for liberating processes that really do generate security for everyone. The presence of nuclear weapons anywhere in the world even at minimal levels generates a level of insecurity for non-nuclear weapon states which is totally unacceptable. The effective pursuit of common security requires an unequivocal rejection of nuclear weapons and a willingness to move rapidly towards non-offensive conventional defense strategies. Small economically secure countries are probably in a better position to pursue such policies but eventually the inadmissibility of force, threat, and coercive diplomacy must be acknowledged by all nations if a new world order based on reciprocal and cooperative principles is to replace that based on competition and threat.

Common Security in the Asia-Pacific Region

As mentioned above, the leaders of the United States an the Soviet union both expect the Asia-Pacific region to be the growth center which will take the world economy into the 21st century.[10] In addition both have indicated that they expect their respective countries to play leading political and economic roles in this development. The dominant economic position of Japan, the recent rapid economic development in China and Thailand, and the dynamic role of newly industrialized countries such as Taiwan, South Korea, Hong Kong, and Singapore, mean that the Asia-Pacific region is assured constant attention from the rest of the world well into the 21st century. Economic considerations will be the primary reason for this sustained attention. The United States, for example, is being forced now to concede financial and technological dominance to Japan. The distant, but not inconceivable, prospect of a Confucian economic triangle that links Japan, China and one or two Koreas in a variety of collaborative economic arrangements will ensure that the North-East, South-East and South-West Pacific regions will be an economic force that cannot be discounted in either the short or long term. Even with renewed competition from Europe and North America, the Asia-Pacific region is going to be critical to the future development of the world as a whole. To respond to such external competition effectively will require greater harmonization of regional political and security interests as well as economic interests.

This will mean the solution of outstanding international grievances within the region, a concentration on confidence and trust building between nations and specific moves aimed at demilitarization. At the moment, there is no institutional framework for regional security discussions and the Asian region is far from constituting a common market. Japan fulfills a critical integrative role (economically), however, and tries to soften potential political conflicts before they disrupt business interests.[11] If the economic integration hypothesis is correct, however, it suggests that regional states will move towards cooperative behaviour for pragmatic economic reasons rather than out of any doctrinal desire to advance common security. (In South East Asia, for example, the Association of South East Asian Nations (ASEAN) is a good example of a regional institution aimed at advancing economic and social cooperation which has had generally beneficial impacts on the development of trust between the member nations.) For formal discussions about common security to have any real significance in the Asia-Pacific region, therefore, they must be aimed at enhancing dominant economic processes. (Of course one of the problems with this is that such processes often generate internal injustice and regional disparities. These negative features are unlikely to alter the fact, regrettably, that politicians and private decisionmakers are more likely to be persuaded by common security arguments if they are seen as good for business! It is salutary for peace and justice movements to contemplate that arguments based on solid market principles in the Asia-Pacific region will probably provide a more compelling impulse to alternative security arrangements than moral exhortation.)

What cannot be denied is that within the whole Asia-Pacific region (despite areas of appalling poverty, e.g., in Indo-China and the Philippines) there is a political obsession with profitability, efficiency and rapid economic restructuring. Growth, product diversification, market size, and regional economic integration (ASEAN in South East Asia, the Closer Economic Relationship (CER) between Australia and New Zealand, and the South Pacific Bureau for Economic Co-Operation (SPEC) linking Australasia with must of the micro states in Melanesia and Polynesia, being three notable examples) signal that the Asia-Pacific region, if it can overcome some enormous historical, cultural differences, has the potential for establishing strong economic foundations on which to build stronger cooperative security arrangements. This potential has to be set in context, however, as there are a number of competing tendencies at work which place a number of internal and external question marks over the achievement of a secure region. (While I have a tendency to be optimistic about outcomes in the short term, it is equally clear that adverse economic circumstances, political competition, wounded pride, territorial disputes or internal insurgency could result in quite severe regional tension if not actual conflict.)

Regional Stress/Tension Points

Against the economic processes which tend to be moving towards integration must be placed a range of territorial or unresolved internal disputes within the Asian-Pacific region.

In the North-East Pacific, for example, the Soviet Union and Japan still have an unresolved territorial dispute in relation to the occupied islands of Etorofu and Kunashiri in the Kurile group. While the Japanese undoubtedly have the stronger legal title to them it is equally clear that the Soviet Union now considers them vital links in its maritime defense strategy. The fact that neither side shows much willingness to compromise on this issue means that it continues to be a source of grievance and potential conflict.[12] Soviet probing of Japanese air space as one of its TU-16 bombers did in December 1987 does little to allay such anxieties.[13]

While there are continuing tensions in relation to Japanese-Chinese relations, these are becoming less important with China's increasing dependence on Japanese technological and economic assistance for its modernization program. China, however, continues to be worried by the expansion of the Japanese military, Japan's continuing trade ties with Taiwan and persistent concern about Japanese "historical amnesia" in relation to Second World War atrocities.[14]

China itself has a range of unresolved territorial disputes, some that may be resolved in the not too distant future and others which currently appear intractable. The Sino-Soviet border dispute over the Amur-Ussuri river border, for example, which generated considerable tension through the 1960s and 1970s, was directly addressed in Gorbachev's speech in Vladivostok and now looks as though it might be settled on terms favorable to China. In this speech he indicated that the Soviet Union is now willing to accept that the border runs through the center of the river rather than along the Chinese bank.[15] If this is accepted it would mean that a number of disputed islands and territories would be accepted unconditionally as Chinese territory. A successful resolution of this border dispute might also mean that the Soviet Union could contemplate reducing some of the 50 Soviet divisions, aircraft; and missiles deployed against

China. Gorbachev did announce the possible withdrawal of 45,000 Soviet soldiers based in Mongolia. These unilateral Soviet initiatives, confirmed in recent bilateral discussions between Soviet and Chinese officials, could further stabilize the border region and reduce antagonism between Moscow and Peking.

China is also embroiled in a dispute with Vietnam, the Philippines, Malaysia, and Taiwan over control of the Spratly islands in the South China Sea. While this disputed territory is unlikely to result in armed conflict, whoever ends up controlling the Spratly islands gains a very important strategic position in the South East Asian region and the dispute shows no obvious sign of being resolved in the immediate future.[16]

Ever since the Vietnamese invasion and occupation of Kampuchea, Peking's relations with Hanoi have been cool and resulted in conflicts on the Chinese-Vietnam border. (This particular dispute looks as though it might be nearer resolution, now, with the May 1988 announcement from Hanoi that it would withdraw 50,000 troops from Kampuchea by the end of the year.)[17]

While some progress is occurring in Sino-Indian relations there is still no permanent settlement of the long-standing Chinese-Indian border dispute nor is there any definite timetable for the reincorporation of Taiwan into China. China is also concerned about its border with Burma (especially in the light of recent internal disturbances there) and there are continuing problems in Tibet. While many of these disputes are being addressed in bilateral negotiations they continue to create real possibilities of conflict between China and its immediate neighbors.

Perhaps the most volatile stress point in the region, however, is Korea. The reason why this is so potentially explosive is because the Korean peninsula is an important focus of attention for four major powers: China, the United States, the Soviet Union and Japan. There seems little likelihood of reunification in the short term or for any simple international resolution of the tension between Pyongyang and Seoul. Few of the international solutions proposed for normalization of relations, (e.g., cross recognition of North and South), have found favor in both capitals and the peninsula remains divided and heavily militarized. The presence of over 40,000 United States troops in South Korea, along with nuclear landmines and other devices add additional complications to an already complex military and political situation. South Korea is more thoroughly incorporated into the economic integration of the region than North Korea but Japanese companies and officials view North Korea as an important new frontier for economic expansion which suggests that the vaunted self reliance of the North might be challenged over the next decade.

In South East Asia, internal economic pressures in Vietnam and external political pressures from Moscow have resulted in the commencement of a phased Vietnamese withdrawal. (Vietnamese politicians have been trying to reform its centralized economy and open Vietnam to foreign investment[18] but the economy is subject to very strong internal and external pressures and many commentators believe it to be on the verge of collapse. There have been two successive crop failures in the North, for example, which have precipitated the threat of starvation for up to seven million people.)[19] Once again it is interesting to note that it is not primarily the dictates of common security, but economic force majeur, which makes it important for the Vietnamese Government to work out a negotiated resolution of the Kampuchean problem. The Government of Thailand, particularly, is awaiting the outcome of these negotiations with most interest since it is concerned to normalize relations with Indo-China generally so that it can deal with Laos over border differences and also resolve settlement of its border differences with Burma. In addition to these international disputes within Asia there are a range of festering national insurgencies as well.

The Philippine Government, for example, has a long running battle with the New People's Army (which neither side seems capable of winning) and there has been considerable popular pressure on the Aquino Government not to renew the leases on the American base at Subic Bay and Clark Air Force Base even though most ASEAN governments and even China publicly or privately favor retaining an American presence as a counter to the Soviet Union and as a long-term check on any resurgent Japanese militarism.[20]

Further south, Indonesia has a continuing battle with the remnants of Fretilin in East Timor and with the Papuan Independence Movement (OPM) in Irian Jaya.

Both the Malaysian and Singaporean Governments, while not confronted with an active military insurgency, have detained a number of internal critics under their respective internal security acts. This challenge to human rights is generating intellectual discontent within both countries.

In Belau, the aspirations of the indigenous people for a nuclear free constitution conflicts with U.S. desires for a military base as an alternative to those located in the Philippines and this has proven to be a source of conflict between both the United States and the Belauan people.

In the South-West Pacific, Colonel Rambuka's 1987 coup in Fiji aroused the possibility of internal armed struggle in an area which has hitherto been considered benign and free of such unconstitutional activity. In French Polynesia, Kanak aspirations for independence and French intransigence (while muted since the compromise solution advanced by M. Rocard) remain a source of conflict in New Caledonia. Although it is remote there is also a possibility that the political grievances of the Maoris in New Zealand and Aborigines in Australia, if unsatisfied, could lead to urban and rural violence. Such violence could be precipitated either by frustrated Maori and Aboriginal activists or by Europeans bent on avoiding a rectification of past injustices. In Vanuatu there are worrying signs of political instability and an emergence of one-party rule.

This very brief overview of stress points and tensions within the Asia-Pacific region indicate that while there are economic pressures in the direction of integration there are also unresolved political problems which continue to cause tensions between and within nations. These problems are likely to fuel conventional arms races and stimulate a reliance on unilateral military solutions. They also pose rather obvious problems for the generation of intra-regional trust and confidence building.

Whether the resolution of these conflicts is a prerequisite for arms control discussions and the building of confidence and cooperation or whether reductions in conventional weaponry and trust building would resolve the regional tensions is a moot point. My inclination is to see processes leading towards resolution of national and international conflicts occurring simultaneously with broader discussions about arms control, trust building and alternative nonmilitary ways of guaranteeing national integrity and wider security.

In the North pacific, for example, which is arguably the most tense part of the Asia Pacific region there have been almost no discussions on regional arms control and certainly no agreements equivalent to those that exist in the South-West Pacific, (e.g., The Antarctic Treaty, the South Pacific Nuclear Free Zone). Nor is there anything comparable to discussions (which admittedly have not resulted in much concrete progress yet) in South East Asia on a Zone of Peace, Freedom and Neutrality. While there have been numerous discussions about resolution of the conflicts between the two Koreas, China and Japan, and Japan, China and the Soviet Union these have not so far resulted in any resolution satisfactory to all parties.

Taking the Asia-Pacific region as a whole, therefore, the area of greatest strategic contention in the North-East Pacific has seen virtually no progress towards common security (except in terms of moves towards economic cooperation and integration) while the strategically less significant South-West Pacific has seen the emergence of an unequivocal nuclear free New Zealand, Vanuatu, and Solomon Islands and the negotiation of a regional arms control agreement which provides the basis for building a more effective sub-regional regime against nuclear weapons when circumstances are propitious for doing so.

Militarization in Asia and the Pacific

If limiting the growth of military expenditure is an important arms control objective, the need would seem to be greater in the North Pacific than in

Europe. Military expenditure in the Far East as a whole (excluding China and the USSR) grew at 4.4% between 1982 and 1985 (compared with a growth rate of 2.9% in the previous three years) and Asian states are buying some of the most modern weapon systems currently available. By contrast, the rate of growth in military expenditure in the European NATO countries during the first five years of the 1980s was well under 3%.[21]

Such expenditure is both a response to the regional tensions outlined above and also a cause of them. Whatever the specific internal or external reasons for such budgetary decisions, high levels of military expenditure make the promotion of conventional arms control, disarmament and common security discussions within the region much more problematic than they might otherwise be. It is likely that economic circumstances will place some downward pressure on defense spending in future but until this happens and unless it is accompanied by a build down in force levels, the Asian region (the North Pacific in particular) will remain a highly militarized part of the world. But it is not just national defense expenditure that makes cooperative Asian solutions to the defense and security dilemmas problematic. Both super-powers must also assume a considerable responsibility for impeding the evolution of trust, cooperation and confidence between potential antagonists in Asia. Just as the North Pacific region (Japan in particular) has become economically more dominant in the past decade so too has its military significance for Washington and Moscow. There has, for example, been "a doubling of Soviet ground forces, a near doubling of Soviet surface combatants and a six fold increase in fighter aircraft since the mid-1960s.[22]

This Soviet expansion precipitated a predictable reaction from the United States which not only built up its own naval forces and antisubmarine capability but harnessed this expansion to more provocative doctrines; for example, the forward maritime strategy of former U.S. Assistant Secretary of Defense John Lehman[23] and the concept of horizontal escalation which is aimed at throwing Soviet forces engaged in any conflict in Europe off balance by quickly opening up a second front in the Far East. To respond to these threats Soviet Forces in the Far East have undergone significant restructuring and much technological effort is now going into trying to make Soviet SSBNs more invulnerable to attack. Despite the Soviet expansion of its Pacific fleet it is clear that the Soviet Union is not currently capable of challenging United States naval supremacy in the Pacific. Most strategists seem to agree that in the North Pacific the Soviet Union has dominance on land and the United States retains naval superiority. (If allied navies are counted into the order of battle this superiority is even more overwhelming.) Air force strength is more or less equal. It is largely because of this imbalance that much Soviet diplomatic effort has been expended in attacking the United States maritime strategy. For their part, the U.S. Navy has developed extraordinary sensitivity to any initiative which might place constraints on U.S. naval operations in the Pacific or anywhere else in the world. This sensitivity helps explain why the United States Administration under promptings from the navy took such grave exception to New Zealand's unilateral ban on the visit of nuclear armed/powered warships to New Zealand ports. [24]

Andrew Mack and other strategic analysts believe, however, that the most serious challenges to regional security do not lie in the strategic imbalance but in the deployment of sea launched, nuclear armed, land attack cruise missiles particularly the U.S. Tomahawk and its Soviet counterparts the SS-N-21 and the nearly developed SS-NX-24. [25] None of these categories of weapons are covered by the terms of the INF Treaty and yet both are capable of fulfilling quasi-strategic roles against the continental United States or the Soviet Union. So even though the INF Treaty and reasonably amicable global summitry has generated a measure of global stability (especially with the inclusion of Soviet Asian-based SS20 missiles) these sea launched weapons remain and pose similar sorts of dangers to those that Cruise and SS20 missiles used to pose in Europe.

Another critical problem which has been noted by many observers in recent years is the tendency for both the Soviet Union and the United States to engage in provocative military exercising in the North Pacific region. [26] These exercises have been getting larger and are subject to less control or supervision in the Pacific than their equivalents in Europe. Although there are some informal bilateral agreements between the navies of the Soviet Union and the United States which establish some basic norms, these exercises generate tension instead of trust and make confidence building and conflict resolution more difficult. While both superpowers continue to probe each others' defensive arrangements and practice large war games in strategically sensitive areas the risks of accidental or unintentional conflict will continue in the North Pacific.

Any discussion of militarization in the Asia-Pacific region would be very incomplete without considering the changing military role of Japan.

There are a number of reasons why this is important. Japan's dominant position within the world economy generates enormous political influence and yet there is considerable uncertainty within the region and further afield about what sort of independent role Japan intends playing in the political and military spheres.

Officials and politicians (on both sides of the political spectrum) in both Washington and Tokyo assume that the Japan-United States Security Treaty will continue and that the consequent harmony of interests on central strategic questions (economic wrangles notwithstanding) renders the assertion of an independent Japanese view on defense and central security issues unnecessary.

While this may have been a reasonable assumption to make in the past there are now internal and external pressures nudging Japan in a more heavily militarized direction.

Internally, for example, the Federation of Economic Organizations--the Keidanren--which is Japan's most influential business lobby has a special defense production committee with 84 member companies. Some of the largest, (e.g., Mitsubishi which already produces McDonnell Douglas F-15 fighters under license and Kawasaki which makes Lockheed P3C antisubmarine patrol aircraft), have been lobbying for more freedom to make weapons over a number of years.[27] Added to these economic pressures, Japanese, right-wing groups want a higher political and military profile to accompany Japanese economic dominance in the region.

Externally, the U.S. Government has been urging the Japanese to expand defense expenditure and assume a more active role in "policing" the North Pacific thereby taking some of the economic burden off the United States. U.S. politicians and business leaders have often expressed irritation that the United States has absorbed most of the financial burden for Japanese and North Pacific security and feel that it is time for Japan to assume a greater share of the defense burden while opening up domestic markets for U.S. goods. The Japanese Government is responding to these pressures for more attention to defense and security in two ways. The first is by stepping up economic development assistance to poor countries, both for altruistic reasons and also in order to bind them as closely as possible to Western security interests. In 1988, for example, Japan will surpass the United States as the world's leading aid donor, U.S. $10 billion compared with U.S. grants of U.S. $9.2 billion. Much of this aid has clear political strings, (e.g., Japanese aid to the Philippines where Japan is the leading partner in a U.S. $10 billion multi-year, mini-Marshall plan to rescue the country) is intended, among other things, to encourage the Corazon Aquino Government to renew the leases on the two major U.S. bases in the Philippines.[28]

In addition to increasing its official development assistance and support for United Nations peace keeping operations the Japanese government is also expanding its direct military spending. It has, for example, increased its share of the cost of keeping 55,000 U.S. troops at 103 installations and bases in Japan. Japanese assistance now stands at U.S. $2.5 billion per annum or U.S.$ 45,000 per soldier. The United States pays U.S. $3.5 billion for the maintenance of U.S.troops in Japan and would like to reverse the proportions.[29] In spite of an undertaking not to spend more than 1% of their gross national product on defense (already a phenomenal amount of money) the Japanese Government now spends approximately 1.6% of their GNP on defense. According to Yukio Okamoto, a senior Foreign Ministry official:

We're already at the same level of the NATO countries and according to some experts, we'll soon have the third largest defense budget in the world behind only the Soviet Union and the United States. By the end of our current five year defense plan in 1990 Japan will have 180 F-15 jet fighters - more than are deployed in the continental United States. We will have 62 destroyers, more than in the entire British fleet... 100 P-3C Orion anti-submarine aircraft, four times what the U.S. 7th Fleet has in the Western Pacific and the Indian Ocean.[30]

U.S. requests for more defense expenditure have also produced an agreement to spend U.S. $978 million on four destroyers that will be the largest warships to be constructed in Japan since the Second World War. The Japanese national Diet, or parliament, has agreed also to finance the first of an undisclosed number of sonar equipped antisubmarine vessels at an estimated U.S. $104 million each. They have also agreed to develop a new antisubmarine warfare centre at Yokosuka.[31]

This sort of expenditure on national defense, while not immediately worrying, is causing come anxiety among Chinese and Korean officials about Japan's short and long-term military intentions.

Japanese harmonization of its security policies with those of the United States, its assumption of responsibility for control of sea lines of communications out to 1,000 nautical miles from Japan means that the Japanese Government currently fulfills a vital strategic role for the Western alliance in general and the United States in particular.[32] While this role is currently acceptable to most countries in the region there is no guarantee that it will continue to be so. Insofar as such a surrogate defense role activates both anti-American and latent anti-Japanese sentiments it will be detrimental to Japanese economic interests in the region. Again it is somewhat ironical that a more enlightened approach to defense may occur because of economic anxiety rather than for any principled reasons.

Further Japanese rearmament, qualitative and quantitative improvements in their armed forces will prompt other nations to ask exactly where independent Japan stands on key security issues.

The Soviet Union is currently more anxious than China or South Korea about the implications of Japanese rearmament[33] but there is simmering anxiety in the rest of South East Asia (stimulated by Second World War memories) about Japan's long-term foreign policy intentions. To help allay such anxieties Japanese foreign ministers have embarked on a series of regional tours to discuss appropriate ways in which Japan might use its economic and political power for the benefit of the whole region, but the lingering doubts remain and act to undermine confidence in Japanese intentions.

This is not the place to go into more details on the diverse ways in which superpower and national militarization generate tensions or contradict integrative tendencies but sufficient has been noted to indicate that the Asia Pacific region is highly militarized and is arguably more dangerous than the European theater where more time and effort has been expended on measures to reduce confrontation and tension.

While judgments about the military intentions of both superpowers in the Pacific are more difficult than those on military capability the evidence strongly suggests that U.S. military doctrines tend to be more destabilizing than those of the Soviet Union most of whose land based forces are oriented primarily towards China rather than the United States. If the Sino-Soviet dispute could be settled and a significant number of Soviet troops and air force units were withdrawn the justifications for U.S. and Japanese strategies would look decidedly implausible.

What Are the Prospects for Common Security in the Asia-Pacific Region?

In spite of obvious challenges to the evolution of a common security regime in the Asia-Pacific region (e.g., border disputes, internal insurgencies, and continuing militarization) there are strong economic and social pressures driving towards higher levels of sub-regional and regional integration. In fact, as mentioned above, the dictates of economic restructuring and expanding readily accessible markets provide more compelling reasons for cooperative solutions of security problems than moral exhortation. Having said this it is also clear that current economic inequalities between countries in the region will determine the shape and contour of the economic development and integration that occurs. Thus there will be stresses and strains between the rich, powerful and poor, powerless nations in the region. Whether such economic inequalities will result in inevitable political or military conflict is unclear. Where Europe is characterized by a reasonably clear confrontation between two military blocs (albeit united by a shared European cultural and historical tradition) the Asia-Pacific region is characterized by a series of crosscutting bilateral military relationships and multiple cultural divisions between East and South East Asia, Australasia and the Pacific island states. Whereas there is a history of arms control and disarmament discussions in Europe the Asia-Pacific region is complex and heterogeneous, politically, economically, and culturally.

Because of this diversity realist and neo-realist theorists encounter some difficulty determining any simple balance of power between opposing parties in the region.[34]

Apart from the obvious border disputes, for example, there is no agreement on who is the enemy or what might produce wider regional conflict. China, for example, which used to be the enemy of the former members of the South East Asian Treaty organization, is now a friend of most of those countries. The Soviet Union has few effective allies or friends in the region. While the United States has both friends and allies and continues to exert strong influence, it is no longer able to exert a determinate influence over regional economic or political processes. Japan is undoubtedly the single most influential regional actor although it too has to walk a delicate tightrope between influence and antagonism.

Despite the stress points mentioned above and the cataclysmic conflicts that have afflicted Asia since the end of the Second World War, the region as a whole (with the exception of the Kampuchea/Thai border dispute) is now reasonably stable and certainly not subject to the sort of bloc confrontation that characterizes European security arrangements.

So what national/regional forces are moving towards common security arrangements in Asia and the Pacific and what are the major obstructions?

Instead of starting in the North Pacific, which is the area of most contention and where there is currently no real momentum towards regional arms control discussions or confidence building it is more appropriate to begin in the South-West Pacific since this region is relatively secure and some sub-regional progress towards common security has been made already. (This region includes Australia, New Zealand and the 13 other members of the South Pacific Forum, e.g., Fiji, Vanuatu, Papua New Guinea, the Solomon Islands, Samoa, Tonga and a number of even smaller micro states.)

As noted already the South-West Pacific sub-region is strategically peripheral, not a focus for superpower confrontation, and the countries within it have spent a considerable amount of energy since the Second World War building up institutions to facilitate regional cooperation (e.g., the South Pacific Commission established in 1947, the South Pacific Forum established in 1971, the South Pacific Forum established in 1971, the South Pacific Bureau for Economic Co-operation (SPEC) a 1972 offshoot from the Forum, the Pacific Forum Shipping Line (1977) and Forum Fisheries Agency.)

Relations between Australia and New Zealand are intimate and secure and rapid movement is being made under the Closer Economic Relations (CER) framework for a full common market between both countries by 1991. Despite the anxiety of some micro states (most notably Vanuatu and Kiribati) about the economic domination of Australia and New Zealand it is generally assumed that an Australasian common market will strengthen the national economies of both countries and have beneficial impacts on the island economies. Neither Australia nor New Zealand nor any of the Pacific Island states feels strategically insecure or directly threatened by any external power.[35] Because of this very benign situation and the absence of any superpower rivalry in the region many of the common security proposals that apply in Europe and which might apply in the North Pacific, (e.g., notification of military exercising, mutual troop reductions, trust building, nuclear weapons negotiations, etc.) do not seem to have any obvious applicability to the sub-region.

Because there are no regional or global military threats to the nations of the South-West Pacific these countries are all more preoccupied with economic rather than security questions. The small micro states, for example, have directed a good deal of their energies towards the development of a free trade zone for the whole sub-region. (The South Pacific regional Trade and Economic Co-operation Agreement (SPARTECA) signed in 1981 was an agreement aimed at giving the small states of the South pacific preferential access to Australian and New Zealand markets.) This economic integration is a very rational response to the precarious economic viability of small states with very limited natural resources and identified as much more important than countering the remote possibility of military conflict at the regional or international level.

While economic questions are paramount, South-West Pacific nations were sensitized to global nuclear issues by the first U.S. test explosions at Bikini Atoll. Regional resistance to nuclear weapons and nuclear testing has been particularly vociferous, however, ever since the French transferred their testing site from the Sahara to Mururoa Atoll in French Polynesia in 1966.

It was largely in response to French testing and concern to take some national and regional initiatives against the threat of global nuclear war that the Pacific Forum countries (at the instigation of Australia and New Zealand) and in collaboration with the United Nations negotiated the South Pacific Nuclear Free Zone Treaty which was eventually adopted on 6 August 1985. Despite the reservations of many peace activists that it does not go far enough to control port calls, the transit of nuclear powered or armed warships or planes, and joint United States/Australian C3I facilities in Australia this Treaty is undoubtedly one of the most significant contributions towards common security in the South-West Pacific region.[36]

Despite the reservations of peace movement activists that the Treaty does not go far enough--it specifically excludes U.S. Micronesia, for example, which hosts the U.S. missile testing facility at Kwajalein, and the Anderson air force base on Guam which has a nuclear stockpile; it also leaves intact United States/Australian C3I facilities at Nurrangar and Pine Gap[37]--the South Pacific Nuclear Free Zone Treaty is definitely a very important first step towards subregional denuclearization. Taken in conjunction with the Antarctic Treaty and the Weaker Treaty of Tlatelolco it indicates that most of the southern hemisphere nations (with two or three notable exceptions) are signaling clearly to the North a strong desire to be nuclear free and for nuclear weapons to have no part in the defense of half the surface of the globe.

Having said this it is clear that this initiative also has deficiencies and that its primary significance is moral and symbolic. Since it is not possible to interfere with passage on the high seas, nuclear powered and armed vessels and aircraft can traverse the zone with impunity and while respecting the terms of the Treaty they are still able to deploy and fire nuclear weapons from within the zone. The response to this objection is that more states party to the Treaty should adopt New Zealand's policy of denying access to nuclear powered and armed vessels or planes and thus create more genuinely nuclear free areas. While the Treaty is intended as a legal document it is also a statement of popular regional desire. It is hoped that nuclear powers will respect this desire and act accordingly.

In fact one of the most serious problems with the South Pacific Treaty is the unwillingness of Western nuclear powers to sign and ratify the protocols to the Treaty.

Protocol 1 (which was formulated after careful consultations in Washington, Paris and London) asks France, the United States and the UK to apply the provisions of the Treaty to their remaining territories within the zone. Protocol 2 contains the negative security guarantees and is addressed to all five nuclear weapon states and protocol 3 prohibits the testing of any nuclear device anywhere in the region.

The Soviet Union and China were the first countries to sign protocols 2 and 3. The Soviet Union initially had reservations about protocol 2. Their negative security guarantees were originally conditional on member states not committing acts of aggression in alliance with other nuclear weapons states or during such aggression permitting transit or visiting rights to air or sea vessels of nuclear weapon states, these conditions under entreaty from Australia and New Zealand were subsequently withdrawn in 1988. China signed unconditionally.

The United States, France and the UK for different reasons have not signed any of the protocols (even though their interests were strongly taken into account during the drafting process.) The United States (despite some support for the Treaty of Tlatelolco) has a long-standing policy of objecting to nuclear weapon free zones in most other parts of the world and Reagan officials believed that support for the South pacific Nuclear Weapons Free Zone would create a dangerous antinuclear precedent for other parts of the world. (Their main anxiety, of course, is that eventually these zones will converge and U.S. forces would not be able to roam freely wherever they wished.) this rejection by the Reagan Administration was condemned by "liberals" like Congressman

Stephen Solarz who quite rightly realized that the Zone places few restrictions on U.S. military activity and should be accepted as a signal that the United States is interested in reducing nuclear risk and uncertainty, but his counsels did not prevail.

France sees itself as a Pacific power and still occupies three island groups. It does not wish to cut itself out of the economic growth of the wider Pacific region, and wishes to maintain its nuclear testing program. The French Government believed that signing the protocols of the Raratonga Treaty would put an end to its testing program but more importantly be seen as a sign of "softness" and over responsiveness to local pressures. They clearly believed that signing the protocols would result in additional pressure for independence in Kanaky/New Caledonia and in other parts of French Polynesia. The UK has no objective reasons for not signing but did not wish to delink from France and the United States.

The UK and the United States did, however, indicate that they would not act in ways that infringed the spirit of the Treaty. The diplomatic advantage, however, clearly goes to the Soviet Union and China who have both demonstrated a greater willingness to endorse antinuclear aspirations than the Western nuclear powers. (Some would say that this support is cynical since neither the Soviet Union nor China has nuclear interests in the region but the fact that they have done so has certainly been noticed.)

In addition to this regional initiative some mention should also be made of New Zealand's unilateral action against nuclear weapons and deterrence generally. New Zealand's unequivocal ban on the entry of nuclear armed, powered warships or aircraft was the culmination of many years campaigning by the New Zealand peace movement and the New Zealand Labour party.[38] While it disrupted taken for granted defense relations with the United States under ANZUS and momentarily disrupted defense links with Australia its primary purpose was a contribution to denuclearization regionally and globally and as an "official" statement to the rest of the world that the New Zealand Government saw absolutely no future in nuclear deterrence as doctrine or theology. While it is arguable whether the stand has had more then moral/symbolic significance there is no doubt at all that it certainly encouraged many other peoples and nations to maintain more rapid momentum for a world without such weapons. It is a policy which New Zealanders feel has made a small contribution to reducing nuclear risk although its critics would argue that it has done just the opposite. As someone who advocated and argued the policy and who had some small responsibility for working through the conventional defense implications after it was implemented I think it was a very important contribution to both regional and global nuclear security.[39]

Moving away from the South-West Pacific where arguably most tangible steps towards common security have been made (the critics would argue that such progress has been made precisely because the security problems are simple and the region is generally benign and strategically peripheral) towards South East Asia and the North Pacific we discover sub-regions which are more heavily militarized; where there are statements of intention but no actual negotiations for nuclear weapon free zones, confidence-building measures, or conventional force reduction.

This is also the part of the Asia-Pacific region that has the most need for such discussions. So what are the positive forces leading towards cooperation, peaceful resolution of dispute and the development of machinery that might begin the long and arduous process of negotiating regional disarmament and arms control agreements?

I have mentioned economic pressures which are leading towards a more closely integrated South East and East Asian region. The Association of South East Asian Nations, (ASEAN), therefore, has to be counted as a significant confidence-building measure within South East Asia. It deliberately eschewed becoming a political or military pact at its inception (and continues to resist pressures in this direction) and has two basic objectives: to prevent national threat perceptions from becoming impediments to economic and social cooperation; and to make a concerted effort to meet the basic human needs for the people in the region.[40] These objectives do help generate confidence between the South East Asian nations and have somewhat pre-empted the necessity for bruising discussions about different strategic perceptions. Despite the fact the ASEAN is not a formal security arrangement, ASEAN nations have incorporated other key players in the region into discussions on many key issues (most notably Kampuchea and Indo-China) in order to harmonize regional responses (e.g., Australia, New Zealand, the United States and Japan all have observer status at ASEAN ministerial meetings). On balance, therefore, ASEAN is clearly a positive and cooperative force within the Asian region. It is autonomous and buoyant (despite pressing internal difficulties in the Philippines and Indonesia and continuing problems in Indo-China) and provides a basis for significant economic integration in future. It provides a structure for mutual understanding, confidence and trust.

This structure while oriented primarily toward economic and social cooperation has not been indifferent to strategic questions, however, and in 1971 in the Kuala Lumpur declaration ASEAN declared its desire to secure recognition of South East Asia as a Zone of Peace Freedom and Neutrality (ZOPEAN). although this was put on the backburner somewhat after the invasion of Kampuchea in 1978 it continues to provide an aspiration which is in accord with common security. As recently as July of this year the Malaysian minister of Foreign Affairs indicated that:

One important step for advancing the early realization of ZOPEAN is the establishment of a South East Asia Nuclear weapon free Zone comprising all South East Asia states. The establishment of a South east Asia Nuclear weapon free zone will serve as an effective measure for reducing tension and promoting peace and security in the region...Establishment of the Nuclear Weapon free Zone would constitute a milestone in our efforts towards the realization of ZOPFAN.[41]

While this conflicts somewhat with the desire of many South East Asian countries to retain an American presence in the Philippines (see above) and would encounter strong resistance from the United States it is a clear signal (from Malaysia and Indonesia most particularly) that key countries in South East Asia do not wish their regions to be nuclearized or defended with nuclear weapons. (The presence of U.S. bases in the Philippines and Soviet naval forces in Camh Ranh Bay in Vietnam are two obvious problems in relation to the negotiation of a meaningful nuclear weapon free zone. While there are difficulties about linking the two bases and a Soviet and U.S. unwillingness to move either of them I think that it would be an important confidence building measure in South East Asia for both Moscow and Washington to withdraw these bases from the region.)

Such moves are positive and need to be encouraged. ASEAN should also be encouraged to continue taking initiatives that result in the peaceful resolution of disputes (e.g., like the recent Indonesian initiative in relation to a permanent settlement of the Kampuchean problem). Such measures will certainly ensure a more secure sub-region in the 1990s and into the 21st century. If Indo-China can be incorporated into ASEAN discussions on a more regular basis there is every prospect that South East Asia will enjoy much more peaceful relations in the future than it has enjoyed in the past.

While South East Asia shows reasonably positive signs that it will develop into a reasonably benign area, the same cannot be said for the North Pacific. The major players, China, Japan, the Soviet Union and the United States, have not indicated that there is any desire to develop a North Pacific nuclear weapon free zone although the Soviet Union in 1969 did make some self-serving and cynical proposals for a "collective Asian security system" (roundly rejected by most of the Asian states) while a rather less cynical proposal emerged from Mikhail Gorbachev's 1986 Vladivostok speech for an Asian security conference along the lines of the CSCE model or that occurring in Stockholm. The U.S. and Japanese position on these suggestions has been consistently negative with little support to suggestions for regional conferences on confidence building, arms control or disarmament. It is clear, however, that even if Japan and the United States wish to adopt a negative or indifferent response at the moment they will not be able to avoid the inevitable necessity for some regional discussions on arms control, anti-submarine warfare, naval deployment and CBMs, or what to do with Sea Launched Cruise Missiles.

Mikhail Gorbachev's September 1988 appeal for fresh negotiations on the naval arms race, and negotiations on Camh Ranh Bay and U.S. bases in the Philippines will undoubtedly keep pressure on the United States to start negotiating a regional common security regime.

Countries outside the North Pacific will not countenance a heavily militarized, high-risk area in the North Pacific if the South West Pacific and South East Asian regions are moving towards tighter socioeconomic integration, stronger nuclear weapon free regimes, and more peaceful procedures for resolving regional disputes.

While Japan, China, the United States, the Soviet Union and Korea may be reluctant to move into large multilateral regional discussions on such issues there will undoubtedly be bilateral discussions on nonconfrontational modes of resolving the disputes, (e.g., Chinese/Russian discussions on troop reductions consequent on an increased thaw in their relations). Soviet/Japanese discussions (although currently in the too-hard basket) might be a possibility in the future and of course discussions about arms control, crisis management and risk reduction in Korea are of paramount importance to the region as a whole. It seems particularly important to move rather rapidly on both bilateral and multilateral confidence-building measures that eliminate the possibility of accidental or unintentional conflicts and which enhance "transparency" between the different forces arrayed in the North Pacific. Advocates of such a proposal argue that:

> Establishment of the commission would represent a critically important first step in the establishment of an arms control regime for the North Pacific. By agreeing to establish the organization, participating governments would be signaling their desire to enhance their mutual security and reduce the risk of conflict. The commission would provide an institutional backbone for the entire arms control process, as well as an organizational vehicle for developing the mechanisms of future arms control agreements. The commission would provide a neutral forum for the discussion and negotiation of mutually acceptable confidence-building measures and, conceivably, other types of arms control arrangements. It could also be used for the airing of grievances, complaints, or differences in interpretation of agreements in force.[42]

Such a suggestion seems eminently sensible but would require the active support of countries such as Japan, China, the United States and the Soviet Union if it were to succeed. The current regime in the Soviet Union has indicated a flexibility to contemplate such an arrangement; it would be nice to think that as Japan assumes more and more international responsibility it too would be willing to demonstrate independent flexibility on this issue and direct its not inconsiderable economic and political resources towards ensuring that this suggestion worked and was successful. This perhaps more than anything else would provide a very useful (reasonably indigenous) regional institution that would undoubtedly make an innovative contribution to common security in the Asia Pacific region.

Conclusion

While there are some grounds for despair in the Asia-Pacific region current trends suggest greater cooperation and peacefulness. The demands and dictates of economic growth (especially in a situation of resource scarcity, opening markets and a highly integrated communications and information system) demand the assumption of pacific rather than bellicose policies, in particular a cessation of expensive arms purchases, the naval race and provocative exercising. None of these are good conditions for business or development generally.

The Soviet Union and China have both embarked on radical economic restructuring, with China already in retreat from earlier initiatives. Foreign and defense policies are also in transition. Vietnam is showing signs that it too wants to reform its economy in a more decentralized and market direction; the sub-regional zones of the South-West Pacific and South East Asia have taken some regional initiatives which indicate that they believe there is more to be gained from rapprochement and peaceful relations than competitive and un-peaceful ones.

The United States is becoming increasingly isolated in its persistent promotion of nuclear deterrence, offensive military doctrines and an unwillingness to submit arms control, disarmament and confidence-building issues to multilateral fora. It cannot and should not expect to regain its declining imperium by persuading Japan to maintain old containment and cold war strategies which are increasingly out of kilter with political forces throughout the world. A prerequisite for real common security initiatives in the North Pacific, therefore, is a gradual strategic disengagement of Japan from the dominant security concerns of the United States. While structural disengagement does not seem likely in the immediate future, and could paradoxically precipitate more rapid Japanese militarization, there needs to be an intellectual and political disengagement so that countries currently subject to Japanese economic penetration can get a feel for the real foreign policy differences that exist between Washington and Tokyo. These two countries hold the key to peace and prosperity in the region as a whole and both need to change their approach to defense and security measures (more in the direction of common rather than national or bilateral military security) in order to give greater recognition to the positive and stabilizing initiatives that have been taken by the Soviet Union but more importantly to acknowledge the legitimacy of the peaceful aspirations of all peoples everywhere.

The success of the principles of common security, therefore, rest finally on. what happens in the North Pacific and cannot be gained by stability in Europe alone. While European and bilateral initiatives between the superpowers are important, the ways in which Japan, China, Korea, the United States and the Soviet Union settle their differences in the North Pacific will in the long run prove more instrumental in the determination of both regional and global peace.

If these major state actors are sensitive to the antinuclear and common security concerns of smaller, strategically expendable countries on the periphery, they ought to be able to generate more harmonious relations between themselves. If they are not then they will become increasingly marginal to the new non-nuclear order that is slowly emerging. It is not just because New Zealand has been willing to unambiguously reject nuclear deterrence that I tend to be optimistic about the future. There are real grounds for hope that the whole Pacific region is beginning to change in a more peaceful and cooperative direction. The challenge facing peoples and states in the Asia-Pacific region is to ensure that the forces moving towards economic integration result in security doctrines consistent with those enunciated by the Palme Commission and do not result in structural inequalities which effectively undermine the alternative security doctrines.

Notes

1.   In retrospect it is now clear that the expansion of U.S. defense spending was a cynical attempt to court domestic political support. Its legitimation was based on faulty information and it undoubtedly diminished U.S. security by fueling a blow out in the U.S. deficit and generating extraordinary military wastage, graft and corruption in the Pentagon. A 1983 Central Intelligence Agency report, for example, indicated that the U.S. aggressive posture and defense spending spree was based on faulty information about the real growth rate of Soviet military spending. Instead of a relentless Soviet expansion (as the Administration had claimed) the Soviet Union had cut their real defense growth rate in half from 4-5% for 1970-76 to 2% a year from 1976-83. and the CIA also discovered the important point that Soviet military procurement was stagnant and had not grown in real terms for the entire seven-year period. See Joshua Epstein, *The 1988 Defense Budget* (Washington: The Brookings Institution, 1987), p. 1.

2.   For a discussion of the background to the work of the Palme Commission and concern about unilateral measures see R. Vayrynen, "Common Security: A Metaphor and an Incipient Doctrine," *World Futures*, Vol. 24, 1987, pp. 177-178.

3.   See Johan Galtung, *There Are Alternatives: Four Roads to Peace and Security* (Nottingham: Spokesman books, 1984.) Particularly Chapter 4 on disarmament where Galtung says of the Palme Commission recommendations "What is good is not new and what is new is not particularly good," p. 139.

4.   Independent Commission on Disarmament and Security Issues, *Common Security: A Blueprint for Survival* (London: Pan Books, 1982), p. 138.

5.   I will not develop the common security idea any further here since the central ideas are now very familiar. The original 1982 book coining the term has now been elaborated by Raimo Vayrynen, ed., et al., *Policies for Common Security* (London: Taylor and Francis, 1985) and in numerous other articles, e.g., Vayrynen, *op. cit.*, note 2; and R. Mutz, *Common Security, Elements of an Alternative to Deterrence Peace* (Hamburg: University Institute for Peace Research and Security Policy, 1985).

6.   For some recent discussions of this suggestion see Kevin P. Clements, *Back from the Brink: The Creation of a Nuclear Free New Zealand* (Wellington and London: Allen and Unwin Ltd., 1988) and some more recent discussions in Andrew Mack, "Arms Control in the North Pacific," Background paper No. 1 to 53rd Pugwash Symposium on Peace and Security in the Asian-Pacific Region, Beijing, People's Republic of China, October 17-20, 1988; also T. Findlay, "Confidence Building and Conflict Reduction in the Pacific: The Relevance of the European Experience," paper delivered to 53rd Pugwash Symposium on Peace and Security in the Asian-Pacific Region, Beijing, P.R.C., October 17-20, 1988.

7.   Independent Commission on Disarmament and Security Issues, *op. cit.*, note 4, p. 142.

8.   See Raimo Vayrynen, *op. cit.*, note 2, p. 190.

9.   It is fascinating to see how asymmetrical the Summit papers are in terms of short or long-term objectives. The Soviet Union is willing to imagine a world beyond minimal deterrence while the United States is aiming for permanent nuclear deterrence with more stability. While stability and risk reduction is useful it is not particularly conducive to the achievement of more truly cooperative defense and security policies and is certainly not conducive to the enhancement of common security in the Asia-Pacific region.

10.   See "Rivalry in the Pacific," *Time Magazine*, November 24, 1986, pp. 4-11.

11.   It is interesting to note in this regard that the Australian Minister of Trade, Michael Duffy, is warning that if the current GATT round does not produce a desirable outcome on agriculture Australia will take the lead in initi-

ating a Pacific-run trading community. This view was also echoed strongly by New Zealand's Minister of Overseas Trade, Michael Moore. See *The Christchurch Press*, Vol. 9, No. 8, 1988.

12. Wolf Mendl, Department of War Studies, London University, who has been following this issue closely, feels that the one or two Soviet initiatives which would have conceded two of the islands could have been responded to more positively by the Japanese Government but were equivocally rejected, (Personal conversation, Tokyo August 20, 1988).

13. See R. Horiguchi, "Soviet Snooper finds a Sting in the Air," *Pacific Defence Reporter*, March 1988, p. 11.

14. See Hong N. Kim, "Sino-Japanese Relations," *Current History*, Vol. 87, No. 528, April 1988, pp. 153-180. The question of not allowing Japan to develop "historical amnesia" was a strong sub-theme at the United Nations University Seminar on Common Security and the Role of the State, held in Yokohama, December 12-16, 1987 attended by the author.

15. See *Time*, November 24, 1986, *op. cit.*, note 10, p. 8.

16. See Kim Gordon-Bates, "A Sea of Troubles," in *South*, June 1988, pp. 35-37.

17. See *Far Eastern Economic Review*, Vol. 140, No. 22, June 2, 1988; also *The Christchurch Press*, June 7, 1988.

18. See Tom Fawthrop, "Vietnam's Opening Door," *South*, October 1987; and M. Barang, "Overstepping the Marx," *South*, February 1982, pp. 23-24.

19. See Barry Wain, "Vietnam Squeezed by Crop Shortage and Currency Crisis," *The Asian Wall Street Journal*, Vol. 10, No. 20, May 16, 1988, pp. 1 and 20.

20. See Susumu Awanohara, "Many East Asian Countries Want the U.S. to Remain," *Far Eastern Economic Review*, Vol. 140, No. 16, April 21, 1988, pp. 27-28.

21. Andrew Mack, "Arms Control in the North Pacific: Problems and Prospects," Background paper No. 1 presented to the 53rd Pugwash Symposium on "Peace and Security in the Asian-Pacific Region" Beijing, P.R.C., October 17-20, 1988. Most of my information on weapon systems in the Asia Pacific region is gleaned from this paper.

22. See Paul Dibb, "The Soviet Union as a Pacific Military Power," Working Paper No. 81, Strategic and Defence Studies Centre, Australian National University, Canberra, August 1984, pp. 7-9 cited in Mack, *ibid.*, p. 2.

23. See P. Hayes, L. Zarsky and W. Bello, *American Lake: Nuclear Peril in the Pacific* (Melbourne: Penguin Books, 1986), particularly pp. 129-131.

24. For two recent explorations of this and related issues see Kevin P. Clements, *Back from the Brink: The Creation of a Nuclear Free New Zealand* (London and Wellington: Allen and Unwin, 1988); and Stuart MacMillan, *Neither Confirm nor Deny* (Wellington: Allen and Unwin, 1987.)

25. *Ibid*, p. 3; and A. Mack, "Global and Regional Superpower Policies," paper presented to IPPNW Conference, February 9-10, 1987, Auckland, New Zealand.

26. See, for example, P. Hayes, L. Zarsky and W. Bello, *op. cit.*, note 23, p. 274.

27. See "Going over the Top, (Published anonymously)" *South*, February 1986, pp. 17-18.

28. See Paul Wilson, "U.S. Pressure Proving Effective on Japan," *The Christchurch Star*, Vol. 21, No. 6, 1988, p. 3.

29. *Ibid*.

30. *Ibid*.

31. *Ibid*.

32. See "The Allies: Time to Share the Burden," *The Economist*, Vol. 307, No. 7549, May 7-13, 1988, pp. 23-24.

33. At a UNU/Soviet Academy of Sciences meeting on Peace and Security Issues in Asia and the Pacific (held at Tashkent, May 1985) Academician Primakov spent a considerable amount of time elaborating how Japanese changes to force structure, the reactivation of an armaments industry and close harmonization of United States and Japanese maritime strategies posed direct threats to Soviet defense.

34. See Gerald Segal, "Pacific Arms Control," Background Paper Nr. 2 for 53rd Pugwash Symposium on Peace and Security in the Asia-Pacific Region, Beijing, October 17-20, 1988, 11-13.

35. See Frank Corner, Kevin Clements, Brian Poananga and Diane Hunt (Defence Committee of Enquiry), *Defence and Security: What New Zealanders Want* (Wellington: Wellington Government Printer, 1986); *The Defence of Australia* (Canberra: Australia Government Publishing Service, 1987); and *Defence of New Zealand: Review of Defence Policy 1987* (Wellington: Wellington Government Printer) for details. While Australians feel greater insecurity than New Zealanders, neither government believes that either country faces any external territorial threat in the short or long term.

36. For further discussion of the Treaty see K.P. Clements, *op. cit.*, note 24, Chapter 7; and Michael Hamel-Green, "The Rartonga Nuclear Free Zone Treaty: A Critical Analysis of its Scope, Domain and Contribution to Regional Security and Disarmament," paper presented to UNU Conference, Auckland, April 3-6, 1986.

37. For an excellent recent analysis on this installation see Des Ball, *Pine Gap* (Sydney: Allen and Unwin, 1988).

38. For details see K.P. Clements, *op. cit.*, note 24; "New Zealand's Anti-Nuclear Stand," *Bulletin of the Atomic Scientists*, Vol. 43, No. 2, March 1987, pp. 32-35; and "New Zealand's Role in Promoting a Nuclear Free Pacific," *Journal of Peace Research*, Vol. 25, No. 4, 1988, pp. 395-410.

39. See Kevin P. Clements, "The New Zealand Defence Review: A Unique Opportunity for Public Participation," in J. Boston and M. Holland, eds., *The Fourth Labour Government: Radical Politics in New Zealand* (Auckland: Oxford University Press, 1987), pp. 214-242.

40. See Jusuf Wanandi, "Political Aspects of ASEAN-U.S. Relations," paper presented to *Fourth ASEAN Institute for Strategic and International Studies Conference*, organized by the Singapore Institute for International Affairs, Singapore, June 27-30, 1988, p.1.

41. Dato Abu Hassan bin Haji Omar, Minister of Foreign Affairs, Malaysia, Keynote address given to *Second Asia-Pacific Roundtable on Confidence Building and Conflict Reduction in the Pacific*, 2-4 July, 1988, KL, Malaysia.

42. Barry M. Blechman, "Confidence Building in the North Pacific: A Pragmatic Approach to Naval Arms Control," in A. Mack and P. Keal (eds), *Security and Arms Control in the North Pacific* (Sydney: Allen and Unwin, 1988), p 221-222.

9

Stable Peace Among Nations:
A Learning Process

Kenneth E. Boulding

A remarkable development of the last 150 years, the study of which has been much neglected and would provide an important opportunity for peace research, has been the growth of an increasing area of stable peace between independent nations. This development began in Scandinavia between Sweden and Denmark in the middle of the 19th century, spread to North America about 1871, to Western Europe, Japan, and Australasia after the Second World War. Stable peace can be defined as a situation between two independent nations in which neither has any significant plans to go to war with the other. This has happened largely without planning, is not much dependent on formal treaties, and has developed almost spontaneously as a learning pattern in national behavior. It is not much related to peace movements or organizations, or even to the development of organized nonviolence.

The conditions for stable peace to appear seem simple: One is that change in the position of national boundaries be removed from national agendas, except by mutual agreement. A second condition is that there should be a minimum amount of intervention by each nation in the other nation's internal affairs. A third might be the development of an economic rather than a romantic, heroic attitude toward the national state, looking on it as a public convenience rather than a quasi-god demanding human sacrifice.

We might also distinguish a phase of the international system which could be called "quasi-stable peace." Latin America could be cited as an example, at least since the Chaco War of the 1930s between Bolivia and Paraguay and even to some extent, to the end of the Lopez War in the 1870s and the "Pacific War" of 1880-84 of Chile against Bolivia and Peru. In this phase international war is extremely rare and national boundaries change very little, although there may be a few disputes like that between Venezuela and Guyana or between Argentina and Chile over a little island in the Magellan Straits. These, however, are not severe enough to lead into international war. The Falkland-Malvinas War, however, suggests that Latin America is not really part of the "great triangle" of stable peace which stretches from Australia and Japan, across North America, to Finland, although it is significant that even a rather aggressive military regime in Argentina did not try to change any of the boundaries with any neighboring Latin American state.

Latin American countries, however, suffered extensive internal war in this period, unlike most of the countries of the "great triangle." Columbia, with its "Violencia," is a particularly sad example. Argentina had the horrifying "dirty war" of its military period in the 1970s and early 1980s until the Falkland War ended that phase. Chile has had the Allende episode and a very repressive government. With the exception of Costa Rica, all the Central American countries have had a good deal of internal violence, especially Guatemala, Nicaragua, and El Salvador. Surinam has also seen great internal violence since it became independent. Brazil seems to have been fairly peaceful since the rebellion of the early part of the 20th century, immortalized in the great Brazilian novel, *Os Sertoes*, and the brief civil war of the 1930s. Bolivia and Peru have each suffered much internal violence. Peru and Ecuador have had a rather minor international war, so one would certainly not regard Latin America as a very peaceful part of the world. Nevertheless, international war has been quite infrequent in the last 100 years and fairly small scale.

In Africa, remarkably stable international boundaries have held since the end of the colonial empires, despite a great deal of internal war. There has been international war between Ethiopia and Somalia, essentially over a boundary problem. Algeria fought a bloody war of independence against France, but this could be regarded as an internal war. Zaire and Nigeria have had severe internal wars. Angola and Mozambique continue to have them. Burundi suffers a prolonged disastrous tribal war. Uganda has almost fallen apart with internal war. There is an internal war with some international implications in the old Spanish Sahara, now perhaps drawing to an end. Egypt has had an international war with Israel. Sudan has had severe internal wars, as has Ethiopia. Nevertheless, compared with Europe over the last few centuries, until the end of the Second World War, international war has been a relatively small part of organized violence, in spite of the fact that the boundaries of the new African states are arbitrary and cut across tribal and linguistic lines and are the result mainly of the geographical ignorance of the European powers at the Berlin Conference in 1884.

In Europe, since 1946, there has been little that could be called international war. The Russian invasions of Hungary and Czechoslovakia are almost the only example. The Basques, as well as Northern Ireland, have each been involved in local internal strife over a long period, but on a small scale. The Soviet Union has had little in the way of internal war in the last 40 years.

Until recently, the "Cultural Revolution" in China had some aspects of an internal war. Southeast Asia has had almost stable war over 40 years, both international and internal. India, China, and Pakistan have engaged in small international wars and local internal violence; for instance, the Sikhs in Punjab. Afghanistan has suffered both internal and international war.

The relations between the United States and the Soviet Union and their respective allies could be described as "unstable peace." There has been very little in the way of actual violence, but a substantial arms race arising out of a system of deterrence which has been fairly stable in the short run, but cannot remain stable in the long run, while large armed forces exist. Nuclear weapons have probably increased the stability of short-run deterrence because of the horrendous costs involved. There is a good deal of evidence that in the pre-nuclear period, the probability of the breakdown of deterrence was something on the order of 4 percent per annum. That is, it would be of the order of what we call a 25-year flood. We have no historical experience, of course, with the breakdown of nuclear deterrence, but the probability of such a breakdown is clearly some positive number, simply because if the probability of nuclear weapons detonated were zero, they would not deter anybody. All deterrence implies some probability of breakdown over the long run; otherwise it would not deter in the short run. The probability of a breakdown of nuclear deterrence may be of the order of 1 or 2 percent per annum, something like a 50 or 100 year flood. With a 1 percent probability per annum, the probability of breakdown in 100 years is somewhere on the order of 63 percent; in 400 years, it is over 98 percent.

If the present system of unilateral national defense continues, therefore, it is clear that nuclear deterrence will break down at some point and the United States and Soviet Union will destroy each other, and probably most of the world. Under these circumstances, the only true national security is through stable peace; as it already exists on a fairly broad scale, it would certainly be possible. The great problem of this generation is how to expand the area of stable peace to include, first, the United States and the Soviet Union and their allies, and then the Third World.

Unfortunately, the underlying dynamics of the movement towards stable peace, whether at the international level or the internal level, has been very little studied and is not well understood. There is a great task ahead here for peace research: first, in terms of the study of the history of the processes by which stable peace is secured, which has been almost totally neglected by historians; secondly, in terms of understanding the patterns of social learning and interaction by which these processes have proceeded, which has been neglected by everybody. It is clear that the development of stable peace is fundamentally a learning process, but how this learning takes place and by whom is still very puzzling and needs investigation. Clearly something happened in Scandinavia between the Napoleonic War and the middle of the 19th century. Something certainly happened in North America between 1812, when the United States and Canada were at war, and the 1870s, when stable peace was secured; and between the war of the United States with Mexico in 1846 and the very minimal intervention by the United States in the Mexican civil war of 1910-1919. Similarly, some learning process has gone on in Western Europe which has effectively brought to an end the wars between France and Germany, or France and Italy, or Britain and these countries. The processes and institutions that foster this learning process, however, are still very obscure, and a very large task of research is ahead. We need, indeed, to study all the various aspects of social systems and inquire as to the circumstances under which these particular aspects diminish or increase the chances of movement towards stable peace.

We can start, for instance, with religion and ideology. It is clear that over a large range, a common religion or ideology in itself does not necessarily produce stable peace. The bloodiest war of the last few years was between Iraq and Iran within Islam. The First and Second World Wars were between nominally Christian countries on the whole. Buddhism perhaps has the best record in promoting peace, though there have been wars between Buddhist states, such as Burma and Thailand in the past. Buddhism's main emphasis has been on personal withdrawal from violence, as we find also in monasticism and in the peace churches in Christianity. Marxism has promoted violence in the interest of revolution and has eschatological hope that the state will wither away, which seems unduly optimistic in the light of its history. A common language also is no guarantee of peace, as we see in Latin America and in Northern Ireland. Religious and ideological differences have often been used as an excuse and justification for war, as in the Thirty Years' War in Europe, in the Crusades of Christians against Muslims, and in the "cold war" between the United States and the Soviet Union. Internal war is perhaps more often justified by ideological differences, as in the case of the Sikhs in India, the Hindu Tamils in Sri Lanka, Protestants and Catholics in Northern Ireland, and communist or anti-communist insurrections in many parts of the world. But, on the whole, wars within ideological boundaries have been just as devastating as those between them.

The relation of economic capacity and institutions to peace, both international and internal, is extremely complex and deserves much more serious study. Such imperfect evidence as we have suggests that wars do not follow very closely the lines of economic conflict and that trade on the whole is a peaceful occupation which tends to be positive-sum, and traders certainly have a very different culture from warriors. On the other hand, economic development certainly increases both the absolute amount and the proportion of national resources which can be devoted to war. Adam Smith stated: "Among the civilized nations of modern Europe . . . not more than one hundredth part of the inhabitants of any country can be employed as soldiers, without ruin to the country that pays the expense of their service."[1] Before the last 200 years or so, it took 80 or 90 percent of the population to feed the 100 percent, so that the proportion of the economy devoted to war could rarely rise above 2 percent, and was usually much lower than this. In the Second World War, the United States was able to devote 42 percent of its national income to the war. Economic development, therefore, enables war to become more destructive, not only because of the technical increase in the destructiveness of weapons, but because more resources can be devoted to it. Even among the poor countries, there is some tendency, at least among the moderately poor, for economic development to increase the proportion of the national income that goes to the military.

At the other end of the economic argument, the rise in human productivity makes war much less profitable, even for the victor, than it is under the conditions of the extreme poverty of population-pressured, hunting-gathering societies, which could occasionally conquer and enslave adjacent agricultural societies with a food surplus. In the modern world, it has become very clear that empire and great power does not pay off economically. In the 19th and 20th centuries, for instance, Sweden and Denmark became wealthier much faster than did Britain and France, whose empires crippled their domestic economic development. Conquest diverts attention from productivity. It is a plausible generalization that the more complex a society becomes, the more damaging and the less economically productive war becomes. People and even governments do eventually understand this fact, and the rise of stable peace may have something to do with this almost unconscious process of human learning. Slavery became obsolete to a considerable extent because the productivity of free labor increased so much that it outweighed any possible advantages of slavery. War becomes obsolete for similar reasons--that it is simply not economically viable for either victor or vanquished.

The role of the arts, music, and literature in legitimizing war is an interesting problem that could be increasingly studied. Certainly military bands, war songs, uniforms, marching as a form of ballet, all contribute to the development of military morale. On the other hand, art itself is overwhelmingly peaceful. I have done some casual studies in art museums which suggest that some 90 percent of pictorial art is peaceful. The same is certainly true of music. Military bands are a very small part of the musical repertoire, and the same could be said of popular songs which are, incidentally, an interesting indicator of the legitimacy of war, as we see by comparing the war songs of the First World War with the relative absence of war songs in the Second, and the anti-war songs during the Vietnam War.

The relation of literature to war and peace is particularly complex. There is a literature of war, and a literature that glorifies war--the writings of Homer and Virgil exemplify the theme. On the other hand, the culture of literary activity and of writers is overwhelmingly peaceful. It would be interesting to trace the proportion of literature in different times and cultures devoted to peaceful themes. It is not surprising that tragedy is frequently built around themes of war, but in time the proportion of peaceful themes in literature increases. The epic frequently developed on a military theme, has virtually disappeared as a form of literature. The novel, in spite of a few exceptions like Tolstoy's *War and Peace*, is developed overwhelmingly on themes of domestic life, in which war intrudes only incidentally. In Jane Austen's novels, for instance, written during the Napoleonic Wars, there is hardly any mention of war. An occasional military ball is the only sign that a great war is going on. The detective story overwhelmingly deals with police rather than with armies, even though it does usually involve violence. Even where war is the theme of a novel, as in *All Quiet on the Western Front*, it is essentially an anti-war theme. There is a certain amount of war poetry, such as "The Charge of the Light Brigade" by Tennyson, written perhaps in his capacity as poet laureate, a government post. War certainly plays a role in Shakespeare's tragedies. Even there, however, the tragedies are essentially domestic involving family, rather than international conflict; they usually end with some resolution looking forward to the restoration of peace. Opera, even grand opera, is mainly concerned with domestic conflict. Comic opera is quite frequently anti-war and makes fun of the military; Gilbert and Sullivan operas are a good example.

The role of organized nonviolence in the establishment of stable peace is an extremely interesting question, the answers to which may be very important in the future. Organized nonviolent conflict is largely an invention of the 20th century. Unorganized nonviolence is a very ancient phenomenon--the simple withdrawal from war and violence into domesticity, production, trade. Religious withdrawal in terms of monasticism goes back to Brahmanism in India, Buddhism, early Christianity and its later peace churches. Organized nonviolence as a political movement, however, does not date much before Gandhi, though a few pioneering examples can be found in the 19th century, for instance, in labor movements and strikes. The Gandhian movement in India, however, is the first example of politically organized nonviolence, which was certainly successful in hastening the abandonment of the British Empire. The other great example is that of Martin Luther King and the civil rights movement in the United States, which, again, had a great deal of success. The very important work of Gene Sharp at Harvard in this area[2] has pointed up the potential role of organized nonviolence as a substitute for military national defense, and a more efficient method of counteracting threats and even invasion from abroad. Because of the development of nuclear weaponry, the long-range missile, even the airplane, national defense in the conventional sense has essentially broken down and a substitute is desperately needed if the human race is not to destroy itself. The potential of organized nonviolence gives hope for the future of the human race in a way perhaps that no other single development of the 20th century can do.

On the other hand, it must be admitted that the rise of stable peace has had very little to do with organized nonviolence. The historical record here is somewhat obscure. In India, Gandhian nonviolence did not produce stable peace externally or internally. The end of British rule was followed by an appalling blood bath between the Hindi and the Moslems internally and the creation of the two states, India and Pakistan, which have by no means had stable peace with each other. India, furthermore, has been engaged in war with China over boundary problems and continues to suffer severe internal violence with the militant Sikhs, and in some tribal areas.

Perhaps the most significant aspect of the development of organized nonviolence is that it now stands in the background as an alternative to violent revolution or national defense. The most common excuse for war is that "we had no alternative," which always suggests that alternatives have not been adequately explored. The widening of alternatives is one of the main tasks of peace research, and with it a vital and exciting new world of knowledge lies ahead of us.

Postscript, March 1990: The extraordinary and unforeseen events, especially in Eastern Europe, of the last year have illustrated, except in Romania, the power of nonviolence and the weakness of military power. The spread of stable peace to the whole north temperate zone is now a strong possibility, and there are signs of it all over the world, in South Africa, in Nicaragua, and in other places.

Notes

1.   Adam Smith, *The Wealth of Nations* (New York: Modern Library Edition, 1937) pp. 657-658.

2.   Gene Sharp, *The Politics of Nonviolent Action* (Boston: Porter Sargent, 1973) and *Making Europe Unconquerable: The Potential of Civilian-Based Deterrence and Defense* (Cambridge, Mass.: Center for International Affairs, Harvard University, 1985.)

PART TWO

CULTURES OF PEACE:
FROM VIOLENCE TO NONVIOLENCE

Introduction to Part Two

Elise Boulding

The conditions for a peace culture are also the conditions for social learning, says Armengol, thus continuing the discussion by Boulding that ended Part One. A peace culture is a learning culture that links heart and mind and prepares for change and difference.

But, how does the movement from violence to nonviolence take place? Satha-Anand calls for a new awareness of how we think and talk, for a rejection of the supposed "normality" of violence. The new awareness involves a highly developed sense of self and other, and of the multidimensionality of being that leads us directly to Mische's paper. In a striking use of metaphor, she offers us the earth as teacher of interrelationships, of the communion of each reality of the universe with every other reality, including our own inner reality. Developing an understanding of "how things work" in the profoundest sense of those words is what peace education is all about. This understanding makes it possible to deal peacefully with change and difference, and to dealing competently with threat. It brings the different "normality," that Satha-Anand writes of, into being.

The second half of Part Two shifts from more theoretically and philosophically oriented reflections on the movement from violence to nonviolence, to highly specific examinations of cultures of violence and domination and their possible future evolution toward more egalitarian, nonviolent relationships. The themes of learning and awareness are found in all three pieces. Chaudhuri's account of grassroots conflicts in India reveals a society where the old complementarities of caste relations are gone, and with them the capacity of the village panchayat system to carry out traditional functions of village decision making. With democratization, intercaste and intergroup relations have become struggles for dominance and conflict has turned extremely violent. Government is relatively powerless as an intermediary force; Chaudhuri refers to NGOs (nongovernmental organizations) as important new actors. In listing the various educational and conflict resolution techniques being utilized by NGOs to deal with this situation, Chaudhuri also describes the emergence of a new civic culture from the conscientization process the conflicts have triggered. This emergent culture is able to draw also on the strengths of traditional culture.

The social conflicts described by de Almeida in rural Brazil are, if anything, even bloodier than the Indian conflicts. The inheritors of the colonial latifundia use violence and terror to retain their dominance and prevent land redistribution. They even use agricultural modernization itself as an instrument against the peasants. The peasants in turn are driven to violence in self-defense and there is a general breakdown of traditional violence-controlling mechanisms. Nevertheless, the oppressed are also developing a new civic consciousness. As with the Indians, the new consciousness draws on traditional problem-solving resources, and new strategies are slowly emerging from the long and bitter struggle.

In neither the Indian nor the Brazilian case can one talk of an emerging peace culture at this time, only of the breakdown of traditional controls and the beginnings of new learnings that hold the seeds of a future peace culture. The themes of duration, persistence, recurring ups and downs, and the development of new skills, that appeared repeatedly in Part One on the development of Common Security, also appear here.

The last example of a culture of violence in transition is different from the other two in that it is not primarily region-specific. The Harris study happens to be of U.S. men. However, male violence--expressed as dominance over the weak, including weaker men, women and children--is a subculture found in most societies. The warrior ethos becomes subtly intertwined with the basic social, economic and political institutions and practices of a society, and would seem to be very durable indeed. Yet, Harris reveals that there is another culture at work also shaping the men of each society--the more peaceable women's culture. As a consequence, men are subject to more intense cross-pressures than is commonly recognized. Those cross-pressures may in the short term lead to more domestic and communal violence in the face of rapid change, as the U.S. is experiencing today. (We saw that same increase in violence in the Indian and Brazilian examples.) Yet, new understanding of the potential multi-dimensionality of both men's and women's roles linked to still viable elements of traditional cultures may promise gentler societies in the future.

Ten Bases for a Culture of Peace

Vicenc Fisas Armengol

In recent years, the role of the peace movement, and even multidisciplinary peace research itself, has centered on the analysis of international rearmament and militarization processes. This has led to a neglect of the design and construction of the "culture of peace" and the consideration of alternative forms of cultural life. What is needed is to combine the work of a critical analysis of destructive processes with the equally important work of developing creative transnational approaches to the present situation.

Satisfying Basic Human Needs

Traditionally, the concept of culture has been related to that of satisfying human needs. Peace research carried out after the sixties has reflected the functionalist approach to basic needs (the environmental and biological conditions to be satisfied if the individual and the group are to survive). Research has now extended this concept of basic human needs to include such non-material aspects as political, social, juridical and other needs, giving a new dimension to the idea of peace and the individual's role therein. In this sense, we could equally well look at culture as the sum of the symbolic and technical responses a human community possesses by which to interpret, evaluate, and make use of its life.

Looked at in this way, the concept of peace not only involves the simple absence of war; it is concerned with the absence of any form of violence that might prevent the satisfaction of any basic human need.

Educating for Change

If I speak of a new culture for peace, it is because I believe we are living in a society which neither satisfies human needs nor seems capable of providing a satisfactory solution to the main problems facing mankind. We live in a society that proclaims a series of values and claims to defend a series of rights, and at the same time offers a reality which is very different and falls far short of those values. A culture for peace must set out to reduce the gap between the values it preaches and the reality of its practices, encouraging the use of those means and instruments which allow us the full realization of the social values it assumes.

A culture for peace will have to reveal those points at which society must be submitted to profound transformations--a society in which taboos, customs and prejudice, moral conscience and faith, no longer attempt to absolve the human being of responsibility. A culture for peace would imply the promotion of education for social change and an educational approach aimed at developing our knowledge and experience of alternatives.

More than ever, the human being appears in need of behavior patterns and instruments that will allow him to face up to and assume his responsibilities for solutions to important social problems. The civic-cultural peace ethic must formulate and work through the tension between ends and means. The peace ethic becomes both a critique of the old order and a proposal for a new civilization. An objective of this magnitude requires a profound worldwide analysis of the present crisis and not, as is customary, an analysis of its purely economic aspects.

Breaking Free from Old Myths and Symbols

In explaining the different forms of aggressiveness, Fromm refers to the "relative aggressiveness" of individuals in the face of threat to their vital interests. Amongst the explanations for this relative aggressiveness, he stresses three factors: (1) Humans create symbols and values which become identified with self and with one's overall existence. Threats to these symbols are seen as threats to people. (2) Humans create a variety of idols to which they enslave themselves (ideologies, the idea of state sovereignty, nation, race, religion, the concept of freedom, socialism or democracy, the maximization of consumption, etc.). (3) Humans are suggestible. It is easy to persuade someone that his vital interests are being threatened, even if this is not the case.

A peace culture would have to tackle the problems generated by the delegation of responsibilities and decision-making to political organs far removed from the individual. Such delegation favours the use of indiscriminate violence by those organs which have made violence part of common political practice and thus part of the culture itself.

Demilitarizing Defense

Peace culture would feature the assumption that conflicts need not inevitably be solved by military force. Alternative defense projects attempt to combine a legitimate desire for defense with the principle of non-provocation and of non-threatening behavior. A peace culture would introduce moral categories into the political context, demilitarizing political behavior and ridding defense and security policies of their militarist components.

Debunking Threats

The mythology of war survives partly as a result of the pathological mechanism of overprotection from threats. Particular individuals or interest groups act, not in accordance with reality, but in accordance with faulty perceptions of reality. The distortion of what is seen, perceived or analyzed allows the establishment of excessive defense mechanisms, on the basis of a previous overestimation of the size of the threat, creating a spiral which in the arms culture, plays a part in the perpetuation of the arms race.

By overestimating threats, it is easy to make enemies where none actually exist, or to give them a subhuman appearance through the manipulation of information. A peace culture would distinguish between "possibility" and "probability," avoiding a paranoid preoccupation with the worst possibilities. This is the only sane and realistic way to conduct the business of individual and national life.

Feminizing Culture

In the culture of war and violence men are the principal actors. The male gender plays a dominating part in the shaping, regulation and control of cultural forms opposed to peace and social justice. There also seems to be a direct relationship between male domination, generally through a hierarchical and authoritarian social organization, and the high level of institutional social violence, including war. It is man, not woman, who has supported and developed a system of war which absorbs suicidal and human resources for the destruction of life.

Virginia Woolf ends her last letter in "Three Guineas" with a consideration that has remained for posterity and that has become part of the heritage of both the feminist and pacifist movements: "We can best help you to prevent war not by repeating your words and following your methods, but by finding new words and methods."

A good part of the discussion that has taken place so far on the culture of peace can be seen as being based on Virginia Woolf's words. The breach between affection and thought, between rational thinking and irrational beliefs, with their basis in affection, is one of the obstacles to be overcome in a project for a culture of peace. The gap between public and private worlds, between the politico-abstract and the everyday and interpersonal, between brain and heart, leads to a dehumanization of political practices and reduced political awareness on the part of many people.

Disobedience as a Virtue

A culture for peace must accept the risk of encouraging the learning of disobedience to taboos, out-of-date rules, and orders that are unjustifiable to the individual's conscience. While disobedience can be the equivalent of irresponsibility in certain circumstances, it can also be a virtue if carried out responsibly and with an understanding of its repercussions. The development of a critical conscience, an understanding of conflictive processes, and the skills of conflict resolution will also be necessary for responsible participation in these processes.

Respect for Cultural Identity

The search for a culture of peace should not make us forget that the practices which allow the destruction of other cultures through imperialist or colonialist policies still persist. A culture of peace must recognize and respect the intrinsic values of all the different national and transnational cultural identities.

The anti-imperialist tradition has concerned itself largely with an analysis of economic imperialism, leaving everything to do with cultural imperialism in the background, when what stands out most about Western penetration of the Third World is not so much economic destruction as the loss of cultural identity.

The colonization of culture operates in the more industrialized countries, as well as in the Third World. Through sophisticated processes of persuasion, the mass media impose behavior patterns, consumer habits and stereotyped images of the world and of ourselves, confusing modernity with deculturalization and massification. Coercive practices that set out to impose a universal culture must be rejected as we learn to use moral criteria that are increasingly comprehensive and less subject to our historical peculiarity.

Overcoming the Logic of Blocs

Only the regeneration of an internationalism based on the imperatives of human ecological survival can provide the necessary force to confront the ideological imperatives of military blocs. As Mary Kaldor puts it, "Disalignment implies acceptance of pluralism, respect for different social systems, tolerance of different approaches to security."

Vitalizing What Is Small

Finally, any debate on a culture of peace will have to vitalize the role of the individual person and the civil society in the face of the state. A peace culture defends people. What is proposed is an alternative project that allows individuals to rediscover their concrete social, political, economic, technological and environmental surroundings, on equal terms and free of oppression.

11

From Violent to Nonviolent Discourse

Chaiwat Satha-Anand

In 1982 Admiral Hyman Rickover, an architect of the U.S. nuclear submarine arsenal, testified before a Joint Committee of Congress that the world would be better off if all nuclear ships were sunk. This incident is by no means unprecedented. In 1961, President Dwight D. Eisenhower warned the American public in his farewell address of the "military-industrial complex" that would influence national policy for the sake of its own interests. There are other examples of those who once worked vigorously in the name of violence but later, usually in the aftermath of their professional services, regretted it and opted for more peaceful alternatives.[1]

When a nonviolent political scientist, Glenn D. Paige, raised the question "Is it possible to have a nonkilling society?" to various scholars from different countries between 1979 to 1985, he found that twenty professional North American political scientists seem to place "the question rather firmly in the category of the unthinkable at this time."[2] If the nature of academic discourse at the international level is partially defined by the hegemony of Western scholarship, especially American scholarship, then the fact that for some American social scientists "a nonkilling society is unthinkable" becomes a phenomenon to reckon with. This brief paper is an attempt to point out that one of the reasons why nonviolence is still marginalized in the intellectual landscape is because it suffers from the hegemony of violent discourse that is considered "normal" academic discourse. By understanding this situation, nonviolent discourse may be able to leave the marginality of academic domain and move to center stage in the world of ideas. Signs of existing counter-discourse will be identified. Policy lessons for nonviolent discourse will be outlined as a step toward creating a dominant discourse that will, in turn, help create a life-world where violence is no longer legitimate. But first, it is important to sketch the mainstream academic discourse that unflinchingly accepts violence.

The Hegemony of Violent Discourse

According to Paige, for some political scientists, nonviolence is unthinkable for three basic reasons. First, man is a dangerous animal capable of killing by nature. Second, there will always be a scarcity of economic resources which, in turn, will lead to violence. Third, violence may be used in the case of self-defense or defending loved ones.[3] In other words, violence is an accepted course of action because of human nature and social reality. On the one hand, Lorenz, Storr and Ardrey, among others, have maintained that human nature is incurably violent.[4] On the other hand, modern social sciences usually believe that conflict is integral to social reality. In order to resolve conflict, violence is generally regarded as a practical, effective and hence, rational means. When such "nature" of man and "practical/effective/rational" conflict resolution are combined, violence is transformed form being merely a means of conflict resolution to a *normal* course of action and the possibility of violence being questioned is dangerously curtailed. Once accepted as normality, violence is naturalized. A study of violence becomes a study of the normal state of humanity. Life itself is no placid pond but a "storm-swept ocean."[5] Knowledge is produced to support the normality of violence. Ideas which are considered respectable, academic and learned are judged by the extent to which they correspond to the norm of knowledge in society. As a result, Paige's "nonviolent" or "nonkilling" political science is unthinkable to many because it does not correspond to such a norm. Nonviolence *is* unthinkable to many not because of their ill-will nor unwillingness to try. Rather, dominant discourse in the academia is marked by the hegemony of violence. As a result, there seems to be no space for nonviolence in the existing discourse. Therefore, to work towards the realization of nonviolence, the nature of discourse needs to be understood.

Discourse

Edelman has suggested that "language is the key creator of the social world's people experience."[6] Consisting of sound waves or marks on paper, language becomes meaningful when people project some significance into it. However, contrary to common wisdom, which believes that it is people who construct the language they use, Foucault has pointed out that there is an important sense in which language constructs those who use it. The notion of discourse Foucault is interested in, means more than mere language. Discourse refers to a web of activities united by acceptance of a set of rules that govern normal behavior. Hence, to focus on discourse means to take into account "how people are enabled to act in meaningful ways and to orient their behavior properly."[6] In order to analyze any discursive formation, Foucault suggests that it "is to weigh the 'value' of statement, a value that is not defined by their truth, that is not gauged by the presence for a secret content; but which characterizes their place, their capacity for circulation and exchange, their possibility of transformation, not only in the economy of discourse but more generally, in the administration of scarce resources."[8] Discourses have systematic structures. Therefore different elements, of which they are composed, can be identified. Discourses need political technologies to exist, dominate and proliferate. Therefore, specific technologies, the localization of different discourses, institutions and disciplines responsible for discursive formations need to be analyzed.

Dominant discourse defines rules of life. In the process of knowledge production, then, dominant discourse becomes the arbiter of what can be legitimately studied, taught, submitted as policy recommendations by which disciplines and by whom. Such production processes at the same time relegate different ideas, based upon unfamiliar rules and nurtured by values deemed alien by mainstream academicians, as idealistic, impractical, unsupported by institutionalized knowledge, and therefore illegitimate. It is this complex process which renders ideas of nonviolence "unthinkable" for those academicians drowned by dominant discourse which, in turn, delimits their potentials to see things differently, to study the seemingly idealistic, and to exercise their creativity for a better world.

Enter Nonviolent Discourse

Recently, there have been a few important studies utilizing Foucault's analysis of discourse on significant contemporary issues such as development and nuclear strategy. These studies shed a meaningful light on how discursive analysis can be applied to violence and nonviolence.

Based on Foucault's fundamental insights into the nature and dynamics of discourse, power and knowledge in Western societies, Arturo Escobar conducts an inquiry on the present situation of the Third World. Basically he questions Western extension of disciplinary and normalizing mechanisms in various fields to the Third World. He also discusses the production of discourses by Western countries about the Third World as a means of effecting domination over it. True to the Foucaultian language, he asks: "In what ways are disciplinary and normalizing tendencies contributing to the domination of the Third World?"[9] He argues that without examining development discourse, it is not possible to understand the systematic ways in which the Western developed countries have been able to manage and control or even create the Third World politically, economically, sociologically, and culturally. Focusing on discourse, development will be seen not as a matter of scientific knowledge, a body of theories and programs concerned with the achievement of true progress, but rather as a series of political technologies intended to manage and give shape to the reality of the Third World.[10] In conclusion, he proposes that the discourse of development must be dismantled if Third World countries hope to counteract the penetration of power and to overcome poverty, unemployment and inequality.

Another study worth mentioning in this context is an attempt to explore strategic studies from a discourse-analytic point of view. Drawing upon Foucault's mode of analysis, Bradley Klein sets out to examine the character of a postwar discipline of strategic/security studies whose major concern is the central coordination of state violence. He argues that "strategic discourse constitutes the world as an object of power, surveillance, force planning, disciplinary intervention, punishment, risk management, calculated escalation and, if necessary, assured destruction through nuclear annihilation."[11] By investing the state with the power to wage war, preparation for war becomes its prerequisite. By proliferating the methods of analysis necessary for the existence of war, strategic discourse perpetuates a condition which Dieter Senghass has called "Organized peacelessness."[12] The language of the whole strategic discourse clouds the world's political nature and provides a convenient popular rationale that seems unproblematic. Klein also warns that those who question such discourse and refuse to see nuclear strategy as a necessity of life are relegated to marginal status. In some societies, they are considered a threat and dealt with as such.

These two studies pave the way in which discursive analysis can be used to crystallize the nature of things under study. Traces of strategy for counter-discourse, as attempts to both critique dominant discourse as well as to replace it, can also be seen. Using discursive formation as a focus, there are signs that the hegemony of violent discourse is now being challenged.

Two important studies serve well as examples. In 1984, a group of former NATO generals and admirals produced a book under the authorship of "The Generals for Peace and Disarmament." They stated that there is clearly no military use for nuclear weapons that will inevitable destroy all that is worth defending.[13] Such an assertion cannot move to the center stage of academic discourse if produced by pacifists. But in this case, the Generals for Peace and Disarmament are former high-ranking officers who command both respect and influence in NATO. Moreover, they have inside knowledge of the realities that dictate NATO policy. This critical assertion is produced from sources close to the center stage of dominant strategic discourse. Since the content of new discourse is in contradistinction to the dominant one, a contest emerges. In other words, the hegemony of violent discourse is challenged at the center stage by those who have been the producers of the hegemonic discourse themselves. The location of discursive challenge is also important. Occurring at the center stage of discursive formation, such a challenge produces at least two significant results. First, the public cannot but be confronted by such discursive challenges which, in turn, means there is a distinct possibility that their traditional belief will be seriously questioned. Second, the center stage of discursive formation is also the center of power and discursive resistance is, in some ways, a contest of power. Power dictates policies. If the dominant discourse is questioned, power that produces such discourse is also disrupted. It will no longer be possible for policies thus produced to continue unchallenged. Policy options will have to be thought out. It will therefore become possible for alternative policies to supplant existing ones.

Judging from numerous reviews, Gene Sharp's *Making Europe Unconquerable* is extremely sensational. As a foremost proponent of nonviolent actions based upon credible social theory, Sharp lucidly shows that countries are already adding nonviolent civilian-based defense to their military policy. With innovative thinking, it shows that the prospect of civilian-based defense is likely to dissuade nuclear attack. In addition, if such a method is systematically organized, an occupying power could be defeated.[14]

Sharp's book can be seen as moving closer to the center stage of dominant discourse. It is another case where nonviolence is moving towards the center stage. The book is reviewed by General C. Georges Fricaud-Chagnaud, President of the Foundation pour les Etudes de Defense Nationale, Paris; and Dr. Heinz Vetschera of the National Defense Academy, Vienna, among others. The reviews have appeared in mainstream journals such as *Foreign Affairs, The New York Times Book Review, Library Journal* as well as pacific journals such as *Reconciliation Quarterly*. Although it is still difficult to assess its challenging result, it may be safe to argue that the book is highly visible in the center stage of normal discourse.

It is interesting to note two basic reasons for such high visibility. First, Sharp seems to be acutely aware of the nature of dominant discourse. In the beginning of his book, he sets out to clarify some basic concepts. For example, he asserts that "defense" used in his book means the protection or preservation of a country's independence; its right to choose its own way of life, institutions, and standards of legitimacy; the protection of its own people's lives, freedom, and opportunities for future development. It can also be defined as instrumentally effective action to ward off, preserve, protect and minimize harm in the face of hostile attack. He also points out that defense and military means are not synonymous because the latter is only one set of means which may sometimes prove incapable of achieving its objective.[15] The discursive formation is being changed once the central concept is redefined. Second, the location of this producer of nonviolent discourse is also significant. Among other things, Sharp belongs to the Center for International Affairs of Harvard University. In fact, Harvard University has since 1965, provided him with an academic home for his research and writing. Fully realizing the significance of discourse location, at the same time power location, Sharp writes: "The establishment within Harvard's Center for International Affairs of the Program on Nonviolent Sanctions in Conflict and Defense in May 1983 has made possible the expansion of my work on nonviolent alternatives and the completion of this book."[16] It is true that Sharp's studies of nonviolence may not be considered dominant discourse by Harvard's academic community, but seen from the periphery of academic discourse, Sharp is at the center. And as one of the most famous universities in the world, Harvard is indeed a center stage of discourse production. It is the seat of high learning responsible for producing knowledge. Nonviolent discourse emerging from such an institution can be seen as a contender of dominant discourse if not dominant discourse itself. It is certainly considered legitimate knowledge ready for public consumption, and serious analysis by policy makers.

Conclusion: Policy Suggestions

Recently attempts have been made to promote nonviolence within the field of peace research. It is fascinating, and somewhat disturbing, that such promotion is needed among academicians interested in peace themselves. Perhaps, even in the terrain of peace, nonviolent discourse is yet to find an established corner. Hence, Theodore Herman's industrious labor is spent in "Promoting Nonviolence Study as Gainful Unemployment" while a vigorous voice was heard from Glenn Paige to suggest that the future of peace research lies in its capability to take nonviolence seriously.[17] Both scholars emphasize nonviolent ethical perspective; systematic pursuit of logic of nonviolent analysis; the need for research and experience sharing, to make nonviolence better understood as a way to peace. These suggestions are useful, in fact, necessary. But in themselves, they are not sufficient for nonviolence to be accepted in such a way that it can indeed influence policies and cease to be considered as exceptions.

This paper suggests that in addition to all the efforts mentioned above, there is a need to come to terms with the nature of academic discourse if nonviolence wants to be seriously considered. Much has been done to "prove" the existence, history and potentials of nonviolent actions. In the process, nonviolent discourse is strengthened. But to be effective as policy guide, nonviolence as discourse has to struggle to leave the margin of normal discourse and move towards the center stage.

As an academician who wishes to see and live in a world where violence ceases to be accepted as a normal course of action and justice reigns, I am convinced about the potential of nonviolence as an alternative to violence. But for such potential to be realized, those who care have the responsibility to present the idea in the most convincing discursive formation. In an age when knowledge production is constituted by a complex interaction between rules which govern normal discourse and institutions responsible for certified knowledge, nonviolence in the form of a counter-discourse may have to try hard to move to the center stage. This discursive movement is important since it serves as a step to take over normal discourse. At some point, it may be more important for the success or failure of nonviolence than for like-minded nonviolent protagonists to get together and find solace among themselves. It is my contention that it may be more fruitful for the benefit of nonviolence if a nonviolent academician is given a chance to serve as a guest editor, not in a peace-related journal, but in an established journal which serves as an institution producing normal discourse.[18] Or in some cases, an undergraduate course titled "nonviolence" may be less of a service than the one under "violence and nonviolence in politics."

In Thailand at present, an open university characterized by its successful distance education program has recently published a textbook on "Peace Studies" in two volumes with fifteen topics. As a member of this course team, I succeeded in persuading the committee to include a topic of nonviolence. What is remarkable about this is the fact that this university is unlike others. At any given time, there are some 200,000 registered students. There is a possibility that this course may reach approximately 2,000 to 3,000 students annually. They will participate in nonviolent discourse in some ways. This can be considered one way of moving to the center stage of normal discourse.

It is possible to argue that the pursuit of counter hegemonic discourse to replace the existing one may result in another type of hegemonic relations in the discursive field. It may be better not to recapture the center of power but to let it fritter away through a proliferation of alternatives. Here I would argue that the nature if the arena in which the discursive struggle will take place is of paramount importance. In order to allow for a proliferation of alternatives, a strong challenge at the center with a counter discourse of comparable power may be necessary.

In addition, a number of scholars are not satisfied with the ways in which the concept of nonviolence gets translated into different languages. In one tongue, it may convey passivity. Yet in another, it resonates religious serenity. This process of translation is important precisely because of the place the concept of nonviolence assumes in normal discourse.

The final *telos* of nonviolence is to completely supplant violence in the world of men. To succeed in the domain of action means the success of one idea over another. This contest requires strategies that will seriously take into account existing discourse and the way in which counter-discourse would be successful in challenging the former. Nonviolent academicians have to be more aware of their own roles as producers of knowledge. Nonviolent knowledge produced with this awareness may have a better chance to chart the course for a better world in the future.

Notes

1. See other examples in Bradley S. Klein, "Strategic Discourse and Its Alternatives", Occasional Paper No. 3, Center on Violence and Human Survival. (John Jay College of Criminal Justice, The City University of New York, 1987).

2. Glenn D. Paige, "Nonkilling and Global Understanding," in N. Radhakrishnan (ed.) *Multiple Streams of Peace Movement* (Kerala, India: Dr. G.R. Institute of Non-Violence, 1986), p. 128.

3. *Ibid.*, p. 121.

4. See Konrad Lorenz, *On Aggression* (London: Methuen, 1966); Anthony Storr, *Human Aggression* (New York: Penguin Books, 1979); and Robert Ardrey, *The Hunting Hypothesis* (New York: Atheneum, 1976). A discussion on an alternative view can be found in Graham Kemp, "Nonviolence: A Biological Perspective" in Chadwick Alger and Michael Stohl (eds.) *A Just Peace Through Transformation* (Boulder & London: Westview Press, 1988), pp. 112-126.

5. Herbert Hirsch and David C. Perry (eds.) *Violence as Politics* (New York: Harper & Row, 1973), p. xii.

6. Murray Edleman, "Political Language and Political Reality," *PS* (Winter, 1985) Vol. XVIII, No. 1, p. 10.

7. See Klein, "Strategic Discourse...", p. 6.

8. Michel Foucault, *The Archaeology of Knowledge* (New York: Pantheon, 1972), p. 120.

9. Arturo Escobar, "Discourse and Power in Development: Michel Foucault and the Relevance of His Work to the Third World," *Alternative* (Winter, 1984-1985), Vol. X, No. 3, p. 378.

10. *Ibid.*

11. See Klein, "Strategic Discourse...", p. 5.

12. *Ibid.*, p. 6.

13. The Generals for Peace and Disarmament,*The Generals for Peace and Disarmament: The Arms Race to Armageddon: A Challenge to U.S./NATO Strategy*, (Berg Publishers, 1984).

14. Gene Sharp, *Making Europe Unconquerable: The Potential of Civilian-Based Deterrence and Defence* (Cambridge, Mass.: Ballinger, 1985).

15. *Ibid.*, pp. 25-26.

16. *Ibid.*, p. xxiv.

17. See Theodore Herman, "Promoting Nonviolence Study As Gainful Unemployment," A Paper for Friends Association for Higher Education Panel Session on "Quaker Studies in Human Betterment" (Washington, D.C., April 18, 1987); and Glenn D. Paige, "The Future of Peace Research: Taking Nonviolence Seriously," A Paper prepared for the special symposium celebrating the 10th Anniversary of the Institute of Peace Science (Hiroshima University, Hiroshima, Japan, July 1985).

18. This strategy has already been tried in Thailand. I myself served as a co-editor for a special issue on "Peace" for *Thammasat University Journal*, a widely respected Thai academic journal in 1985.

12

The Earth as Peace Teacher

Patricia M. Mische

Introduction

Peace education is still in the early and groping stage of its development. There is as yet no commonly agreed-on conceptual framework, philosophy, or definition of the field. What has been missing is an adequate cosmology of peace and of peace education: a cosmology that can provide a common story and framework for peace educators, researchers and activists everywhere.

The purpose of this paper is to consider a central dimension of such a new cosmology for peace education: the Earth as primary peace teacher. On the surface, a focus on the Earth may appear to be less essential or relevant to war and peace than other, more homocentric dimensions. When we sit in conferences in urban centers, the relevance of ecological systems to questions of war and peace may elude us. Yet the deeper we go in considering the relationship between ecological and peace questions, the more inclined we may be to consider the peace of humans with the Earth not only as important, but as central to peace between humans. Moreover, the Earth as a living, creative system may be the central paradigm for a positive peace.

In this short paper I cannot touch on all the aspects of an ecology of peace, but I would like to focus on four core points. I will assert that:

1. ecological well-being is the bottom line and foundation of a positive or just and sustainable peace;
2. we presently exist in a state of non-peace or war with the Earth;
3. this war is being waged in our own psyche as well as the external world and at its deepest level is a war against our own essence;
4. the Earth is the primary teacher and guide for ending this war, healing this brokenness and building the peace.

Ecological Well-Being is the Bottom Line
in a Positive Peace

Peace scholars distinguish two broad categories of peace: Negative peace and Positive peace. Negative peace refers to the absence of armed conflict or physical violence. But the lack of physical violence does not necessarily mean the lack of structural violence. Such a negative peace may be an unjust peace or an imposed peace, such as the Pax Romana. Positive peace refers to conditions of economic well-being and social justice and participation being realized such that the root causes of conflict are diminished.

It is my assertion that the conditions of a positive peace cannot be realized apart from sustainable ecological health. What I am saying is that at its deepest level the foundation for a positive peace is peace with the Earth. It is ultimately the Earth that is the source of our survival, physical sustenance, health and wealth. It is not possible to provide even a basic modicum of survival for the Earth's people apart from the capacity of the Earth to continue its creative and life-giving processes. The bottom line in economic well-being is the Earth's productivity. Presently the human is in a state of non-peace or war with the Earth, making it increasingly more difficult for the Earth to continue providing the material (and I would also venture to say the spiritual) conditions for a positive peace. Because we have not seen that the Earth itself is the foundation of any peace system, and because we have ignored the lessons of the Earth for the meaning and practice of peace, we find peace constantly eluding us.

Symptoms of Non-Peace or War with the Earth

The symptoms of the human state of non-peace or war with the Earth are becoming increasingly more severe and life-threatening. Singularly, these symptoms each constitute its own severe crisis. Collectively they constitute an interrelated crisis of crises, or megacrisis, with far more destructive power than an atomic bomb. The following are only a few of these symptoms, all humanly caused and humanly preventable:

Ozone
For some time researchers have been concerned that the use of chlorofluorocarbons and certain other man-made pollutants may be depleting the protective shield of ozone in the stratosphere which shields crops and people from solar ultraviolet radiation. In May 1985, British researchers noted a sharp decline in the ozone layer and the appearance of a "hole" in the shield over

Antarctica. Further research has corroborated this report. It is warned that further depletion of the ozone will increase skin cancers, retard crop growth (increasing prospects of famine) and impair the human immune system.

Carbon Dioxide And Climate

Human activities are now changing the climate, with far-reaching implications for food production in the next century. Excessive amounts of carbon dioxide (resulting mainly from the burning of fossil fuels and the release of other gases and chemicals into the atmosphere) are producing a greenhouse effect over the planet, allowing the sun's radiation in but not out. The effect is an increase in the temperature of the air near the Earth's surface. A meeting of experts in Villach, Austria in 1985 [sponsored by the United Nations Environment Programme (UNEP), the World Meteorological Organization (WMO) and the International Council of Scientific Unions (ICSU)] agreed that "this warming effect would lead, in perhaps 50 years, to a gradual rise in the Earth's temperature of up to 5 degrees Centigrade--roughly equivalent to the change which has occurred since the last Ice Age." Along with the melting of the polar ice caps, "this will both alter the pattern of the Earth's rainfall in ways not yet understood, seriously affecting agricultural production and raise the sea level by up to 1.4 metres, inundating low-lying coastal areas in many countries." Another report, commissioned by UNEP, WMO and ICSU from the International Meteorological Institute in Sweden, warned that by the year 2030 the world's average surface temperature will rise between 1.5 and 4.5 degrees Centigrade.[1] Such predictions overturn most long-range development plans, which usually assume an unchanging climate. If such trends continue unchecked, the resulting scarcities, competition and wars for scarce food and other survival needs, would make it difficult to sustain even a negative, much less a positive peace.

Oceans

All life emerged from the oceans. Yet, after billions of years of life-creating and sustaining activity, oceanic researchers in the 1970s began pointing to evidence that the oceans were dying. Oceans have been a vital source of food for human populations since the beginning of human life. They determine climate and are also a vital source of oxygen. If the oceans die, humans will die with them. We know little about what happens in the ocean depths. But in the coastal waters, which provide over 90 percent of the oceans' food harvest, it is quite apparent that the oceans are being treated by human populations as the toilet bowl of the world. Untreated sewage, pesticides, herbicides, industrial chemical wastes, radioactive contaminants, all end up in the seas, often trapped in waters near shore, poisoning marine life. Coral reefs, the rain forests of the oceans and home to a third of the world's fish species, are being destroyed.

There have been some efforts around the world to turn back these death-dealing processes (e.g., UNEP's 10 regional seas programmes), but there is still a long way to go in saving the life of the oceans.[2]

Water

Earth is a water planet. It is, in fact, over two thirds water. But of that, 97 percent is salt water. Of the remaining, 99 percent is in a frozen state or underground. Only a tiny fraction remains for humans to drink (like the Earth, we are water beings, comprised of two thirds water and requiring fresh water daily to survive), to water our crops, cleanse ourselves and wash away our wastes. Today 1.7 billion (1,700,000,000) people (more than a third of the world's population) lack safe drinking water. Diarrheal diseases related to unclean water cause the deaths of more than 4,600,000 children under the age of five years annually. Every day more than 25,000 people die as a result of bad water management.[3] The problem is primarily humanly caused and therefore humanly preventable.

Loss of Topsoil and Desertification

Loss of topsoil and desertification are other major symptoms of our state of non-peace with nature. Every year more than 24 billion tons of topsoil are washed into the oceans and millions of hectares "are sterilized by salts, polluted with chemicals, bled dry of nutrients, buried under swamps, or buildings."[4] The loss of topsoil can lead to famine. The African famine of 1984-85 killed over a million people.[5] No war since World War II has been as devastating.

Deforestation

A UNEP study points to the dangers inherent in loss of our forests:

> Forests cover some third of the world's land area. From the pine forests of the north to the tropical rain forests of the equator and the temperate forests of the southern hemisphere, they regulate our climate, protect water resources and provide us with forest products to the tune of some $100 billion per year. Half the world's population depends on them for fuel and they are home to millions of plant and animal species.

Unfortunately, forests are disappearing all over the world. Every year tropical forest areas, equivalent to the size of Austria or Sierra Leone, are being cut down. In the last 40 years, about half of the Earth's tropical forests were felled. The result has been irreversible loss of millions of plant and animal species. It has also resulted in the loss of vital watersheds and in flooding when there were no longer the trees to hold back the water. The tropical forests regulate climate, are the major source of the Earth's oxygen supply upon which all animal/human life depends and absorb the heat of the sun and carbon dioxide. Their loss compounds immeasurably the carbon-dioxide/ global warming threat. Saving what remains could delay or even prevent these death processes and save world food supplies in the next centuries.

One could go on with a multiple of other symptoms of our non-peace with Earth. But this may be enough to underscore that human assaults on Earth are now outpacing her healing capacities to such a degree that future life and health on the planet can no longer be assumed but has become a question.

All of these crises underscore the indivisibility of the Earth, that to touch one part is to touch the whole. The destruction of the Amazon rain forests threatens not only the native peoples in the region. This, the lungs of the world, which produces one fourth of the world's oxygen supply, is vital to the total human population and to all breathing creatures. Each of these issues challenge the notion of national sovereignty. The question of sovereignty needs to be reconsidered. Who owns the rain forests? Who owns the Earth? Who speaks for the Earth?

The Impact of War and Preparations for War

While many of the above symptoms of non-peace with the Earth have resulted not from shooting wars between humans, but from unconscious, unthinking, or uncaring ecological behavior, human wars and preparations for war further compound the problems. Much of the environmental destruction that occurs in warfare is dismissed as "collateral damage." In past wars, the Earth was not the target, so the euphemism may have applied. But in the Vietnam War, agent orange, napalm and various other weapons were devised for the specific purpose of defoliating and assaulting the Earth. In the medieval European period, rules of war were developed and vows taken by warring knights in which they swore not to destroy forests, crops, livestock or noncombatants. But in modern warfare the Earth itself has become a target.

The syndrome occurs not only in live warfare, but already in the training of troops, testing of weapons and other preparations for warfare. The resulting destruction is rationalized as necessary to national security. Examples abound, from the devastation of the fragile desert culture where nuclear tests are conducted in the U.S., to the vaporization and destruction of whole islands in the Pacific which were chosen for target practice. Missile testing in the Pacific is destroying coral reefs and causing toxicity in some of the fish life, ultimately affecting the health of human populations.[6] UN reports show that between 1945 and 1980 (after Hiroshima and Nagasaki and without a relationship to an actual war) there were 1233 nuclear tests, including more than 200 in the Pacific region, resulting in the release of radioactive contaminants into the air, water and soil and affecting food supplies.[7] Nuclear vessels have routinely discharged toxic chemicals and radioactive debris into the oceans, poisoning marine life.

Sometimes there are "abnormal" releases, such as the highly radioactive spill in Apra Harbor, Guam, in 1975, after which the level of radioactivity on nearby beaches rose to 50 times the allowable level.[8] According to a report by the Fund for Constitutional Government based in Washington, the U.S. navy may have had at least 13 such "abnormal" discharges and the Soviet Union a comparable number.[9]

In the past, the effect on the environment of human warfare was chalked up to "collateral damage." But in the new situation in which the Earth is the target, it is the loss of human life and health that has been rationalized away as "collateral damage." Thus the hibakusha of the Pacific--the victims of nuclear testing--are often deprived of retribution for radiation damage because "they were not the target." Some suffer genetic damage and are no longer able to have children. Thus whole families die out.[10]

In the name of peace and security we are jeopardizing the very foundation of our survival. The cost of human preparations for war include hunger, lost homelands, infertility and long-range damage to the human gene-pool. Where do these "collateral effects," so destructive of Earth and her human dependents, ever figure into the true costs of maintaining military power?

As we look to the future, we see on the military drawing boards not only preparations for taking warfare into outer space, but also climatic alterations and other forms of environmental warfare. Once maintained in the name of defending human populations, systems of national defense are now becoming dysfunctional to future human and planetary survival. In the name of national defense, nations are being distracted from the real and legitimate security concerns before us, including food, water, air, health and ecological sustainability.

We are at an axial moment in history. We have developed new powers over life and death. We can intervene in the DNA, the delicate genetic coding that has built up over eons of natural selection. We can create new species in test tubes. We can cause millions of plant and animal species to go out of existence through over industrialization, deforestation and contamination. With our weapons of mass destruction, we can render the whole planet uninhabitable. In the billions of years of human evolution, no preceding generation has had such powers over life and death--powers that in the past were only ascribed to God. We will now literally determine the fate of the Earth.

We have new powers over life and death, but there has been a tragic lag in our development. We have not developed the moral maturity or spiritual wisdom to use these powers in ways that will assure our future survival and the life-and health-giving capacities of the Earth. As Hannah Arendt noted about those who perpetrated Nazi war crimes and were responsible for genocide, we have no mental or moral tools "to think what we are doing." Instead of thinking first and acting only after we have considered the consequences, we reverse contemplation and action and consider the consequences only after the damage has already been done.[11]

Psycho-Spiritual Interface: War with Our Own Essence

This brings us to our third consideration. *The first step in healing our planet and making peace may be to heal the war in our own psyches.* For the war on nature and the inter-human wars going on in the world may at their deepest level be manifestations in the outer world of wars waged in our inner world against our own essence.

What is being said here? In the modern era we have seen increasing commodification of the Earth and her resources; and increasing competition between humans for control of those resources, leading to assaults on the Earth and states of war in the human community. This increasing commodification has involved at a certain point a shift in human consciousness regarding the relationship of humans to the Earth. Here we include both personal and collective shifts of consciousness and relationship. In the tribal period of human history, the predominant sense of the human's relatedness to the Earth was not one of ownership or control over the Earth, nor even of the Earth as other from self, but rather one in which the human was seen as part of the Earth, subject to her more powerful and sacred forces and laws. The Earth was often imaged as a mother upon whom one's nurturance and survival depended. The personal and community destiny was inseparable from the Earth's functioning powers. But over time, beginning with the development of agriculture and especially in the modern era, there has been an increasing objectification of the Earth, a paradigm of the Earth or nature as other and apart from self and the human. Thus a duality was set up in the human psyche between the human and nature. From this duality, there followed the myth of human dominance over the Earth. As other than human, the Earth was gradually devalued to less than human. Among enlightenment philosophers reason was elevated above nature. Humans were superior by virtue of and to the extent that they could reason. The "natural" world and those whose modes of knowing were more instinctive or intuitive, were seen as inferior. In this hierarchical and hegemonic paradigm, the Earth became not only other, but also something to be conquered, exploited, controlled and subdued.

This separation of human from nature may be the original sin, the original brokenness, the original act of war. In the Judeo-Christian account of Genesis, it may be that the story of the exit from the Garden is the story of the exit of our mind and heart from union with the Earth in which our own life has its origins. It is a story of our lost relatedness to the Earth; a loss of our sense of being part of nature.

The myth of separation and dominance over Earth paved the way for other dualities and splits in human consciousness, other expressions of dominance: the domination of the masculine over the feminine; the domination of class over class, race over race, religion over religion, nation over nation. It paved the way, too, for the image of the hero not as creator of life or nurturer, or planter of seeds, but as warrior and conqueror, always in battles requiring one to be a winner and the other to be a loser. So, to prove his capacity to lead his nation, Ronald Reagan periodically had himself photographed chopping wood, never planting trees. The ultimate picture of the macho hero today is Rambo engaged in mindless, inarticulate conquest and violence. The myth of the hero conqueror, whether conquering over nature or over other humans, is accompanied also by an often explicit devaluing of the feminine. The feminine is depicted as weak, vulnerable, dependent and, like nature, an object for conquest and control. The parallel between the devaluing of nature and the devaluing of the feminine (and with it of women and also those men who seem to manifest feminine qualities) should not be overlooked or considered mere coincidence. There is at some level an integral relationship between the rape of the Earth and the rape of women. This relationship cannot be explored in the space of this paper, but we need to note its existence as part of the syndrome of non-peace with nature. The role of women as child-bearers and nurturers has often been considered by the philosophers of rationalism as having more kinship with the natural world than the world of human reason. Seeing these as not distinctly human activities but ones shared with the animals, modern philosophers (and some feminists as well) considered child-bearing and nurturing roles as having less value than so-called rational pursuits.[12]

What is being stressed here is the state of war and conquest that exists within our psyches when we pit reason against nature, or the human against nature, as if they were separable or one dominant over the other. To try to separate nature from human nature, or to diminish the nature in human nature, is to wage war against our own essence. This inner psycho-spiritual war will be played out forever in the external world in wars against nature and each other, until we recognize what we are doing, reconcile and heal the split state of our inner world. Unless we get to this tap root of human destructiveness within our psyches, we will be increasingly more destructive of nature and each other. The first step in the dismantling of the war system and the building of peace is the healing of the brokenness and reconciling of the dualities in our own minds and hearts. This includes as a vital component of the healing, the reclaiming of the nature in human nature and the rediscovery and conscious acting upon a sense of our participation in, rather than domination over, nature. We need to discover and act upon the truth that the Earth is like a single cell in the universe. And we are not over the cell, but a part of its life. We will live or die as this single cell Earth lives or dies.

There are many positive signs that such a new consciousness is beginning to develop. But, it needs to go much deeper and broader in the collective and social consciousness and conscience if we are to break through the death processes to the healing and regeneration of Earth. To that end, we need to learn our own story which is also the story of the Earth. This story begins with our origins in the original fireball and galactic formations. It continues through the emergence of the Earth as part of a remote solar system within a remote galaxy. It includes the formation of Earth's outer crust in a period of cooling and the emergence of water and land formations. It proceeds after billions of years when the conditions were just right for the emergence of the first life forms in the oceans and the development over billions more years of an infinite variety and complexity of life forms in the waters, on land and in the air. It continues these creative life-giving processes in the development of the human. As Teilhard de Chardin observed, the human is the Earth in a new, consciousness stage of its evolution. In Teilhard's view the human emerged as an expression of the curvature of space--the return of the Earth to itself in conscious reflection on itself through the human. Thus the human stage in Earth's development is implicitly directed toward global unity. [13]

The big question now is whether these deeper purposes will be realized. We are at a delicate and critical juncture in the Earth's development. As Thomas Berry has asked: "Can Earth survive the intelligence it has brought forth?" We who are of the Earth and from the Earth now have incredible powers in determining the future of the Earth. But we don't know what we are doing. As noted above, there has been a critical lag in our development. We lack the moral and spiritual perceptions and tools to even comprehend, much less make critical choices related to the continuation of life on the planet. In essence, this is a learning gap and reflects the true nature of the crisis in education around the world.

The Earth as Primary Peace Teacher

This brings us to our fourth point. In seeking a way out of the present death processes toward peace with the Earth and peace among ourselves, the Earth itself will be our best teacher. A problem with most present notions of peace (and maybe why we do not succeed in our peace efforts) is that they are essentially homocentric (human centered). We need to go beyond images of Pax Romana or Pax Humana and reconceptualize the definition and processes of peace in terms of Pax Gaia, or Peace of the Earth. In developing this theme,

I am going to refer substantially to the thought of Thomas Berry, who in turn draws substantially from scientific understandings of cosmic laws and Earth processes. What does a study of the Earth and cosmos reveal relevant to our concerns for peace?

Differentiation or Diversity

From the beginning, the cosmic and Earth processes have involved increasing complexification and differentiation.

> Everywhere we find this differentiating process taking place. In our own solar system, within the sequence of planets, we find the planet Earth taking shape as the most highly differentiated reality that we know about in the entire universe. Life on the planet Earth finds expression in an overwhelming variety of manifestations. So too when homo sapiens appear there are immediately multiple modes of expression in human existence, which themselves change through the centuries.[14]

Respect for the diversity of life forms and a diversity of human cultures and expressions is vital to a Peace of the Earth.

Interiority or Subjectivity

"From the shaping of the first hydrogen atom to the formation of the human brain, interior psychic unity has consistently increased along with a greater complexification of being." This "deepening interior or psychic identity in the structure of reality"[15] is not determined by the human, but in its own integral functioning. There is an inner intelligence in the working of life that needs to be respected.

Communion

Physicists call it magnetism or attraction. Biologists call it bonding. Teilhard called it love. He considered the flow of intelligence and communion between all our body parts and asked, if every cell in our body is coded for working effectively, intelligently, in communion with other cells and organs, how can we doubt that we were created in and for love? The "communion of each reality of the universe with every other reality in the universe"[16] flows from the macro workings of planets around their sun and suns within galaxies and the micro workings of electrons and neutrons around a nucleus in the simplest of cells. The parts do not collapse into each other and lose their own identity. But neither do they function independently of each other. Interdependence and community are not abstract ideals but what makes the universe and human life possible. A Peace of the Earth in its very essence is community. The community of which we speak is a community of geological, biological and human components and not only of human parts. But it also involves humans in community with each other. Educating for peace then, involves educating for responsible life in community.

Indivisibility

The peace of the Earth is indivisible. The Earth is a single community composed of all its geological, biological and human components. Human peace is not sustainable outside this larger community. In an age of global scale interdependence, we can assert that human peace is not possible outside the global human community.

The Earth is a "single, organic, living reality that must survive in its integrity if it is to support any nation." Thus, "to save the Earth is a necessity for every nation."[17] From this view, notions of sovereignty and nationalism are turned upside down. The air cannot be nationalized or personalized or privatized, nor the water, nor other Earth processes. They circulate everywhere and function integrally, apart from human political divisions.

Creativity and Conflict Resolution

The word "peace" is problematic because it is so identified with passivity. In contrast, an essential characteristic of the Earth's development has been not passivity or quietude, but tremendous creativity. The whole universe has emerged not in harmony, but in conflict and disequilibrium and with a creative resolution of antagonisms. Thus the key question for humans faced with tremendous conflicts today is not whether to choose between conflict or peace, but rather "How can we deal creatively with the enormous tensions that presently afflict our planet in its every aspect?"[18] The goal of peace education then is not the elimination of conflict. Conflict is inevitable and probably even essential to growth and development. Rather, the goal is the development of capacities to resolve conflict creatively. Today we are in the midst of tremendous conflicts, testing our ability to grow together and survive. In past history, there was room for failure in resolving our conflicts. But now, in a nuclear age, with severe ecological damage already before us and the Earth's survival at stake, there is no room for human failure. Whether East/West, North/South, male/female, religion vs. religion, human vs. Earth, a failure of creativity now would be a failure of the greatest magnitude. As Berry has noted:

"In our present context failure in creativity would be an absolute failure. A present failure at this order of magnitude cannot be remedied by a larger success. In this context a completely new type of creativity is needed. This creativity must have as its primary concern the survival of the Earth in its functional integrity."[19]

Peace as Discovery, Change, Transformation

Peace of the Earth is not a pre-determined or fixed condition, but a dynamic, ongoing, transformative process. It is characterized by a sense of incompletion. It is activated by polarity tensions and gropes toward resolution, toward a more complete expression, toward discovery and transformation. In this process there is no pre-determined pattern of action. It is never the same from one period of history to another. It has been different in the tribal period and the traditional civilizations and in the modern period. We are now entering a global period of increasing human interdependency and new imperatives. In the modern period, we tried to "substitute a peace of human contrivance for a peace of an integral human presence to the Earth community in its organic functioning,"[20] and it was a terrible failure. We cannot afford such a mistake this time.

Increasing Role of the Human

The Peace of Earth has been progressively dependent on human decisions. Presently decisions regarding the fate of the Earth are being made predominantly by the industrialized nations (and predominantly by a few leaders in those countries). Superpower conflicts dominate the world. In this regard we note the lack of leadership on the part of national governments regarding the fate of the Earth and ask, Who will fill this leadership gap? We cannot wait for governments to act. They have too much invested in the status quo. From whence will the necessary leadership come today? The real hope may be in social movements and in religious networks who are able to transcend sovereignties and narrow nationalisms and ideologies and to act out of a deeper consciousness of the Earth in its functioning integrity and wholeness.

Certitude and Surprise

The Peace of the Earth is characterized by certitude and surprise. At each stage of its development, when there was an impasse in the Earth's development, the most improbable solutions emerged to enable Earth to continue its development.

"So at the very beginning of the universe if the rate of expansion had been a hundred billionth of a fraction faster or a hundred billionth of a fraction slower the universe would have exploded or collapsed. So at the moment of passage from the radiation stage to the next stage only a fragment of matter escaped anti-matter annihilation, but out of this fragment has come the galactic systems and the universe entire. So at the shaping of the solar system, if the Earth were a little closer to the sun, it would be too hot; if slightly more distant it would be too cold. If closer to the moon, the tides would overwhelm the continents, if more distant the seas would be stagnant and life development could not have taken place."

"After the appearance of cellular life when original nutrients were consumed the impasse was averted by invention of photosynthesis upon which all future life development has depended. With the great story of life in its groping toward unlimited variety of expression, the mysteries of life multiply, but the overall success of the planet becomes more evident."[21]

Can we dare to hope for surprises and resolution of our present conflicts? We need alternatives to the present impasses between conflicting forces that threaten our survival and well-being; perpetuating and escalating the war-system is a non-solution to our present problems. Alternatives are needed at local, national and global levels. Hope can be found in the emergence of people's movements all over the world seeking peace. Everywhere people are not waiting for governments to make peace, but are undertaking their own creative initiatives: citizen diplomacy, citizen summitry, people witnessing for peace by walking and running around the planet, by negotiating and dialoguing, by teaching for peace and some by offering their own bodies as a nonviolent presence between conflicting forces.

These people's movements may be the Earth's surprise in paving the way out of our present impasse and toward the next stages of life on the planet. We, the people, may yet be the Earth's surprise, the agents of reconciliation, creativity and breakthrough in building the Peace of the Earth. Preparing the world's peoples for this great task is the challenge of educators everywhere.

Notes

1.   United Nations Environment Programme, *UNEP Profile* (Nairobi, Kenya: United Nations Environment Programme, 1987).

2.   *Ibid.*

3.   Figures from *UNEP Profile, Ibid.*

4.   *Ibid.*

5.   *Ibid.*

6.   Rosalie Bertell, "An Appeal for the Marshall Islands," *Breakthrough*, a publication of Global Education Associates (Spring, 1986), Vol. 7, No. 3.

7.   Rosalie Bertell, "The Health of the Oceans," *Breakthrough* (Summer, 1984), Vol. 5, No. 4.

8.   *Ibid.*

9.   *Ibid.*

10. Rosalie Bertell, "Fact Not Fiction: Ignorance and Disinformation After Chernobyl," *Breakthrough*, Vol. 8, No. 1-2, 1987 and Edmond Billiet, "Hibakusha: A Survivor Speaks," *Breakthrough*, Vol. 5, No. 4, Spring, 1986.

11. Hannah Arendt, *The Human Condition* (Chicago: University of Chicago Press, 1958).

12. Carol McMillan has done a fine analysis of this relationship between the devaluing of nature and the devaluing of women in her book *Women, Reason and Nature* (Princeton University Press, 1982).

13. Berry, Reference not completed.

14. Thomas Berry, "The Ecological Age," *The Whole Earth Papers*, a publication of Global Education Associates, No. 12.

15. *Ibid.*

16. *Ibid.*

17. Thomas Berry, "The Cosmology of Peace," *Breakthrough*, a publication of Global Education Associates, Vol. 5, No. 3, (Spring, 1984).

18. *Ibid.*

19. *Ibid.*

20. *Ibid.*

21. *Ibid.*

Conflict and Values: A Study of Grassroots Conflicts in India

Ranjit Chaudhuri

Though conflict is said to be ubiquitous, that which is taking place in contemporary rural India needs special attention. The social conflicts that threaten the fundamental cohesion of village society and its central values have not been properly analyzed and discussed. In fact, India has not yet realized the importance of conflict study at the grassroots level. Social scientists and peace researchers have attached more importance to analyzing the conflict situation prevailing at the national and international levels. The convulsions that are taking place at the village level have been more or less ignored. Widespread caste riots, ethnic conflicts and group violence have become a recurring phenomenon. Yet no significant study is available on this growing social crisis. This paper is an attempt to identify the sources of conflicts and analyze them against the background of contemporary social values, as well as to offer possible alternatives for conflict resolution.

Every corner of India is experiencing unprecedented inner struggle in the form of group war, ethnic conflict and caste violence. Through this struggle, Indian society has been trying to bring to surface a social expectation which has long been suppressed. In the process, social values are being rearranged, and some are being fully replaced. The far-reaching effects of this inner conflict on the social institutions, human psychology and core values at the grassroots level are extremely significant.

Caste and Caste Riots

Caste is the most important social institution in India. Caste values are so deeply rooted that caste members cannot remember actually acquiring caste consciousness. Each caste group develops a culture of its own in which people live, grow and die; creating a world of association of their own. This is particularly true for the vast majority of rural people, who live in small villages and are intimately attached to the role socially ascribed to them. Caste character has remained unchanged for centuries because Indians predominantly live in villages. The village represents a complete world to the people who live in it. Generation after generation, people of different caste, creed and faith live there side by side, yet they could not live as a homogeneous entity. Village society is a closed society; each member is given a socially ascribed role to play having no scope of vertical and horizontal mobility. To the vast multitude of people, the village is the only real entity, and all other units like state, nation, etc. are either abstract or unknown. A villager does not function in relation to state or nation. His life is centered around the village and like an actor, he has a role to play.

Traditionally under the feudal system, the role of each caste member was complementary to the roles of other. The social and religious institutions that sustained the complementarity for so long began to crack apart with the introduction of new politico-economic institutions into villages. Franchise, land reform, local self-government, primary education, welfare schemes for some people and commercialization of labor and agriculture gradually exposed the inner contradiction of the caste system. The sustaining capacity of the social system became weak, and those at the lowest strata of the social ladder began to protest. Conflict became endemic and each caste group, realizing the danger, hardened its position by forming caste associations. Caste loyalty was sustained because of common customs, heritage and rituals. This loyalty was reinforced as a result of rising conflict and competition among the caste groups. Caste character is prevalent in the ethnic groups also. Plains tribals in India are the extended version of the Indian caste system. The tribals' mechanism of maintaining an inner group through rituals, portrays all the character of a caste group. The distinct and separate character of castes, with all its asymmetry and multiplicity, has become the source of tension and inner struggle.

The asymmetry and multiplicity of caste groups have made them contesting partners of social, economic and political power. The traditional privilege pattern of the society has been challenged, giving rise to bitter conflict. The underprivileged have never truly acquired access to the spoils very easily. Gradually new dimensions were added when development activities were introduced in rural society. With the increase of development activities, responsibilities and privileges were also increased. New spoils have been poured into the villages and new opportunities have been offered. But they were too few and the demand too great. As a result, conflicts began to rise, often leading to violence. In an atmosphere of violence, the individual tends to protect himself under the cover of a collective entity. Caste organization provides the most convenient tool for this.

Caste conflict comes also in the form of demands for human justice. In the stratified Indian society, it was thought that the backward communities, if left in open competition with the advanced ones, would face an unequal situation. Justice demanded certain protective measures that were necessary in order to ensure human rights. How far those measures are to be extended is yet to be decided. This has become a sensitive point of contention between the warring caste groups in different parts of India and especially in Gujarat. Here human rights, economic privileges and political power have combined to precipitate a crisis that has failed to find any redressive solution. Therefore, it has taken a form of political violence, indicating that caste factors have become more a political issue than anything else. The traditional value of obedience in the lower caste is gradually being replaced by the attitude of competition.

Moreover, political franchise has instilled a sense of importance in all the sections of the society. Panchayat, the local rural government, provides the platform to show and prove a group's importance. Panchayat, purported to be the vehicle of development, often became a volatile field of conflict and quarrel. Franchise played an important role in raising a challenge against the traditional privilege pattern. With the introduction of local self-government in the form of panchayat, every group had the opportunity to fight for its own rights. In the eyes of the law everybody is equal, so each individual is a potential contender for the highest position in the panchayat. This instilled a sense of importance in them. Gradually political confrontation began to grow for the control of panchayat. Caste groups turned into interest groups and as a result, there was a rise of fragmented leadership in the village. Behind the original philosophy of panchayat, there was a presumption that the village was a homogeneous unit, but in practice it became a sensitive center of group rivalry.

The most ominous development in recent times has been the caste riot. Caste groups forming their own "army" sometimes make aggressive attacks on one another resulting in mass killing, burning and looting. On the surface it would appear that riots break out because of the question of land holding, harvesting, labor wages, reservation of privileges, etc.; but these are more symptomatic expressions of wider and deeper problems of social change and deepening democratic values and culture. The conflicts are consequences of the human urge for equality, justice and social rights. Democratic processes have deepened these values in the minds of the people, but the traditional social institutions are not changing, and so conflicts arise due to the incompatibility between the rising aspirations and the traditional social institutions. A literature of theory, opinion and polemics has been turned out in recent times defending and advocating this struggle with new vigor, new relevance and meaning. This has created a psychology of defiance.[1] A number of NGOs are also working for the awareness-building of the backward people.

National political parties have thus far failed to understand the rising aspirations and the nature of inner struggle. These parties, irrespective of any shade and color, have been condemning this struggle as separatist and reactionary. So the aspirations of backward people and communities are suppressed with severity, under both progressive and conservative governments. But notably where caste riot has become intensive, some sort of Marxian extremism has gradually developed. These extremists swear by Marxism and profess a goal of the physical annihilation of upper caste. These extremists organize themselves in small political groups and remain confined to small regions and thrive on local issues. While the national political parties tend to ignore or condemn the caste violence as a narrow local affair, the Marxist extremist groups live off of caste violence.

Socialist leader Dr. Rammanohar Lohis realized this new phenomenon of caste-class association in Indian politics years ago.[2] He saw that a new struggle was coming to Indian politics in the form of caste struggle which, in fact, was likely to transcend all forms of class war in the Indian context. While the class concept is relevant for all advanced industrial stages, caste continues to remain an intimate social fact in India. Caste hierarchy is so deeply embedded in the socio-economic texture of the society that economic stratification becomes largely irrelevant. The present trend indicates that social stratification creates intricate issues that become a volatile political subject where the actors are not an economic class but social groups like castes, and they divide themselves into warring sections.

Along with the caste, many other factors have mingled to create strife in India. Indian local politics has become a riddle of interplay of social, economic, communal, ethnic and various other forces. Each one is inextricably linked with another. All of these forces have created a very complicated situation at the grassroots level.

A Typology of Rural Conflict

A typology of strife in villages might be helpful in understanding and identifying the conflicts. The conflicts that occur move from protest to competition and then to riot. Protests can begin with any socio-economic issue like daily wages. Competition for control of panchayat, land, wages and similar issues, becomes greater. The typology may be formulated as follows:

1. Caste/Ethnic Protest: Domination of one over another is resented. Repression, exploitation resented. Low wages protested. Backward ethnic groups show dissatisfaction over their poverty. These and similar means of protest may arise.
2. Caste/Ethnic Competition: Competition is shown during Panchayat election. Competition for getting nomination from different parties. Competition for control of economic/political spoils.
3. Caste/Ethnic Conflict: Litigation against the unlawful acts of the privileged caste. Agitation against caste domination and illegal acts of the dominant caste. Demonstration against the dominant Caste/Community/Authority.
4. Caste Riot: One caste attacks another, burns, kills and destroys each other.
5. Ethnic Riot: Ethnic groups sometimes attack other ethnic groups.
6. Tribal/Non-tribal Conflict: Tribals and non-tribals develop mutual suspicion. Tribals want to get rid of non-tribal domination.
7. Tribals/Government Conflict: Tribals put up resistance against government policies. Government pursues repressive policy against the tribals.

The typology of conflict has been formulated, keeping in mind the pattern of conflict prevailing in the social process. The typology is basically illustrative and not exhaustive. A point to be noted is that though the conflicts are localized, the actors involved in the conflicts are caste, ethnic group, communal group, non-tribals and also government. The conflicts arise in fragmented manners but they affect all sections of society and the highest authority. In other words, these conflicts are affecting basic human values and rights. Successful resolution of conflict at the grassroots level will determine the strength of democratic culture, or what Almond and Verba call *civic culture*.[3] This widespread conflict situation may lead to anomie, but if properly resolved it will usher in a more egalitarian democratic society.

The conflict phenomenon has given rise to various social, political and economic organizations. The following illustrations may be interesting:

- Caste Organization: Kayastha Sabha. Lingayat Parishad, Marwari Society, Christian Dalit Group.
- Communal Organization: Hindu Suraksha Samity, Viswa Hindu Parishad, Muslim Beradari.
- Ethnic Group: Adivasi Sabha, Kurmi Sabha.
- Caste Political Party: Dalit Party, Bahujana Samaj Party.

- Ethnic Political Party: Jharkhand Party, Jharkhand Mukti Morcha, Gorkha National Liberation Front, Tripura National Volunteers, Assam Gana Parishad.
- Marxist Extremist Group: Indian People's Front, Krishan Mazdoor Kranti Party, Different factions of Naxalite group.

Among the above organizations and parties, some rose from local groups to regional groups and parties. They now act as important interest groups and influential regional political parties.

The typology of conflict and organization reveals that caste, communal and ethnic equations have percolated deep into the Indian society. Localized conflicts get linked with each other to become a regional issue, in order to influence a sizable number of people. When the conflicts assume that proportion, the actors display both emotional and rational impulse. If the element of emotion exceeds the rational content in any action, the conflict generally becomes destructive. By identifying the character of the conflict, one can understand its horizon; but when the conflict stands on any rational issue, it becomes less destructive and more enduring. If any conflict deepens democratic pluralism it tends to reduce centrifugal tendencies. This point was highlighted by William W. Lockwood. Commenting on the Indian situation he said, "Yet the very complexity of these plural divisions as they overlap and cross-cut each other is a safeguard against the kind of bipolar confrontation that split Pakistan apart and threatens Ceylon and Malaysia".[4]

Power and Conflict

In any conflict, power is considered to be a basic component. For a long time, backward castes and communities have characterized themselves as relatively powerless. Now they want to gain as much power as possible to equalize themselves with those perceived to be more powerful. The most effective way to gain power is to form organizations. The power of collectivity brings a sense of security to its members. The endurance of the lower caste groups in the conflict indicates that they are psychologically gaining more power whereas upper castes are losing it proportionately. The reduction of upper class power is, in fact, a shrinkage of their offensive power which increases the defensive alternatives of the lower caste. Collective actors are confronting the situation in an effort to countervail each other. Power mobilization by the groups is conditioned by the inherent moral strength of their case. Moral strength, on the other hand, comes from the rational justification and legitimacy of their case. The rational justification of the claims of the backward caste and therefore, their power is drawn in India from the highest legal document, namely, the Constitution. The sanction of legal equality by the Constitution has lent legitimacy to the movement for social equality. The caste conflict is, in a sense, an arduous effort to socialize legal equality.

In India, grassroots conflicts are signs of the awakened need for more power by the traditionally oppressed people. It is a demand for broadening democratic practices and values. As the movement gathers momentum the conflicts will become more intense, engulfing every oppressed caste and community.

Condition of Conflict Resolution

Conflict resolution in the present situation of India has certain difficulties. When entering into conflict situations, contending partners often involuntarily become irrational, and act with emotion led by an imposed ego. Any collective actor has limited control over role performance. There is an unknowing submission to collective dictation. When emotion and irrationality soar high, conflict resolution becomes difficult.

Difficulty may also arise when the situation demands complete change of pre-conflict relations. This is particularly relevant for a country where social institutions, like caste, have prevented social mobility. In order to infuse democratic values, the social relations must be changed. Under the compulsion of social change, conflict management becomes particularly complex. Difficulty is also visualized when social development demands total change of social relations. Generally the methods of conflict resolution tend to stick to the status quo. Here the social activists and planners face a real problem because they have to ensure social progress. If, for the sake of avoiding conflict, they try to maintain the status quo, they will be taking recourse to social regression; if they want to see progress, conflict may become unavoidable.

Under the circumstances, we suffer from certain constraints in evolving alternatives. Still, we can think of a few methods allowing government agencies, elected bodies and non-government organizations, to play a sufficient rational role. In spite of their limited efficacy, the methods of conscientization, persuasion, negotiation, organization, professionalization, separation and unification may be considered.

Alternative Methods

Conscientization
    Through this process caste groups may be taken to a higher level of understanding social dynamics.[5] At a point of qualitative change, if consciousness is

raised to a high level, the change becomes smooth without being violent. If the actors understand that change is inevitable, they may accept it as a conscious choice. NGOs can play effective roles in raising the mass consciousness for the peaceful change of society.

Persuasion

Where conflict is avoidable persuasion can be adopted as a method of conflict resolution. Persuasion works better if the gains and losses are made visible to the contending parties. In other words, the gains and losses of violence must be clearly opened. Persuasion generally works either in the pre-conflict situation, when gains from conflict remain uncertain, or when the contending parties incur heavy losses through conflicts.

Negotiation

Conflict can be avoided if the doors of negotiation are kept open. Here again, the role of NGOs is very important, NGOs can keep the dialogue between the contending parties open and thus reduce their emotional heat. Negotiation can finally diffuse the conflict.

Organization

When a stronger group oppresses a weaker group it is necessary to unite the weaker party in an organization. The organization of the weaker group then countervails the oppressive instruments of the stronger group. Organization brings a sense of confidence among its members and enables them to fight oppression. A new alignment of power relations takes place in the society and strikes a new balance.

Professionalization

If the population can be taken to a high level of professionalization, professional competition countervails other conflicts. A professional society is highly skilled and its members have a wider functional ability. If professional skills are raised, the population can be organized into professional guilds, cuts across caste loyalty. Professional loyalty is not as aggressive as ethnic and cultural loyalty. Professionalism transcends caste hierarchy.

Separation

When unity is found to be impossible, it is necessary to make arrangements for separation with the purpose to remove the parties from the point of contention. This arrangement is necessary when reconciliation between the groups is ruled out and there is more chance of destruction and violence. Separation can be found through certain institutional arrangements.

Unification

Social leaders may attempt to unify the process of development through the rationalization of social values by regenerating common morality, honesty, trust, friendship, tolerance, cooperation, etc. Universal practice of these values leads to social cohesion. New orientation of the people in these universal values is helpful in social unification and maintaining social peace.

Conclusion

Violence, conflict and strife that have taken form in contemporary rural India, should be studied and analyzed from the point of both conflict management and the development of the democratic process. While considering conflict management, it is necessary to bear in mind the contradiction that may arise while achieving social progress and maintaining peace. Due to the fact that conflict is ubiquitous, the basic task is to maintain legitimacy where contending parties remain at equal distance from the official power. Indian bureaucracy has failed to resolve the social and economic contradiction in rural society. Elected bodies like the panchayat have failed to foster the feeling of unity in the villages. Rather various caste and group interests have become sharpened. Methods open for conflict resolution invite both government and non-government organizations to play the role of animators. Democratization of values and realignment of group relations will be the final indicator of this social process.

Notes

1.   NGOs and leftist extremists have produced a large amount of political, economic, and sociological literature as well as drama and music. These had made a tremendous effect on the people.

2.   Lohia Rammanohar, *Fragments of a World Mind* (Calcutta, 1950), p. 114.

3.   Gabriel A. Almond and Sidney Verba, *The Civic Culture* (Boston: Little, Brown and Company, 1965).

4.   William W. Lockwood, "Asian Triangle: China, India, Japan," *Foreign Affairs* (Vol. 52, No. 4, 1974).

5.   Social activists are indebted to Paulo Friere for making this concept meaningful in his book, *Pedagogy of the Oppressed* (New York: Herder and Herder, 1979).

14

Citizenship and Rural Social Conflicts in Brazil

Alfredo Wagner Berno de Almeida

The originality of the instruments of violence, used in land conflicts during the last two decades, may be seen both in their systematic and generalized character which exceeds the coercion mechanisms historically observed in latifundia. Latifundia is a forum of concentration of large estates. In their continuing and immoderate application, the most obvious result has been a gradual and uncontrollable increase of the crime rate in rural areas, in excess of limits that are regarded as tolerable. This violence is not caused by irrational impulses, an impression which is sometimes fostered by continuing killings and cases of massacres where natives and whole families of peasants are wiped out. Rather, it is the result of carefully contrived strategies and ruses characteristic of situations where there is an intense process of concentration of landed property.[1]

Despite the fragmentary statistical data, since crime records have been of slight value in evaluating acts of violence in land conflicts, nevertheless there already exists a reasonable quantitative base and a relatively significant number of descriptions of events. One can assert that, together with the increase in the rate of crime and violence in rural areas, there is an increase in the provocative character of the crimes.

According to statistics produced within the Ministry of Agrarian Reform and Development (MIRAD), during 1985 and up to January 1987, about three thousand land conflict situations have been inventoried. They cover a wide range of antagonisms and confrontations of interests involving not only property, but also work relations and the circulation of agricultural products. They are defined as "critical or social tension zones."[2] The trend toward concentration and the improper use of land by latifundia (large estates) is accompanied by a generalized increase in social conflicts and rates of violence. Characterized by the use of force and physical and mental constraint, acts of violence include murders, assault, serious injuries and armed robbery. Their purpose is not only to appropriate land worked by families, but also, in many cases, to pillage agricultural production; control peasant labor; and set up obstacles to prevent peasants from having access to land.

More recent data from the above-mentioned sources indicated that during 1985 and 1986 there were recorded 558 deaths in land disputes.[3] In over ten cases, the peasants involved in these disputes have disappeared or their whereabouts are unknown, according to the complaints filed by their families with the authorities. They include 550 murders and 8 suicides. The former include 494 events involving public and private land and 56 involving trespassing on Indian lands. Note that in at least two thirds of the cases of murder, the victims were peasants.

The cases of murder are distributed over different States of Brazil and denote regions that present an overall picture of social conflict and tension occurring both in recently settled areas and old settlements. However, the highest rates are in the Amazon areas (Para, Mato Grosso, Maranhao) where settlement is expanding.

Table 1
Distribution of Deaths by Region and State
(1985 - 1986)

North

- Rondonia	34
- Amazonas	07
- Roraima	01
- Para	190
Total	232

Northeast

- Maranhao	51
- Ceara	13
- Piaui	08
- Pernambuco	25
- Alagoas	03
- Bahia	42
- Rio Grande do Norte	02
Total	144

Southeast

- Minas Gerais	55
- Rio de Janeiro	14
- Sao Paulo	12
Total	81

South

- Parana	03
- Rio Grande do Sul	02
- Santa Catarina	02
Total	07

Center-West

- Mato Grosso	59
- Mato Grosso do Sul	05
- Goias	30
Total	94

In mid 1986, the Ministry of Agrarian Reform and Development (MIRAD) and the National Agrarian Reform Institute (INCRA) were incapable of initiating any action that would overcome inertia and the barriers raised by the counter-reform. Refusal of the Proposal to the National Agrarian Reform Plan (I PNRA), approved at the IV National Peasant Congress held in Brasilia on 25-30 May 1985, was followed by another more puzzling refusal. The Sarney Administration refused to comply with the timid goals included in the Administration's own plan, (i.e., the I National Agrarian Reform plan, according to Decree No. 91,766 of 10 October 1985). Expropriations on social grounds were cut and their character was redefined by negotiations and "agreements" with big landowners.[4] Emergency action in conflict areas was suspended. Implicitly, the administration now endorsed all forms of domination, including the use of brute force which was commonly resorted to by the large landowners and land grabbers (grileiros). As a result, the statistics on land conflicts, produced in 1985 and 1986 by the proper government agencies, were not processed further and systematized for publication. Here again, we have a refusal to acknowledge the existence of such conflicts which was a normal feature of the land agencies during the period of dictatorship.

Therefore, the available data concerning murders committed during land conflicts during 1987 are those published by religious organizations, such as the Comissao Pastoral da Terra (Pastoral Land commission,) and voluntary organizations, such as the National Campaign for Agrarian Reform. These statistics refer only to the deaths of peasants, a total of 95 murders in 1987. The Comissao Pastoral da Terra recorded 561 murders in land disputes from 1985 to 1989, particularly of Indians and peasants, involving 600 thousand people and an area in excess of 70 million hectors.

Organized Crime and Impunity

As regarded by investigators, traditional rules and procedures are a specific code of violence based on common law regulating, among others, "crimes of honor," "family feuds," blood debts" and cases of banditism. In opposition to these procedures and rules which have been followed in rural areas to discipline antagonisms, we have a set of murders committed openly, without even bothering with the simplest precautions. Even though these acts are also in violation of lawfully instituted regulations, they are not uncommon and even cases of double murder are frequent. Double murder cases occur when more than one person in a family is killed for the avowed purpose of affecting the management and composition of the labor force of peasant families. It should be noted that murders are committed in locations where there are many persons--in buses, boats, bus stations, markets, fairs, and public squares. There seems to be little concern about eyewitnesses or the identification of those who commit such actions. There is a puzzling certainty of impunity. The public nature of such acts, on the other hand, is certainly intended to intimidate. The spreading of fear and some panic are thus foreseeable corollaries since impunity implies, above-all, power exceeding that of lawful authority. These characteristics are accompanied by the cruelty with which these crimes are committed and a great number of other forms of physical constraint, such as: beatings, bodily injuries, torturing, rape, beheading, and lynching.

In any case, more dramatic than the quantitative increase in these statistics is the new varieties of violence--perverse crimes, murders by shooting, suicides--and hundreds of atrocities that are becoming routine in rural areas. Organized crime has become a very common feature of these new forms of violence. It is noted that group violence is not limited to a few exceptions, but in fact is a feature of nearly all killings of peasants, Indians, professionals working for representative organizations (lawyers, educators) and clergymen. The increase in the proportion of such organized crimes draws attention to groups of criminals and bands of gangs, commonly known as "crime syndicates." These groups infest the Northeast and Center-West and the Amazon region. Organized crime mainly takes the form of what is commonly known as private militias, vigilante groups, security officers or watchmen, which have been continuously charged by trade unions with the use of coercion and threats against peasants in different Brazilian States.

Such highly bellicose attitudes should be seen and interpreted as forms of aggression that are dependent on specific historical circumstances. In other words, the means of violence and coercion which are traditionally resorted to by latifundia are undergoing deep changes. The existing rural violence and a certain type of banditry has divested itself of traditional forms in order to adapt .to the new forms of land occupation dictated by the interest in concentration of large economic groups.

A New Type of Latifundism

Agrarian conflicts in which murder occurs are extreme cases of violence and involve antagonisms where conflicting interests have attained the limit. However, there are other features of these conflicts that are equally serious and clearly violent that have come into being as a result of the trend towards concentration of landed property and a new type of latifundism.

During the last few years, government allocation in the rural area of a large volume of incentives and subsidies, and the granting and sale by the government of public lands before democratizing access to land, have contributed toward aggravating the concentration of landed property. This situation is to a great extent reflected in most of the farming and cattle-raising projects that have received tax benefits from the government.

The establishment of this new type of latifundism, despite its avowed purpose of agricultural modernization, has not renounced the use of traditional methods of immobilizing labor (*peonagem da divida*). In addition, this trend has instituted coercive mechanisms based on violence for the purpose of disorganizing the economies of small agricultural producers who for decades, if not for centuries, have tilled the soil and inhabited these regions. The most immediate result of these attempts has been the expulsion of large numbers of peasants from the land they till and the spread of a climate of unprecedented violence and tension in rural areas.

In addition to an increase in the transfer of peasants to metropolitan areas, thus aggravating urban problems and causing the country's population pattern to change and become distorted, there is an increasing tendency for families to crowd together in so-called "camps." This crowding creates innumerable potential conflict situations. In August 1986 there were 18,478 families living in 99 camps located mainly in the South Region.[5]

Other conflict situations are to be found in gold prospecting areas which have become zones of serious social tensions. About 400 thousand gold prospectors have been counted[6] and the National Department of Mineral Production has identified 64 conflicts.

Social tension situations related to labor law violations and the unlawful use of labor immobilization instruments involved about five million workers in rural areas, according to the estimates of the Ministry of Labor published in the Preamble to the draft law regulating casual labor.

Democratic Transition and Land Conflicts

The amplitude and intensity of social conflicts in rural areas with a high rate of violence are in strong contrast with a political environment that is more favorable towards recognition of the peasants' right to land. How can one explain, after nearly three years of transition towards a democratic regime, that violent actions, truculent methods and organized and widespread murder, continue to be as frequent and savage as before in rural areas?

These tragic statistics show that the innumerable segments of the peasantry, who are involved in critical tension zones, have been excluded from inalienable rights. Groups of *peoes, boias-frias*, squatters and small landowners and groups of Indians permanently exposed to threats, are subjected to multiple deprivations with respect to basic rights. This is a result of failure to comply with the labor laws concerning *peoes, boias-frias*, permanent wage earners, and the Land Statute regarding squatters and tenants. It is a result of the lack of law and order--peasants and Indians are victims of acts of violence--and of violation of what the Indians' Statute proclaims.

These are formally granted the status of citizens, but in fact this is no more than a kind of semi-citizenship which allows them to enjoy only a certain number of rights, while other rights that are essential to the full exercise of their activities are denied them. In fact, the camped peasants and those who are immobilized by the mechanisms of force--gold prospectors, squatters who have been arbitrarily evicted from their land, Indians whose territories have been occupied by intruders--represent "second-class citizens" who do not fully participate in the *polis*.

It should be said that stable forms of democracy are not restricted to the vote. The very idea of a Constituent Assembly presupposes the formalization of an order where social conflicts could be resolved non-coercively. Thus, government intervention cannot limit itself to regulating antagonisms between individuals and social groups in a situation in which the very existence of agrarian conflicts is officially described as something that cannot be eliminated. When the opponent's objective, to eliminate or neutralize his rivals through violence, takes the upper hand in all of its forms while refusing to accept any means of settlement other than brute force, we have a fundamental contradiction: the other party is being socialized by absolute submission, by compulsory subjection, as a result of brutal confrontation.

A noteworthy feature of this functionalist conception is the idea that land conflicts and violence in particular are inherent and essential to the development of production forces in rural areas. From this point of view, coercion and acts of constraint will deliver peasants from a state of backwardness by redeeming them from traditional subordinations.

The idea of subordination by force is, however, historically tied up with the idea of the latifundium as a forum of concentration of landed property which routinely resorts to coercive acts to appropriate the peasant surplus. The principle of acting violently in situations involving antagonisms and disputes over land has been strengthened and stimulated by ideological patterns that are inherent to the formation of latifundia. Brutal action and the forms of banditism, which have now become explicit as organized crime, would represent a traditional response to social problems of renewed complexity.

Glorification of Violence

We face a bundle of confrontations which cannot be easily assimilated. They are empirically synthesized in the multiple tensions between traditional forms of domination taken to an extreme and organized forms of participation by the peasants.

The conflicts act as a mechanism through which adjustment to new conditions of agreement presupposes in advance the acceptance of the claims and demands of the peasants. Nevertheless, the aggravation of murders represent new forms of conflict associated with the political participation of peasants in the process of breaking with the authoritarian regime and moving toward democracy. This is one of the most forceful ways of calling attention to their claims and a means of ensuring a non-discriminatory access to citizenship. In this sense, the land conflicts are the greatest expression of the social tensions mentioned earlier.

Mobilization of peasants for access to land, while a right according to one condition of full citizenship, also implies that private property rights relating to land are legally subordinate to the social obligation of full tillage and economic use. The social function to be performed by the ownership of land [7] and other legal provisions that provide for the access of peasant to land and adequate regulation of work relations, support social practices that run counter to those that large landowners today have managed to effectively impose.

The large landowners, with the unrestrained adoption of the most extreme instruments of violence, defeat the maintenance of their own domination. They become increasingly exposed to legal sanctions, despite the impunity of their present behavior. The forms of organization that they set up, on the lines of the Ruralist Democratic Union (UDR), are intended to revive the principles of a form of domination based on practices of the monopoly of land and the control of votes no longer seen as legitimate in social and economic life. These militant organizations are in fact out-of-date, an anachronism.

In this context, the technical improvement of instruments of violence in rural areas has reached such a destructive potential that there is no political objective to justify their use. The large landowners increase their destructive potential by successive annihilation, the demolition of entire villages and the spread of panic and fear. This is seen particularly in the Mearim, Pindare, Tocantins and Araguaia river valleys.

There are immense difficulties in maintaining or renewing such forms of domination; although the concentration of landed property does not seem to have lost its prerogative of local political power and insinuates itself strongly due to its overlap with the interests and resources of industrial capital.[8] It is in the byways of this break that the mobilization of peasants is more organized and more compact, although the number of peasant victims is high in critical zones of conflict and tension. The peasants are fighting to secure their independence, while the producers want to preserve domains that in effect belong to the peasants. The peasants demand recognition of their rights even in circumstances in which they aim to take back areas from which they have been arbitrarily expelled and evicted. Thus, the scene of clashes and confrontations has been, of necessity, their own land which they know so well from their daily work.

Full Citizenship for the Peasants

Agrarian conflicts show themselves subject to political determinations. These determinations are dictated by the degree of mobilization of peasants and the capability of government intervention to resolve them.

The Proposal for the National Plan of Agrarian Reform, launched at the IV National Peasant Congress, nurtured in peasants the belief in the possibility of solving agrarian and rural social justice problems, as well as transmitting an idea favoring recognition of all the individual and public rights involved in the claim for agrarian reform. Thus, events that seriously attacked the peasants' right to full citizenship were clearly evidenced as being unlawful.

The rise itself of the Ruralist Democratic Union (UDR) in May 1985 is a sign that there is a new strategy by the Right for rural areas. This is a result of limitations being imposed upon forms of domination using brute force.[9] Their strategies have resulted in a delay and slowdown of actions relating to land. The corollary is the failure to meet, to a suitable extent and in accordance with the officially established goals, the peasants' fundamental claims. As the abyss between actions relating to land and the demands of the social movement keeps increasing, we have a situation which favors conditions causing agrarian conflicts to persist and to grow.

Notes

An earlier version of this chapter was published in *Tribunal National Dos Crimes Do Latifundio*, edited by Vozes/FASE/ADJUP, 1988. It is reprinted here with permission of the author.

1.   About this process, the Proposal for the drafting of the I National Agrarian Reform Plan provides the following data: "According to the data of the 1980 Farming and Stockraising Census, establishments whose area was equal to or greater than 1,000 hectares accounted for about 1% of total rural properties and approximately 45% of the total area. On the other hand, establishments having an area of less than 100 hectares accounted for nearly 90% of the total, but they accounted for only 20% of the total area covered by the census. The data of the National Agrarian Reform Institute's (INCRA) Register of Rural Properties, which was organized subsequently to the promulgation of the Statute, reflect more accurately the concentration of landed property, since individually "rural property" is a unit of land ownership and possession,, while the Farm and Stockraising Census of the Brazilian Institute of Geography and Statistics (IBGE) defines a "farm and stockraising establishment" which is a production unit. Thus, the properties covering over 1,000 ha which in 1967 accounted for 46.9% of the total surface area of the country's rural properties, in 1984 accounted for 58.3%. At the other extreme, properties covering less than 100 ha dropped from 18.7% in 1967, to 14% in 1984. The poor distribution of land may be evaluated better from the figures gathered during the survey: Properties covering more than 1,00 ha accounted in 1984 for only 2.9% of the total and those covering less than 100 ha, 83.2%. Of the latter, 66.4% (more than 1,700,000 properties in absolute figures) had surface area of less than 25 ha.

The concentration of landed property, historically assured and stimulated today, causes social injustice to prevail in rural areas. While in 1984 there were 10.5 million landless peasants, the properties that the Statute regarded as latifundia (and which, therefore, did not perform their social function) appropriated 409 million hectares. These properties had about 25% of their workable surface unused in 1972. This situation worsened substantially, to the extent that, in 1984, the unused workable area rose to 41%" pages 5,6. (Proposal for drafting the I National Agrarian Reform Plan, MIRAD-INCRA, May, 1986.)

2.   Cf. Article 15 of Law No. 4504 of 30 November 1964.

3. Cf. Coordenadoria de Conflitos Agrarios (MIRAD-INCRA), *Conflitos de Terra* Vol. I and II. See also Informacao Tecnica CCA, about land conflicts, dated 20 November 1986 (MIRAD).

4. The I PNRA's land expropriation goals for 1985/1989 totaled 43,090,000 ha. Until December 1987, the Sarney Administration had decreed the expropriation of 2,325,109 ha. Available to the Administration are 5,270,000 ha of unused land. Adding together these two figures, we obtain a total of 7,595,100 ha which subtracted from the I PNRA's overall target figure leaves 35,494,892 ha that would have to be expropriated. If the government will maintain a monthly expropriation rate of about 140,00 ha, which is the actual average rate up to January 1987, it would take 258 months, or 21 years 5 months, to meet the goal of 43,090,000 ha. In other words, according to this projection, the I PNRA will be completed in the year of 2008.

5. Cf. Coordenadoria de Conflitos Agrarios (MIRAD-INCRA), *Acampamentos*, Brasilia, September 1986, pp. 22-29.

6. Coordenadoria de Conflitos Agrarios (MIRAD-INCRA), *Garimpo e Tensao Social*, Brasilia, October, 1986, pp. 45-50.

7. Cf. Article 2, Paragraph 1 of the Land Statute.

8. For further details see the interview by Dr. Jose Gomes da Silva and Nelson Letaif in *Senhor Magazine*, No. 256, 11 February 1986.

9. Cf. Cf. CPT-CNRA--"A Ofensiva da direita no campo," 1988.

15

The Role of Social Conditioning in Male Violence

Ian M. Harris

In most countries with standing armies, the male population is conditioned to acts of violence and to killing.[1] Social conditioning prepares males to obey orders and go to war. Mass media--videos, popular songs, television, commercial magazines, and movies--depict men violently expressing anger and killing others. It is estimated that children in the United States, by the age 18, will have seen on television an average of 18,000 violent deaths.[2] Such violent images, deeply imprinted in the male psyche, condone male brutality and reward men for violent behavior (e.g., they have sex with attractive women; they earn promotions; they destroy their foes; they receive congratulations from peers, etc.). Social messages, subtle and overt, condition men to use violent means to enhance their position in this world.

Messages supporting violence definitely influence male behavior, but don't necessarily cause men to be violent. Women, who occupy the same cultures and witness similar acts of violence, do not on the average act as violently as men. The reasons why certain men are violent are complex. Male sex role socialization is the process by which males learn how to be men. Part of that socialization involves receiving cultural messages that condition men to be violent by condoning and even encouraging violence. According to a social conditioning explanation of male violence, men are conditioned by the societies they inhabit to respond to aggressive and frustrating situations with violent behavior.

This explanation does not adequately explain male violence. If all men receive similar cultural messages that condone violence, why aren't all men violent? Why do some men who receive violent social messages never in fact become brutal or cruel? Not all men strike out when they become frustrated or angry. Some overcome primitive instincts and express rage and resentment in civilized ways that don't hurt others. Whether or not a particular man engages in violent acts depends on a variety of influences that include messages from the culture, early familial environment, models he has in his own life for expressing emotions, and the particular demands of social organizations. In order to understand the effect of social conditioning upon violent male behavior, it is first necessary to examine closely the process by which men are socialized.

Male Sex Roles

The male sex role consists of cultural norms that set standards for what it means to be male. These norms or sex role messages establish culturally condoned notions for male behavior. Individuals receive sex role messages from a variety of places--from families, peers, the media, significant others, and the various cultures they inhabit. Becoming a man is an interactive experience, where each individual deciphers cultural standards for male behavior and forms for himself a schema, or pattern that establishes his masculine identity. Depending upon individual circumstances (what friends value, what family members reward, what teachers emphasize, etc.) each man adopts by the time he is 16 his own unique gender identity.[3]

Becoming a man implies learning a set of rules[4] or standards, referred to in transactional language terms as scripts, which are used as behavioral references. These messages help determine an individual's sense of appropriate male behavior and form a blueprint that sets direction for his life by defining how he ought to behave. Throughout the life cycle these schema can be altered as an individual adjusts his standards to reality. Are his behavior and values appropriate? Is he being rewarded or discouraged for his masculine behavior? Erikson indicates that it takes a crisis to alter an individual's identity after this original schema has been set.[5] As a man matures, he modifies his notions of appropriate masculine behavior if certain behaviors become dysfunctional and lead to divorce, problems with the law, unhappy relationships, job loss, etc. Thus, negative reinforcement can prod a man to alter his gender identity or even change his violent behavior.

Male Messages in the United States

In order to determine the effect of sex role messages upon male violence in the United States, in 1983 this author started asking men to name two messages they had received that helped determine what it meant for them to be a man. These messages were refined and developed into a questionnaire with twenty-four messages that have been filled out by over four hundred men from different parts of the United States. This sample represents men in the United States who were better educated by three years above the U.S. average and the majority of respondents came from the country's mid-West.

The following list contains a rank ordering of these messages based on which message respondents named as the most influential in his life. The message that received the greatest number of responses is at the top and the message that received the least at the bottom:

1. Scholar: Be knowledgeable. Go to college. Value book learning. Read and study.

2. Work Ethic: Men are supposed to work for a living and not take handouts.

3. Be the Best You Can: Do your best. Don't accept being second. "I can't" is unacceptable.

4. Self Reliant: Asking for help is a sign of weakness. Go it alone. Be self sufficient and don't depend on others.

5. Nurturer: Among other things men are gentle, supportive, warm, sensitive, and concerned about others' feelings.

6. Good Samaritan: Do good deeds and acts. Put others' needs first. Set a good example.

7. Nature Lover: Love of outdoors. Respectful treatment of plants and animals. Harmony with nature.

8. Tough Guy: Men don't touch, show emotion, or cry. They don't let others push them around.

9. Breadwinner: Men provide for and protect family members. Fathering means bringing home the bacon, not necessarily nurturing.

10. President: Men pursue power and status. They strive for success.

11. Adventurer: Men take risks and have adventures. They are brave and courageous.

12. Control: Men are in control of their relationships, emotions, and jobs.

13. Stoic: Ignore pain in your body. Achieve even though it hurts. Don't admit weakness.

14. Faithful Husband: Men give up their freedom when they get married.

15. Technician: Men relate to, understand, and maintain machines. They fix and repair things around the house.

16. Rebel: Defy authority and be a non-conformist. Question and rebel against system.

17. Hurdles: To be a man is to pass a series of tests. Accomplishment is central to the male style.

18. Be Like Your Father: Dad is your role model. Males express feelings in ways similar to their fathers.

19. Sportsman: Men enjoy playing sports, where they learn the thrill of victory and how to compete.

20. Playboy: Men should be sexually aggressive, attractive and muscular.

21. Superman: Men are supposed to be perfect. They don't admit mistakes.

22. The Law: Do right and obey. Don't question authority.

23. Warrior: Men take death-defying risks to prove themselves and identify with war heroes.

24. Money: A man is judged by how much money he makes and the status of his job.

This rank ordering of messages appears to be wrong. Respondents did not rate the traditional messages--Breadwinner, Warrior, Superman, Stoic, Playboy, President, Adventurer and Control--as very influential in their lives. Messages like these have been singled out by sex role researchers as dominating male behavior. This study shows that sex norms promoting traditional male behavior exist in the United States and provide cultural messages which influence men but not as strongly as more positive messages they receive from their mothers, fathers, and other significant people in their lives. Messages that men receive promoting traditional male behaviors are of secondary importance.

In their attempt to describe how men are conditioned by societies to be violent, sex role researchers have focused on those violent aspects of male behavior that differentiate men from women and ignored those aspects of male behavior that are traditionally feminine. Previous studies about men have made the mistake of observing the grossest of male actions--the killing of soldiers, the greed of business men, the violent acts of crime, the obsession with winning that dominates sports, the competitiveness of politicians, the lack of involvement of some fathers in their family life--and deduced from these observations that men exhibit destructive behaviors. If boys were raised in locker room settings with men whose sole purpose was to turn them into winners, they might grow into the monsters they are popularly depicted as in the media. However, boys are most often raised by their mothers. They have sisters, aunts, teachers, ministers, and significant others who give them peaceful, loving messages about how they ought to behave that contradict tough masculine images rampant in modern cultures. Primary messages that encourage men to do well in school, to work hard, to be the best they can, to be nurturing, to be self-reliant, and to participate in civic affairs, have a more lasting value for the male psyche than the cultural messages promoting violent male behavior.

These messages do not necessarily produce within men the behavior described within the message, but rather set normative standards that men carry around in their heads and try to realize. Such scripts help males determine their plans, what they want to do with their lives, how they will act in certain situations, etc., but the actual course of their lives may deviate considerably from the scripts and sex role schema developed in younger years. Once men assume adult tasks in competitive social organizations, they may not behave in accordance with the various messages they learned as children, but the messages still tug within their psyches. A married man who commits adultery may feel guilty because of the faithful husband message.

The Violence Equation

Each man has a choice in a given situation about whether or not to use violence. Men are not clay puppets molded by the circumstances around them. They can choose whether to act violently or nonviolently. How a given individual acts in a certain situation, depends upon a complex set of factors that together constitute "the male violence equation." Every act of violence an individual commits can be explained with the following equation:

$$VB_m = SM + IR + AB + OE$$

In this equation violent behavior by men VB_m is a function of social messages (SM), inner rage (IR), anger behavior (AB), and organizational expectations (OE). When an individual chooses at a particular time to commit an act of violence, his decision is based upon a complex mixture of these factors. His previous history comes to play and his mind calculates an appropriate response to a given situation based upon what he has learned and been rewarded for in the past.

Social messages (SM) are an important part of this equation because they set standards for male behavior. The messages from the list of messages above that directly promote violence are "Tough Guy" and "Warrior." Tough guys don't show their emotions. They don't let other people push them around. The influence of the Tough Guy message urges men to prove they have guts, fighting to establish their place in the world of men. Some men even go so far as to join elite military groups like the Foreign Legion or the Marines to prove their toughness.

The Warrior message instills in young boys a desire to imitate the behavior of other warriors--brave men who have proven themselves through combat. The Warrior message is similar to the Tough Guy message when men take risks to prove they have balls. Some men drive cars at incredible speeds; others drink prodigious amounts of alcohol; and others play with guns. War games with young boys demonstrate they have what it takes to be a warrior. Many primitive societies have complicated initiation rites into the brotherhood of warriors, where adolescents leave the warmth and security of mothers' protection to join the hard world of grown men. In modern technological societies, boys goggle at war heroes on television screens and play with war toys to learn the ways of warriors. A warrior has a mission. For many men this means joining a cause or becoming patriotic to the point where they achieve honor and demonstrate their heroism by being willing to die for their countries.

These messages, important parts of the violence equation, contribute to the sex role conditioning of men but are not sufficient causes of male violence. Men are violent for many reasons. Every man has deep within his psyche a pool of resentment that comes from various putdowns he has experienced--times when he has been violated, that vary from abandonment as a child, physical abuse, sexual abuse, loss of a job, rejection by lovers, being told he has no worth, etc. This reservoir is the driving force behind male anger. A majority of male rapists were sexually abused as children. Veterans returning from the Vietnam war are prone to sudden outbursts. They have deep psychological scars caused by their war experiences that are often released in violent expressions of rage. Recently, such a veteran in Arkansas shot his family and neighbor, killing nine people, some of whom were gunned down in a shopping mall. This pool of resentment, inner rage (IR), is the driving force behind male anger and operates in unique ways with individual men. A boy raised nonviolently may not have within deep feelings of rage that need to be expressed and hence his tendencies for violence would be less than someone raised in a physically abusive home.

This phenomenon has a particularly powerful effect upon working class and minority men who are constantly put down by bourgeois white societies. Classism and racism are built upon the superiority of white Anglo-Saxon middle class males. Men who differ from the norms established by white ruling classes feel inferior because institutional barriers keep them from fulfilling their dreams, from being able to hold meaningful jobs, from acquiring a sense of satisfaction from their lives, and from participating equally in the social order. They have what it takes but aren't able to succeed because social institutions deny them opportunities other men take for granted. Minority and working class men have deep resentments about not being able to earn many of the privileges so casually touted in the media as being the common lot of all men.

All men have within them feelings of rage and fury. How they express these feelings depends to a large extent upon the models for resolving conflicts they have in their own personal lives. For each man a complex set of factors determines his anger behavior (AB), how he responds to aggressive and frustrating situations. If his peers are violent, he will ape their behavior. Without adequate role models of nonviolent behavior most men do not realize how to express their deep seated frustrations peacefully and learn violent behavior from cultural images that depict men expressing their emotions violently. If a boy is raised nonviolently, he may not have within deep feelings of rage that need to be expressed and hence his tendencies for violence would be less than someone raised in a physically abusive home. Men model the violent behavior they see around them. They learn to strike their loved ones when they get angry because that's how their fathers expressed anger. Fathers spank their children because that's the way they were raised. Think of an angry man. How is he expressing his anger? Images like Clint Eastwood pulling out a .357 magnum and blowing away all those closest to him dominate many men's psyches. They learn to express their anger in violent ways and respond violently to fearful situations because that's how they observe other men's behavior. If males only witness other men expressing violence in angry ways, individuals may not know how to release frustrations nonviolently. However, if they have models in their lives of people expressing anger nonviolently or responding to fearful situations in civilized ways, they may themselves seek peaceful solutions to tense situations. Religion plays an important role in some men's lives, teaching them to respond to other human beings with love and feelings of brotherhood.

The rest of the violence equation comes from organizational expectations (OE) that are placed upon men in specific social institutions. Concepts of masculinity are deeply embedded in social organizations. Many men join violent organizations, like the army or police where they are trained to use force and to kill. Such organizations require them to be violent. Once they are in these organizations, other messages they receive, like 'Be the Best You Can' and 'Adventurer' have an important influence. For a bomber on a bombing run over Dresden, this means bomb the hell out of the Huns. For Lieutenant Calley, a U.S. lieutenant in Vietnam, it meant wiping out civilians in jungle villages like Mai Lai. For executives in corporations, it means making workers redundant in order to increase the profit margins of their firms. Such violent behaviors are justified by the organizations from which men draw their livelihood. They want to succeed within those organizations.

Being in the army means you don't question orders. Here 'The Law' message exerts its influence. Men are told from the time they are young boys to be obedient and not question authority. In schools, they are punished for speaking out of turn and reprimanded for non-conforming behavior. At home they are told to obey parents. Such constant reinforcement of conformity make them good soldiers when as adults they are ordered to commit heinous acts upon fellow human beings.

The 'Adventure' message adds to the violence equation. In violent social organizations, men who are brave and courageous are rewarded for committing brutal acts. They go the extra mile to prove their worth by taking risks. This message is not necessarily negative and can have positive effects. A sense of adventure and risk-taking will be required to challenge existing social norms that support violence and to promote nonviolent ways of resolving conflict.

This violence equation depends to some extent upon the conditioning that men have received to be violent. This conditioning comes in the form of social messages (SM) and organizational expectations (OE). Both of these factors set expectations for men to be violent and, when men are rewarded for violent behavior, contribute to male violence. The independent factors in this equation that can counterbalance violent male social conditioning are inner rage (IR) and anger behavior (AB). Some individuals are angrier than others. Full of pain from past experiences, they are time bombs waiting to go off, exploding at the slightest provocation and present definite threats to society. Other men, raised in nonviolent circumstances in nurturing environments, may not have "a tiger" inside, tearing at his chains. They may upon occasion get angry, but that anger is not propelled by powerful forces that often result in destructive behavior. To a large extent, whether or not a man will be violent in a given situation, depends upon how he has learned to express his emotions and the depth of rage he has within him. Men who have learned nonviolent ways of expressing anger and frustration can draw upon these past experiences to contradict both social messages and organizational expectations that urge them to be violent.

The Contradictions of Being a Male

This study indicates that some men feel frustrated when they can't realize deep-seated messages they have within themselves. Many men raised by nurturing parents find themselves in competitive work environments where they are expected to be unemotional and nonsupportive. They are supposed to give orders, fire others, and act in ways that may generate profit for their employers, but deny their essential humanity. Men are also systematically raised to kill. Killing other human beings wounds men psychologically, because men have also been raised to respect life. Gandhi said that the individual who commits an act of violence, suffers more than the victim.[6]

This study underscores the contradictory nature of being a man, which some researchers have pointed out as "sex role strain."[7] Men receive conflicting messages from their cultures. Messages such as Playboy and Faithful Husband, the Law and Rebel, Nurturer and Stoic, place contradictory expectations on men. Inability to fulfill such contradictory expectations increases male frustration, inadequacy and sense of failure.

Conclusion

For a long time sex role researchers, social commentators, and feminists have pointed out the problems caused by violent male behavior and raised important challenges to the nature of patriarchy. Most radical critics of patriarchal society have overlooked how the vast majority of men are victimized by violent social messages. To be sure, all societies in this world are controlled by men and most of those societies encourage men to use violence to solve problems and advance their interests. But, the vast majority of men are not in positions of power where they enjoy the benefits of patriarchy. The vast majority of soldiers in the army are not generals or captains, but rather privates sent to slaughter. The vast majority of working men do not direct corporations, making economic decisions that dislocate other people's lives. Rather, they "man" the factories in menial and clerical jobs with low pay and no status. Patriarchy, an oppressive social order that provides privileges to some men and rests upon male violence, oppresses men, too.

A few men at the top benefit greatly from the patriarchal order, but the vast majority of men live lives of quiet desperation trying to find meaning in a violent world full of oppression and pain. Having been taught not to show their emotions, they don't know how to release their feelings of rage at social systems that deny their personhood. They form their identities in a world that expects them to be tough, and then doesn't support masculine expression of emotions about the inhumanity of living in a world based on greed and competition. For every man who gets to the top thousands of others are crushed in the mad stampede for glory and profit. Those who can't realize their dreams have deep feelings of rage and frustration that need to be released.

Maintaining a tough veneer takes its toll. More men than women die of cancer and heart attacks--diseases related to the strain of trying to make a living in capitalist cultures. What's more: The dominant norms of these cultures are such that people tend to blame themselves when they fail. Rather than expressing their anger at social injustice through constructive social action, they turn to drugs and alcohol or take out their frustrations upon their loved ones.

The rank ordering of the above list of messages indicates that the masculine sex role has both traditional masculine and feminine components and that male sex role expectations are not limited to unemotional, aggressive responses to the world, as some feminists have strongly stated. This, of course, is good news. Men are not simply conditioned to kill. Although some men are indeed violent, this study indicates that there are many positive messages embedded within the male sex role. Men have choices about how they want to behave. In order to produce more nurturing individuals who will live in harmony with the life forces on this planet, the positive tendencies that already exist within the male psyche will have to be reinforced, the horrible effects of violent behavior will have to be understood, and nonviolent responses will have to be learned.

The key to overcoming sex role conditioning for violent male behavior is teaching men how to respond nonviolently to conflict. Citizens of the Philippines--angry, frustrated, and oppressed by the regime of Ferdinand Marcos--put that anger to constructive use by organizing nonviolently to bring in a new social order. Similarly, Gandhi used nonviolent tactics to overthrow the British Rule of India. Neighbors can resolve disputes by talking to each other. The United States and the Soviet Union can diffuse cold war tensions by signing treaties. England and France overcame years of enmity and become trading partners and allies. Lovers can learn peaceful ways of communication. In the same manner, men can learn nonviolent ways to express their anger.

Notes

1.   For an interesting discussion of this phenomenon see Sam Keen, *Faces of the Enemy* (San Francisco: Harper & Row, 1986).

2.   Tipper Gore, "Raising Kids in an X-Rated Society," in *Engage/Social Action*, May 1987.

3.   Joseph Pleck, *The Myth of Masculinity* (Cambridge: MIT Press, 1981).

4.   Joseph Pleck, "Masculinity-Femininity Paradigm," in *Sex Roles*, 1975, Vol. 1, No. 2, pp. 161-178.

5.   Eric Erikson, *Identity: Youth and Crises* (New York: Norton, 1986).

6.   Thomas Merton, *Gandhi On Nonviolence* (New York: New Directions, 1965).

7.   L. Termin and C. Miles, *Sex and Personality* (New York: McGraw-Hill, 1936).

PART THREE

CULTURES OF PEACE:
VOICES FROM THE PERIPHERY

Introduction to Part Three

Elise Boulding

The Center-Periphery model of social change has gone, in a few short decades, from a model demonstrating the power of centrally-located elites to dominate and oppressed peasants and workers (and women, for the elites are male), to a two-way flow model that emphasizes the power of knowledge and skill at the periphery, as well as, the power of command over resources at the center. The knowledge and skill among workers, peasants and women at the periphery, which tends to be unknown to the elites, is each society's resource for adaptation and problem-solving in times of rapid change. At the global level, it is the Third World that is the periphery and it is in the Third World that new resources to meet our global crises are to be found.

Part Three is then dedicated to the voices of the supposedly powerless: Third World societies, children and women. From the African periphery, Uchegbu's paper raises some important questions about human rights--often thought of as the West's gift to the world. Western rights concepts and Western law are in fact disenfranchising for members of African societies, and ignore or even stifle the powerful resources for adaptation and problems-solving in families and communities. We saw in Part Two how modernization has put intolerable pressures on traditional life ways in India and Brazil and destroyed customary checks on violence. A creative restatement of human rights that roots them in local cultural strengths, as Uchegbu is proposing, will not only empower Africans, but all Third World societies.

The rights of children are sentimentally invoked when war is being denounced, but in practice they are the most ignored constituency, the periphery of peripheries, in every society. Sorensen's proposal for a Treatment of Children Index (TCI) as a measure of societal well being, involves the radical step of actually looking at and listening to children. This looking, where no one looks, would show what a heavy economic burden the children of the poor bear in every part of the world, including Euro-North America. Their malnutrition literally affects each society's productivity, to say nothing of its moral health. The survival skills of children have astounded those who have studied them. A society that listens to its children will find itself growing wiser.

Women are a special kind of "universal periphery." Whatever the status group--whether the elites or the poorest worker--women are present as peripheral to that particular status. Their relative voicelessness, wherever they are, is perhaps the single greatest obstacle to a fuller human development. Half of humanity's skill, knowledge and wisdom is largely unavailable in the public sphere. Brock-Utne goes to the heart of the peripheralization of women: the cultural inability to create relations of genuine interdependence between women and men, the cultural fixation on male dominance. This is the cause of the persistent mal-development characterizing the 20th century. The re-creation of culture away from dominance-submission patterns toward partnership relations is critical for every form of human and social development, and a major condition for the removal of violence and the emergence of peaceableness.

Valenzuela also writes about the female periphery, but provides a rather amazing case study of how Chilean women organized at the periphery to solve pressing social and economic problems under very repressive political conditions. There could be no more striking example of the basic point being made in Part Two about the competence and inventiveness of those treated as society's marginals. The development of women's political voice foreshadows, one hopes, the development of the kind of male-female partnership relations that Brock-Utne writes about.

All of these voices from the periphery--the African voices, the children's voices and the women's voices--bring new potentials for social transformation to the societies and the world of which they are a part.

16

Human and Peoples' Rights
in the Banjul Charter

Amechi Uchegbu

Introduction

The question of what rights are inherent to man has been a preoccupation of jurists and philosophers for many ages. What is, however, not a problem and seems to be taken for granted is the fact that societies exist in which human beings live and interact with one another. Perhaps a distinction, which may be made between a society and an anarchic aggregation of individuals, lies in the fact that in the former situation members of the society recognize and implement certain basic rights which they find necessary to sustain that society whereas in the other, no such rights are articulated. It is impossible, however, for human rights alone to sustain social coexistence. Human rights are given and enforced to enable members of the society to live peacefully together in order to produce means for their sustenance. A society and an anarchic aggregate therefore part company with regard to the existence and maintenance of law and order.

A mere existence of human rights alleged to have derived from a divine source and therefore to be sufficient to sustain social cohabitation cannot, per se, keep people together. Fundamental human rights must be given a legal backing. The law must clearly define the rights and circumscribe its sphere of operation. This is basic. To be enforceable, laws must conform to morality, justice and reason. The conception of human rights itself is evidence of the struggle of human against fellow human with the ubiquitous intention to dominate.

To guarantee human rights is to safeguard the rights of persons. This is not to eulogize the law. Legal human rights and theological or moral human rights have their advantages and disadvantages. Legal human rights are relatively known and certain and can be enforced with violence if necessary.[1] With regard to human rights under natural law, it is everybody's ball game. The scope of the rights is unknown, as are the nature and characteristics of those rights. What rights are, for instance, given to man by God or by nature? This is subject to different interpretations. No orderly society can, however, operate on the metaphysics of natural law alone. Positive law can be dangerous as inherent in its own logic is the fact that law can create rights and can abolish them. The principle of 'law is law' has enabled the judges in South Africa, for instance, to enforce the most blatant apartheid which has been aptly described as a crime against humanity.[2] In this type of crisis situation, the natural law concept of human rights forms the basis of the criticism of and struggle against such a neo-barbaric legal system.[3] Both positive and natural conceptions of human rights actually complement each other. The natural law concept of human rights is, however, not settled. If persons have rights, who gives such rights? If rights are universal, why should Africa, being part of the universe, need its own human rights?

Christian theology states that God created man and woman endowed them with certain rights, such as the right to life, to be taken only in accordance with divine authority. This is the superterrestrial concept of human rights. The right existed before creation. African societies were not, before colonialism, Christian societies. Is it then to be said that they were excluded from being beneficiaries of these divine rights? The religious concept of human rights is as universal as the human being. Indeed, the African traditional religion recognises God as the creator who is worshiped through the gods. Breaches of divine rights require appeasement of the gods through whom such prayers are then transmitted to the God.[4] The problem with this superterrestrial concept of human rights is lack of empirical grounding and the fact that such rights resist the dynamics of social change. There is then the European philosophical concept of human rights, said to have originated with the Stoics.[5] With them, the world is conceived as a unified system governed by natural law having the character of Right Reason which dictates that all human beings are equal. According to Marcus Aurelius in his meditations a society is

> "A polity in which there is the same law for all, a polity administered with regard to equal rights and equal freedom of speech and kindly government which respects most of all the freedoms of the governed."[6]

The proposition is equality before the law, equal rights and freedom of speech.

Although the entire gamut of early European philosophy maintained this trend of thought, they did so against the glare of man's inhumanity to man.[7] Greek society, for instance, which trumpeted man's equality with man denied equality to women and maintained a slave system where the slave was denied, not only human rights, but humanity itself. European colonialism, racism, feudalism coexisted with the philosophy of human rights. Africa suffered under the savage attack of colonialism while European philosophers made noise about the elegance of human values. Who is human and what rights appertain to humans were issues yet to be freed from the idealism of philosophy. The problem with philosophy is the impression given by the individual philosopher that a theory is of universal application. Yet, on closer analysis and checked concretely with given facts this claim often falls through. This is especially the case with the application of the philosophy of human rights to Africa, which a philosopher like Hegel found to be without history, instead sharing its history with its colonizers.[9] Philosophy has its internal contradictions. It can pontificate oppression whereas, in fact the people may struggle for their own liberation. Marxism, however, ushered in a new dimension to the theoretical controversy as to the origin of human rights. If human rights were rights given to person *qua* person, then such a right must have come from somewhere. The European social contract theorists attempted to locate the source in the so-called social contract but failed because a contract presupposes the existence of a society and does not itself create it.[10] If human rights are societal rights, the society must have existed before the rights. Man, Marx found, is no longer simply a biological being but a social being. Rights are not natural. They are the claims made by humans against fellow humans in the course of productive activity. All human rights are basically the products of a given economic system and change according to changes in the struggle of mode of production. Thus, human rights in a slave economy differ from human rights in the feudal economy, the capitalist economy and the socialist economy.

Human rights, as discussed so far, are comprehended in universal terms without regard to the socio-cultural peculiarities of different societies. The African social systems differ from the European in history, culture, climate and the level of economic development. The African content of African religion, for example, is different from that of the European. Regional or particular regimes of human rights can of course only particularize the existing human rights and may no doubt add more according to experience.

Prelude to the African Charter

Africa has made significant contributions to world civilization; at the same time, its own civilization dates from time immemorial. More recently, however, most of the States in Africa have been under European colonialism. In the course of that colonialism, the Europeans introduced their values into the socio-cultural life of Africans. Although the concept of human rights had become very vocal after the Second World War, Africa was seldom considered as a region of human rights. It was outside the arena of human rights and hence the practitioners of colonialism found no compatibility between colonialism and human rights.

In 1948, the General Assembly of the United Nations proclaimed the Universal Declaration of Human Rights. From Africa, only Ethiopia and Liberia were parties to the Declaration. The Declaration is not law. The Declaration expressed itself in universal terms, asserting existing rights which all human beings were to enjoy. The General Assembly declared the rights but did not create them. However, what the Assembly declared to be universal rights are certain rights--the Judaeo-Graeco rights--with which the dominant members of the Assembly were familiar. For example, rights were there mirrored as 'individual rights' and not as 'people's rights,' and yet the traditional African societies saw the individual only as a member of a group and not as an individual per se. However, the general language of the Declaration camouflaged the socio-cultural specifics of human rights even while recognizing those that are universal. When the Declaration asserts the right to marry at full age, it neither said whether the marriage is polygamous nor what age is 'full age.' Marriage in both Islamic law and the traditional African culture is potentially polygamous and can be contracted well below the age of fifteen.[11]

It can, of course, be contested that the right to marry can only be meaningful for persons over the age of seventeen. This, however, would require scientific proof of the proper age when persons in all cultures would be able to discharge marriage responsibilities. The universal aspects of the Declaration's human rights include right to life, freedom of movement, assembly, etc.

Since the 1960s however, Africa has become a force to be reckoned with in the United Nations and has assisted the Assembly to push a few significant treaties on human rights as well as many Resolutions.[12] Outside the United Nations, Europe had, in 1950, promulgated its own human rights treaty[13] as did the American Convention on Human Rights (1970).[14] The African effort to produce its own treaty on human rights was hampered by many problems. Although it is true that various African constitutions contain human rights provisions, these are really, in most cases, the reproduction of the Judaeo-Graeco values brought about by colonialism and remote from the experiences of the bulk of the African masses. Besides, African countries were enjoying the honeymoon of independence and were in no mood to depart from measures that would further consolidate their independence. The neo-cultural economies in many ways compelled the governments to seek first the kingdom of the economy and thereafter those of human rights. Human rights were considered luxury rights. Moreover, the infrastructure for the practice of human rights was still at its developmental stages. Colonialism did not bother much about it. There was then the poverty of human rights consciousness which was part and parcel of the product of colonialism. Human rights education would have ended colonialism long before it was overthrown and would perhaps have prevented the introduction of neo-colonialism in its place. It was, however, in the interest of the colonisers to play down a formal education in human rights. There is, finally, the practice of cultural imperialism which entailed the suppression by colonialism of African culture and the promotion, as a matter of policy, of European culture; a dose of which was taken by the nationalists, who struggled and won independence for Africa. Where elementary provisions of human rights existed, most of the ruling nationalists equated these with European values.

In spite of these constraints certain notable events in Africa and the world would have no doubt pricked the conscience of African leaders that a regional human rights treaty should be promulgated. The principle of non-interference in the domestic affairs of the members of the Organization of African Unity (OAU) prevented African States from contesting such historic events as the massacres in Burundi in 1973 and that of Emperor Bokassa in Central Africa 1966-1979. There is, of course, the neo-barbaric apartheid policy in South Africa which is unanimously condemned in Africa. Between the 1960s and 1986, when the African Charter came into force, African States have individually ratified some human rights treaties and have, in accordance with modern trends, inserted human rights provisions in their various constitutions. Nevertheless, a regional human rights treaty consciously enacted to accommodate the specific values, traditions, and morals of Africa remained compelling. Observance of the Judaeo-Graeco human rights would sooner or later stifle the cultural development of Africa. It was in response to these problems that the Charter sought to redress the cultural perversions tied with the European concept of human rights.

Development of Charter

As has been pointed out, African States have participated in world development of treaties in human rights since the 1960s. African nations have entrenched in their various customary laws, fundamental human rights. The notion of human rights is not a creation of the Charter, but an affirmation of those rights in African traditions and those found in the treaties to which African States have been parties. In the early 1960s, the Charter of the Organization of African Unity had foreshadowed the development of regional human rights.

The Charter was drafted under the auspices of the *Organization of African Unity* (OAU) and signed in Banjul in The Gambia on January 1981. The Charter was preceded by the Dakar Draft of 1979, which was adopted by the OAU with some modifications. The Dakar Draft was prepared by experts with a mission to give human rights an African look. The OAU itself is a regional political organization, of a part of the world legal order, in which questions of human rights were increasing in importance. The OAU itself was born in May 1963 and by 1981 was already able to produce a regional Charter on human rights. Between these dates however, there have been numerous efforts to create an institution of African human rights. The peculiar history of Africa--colonialism and apartheid--did contribute to the slow pace of development. African States have been busy struggling to prevent recolonization by imperialism, struggling against neo-fascism in South Africa and Namibia; struggling to preserve their political integrity against trends of secessions and civil wars. The African States were slow in accepting international, as distinct from domestic, legal regulations of human rights, the implementation of which will, in essence, mean an interference in their domestic affairs. In spite of those problems, the OAU eventually produced the African Charter which came into force on 21st October 1986 and represents the African concept of human rights.

The Features

The Charter was unanimously adopted by the Summit Meeting of the OAU held in Nairobi Kenya. This adoption did not, at the time, give it legal force. This is because the Charter itself provides in its Article 63 that to come into force, at least half of the members of the OAU shall have either ratified or adhered to the Charter. It may be naive to imagine that because the Africa Charter creates regional human rights law, the principles embodied in it have no universal application. From the standpoint of international law, this may be erroneous. The Charter embodied a lot of principles contained, not only in the *Universal Declaration of Human Rights,*[15] but also in many other United Nations Declarations and UN sponsored treaties to which some members of the OAU are parties. Quite apart from these, some of these rights are also found in other regional human treaties, such as the *European Convention on Human Rights* and the *American Convention on Human Rights*. These rights and freedoms include: the right to life; equality before the law; right to fair hearing; freedom of religion; freedom of conscience; right to information; freedom of association and movement; right to marry.

The Charter has a preamble and 68 Articles, some of which are divided into Human (Individual) and Peoples' rights. About 16 of the Articles are devoted to individual rights (i.e., Articles 2 to and including Article 18); while the provisions on the Peoples' rights range from Article 19 to and including Article 24. The rest of the Articles are devoted to duties imposed by the Charter on the contracting parties and the establishment of an enforcement machinery known as the Commission. From the point of view of rights-duties relationship, the Charter creates a trilogy: the rights and freedom of the individual, the rights and freedoms of the African peoples and the duties of the contracting parties.

The Charter is a treaty through which rights are conferred on individuals and peoples normally regarded as objects of international law. The Charter does not elevate the status of the individual and peoples as subjects of international law in their own rights. The rights to be enjoyed are contingent upon ratification of the treaty and disappear with withdrawal. Also, neither the individual nor the African peoples have direct right of enforcement for the breaches either against their own States or against other contracting States. The Commission is the enforcement institution admittedly composed of individuals but elected by the Assembly of Heads of States and Governors of the OAU.[16]

The Sociological Perspective

Before analyzing the substantive provisions of the Charter, it is necessary to discuss its essence as announced in its Preamble. Traditional lawyers like to argue whether a Preamble is a part of a legal instrument or distinct from it, but for a jurist this is a fundamental aspect of the legislation. It is here that the legislators announce their positions, in this instance, regarding human rights. The preamble of the Charter is couched in a typical form but its content is innovative. The preamble recalls that the treaty of the OAU, from which it was born, provided that "freedom, equality, justice and dignity are essential objectives for the achievement of the legitimate aspirations of the African peoples." As such, the members taking into account the specific historic condition, traditions and African civilizations, set out to give the citizens of the continent human rights that would be reflective of these values. The skeptic might argue that this preamble cannot be taken seriously because African traditions and civilizations are too diverse, heterogeneous and undeveloped to be accorded a neat legal backing as was done under the Charter. The implication of this would be that the values expressed in the Charter must either be totally un-

African or might be representative of the value of some perhaps major African signatories to the Charter, seeking to impose these values on others. Such thinking is premised on the ignorance of the evolution of the Charter itself, which recorded a consensus of all the African Government members of the OAU. Besides, the Charter was drafted by Africans in Africa for Africans with a specific mandate to emphasize those rights peculiar to Africa. It is correct, however, to argue that African civilization is no longer synonymous with African traditions, which colonialism destroyed in part. It has become a fusion of universal values and indigenous African values. While it is easy to identify African traditions such as polygamy, family systems, religious practices and so on, what is often attributed to European values are in fact no more than universal values to which Africans have made their own contribution and in which they share. The Charter indeed is an amalgamation of strictly African and universal values.

Socio-Cultural Traditions

The Charter distinguishes between economic, political and socio-cultural rights. In its preamble, the authors took into consideration "the virtues of their (African) historical tradition and the values of African civilization which should inspire and characterize their reflection on the concept of human and peoples' rights." With this, the Charter imposed a duty on the contracting parties to ensure that they promote the morals and traditional values of the African community.[17] The Charter gave specific recognition to the family as the natural unit of and basis of society and as such should also be protected by States. The African family is the custodian of moral and traditional values, and this the Charter recognizes.[18]

The problem with the implementation of these provisions lies in the mixed nature of African culture and morals. It is true that the family unit is still the bulwark of African tradition. The concept of the family however embodies as it were sex, marriage, parenthood and kinship.[19] Most African family systems are patrilineal, while some are matrilineal. In the former, the father is the symbol of authority and a depository of the customs, morals and values of the society. He enjoys the allegiance of his children and in return protects and teaches them and represents their interests in inter-family relations. In matrilineal institutions, inheritance basically follows the mother line.[20]

When the Charter imposes a duty to protect the family and values of the society, it implicitly endorses a struggle against alien colonial cultures that have a legal basis in African legal order. The African tradition expresses itself in the African customary law which itself is also reflective of the African religion. Yet, Western and African traditions still conflict. In Nigeria for example, the

Nigerian High Courts are still obliged not to enforce any rule of customary law which is repugnant to "natural justice equity and good conscience." This provision means no more than providing a legal justification for striking down rules of customary law that are not in line with the British imposed law with its built-in British values.[21] In the Helen V. Aika[22] case in a High Court in Bendel State, a judge held that it was repugnant to natural justice, equity and good conscience for a woman to marry another woman. Yet, according to the custom among the Ishan people, a widow is entitled to marry another woman and arrange a partner for her with a view to producing male children to avoid the disappearance of the husband's family line. The rationale behind the system is to ensure the perpetuity of the family line because descent is unilineal. What is significant here is that the court is part of the State whose duty it should be to ensure the preservation of the African culture and tradition.

The African value-system is in a state of confusion, in that only a progressive state, equipped with a clear ideology, can carry out the duties of the Charter. In some African States, the European capitalist values have in the guise of Christianity, penetrated deep in the rural areas of Africa--taking its toll of millions of Africans so much so that it has become a gargantuan task to uphold the traditional African morals and values. The average African elite, for example, first marries according to customary law and subsequently goes through the so-called 'white wedding' (i.e., Christian or Church weddings). Although the family is the agent of society that inculcates into the individual initial values, where this unit is itself inflicted with colonial values, one wonders what option is available to a contracting party. The Charter for instance grants rights to religion and at the same time is expected to uphold traditional African values. When an African adopts Christianity and begins to reorder the values of his family accordingly, is the State expected to promote this or not?

Freedom of Religion

Article 8 of the Charter, provides that:

> "Freedom of conscience, the profession and free practice of religion shall be guaranteed. No one may, subject to an order, be submitted to measures restricting the exercise of these freedoms."

The cautious provisions of this Article is reflective of the African experience. The Charter denies a complete freedom of conscience and religion. The rights, although created by treaty law, are nevertheless subordinated to law and order.

Religion has its two-fold dimensions--the spiritual and the social.   The belief in the omnipotence--the force beyond man whether called "power," "God" or "Allah"--nevertheless remains outside the sphere of scientific knowledge.   The skeptic could indeed say that if anything, Man created God.   There must have been consciousness in a living being to begin the in-depth inquiry as to who was his creator.   The concept of God must have been the answer to this inquiry.   Now the correctness of this answer is accepted without proof.   It is for this reason that the word "believe" is used in regard to religion rather than knowledge.   The second aspect of religion is the social.   Adherence to the commands of a superior force with power to compensate the mundane individual *post mortem* makes the individual aspire to be a good citizen with the hope of a reward.   Since the dead cannot relate to the living nor the living experience death while still being alive, it becomes impossible to know whether this reward was actually given.   While religion induces submission to what is deemed to be the will of God, in its extreme practice it creates serious obstacles to social revolutions aimed at bringing about qualitative socio-economic change in the mundane world.

Africa has three main religions--traditional, Islam and Christianity.   There are of course, numerous denominations in Islam and in Christianity. Africa has witnessed such grave religious riots that it has been a serious matter to accord absolute freedom of religion to Africans without qualifications.   The numerous sects of religious practices are motivated, not only by the desire to exercise the freedom of conscience and religion to go to heaven through any chosen route, but also by the desire to make money.   The capitalist ethos has so penetrated religious worship in Christianity that it is now difficult to isolate worship of God from worship of capital.   This indeed challenges the traditional meaning of religion as a belief in spiritual beings.[23]   It can, of course, be argued that man does not live by spirit alone and that "bread" sustains the spirit and makes the spirit the presupposition of bread.

Since colonialism introduced Christianity in Africa by using the very freedom of religion to attack, subjugate and enslave Africans, the claim of freedom of religion and conscience was rightly watered-down by the Charter. The imposed religions of Islam and Christianity have eroded the base of the traditional African religion to a degree that now confuses the African religious practitioners. The Charter distinguishes "conscience" from "religion." Conscience is inner motive and may be unrelated to religion. The agnostic who has liberated himself from the metaphysics of religion is a man of conscience and enjoys freedom from all religions.   Conscience can be motivated by an inner revulsion against a given conduct.   It can be based on religion and may be simply psychological or rational feeling. African traditional religion approaches God through the gods and between God and the gods stands the high priest who acts as the agent of humans, linking them with their God.[24] African traditional religion expresses the profound culture of the African people. With Christianity, the Europeans adapted the Bible to their own culture. Hence, while purporting to impose Christianity on Africa, they did so by imposing the European values as if biblical teachings are synonymous with European morality and culture.

The Charter makes a timid attempt at rescuing the decline of African culture which has resisted barrages of attack, not only from pure colonialism, but from neo-colonial forces of today. Article 17 provides:

1. Every individual shall have the right of education.
2. Every individual may freely take part in the cultural life of his community.
3. The promotion and protection of morals and traditional values recognized by the community shall be the duty of the State.

The African is thus allowed to take part in the cultural life of his community. This is not a right but a privilege. The State, however, is under a duty to protect the morals and traditional values of the community. Religion is a normal source of morals, and confused and conflicting morals of the urban African are attributable to the alien plural religious and cultural practices. It is true that law and morals can be distinguished, but the duty of the State here is to use the State apparatus to protect the morals and values of his subjects from cultural imperialism. Which aspect of the African culture is to be protected and which denied, is the business of the State.

In traditional Western jurisprudence, law and morals have been distinguished, although sometimes they converge and other times they diverge. In English law, for example, A is not ordinarily under a legal duty to rescue a drowning man even if he, A, is a very good swimmer. As a moral value, most people will agree that A is under a duty to so. In African traditional situations, it is not easy to divorce morals from customary law and religion. This is because the African law is on the one hand positive (i.e., man-made), while on the other hand natural law (i.e., god-given). When man-made laws conflict with the laws of the gods, the latter prevails. As concerns morality, what the laws forbid is immorality, but not all immoral acts, such as fornication, are illegal. The point being made is that the gap between law and morals in traditional African society is narrower than in European jurisprudence. The reason for this difference is African societies are closely knit and societal bonds chaining family and clan relationships are strong. Socially unapproved conduct is frowned upon and the consequences are more far-reaching for the violator of accepted codes of conduct psychologically and physically because of the tradition of living closely together.

Freedom and Slavery

Slavery is the status or condition of a person over whom any or all of the powers attaching to the right of tenancy of things had been extended to fellow human beings whose labor power was purchased permanently.[25] In part of Greek and Roman societies, positive law regarded a slave as a "thing" to which no rights were attributed. In African societies, slaves were mainly prisoners of war who were either shared among members of the ruling class or sold to anyone who could afford them.[26] There are other species of enslavement which do not easily fall under the category of prisoners of war. In some African societies, an oppressed person or a fugitive from justice may take refuge within the domain of a god where his person and his successors become the permanent property of the gods. He is not worshiped of course, but rather ostracized. He could own property and marry, but only with persons of his kind, nor can he become a titled dignitary. He is a nevertheless a person and not a thing. This system is known as *OSU* in Nigeria.[27]

African traditional societies are stratified according to a hierarchy that corresponds with the enjoyment of privilege. The criteria for distinction are partly birth and partly achievement. In some situations, the laws of the gods prevent movement from one status to the other. For example, once an *OSU* always an *OSU* because it has been so decreed by the gods. Divine laws are immutable and prevail over man-made laws. With regard, however, to the status of chieftaincy, this can be attained through concrete achievement assuming of course the contender is free from the stigma of *OSU*. There is also the system "by which one person (or persons) renders personal services periodically to another in lieu of the interest on money lent by that other person to the servant or a relative of such servant."[28] The services thus rendered went towards the liquidation of the debt. The bonded is not the property of the creditor and indeed is bound to treat him or her as he would a member of his family.

One significant feature of enslavement in the African traditional system is that it does not fit into the European concept of slavery enunciated in various treaties. The meaning of "ownership" of a person comprehended as a bundle of rights and privileges is alien to the African customary law which is rooted in family units as corporate persons and not individuals as such. The individual consent is really an affirmation of the consent of his family to which he is a party or usually subscribes. The European concept neatly distinguished between a worker and a slave corresponding to "contract" and "status." Again the notion of offer, acceptance and intention to create legal obligations which exist in English law of contract is alien to African culture where promises made are supported by the will of the gods. Human relations in an African family are humane and even the bonded man, the *OSU*, *ORU* or *Iwofa* is treated as a human.[29] Elias thus observed that the relationship between the bonded and the free is not that of an object, but of keeping the other at arm's length.

Although the Charter in Article 5 accords to all Africans the right to dignity and prohibits "All forms of exploitation and degradation of man particularly slavery, slave trade, torture, cruel, inhuman or degrading punishment and treatment," it does not elaborate its concept of slavery. The broad language of Article 5 no doubt extends to the degrading treatment in African traditional systems. In actual fact, the municipal law of some contracting parties had attempted to abolish some of these but not successfully. The *OSU* for instance, is a creation of religious customary law and can only be effectively abolished by that legal system or the *OSU* might disappear when the uncontrolled capitalist intrusion into the rural areas begins to break up the undefended customs of the people and force upon them a new mode of existence. It is significant to note that the Charter did not, as some other conventions did, distinguish between slavery and servitude, although the Charter's prohibition of "all forms of exploitation and degradation" is all-embracing.

Actually the Charter, in prohibiting slavery and slave trade, is merely asserting the position of customary international law. What is controversial, however, is the prohibition extended to all forms of exploitation.

Conclusion

The Charter marks the first organized step on a continental basis to accord human rights to Africans and to reanimate the struggle of some African countries to resist cultural imperialism. The idea is laudable but socio-cultural rights are products of the economic system and so the battle for the full realization of the former ultimately depends on the success of the latter. However, within the prevailing economic system, much can be done to realize the ideals of the Charter, especially as regards African cultural revival. Although the Charter just mandated the contracting parties to protect the family system, the morals and the culture of traditional Africa, there is more than the traditional culture to be protected.

Africa is a component part of world revolutions and it will be naive to continue protecting obsolete and decadent cultures and morals simply because they are of African tradition. The problem is where to draw the line. The OAU should really follow up these provisions of the Charter on the socio-cultural aspects of human rights, set up an African law reform committee to look into various African customary laws and be able to develop those that have potential in assisting Africa in its struggle for economic self-sufficiency.

Notes

1.   This is the basic position of positiveness concept of law. John Austin, in *Province of Jurisprudence Determined*, Prof. H. Hart, ed. (New York: Noonday Press, 1954).

2.   Oliver D. Schreiner, *The Contribution of English Law to South African Law and the Rule of Law in South Africa* (The Hamlyn Lectures, 19th ser.). (London: Stevens, 1967), p. 97.

3.   Amechi Uchegbu, "National Law and the Nigerian Legal Order," *UCHE, Journal of Philosophy* (University of Nigeria, 1986) p. 20.

4.   Edward Geoffrey Parrinder, *Religion in Africa* (Baltimore: Penguin Books, 1969), Uchegbu *op. cit.*, p. 34.

5.   Bertrand Russell, *A History of Western Philosophy* (New York: Simon and Schuster, 1945), p. 275.

6.   *Ibid.*, p. 275.

7.   Aristotle's *Nichomachean Ethics* (Ross trans. Oxf., 1961), p. 106.

8.   Kwame Nkurmah, *Consciencism* (Heinemann, 1966), p. 60.

9.   Dover, *Philosophy of History* (1965) p. 19, "At this point we leave Africa, not to mention it again. For it is no historical part of the World; it has no movement or development to exhibit."

10.   Mav and English, *The German Ideology* (C. J. Arthur, ed.) Lawrence and Wishart (1970), p. 42.

11.   Mohammed V. Knott (O.B.), In this case, the plaintiff married a 13 year old girl according to Islamic law operating in Northern part of Nigeria. When they got to England, the plaintiff petitioned the English court to remove the wife from the custody into which she was placed to protect her from immorality. The Court agreed with the plaintiff.

12.   See for example the four Geneva Conventions (International Committee of the Red Cross, 1949); numerous International Labor Organizations Conventions; International Conventions on Civil and Political Rights (1966), International Covenant on Economic Social and Cultural Rights (1976), etc.

13.   European Convention on Human Rights (1950), United Kingdom Treaty Series (U.K.T.S.), 70 (1970).

14.   *International Legal Material (I.L.M.)* (1970), Vol. 9, p. 672. This treaty came into force in 1978.

15.   General Assembly (G.A.) Resolution 217 A (III), GA OR 3rd Sess; Part 1 Resolution, p. 1.

16.   *Banjul Charter*, Art. 45.

17.   *Banjul Charter*, Art. 33.

18.   M.S. McDougal, et al., *Human Rights and World Public Order* (Yale,

18. M.S. McDougal, et al., *Human Rights and World Public Order* (Yale, 1980), p. 77; J. Cohen and H. Chiv, *Peoples China and International Law* (1974), p. 97; K. Davis, *Human Society* (Collier-Macmillan), p. 70; M. Peil, *Confueius and Conflict in African Societies* (Longman, 1977), p. 133.

19. Peil, *op. cit.*, p. 135.

20. See Forde in Radcliffe--A.R. Brown and D. Forde (eds.), *African Systems of Kingship and Marriage* (Oxford, 1950).

21. Ameghi Uchegbu, "Repugnance of the Repugnancy Doctrine," *The Lawyer, Journal of the Law Society* (University of Lagos, 1980) Vol. 10, p. 5, C/f Derret, "Justice, Equity and Good Conscience" in *Changing Law in Developing Countries* (Anderson Unwin: London, 1963).

22. Helen Odigie and Iyere Aika, Suit no. 4/24A/79, Ubiaju High Court, Bendel State of Nigeria (1982).

23. See H. Shapiro, ed., *Mau, Cultural and Society* (Oxf., 1971), p. 398, C/f Durkeim, "a religion is a unified system of beliefs and practices relative to sacred things, that is to say, things set apart and forbidden..." Peil op. cit. p. 215.

24. Ameghi Uchegbu, *Philosophy*, p. 28.

25. Supplementary Convention on the Abolition of Slaver, the Slave Trade and the Institutions and Practices Similar to Slavery (1956). In force 1957.

26. Elias distinguishes prisoners of war slaves from the bondage slave (i.e. "those who gave themselves into bondage of creditors for unpaid debts..."), *The Nature of African Customary Law* (Manchester, 1956), p. 107.

27. M. Balonwu, "The Growth and Development of Indigenous Nigerian Laws as Part of our Heritage..." in *African Indigenous Laws* (ed.), Elias et al., p. 48.

28. Elias, *op. cit.*, p. 107.

29. C. Ifemesia, *Traditional Human Living Among the Igbos, An Historical Perspective.*

17

Development Through the Eyes of a Child

Georg Sorensen

Introduction

The standard way of looking at development problems is from the perspective of the grown-ups. This is hardly a justifiable procedure, considering the fact that the large majority of the world's population are not adults. Out of roughly 5 billion people, 2 billion are children, and close to 1 billion are youngsters[1] (between 15 and 24 years of age). The vast majority of children and youth do, of course, live in the Third World.

For us in the First World, agenda-setting in the media and in the public debate at large, is clearly dominated by the priorities of First World adults; not too surprising, since both contributors and audience in the debate are First World adults. When it comes to illness, for example, this means that the highly dominant issue on the present agenda is AIDS. The AIDS-problem should, of course, be taken very seriously, and vast resources have indeed already been canalized towards finding a cure. But consider the attention devoted to AIDS when we change perspectives from First World adults to Third World children; here, the main problem is dehydration. Dehydration actually kills an estimated 5 million children each year--one child every sixth second.[2] Fortunately, a cheap and efficient cure has been developed recently,[3] but it still remains to put the cure--oral rehydration therapy--at the disposal of the millions of families who need it. This whole problematique, and the urgent measures which are needed in order to save the lives of millions of children every year, has not had even a fraction of the attention devoted to AIDS in the First World.[4]

It is not only in the public debate that children have difficulties in getting on the agenda. In the scholarly debate on development problems outside the auspices of UNICEF, children are rarely given special attention. One example: in a recent comprehensive introduction to development problems--a contribution which is in many ways outstanding--there is no reference at all to "children" in the index, and the closest the text comes to treating children's problems is chapters on population and education.[5]

The basic intention of the present article is to put children on the agenda of development. The following section discusses to which extent development problems of children differ from those of adults; subsequently the notion of childhood/youth as a Western invention is brought forward. It is shown how the problem of children is often that of being caught in the nexus between an "old" and a "new" world. The problem of material needs and the urgency of structural change instead of short-term relief-programs is addressed.

Finally, a case is made for a "Treatment of Children Index" (TCI) which covers both material and non-material aspects of development, and which should be a significant element in evaluating development progress of specific countries. It is briefly shown how the use of TCI gives results that are different from those stemming from standard criteria of development evaluation.

What Is Development for Children?

The first half of the question is no less difficult than the second. We know that there can be no uniform path of development, applicable to all countries and areas. Different types of countries need different strategies of development, and any single country invariably changes development strategy over time.

What can we say, then, about the meaning of development in a more general sense? Perhaps it is possible to point to what Bjorn Hettne has called "indications of what development should imply."[6] This means that certain elements should be incorporated in any process of development, irrespective of the exact nature of the development path in a single country or area.

Working in this direction, Galtung[7] has suggested that the notion of development should include a universal dimension, having to do with the material and non-material needs of human beings. Development may then be said to imply the satisfaction of these needs for individuals and groups in a way that does not harm other people or nature. Four groups of needs have been identified: welfare (material needs in a broad sense); freedom/rights (as opposed to repression); survival/security (as opposed to destruction); and identity (as opposed to alienation).

There is little doubt that these material and non-material needs are at the same time idealist, quite abstract and historical in relation to the limitations bearing upon concrete processes of development in specific areas. There is the additional problem that this notion of development is formulated exclusively on the level of the individual human being. There are a host of relevant development problems on two other levels--those of the state and the international system--which cannot merely be reduced to the level of the individual.[8]

In the face of these objections, I will, however, hold on to Galtung's four groups of needs as a useful starting point for discussing children and development. The merit of his conceptualization is first that human beings are put at the center of the process of development; second, that development has to do with both material *and* nonmaterial needs. In addition, the categories of needs are precise enough to be meaningful, and vague and open-ended enough to make sure that this is not a step towards any "final" definition of development.

This means that the notion of development implies improved welfare (raising the general level of living in a broad sense); more freedom (ability to choose, and to control one's future); increased security (against threats of violence and other types of threats); and more self-esteem and self-respect (not being used as a tool by others for their own ends).[9]

What happens when these development priorities are related to the situation of children? The basic premise must be that children are human beings with material and non-material needs like other (adult) human beings. Advancement along the four dimensions of needs mentioned above amounts to development progress for children as well as for adults.[10]

We should also, however, expect some variation and new angles when considering children's development issues specifically. First, the decisive sphere for children is the immediate surroundings in terms of social and economic space. It is the situation of the "household" or "family" unit which is crucial; the regional and national community are less important, but the processes on these levels do of course impinge on the situation of the "households."

Secondly, children are very often in the role of innocent victims, exposed to actions and events which are none of their making. Most obviously, children are victims of violence, war and persecution.[11] But there is also evidence that children of the poor are the group hit hardest by economic recession in Third World countries. The mechanism is that "in many societies, females and young children depend on what is left--of the evening meal and of the weekly wage--after their husbands and older sons have met their needs."[12]

Thirdly, children have needs that must be covered in order to avoid severe permanent damage. This is most obvious in the case of material needs, where lasting damage can be inflicted by malnutrition, interlocked with illnesses and infections. The urgency of children's needs stems from their low resistance capability; this means that non-satisfaction of crucial needs can result in permanent loss of physical and intellectual capacities, if not death.

Finally we should perhaps expect children to put less emphasis on material needs (above a basic level of welfare which must be met) and relatively more emphasis on the non-material aspect of needs. The excessive materialism of the

Western lifestyle, for example, is not of the children's making. On the contrary, there is little doubt that the preoccupation with welfare in a material sense often exhibited by Western parents, involves a neglect of the non-material needs of their children.[13]

Childhood and Youth: A Western Invention?

The answer is affirmative. The interesting point is, however, that childhood was invented at a specific point in time, as noted by M. Bekombo: "In European society childhood was not recognised as a distinct life-phase until the Industrial Revolution. Following a period of intense exploitation of child labour, the need for a more highly skilled workforce with the consequent expansion of training and obligatory school attendance, amongst other factors, led to the gradual withdrawal of children from the productive sector. This heralded a radical change in the concepts of, and attitudes towards, childhood. Rather than a source of economic gain, the child progressively became an economic charge and an object of parental psychological investment. The immediate consequence of this change in the child's situation included a general reduction in the birth rate; adoption, formerly widespread, became rare."[14]

Bekombo also cites the historian P. Aries for the assertion that the idea of childhood is not mainly related to economic changes, but to the spread of literacy and schooling.[15]

In Third World countries, the view of children as a source of economic gain is still widespread: "Though many factors are cited by parents as reasons for having children, the work of children, domestic or otherwise, recurs frequently. The implication is that parents see the 'production' of children as a means of adding to the household labour force."[16]

Meanwhile, schooling is widely recognized in the Third World as a necessary step towards economic and social development. Accordingly, substantial resources are devoted to securing schooling facilities and children are encouraged to attend school. But school attendance requires relief from other activities and obligations. This is why schooling lies at the core of childhood in the Western sense, as a specific phase of life free from (directly) productive activity.

In this situation, contradictory pressures are often exerted on children in developing environments, because their presence is required in two places at once: in school, as a necessary means of entry to the modern world, and in the household/local community, in productive activity. Bekombo gives, with reference to Africa, a precise description of the dilemma: "From the age of about 3 years, two principal phases can be identified: up to 6 or 7 years, during which a child's activities are centred on the life of the household, and from 7 to 16 years, during which activities range over the whole area of the village. In the household phase the child helps not only in strictly domestic activities--care of younger children, food preparation, maintenance of the living area, obtaining supplies of water and wood, transport and harvest, and so on--but also in more specialised tasks oriented towards household consumption, such as hunting, fishing, hut construction and the sale of produce in the market. In other words, the child participates in all the subsistence activities which make up the economic life of the child's group...Even a superficial survey carried out in rural areas that have schools will clearly show that children of pre-school and early school age spend more time on these tasks than, for example, in learning to read."[17]

A child/youth is required to go through school, but at the same time, school is embedded in a social structure which has no place for childhood/youth in this sense. This dilemma is aggravated by two circumstances. On the one hand, skills acquired at school have little or no relevance for the tasks which children attend to outside school. On the other hand, it is by no means certain that going through school secures a job in the modern sector: "The academic education received at school can be applied in only a limited number of jobs...a young educated individual rarely finds a job on the sole basis of his and her ability to read."[18]

In the urban environment, traditional family and social structures are rapidly broken down. This means that the shortages of jobs after school is combined with the impossibility of returning to the traditional environment.

We see that the problem of schooling and education is very complex. It is not just a matter of getting the children to school and teaching them how to read and write. It is more a problem of changing ill-adapted education systems copied from a Western tradition and of providing a more reasonable margin of certainty that children and parents will stand to gain from the expensive investment in schooling. The problem of being caught in the nexus between old and new is replicated in the area of work/employment. The common attitude in traditional settings that children work in the household/local community, means that children easily run the risk of being recruited to hard labour in industrial or semi-industrial surroundings. In Thailand, for example, it is estimated that 3.8 million children (11 to 16 of age) are working. The majority are working in the context of the family household, but it is more and more common that children from the poor Northern areas are sold by their parents to work in Bangkok or some other city, in industry, handicraft, commerce or prostitution at a yearly "wage" of 60-80 U.S. dollars. In many cases, the parents are unaware of the conditions to which the children are exposed, with work up to 12-16 hours per day.[19]

Many children in Europe worked under conditions similar to the children in Bangkok, before and during the early phases of industrialization. In neither case are such conditions compatible with the goals of development for children formulated above. It should be stressed, however, that it is not necessarily the more recent Western notion of childhood/youth which is the optimum form of realizing the development goals for children. The Western form of childhood/youth is the byproduct of a specific type of socio-economic development and, as such, it is also subject to change over time.[20] The important elements to have in focus are the categories of needs described earlier. It is far from certain that the Western type of childhood is the best way of satisfying these needs.

The Problem of Material Needs

Welfare--the providing of material needs--remains the overriding concern when looking at development problems from the children's viewpoint. It is five hundred million children that are affected by malnutrition, infections and ill-health. If the present trend continues, it will be some 600-650 millions in year 2000.[21] In 1981, forty thousand children died from malnutrition and infection every day and if anything, the figure has gone up since then. "No statistic can express what it is to see even one child die in such a way; to see a mother sitting hour after anxious hour leaning her child's body against her own; to see the child's head turn on limbs which are unnaturally still, stiller than in sleep; to want to stop even that small movement because it is so obvious that there is so little energy left inside the child's life; to see the living pink at the roof of the child's mouth in shocking contrast to the already dead-looking greyness of the skin, the colours of its life and death; to see the uncomprehending panic in eyes which are still the clear and lucid eyes of a child; and to know, in one endless moment, that life has gone."[22]

Malnutrition and ill-health are caused by poverty and lack of food. The well to-do sections of the population--including the upper strata in poor Third World countries--suffer no such problems.

The immediate remedy when there is lack of food is to supply that commodity, and this is what is done in a good many aid programs, especially in situations of acute need. In addition, recent scientific advances form the basis of programmes where relief is also quickly forthcoming. The most comprehensive program in this regard is UNICEF's GOBI-FF-strategy, standing for Growth Charts, Oral rehydration therapy, Breastfeeding, and Immunization - plus Food supplements and Family planning.[23]

There is a tendency for public attention in the West to focus on immediate aid programs when dealing with Third World hunger problems, with 'Band-Aid' and the other 'Food for Africa' campaigns as the most recent example. There are probably several reasons for this one-sided focus: the immediate hunger problem is easy to understand, and has a strong appeal to emotions; the aid situation is action-oriented and makes good copy for the media; the long-term, structural problems of malnutrition are much more complex and it is much more difficult to gather a broad coalition behind the demand for structural reform. Nonetheless, the only feasible long-term solution to the problem of malnutrition and ill-health is structural reform that alleviates poverty. "For those who simply do not have enough to eat, the long-term solution lies in having either the land with which to grow food or the jobs and the incomes with which to buy it."[24]

It is not difficult to argue convincingly that Third World countries need economic development; the problem with structural change is not on that level. The problems are twofold; on the one hand devising an optimum strategy of development, the road towards structural change; on the other hand, the forging of coalitions with sufficient political muscle to make the necessary structural change happen.

The interesting question, then, has to do with devising strategies of development that are favourable through the eyes of a child, in the sense of emphasizing children's needs in the overall setting of development priorities. In the following section, a closer look is taken at some much-used development strategies with this in mind.

Development Strategies Through the Eyes of a Child

It is clear that the conventional measure of Gross National Product (GNP) per head is not an adequate way of measuring the satisfaction of children's needs, even when we limit the discussion to welfare, material needs. Overall growth rates and overall GNP levels say nothing about the content or the distribution of growth. Out of the other available data, there are two measures better suited to say something about the situation for children's welfare. One is the infant mortality rate (infant mortality per 1,000 live births); the other is the Physical Quality of Life Index, the PQLI. There are three indicators in this index: literacy, infant mortality, and life expectancy at age one.[25]

We should expect countries with a not too high degree of socio-economic inequality and where redistributive measures have been taken, for example through agrarian reform, to look best in terms of infant mortality and PQLI. On the other hand, countries where economic development is combined with a relatively high level of inequality, should be expected to be much less successful in terms of children's overall welfare.

GNP per capita, PQLI[*] and infant mortality in selected countries, 1982.

	GNP per capita in US$	PQLI[*]	Infant Mortality per 1,000 live births
Brazil	2,240	72	76
China	310	75	35
Tanzania	280	58	102
Guinea-Bissau	170	29	147
Taiwan	2,503	87	9
Rep. of Korea	1,910	85	34
India	260	42	125

*See explanation in the main text. Source: Todaro 1985, pp. 47-61.

These expectations seem to hold true. Let us start with the example of Brazil, one of the Newly Industrializing countries with a large and diversified industrial sector, which accounts for a substantial share of total industrial output in the Third World as a whole. Industry accounted for more than 35 per cent of GDP by 1980, and Brazil has shown impressive rates of economic growth, in particular during the seventies and the late sixties. Brazil has a GNP per capita of 2,240 U.S. $ (1982), a figure on level with for example Taiwan, Rep. of Korea, Portugal and Romania.[26] However, growth has also been highly unequal in Brazil. The infant mortality rate is 76 and the PQLI rating is 72. We can compare these figures with those of the People's Republic of China. China's GNP per head is not even one fifth of the Brazilian, 310 dollars, on a level with such countries as Niger, Guinea, and Tanzania. But China has undertaken profound structural reform with particular emphasis on improving living conditions for the poor in the countryside. In addition, there have been a number of direct measures aimed at improving children's welfare. As a consequence of these efforts, China's PQLI-rating is at 75, slightly better than Brazil, and the infant mortality rate has been reduced to 35, less than half of the figure for Brazil. Infant mortality in China has been reduced to a level similar to the Soviet Union (where the figure is 32); the USSR has a GNP per capita almost twenty times higher than China.

The indication that children's welfare is improved through structural reform aiming at less inequality should, however, be qualified in some respects. First, it should be said that intentions of reform are not enough; time is required, even a rather long time in the case of very poor countries with few economic and other resources. This can be seen from the examples of Guinea Bissau and Tanzania where reforms have been launched some years ago (more than 15 years ago in the case of Tanzania), but where poverty is still widespread, accompanied by a poor level of children's welfare. GNP per head is 280 dollars in Tanzania, infant mortality is 102 and PQLI, 58. In Guinea-Bissau, infant mortality is at 147 and PQLI at 29, with a GNP of $170 per capita.

Secondly, there are some countries with fairly good ratings in terms of children's welfare, even though their present strategies of development are not particularly equality-oriented. Examples are Taiwan (Infant mortality 9, PQLI 87, GNP per head $2,503) and Rep. of Korea (Infant mortality 34, PQLI 85, GNP per head $1,910). In both cases, however, the present strategies of economic development through industrialization and manufactured exports, have their basis in profound structural reform during the years following World War II, including agrarian reform with redistribution of land. Recent studies claim that Korea and Taiwan could never have achieved their present "development success" were it not for these earlier reforms.[27]

Against this background, the pointing out of an optimum development strategy in terms of children's material welfare is not straightforward. The countries with a fairly high degree of success (at least when considering PQLI and infant mortality) have followed quite different development paths. But there are a few pointers. First, children's welfare cannot be left to the so-called free forces of the market. Children have no economic voice in the form of purchasing power, so the "magic of the market place" does not work for them. They have no political voice either, which means that their welfare problem is left to the political goodwill of adults. Secondly, political measures must be directed at alleviating poverty; this may include both land reform "providing the land with which to grow food" and economic growth in agriculture and industry, providing the jobs and the income with which to buy food. This means that labour-intensive growth is better than capital-intensive growth, where the job-potential is much smaller. Thirdly, in very poor countries, general measures must be accompanied by specific efforts directed at improving welfare for children. Otherwise, improvements will take too long to materialize.

All of this is, of course, much easier said than done. There is always a contradiction in requesting greatest efforts and most urgent change in those countries with fewest resources; it is these same countries, moreover, which often have a constellation of social forces that makes rapid structural change very difficult.

We have, however, already indicated some examples that should not be followed and some that follow desirable strategies of development from the viewpoint of children's welfare. The Brazilian path of development can not be recommended from the children's view. Although there have been impressive results in terms of industrial growth, the strategy for development has been specifically elite-oriented, both on the supply side (emphasis on consumer durables) and on the demand side (capital-intensive industrialization with most benefits to a small layer of skilled white collar employees and workers). It is also a problem that the Brazilian model has not involved reforms in the agrarian sector. Only in recent years has attention been devoted to agriculture, and this has been with emphasis on large-scale agribusiness which does not mean much improvement for the large mass of poor peasants.

Growing enough food does not solve the problem if the children and their poor families do not have access to it. The case of India is illustrative in this regard. In many respects, India is a development success: the industrial sector is fairly advanced and controlled by local entrepreneurs; a "green revolution" in the countryside has boosted agricultural output to the point of making India a net exporter of agricultural produce. But neither industrial nor agricultural development has seriously questioned the elite-oriented nature of the development strategy; and it seems that inequality of the economic structure is reinforced through the interlocking religious and ethnic inequalities.[28]

In China, both industry and agriculture have not reached a level of sophistication similar to the most advanced undertakings in India. But here emphasis has been on basic needs for the mass of people since the "beginning" in 1949. As a consequence, China has reached much more impressive results when looking at the indicators of children's welfare.

Taiwan has followed a development strategy substantially different from mainland China, with emphasis on exports of products from industry. But it should be noted that there are also some structural similarities between the two countries: in both cases, agricultural reform has boosted the production of food since the late forties and early fifties; in both cases agrarian reforms were executed in a way that benefited the mass of rural workers and their families[29] (in contrast to India). And although industrial development in Taiwan came to emphasize exports and world market integration, it has also been able to provide gainful employment to a very large share of the population (in contrast to Brazil).[30] Both China and Taiwan have, in other words, followed development strategies giving the vast majority of the population either the land on which to grow food, or the possibility of making an income with which to buy food.

It should be stressed that the problem of material needs when discussing children's welfare cannot be reduced to the issue of getting enough to eat. And certainly, when it comes to housing, education systems, health services and systems of social security, the situation in both China and Taiwan leaves a lot to be desired. But so does the situation in the countries mentioned above with non-desirable strategies of development and there is little reason to believe that an assessment of these other dimensions of children's material welfare would change the conclusion reached here regarding good and bad strategies of development.

So far, we have concentrated on material needs. There is no doubt that the situation is most critical in Third World countries in this regard, although it is sometimes forgotten that large segments of the population, both children and adults, in many industrialized countries, suffer the lack of material needs as well. Several millions of Americans exist below the official poverty line; in Britain, it has been estimated that no less than 29 per cent of the children live at or below the official poverty level.[31]

But there is no doubt that the problem of children's material needs in the industrialized countries is very small compared to the situation of many places in the Third World. Indeed, it can be said that Western industrial society is beset with an excessive materialism, a single-minded focus on material comfort and wealth. For the children in the West, this situation has serious implications; there is a lack of value-orientation, except for the notion of materialism. A recent investigation among young people in a small Danish town revealed that the dominant attitude was one of looking at society like a giant supermarket where the main focus is on securing a high level of material comfort for oneself. "Serving oneself," for example through theft in a supermarket is widely accepted among the young. Indeed, access to material comfort is often not available through working and earning an income; due to the economic crisis of the last decade, a whole generation of young people--the so-called "no future" generation--has had an almost impossible task in finding an occupation. There is no sense of responsibility towards society on the part of the youngsters and there is very little communication with the parents regarding their whole situation.[32] On the other hand, parents often work very hard (again in order to have a high level of material comfort) and this often leaves little room for relating to the problems of their children.

For many Danish children and young people, this is a situation of spiritual starvation in a society where there is too little attention given to the nonmaterial aspects of life; a similar (or even worse) state of affairs can be found in most countries in the industrialized West. In terms of the groups of nonmaterial needs mentioned above, the problem covers all the aspects; there is a lack of identity, of being able to define a place for oneself both in relation to other people and in relation to society; a lack of security, both in the sense of breakdown of the immediate social networks (family) and also in the macro-sense of living in a type of society which keeps piling up military hardware in order to defend increasingly fragile physical surroundings.[33] And perhaps also a lack of freedom, in part from inability to participate in decisions shaping one's own future and from being denied the freedom to choose an occupation, or even to get a job.

It is probably true that children and young people in many Third World countries are in a better situation than the children and young from the industrialized West when it comes to non-material needs; especially in the sense of being firmly embedded in close social networks which helps to give a sense of identity and security. A recent publication claims the state of Bhutan to have one of the lowest GNP's in the world, but one of the highest scores in terms of "GNH" -Gross National Happiness! This judgment is put forward in the context of describing the situation of children and young people in Bhutan, with special emphasis on the way in which a cultural identity with a long historical tradition is preserved, even in the face of rapid social change.[34]

Other examples could be cited that testify to the strength of close social networks among children and youth themselves and among the younger and the older generations.[35] But it should also be said that it is easy to idealize the Third World from the viewpoint of the West, when it comes to non-material needs. As was hinted at in section 3 above children and young people in the Third World will also in many cases experience the lack of value orientation and the fragility of close social networks which are so typical of the industrialized West.

Conclusion: Who Wins the TCI Contest?

The opening argument of this paper concerned the importance of looking at processes of development from the viewpoint of children. Four categories of material and non-material needs were identified as "ideals" when looking at concrete development experiences through the eyes of children. Against this background, an attempt was made to identify "good" and "bad" strategies of development; the argument was that the categories of needs could form the basis of a TCI--"Treatment of Children Index"--against which concrete processes of development could be evaluated.

But there are many problems with the construction of a precise TCI. More knowledge is needed regarding the best indicators for the satisfaction of children's material needs, and there is also the problem of getting reliable data from each country.[36] Even larger difficulties turn up when it comes to assessment of non-material needs. In this area, it is much more difficult to construct operational indicators (it has been said that social science "possesses no euphorimeters") and there is a serious problem with the availability of information. Moreover, there are problems when it comes to giving relative importance to each of the categories of needs.[37] Finally, we know that there are large differences not only between countries but also within regions and areas of countries; it is not certain, in other words, that the TCI should be applied only on the level of a whole country in order to get a reliable picture of the children's situation.

On the other hand, none of these problems are new; they have already turned up in the context of attempting to construct better measures and indicators of development progress than the traditional measure of GNP per capita. Problems regarding methodology and availability of data should not keep us from thinking of development progress in terms of TCI, and to proceed with the efforts of improving TCI measures.

Which country in the world has made the most significant development progress over the last decades from the viewpoint of children? My own candidate for winning the TCI contest is *China*. We have seen that China has succeeded in taking enormous steps forward in terms of children's material needs, even though the GNP-level per capita is still very modest compared to other Third World countries. Behind the figures is a conscious strategy of treating the children as a privileged group in society, emphasizing all aspects, both material and non-material, of the children's lives.

What is perhaps most impressive from the viewpoint of Western society, is the priority given by the Chinese to moral values in the upbringing of children, endowing the children with a sense of human dignity and identity, a definition of the place of the single child, in relation to society and to other people.[38]

There are, of course, also problems and drawbacks. Since 1949, there has been an increasing birthrate. In conjunction with decreasing mortality, this has meant a population growth from 552 million people in 1950 to more than one billion today. Beginning in 1980, an ideology of one child per couple has been promoted. The argument is that uncontrolled population growth is simply not possible in the face of scarce economic and other resources.[39]

This way of controlling the number of children is often criticized by Westerners on moral grounds.[40] Another area of criticism has to do with Chinese collectivism, giving priority to the collective over the individual, the other face of the emphasis given to moral values mentioned above. There is no doubt that the Chinese interpret the individual obedience to society in a more positive way than do Westerners, seeing in it an element of unity and coordination, a striving towards common goals, instead of discipline and conformity.41

In any case, the basic argument in this context is in favour of the TCI as an alternative measure of development progress. And even given the pros and cons of the Chinese path, there is no doubt that China has made substantial progress in TCI terms. China is a prominent member of a group of countries where children are treated well, both in material and non-material terms. We could call the group "TCW countries" (Treating the Children Well countries). The group should rank higher in our esteem than NIC countries and OECD countries alike.

Notes

1. Admittedly, in many Third World countries, individuals above 15 years of age are considered adults; see also section 3 of the present paper.

2. James P. Grant, *The State of the World's Children 1982-83* (Oxford, 1982), p. 7n.

3. The cure is ORT (Oral Rehydration Therapy), "a breakthrough which was made possible by the discovery that adding glucose to a solution of salt and water can increase the body's rate of absorption of the fluid by 2500 per cent." *Ibid*, p. 8.

4. In spite of various promotion efforts of the children's cause, such as the International Year of Children in 1979. (Editor's note: See Elise Boulding, *Children's Rights and the Wheel of Life* (New Brunswick: Transaction Books, 1979). It was written specifically for the year of the child.)

5. The book I have in mind is Michael P. Todaro, *Economic Development in the Third World* (New York, 1985).

6. Bjorn Hettne, *Current Issues in Development Theory* (Stockholm, 1978), p. 7.

7. Johan Galtung, et al., "Why the Concern with Ways of Life," GPID Project, UN University, printed in *The Western Development Model and Life Style* (Council for International Development Studies, Oslo, 1980).

8. For an interesting attempt to address the survival/security problem on both system, state, and individual level, see Barry Buzan, *People, States and Fear* (Sussex, 1983).

9. See Todaro, *op. cit.*, pp. 85-89 for a similar conception of development.

10. The category of "freedom" is probably more tricky in the case of children, because it bears upon the relations of authority in the child/adult-relationship. For an operationalization of "freedom" see Johan Galtung/Anders H. Wirak, "Menneskelige behov, menneskerettigheter og utvicklingsteorier," in A.H. Wirak (ed.), *Behov, utvickling og verdier* (Oslo 1979), p. 155.

11. See Peter Townsend, *The Smallest Pawns in the Game* (London, 1980).

12. James P. Grant (UNICEF), "The State of the World's Children," 1984, p. 69.

13. On materialism in Western lifestyle, see Galtung 1980, *op. cit.*, and Georg Sorensen, "Notes on materialism and boredom - Western development ideals," Working paper no. 5, Development Research Group (Aalborg University, 1984).

14. Manga Bekombo, "The Child in Africa: Socialisation, Education and Work," in Gerry Rodgers & Guy Standing (eds.), *Child Work, Poverty and Underdevelopment* (Geneva (ILO), 1981), p. 133.

15. Loc. cit. It should be noted that the constant element of childhood has to do with the withdrawal of children from the productive sector. The actual organisation of children's lives outside of production has, however, been subject to substantial change since the industrial revolution. The current way of life of children in Scandinavia is presently being mapped out in a large research project, cf. Lars Dencik, *Smaborns hverdag i den moderne barndom* (Small children's every day life in modern childhood), Fructus no. 4, Jan. 1986, p. 8n., Roskilde University, Denmark.

16. Rodgers & Standing, *op. cit.*, p. 25.

17. Bekombo in Rodgers & Standing, *op. cit.*, p. 124.

18. Loc. cit.

19. Wolfgang Foste, *Verkaufte Traume. Kinderarbeit und Kinderprostitution in Thailand*, Munchen 1982.

20. Cf. the research project mentioned in fn. 15.

21. Grant 1982, *op. cit.*, p. 5.

22. *Ibid.*, p. 4.

23. *Ibid.*, p. 38.

24. *Ibid.*, p. 27.

25. "For each indicator, the performance of individual countries is rated on a scale of 1 to 100, where 1 represents the "worst" performance by any country and 100 the "best" performance.... Once a country's performance in life expectancy, infant mortality, and literacy has been rated on the scale of 1 to 100, the composite index (PQLI) for the country is calculated by averaging the three ratings, giving equal weight to each, Todaro, *op. cit.*, p. 102n.

26. All figures from Todaro, *op. cit.*, pp. 47-61.

27. Dieter Senghass, *The European Experience. A Historical Critique of Development Theory* (Leamington Spa/Dover, 1985), ch. 5.

28. See Georg Sorensen, *Internal and External Intertwined: 5 obstacles to development in India*, Working Papers no. 20, Development Research Group, Aalborg University, 1986.

29. The fact that the collective element had a significant role in the Chinese reforms and small private plots dominated in Taiwan does not seem to have made a large difference from the viewpoint of children's welfare.

30. Cf. the following figures from 1981:

	Distribution of GNP, %			Distribution of Employment, %		
	Agri-cult.	Indu-stry	Ser-vice	Agri-cult.	Indu-stry	Ser-vice
Taiwan	9	45	46	19	42	39
Brazil	13	34	53	30	24	46
India	37	26	37	69	13	18

Source: World Bank Development Report 1983, quoted from Dieter Senghaas/Ulrich Menzel, *Indikatoren zur Bestimmung von Schwellenlandern* (Bremen University, 1984), p. 12.

31. Lecture given by a local doctor from Brighton during the IPRA XI General Conference in Sussex, April 1986.

32. Radio interview with project leader Dominique Bouchet, Odense University, April 1986.

33. Jan Oberg, "At udvikle sikkerhed og sikre udvikling (To develop security and secure development)," Gylling, 1983. See also Georg Sorensen, "Peace and Development. Looking for the Right Track," *Journal of Peace Research* 1, 1985, pp. 69-78.

34. N. Hartmann & G. Olesen, *Unges fremtid liv, lykke og udvikling* (Kobenhavn, 1985.)

35. Cf. Bjorn Forde, *Vi holder sammen*, (Kobenhavn, 1985)

36. Cf. W.P. McGreevey, *Third World Poverty. New Strategies for Measuring Development Progress* (Lexington, 1981).

37. Cf. Johan Galtung, "Twenty-Five Years of Peace Research: Ten Challenges and Some Responses," *Journal of Peace Research*, Vol. 22, No. 2, 1985.

38. Rita Liljenstrom, et al., *Kinas barn och vara* (Chinese children and our own), Lund, 1982.

39. *Ibid.*, p. 21. Cf. Liu Zheng, et al., *China's Population: Problems and Prospects* (Beijing, 1981).

40. Strongest from groups in the U.S. I must admit that I find the Chinese arguments in favour of birth control quite convincing, cf. the sources mentioned in fn. 39.

41. Liljenstrom, et al., *op. cit.*, p. 10.

18

Underdevelopment and the Oppression of Women:
A Feminist Perspective

Birgit Brock-Utne

Introduction

"As a woman I have no country. As a woman I *want* no country. As a woman my country is the whole world." This confession was made by Virginia Woolf in her beautiful novel: *Three Guineas*.[1] In this novel, she tries to answer a man on how women can help men abolish war. I am not going to attempt to answer the question of how women can help men abolish underdevelopment. In fact, this lecture will give few answers. Instead, it will be an attempt to raise some questions about underdevelopment and about the global oppression of women. This will be accomplished by first pointing at some similarities between the underdevelopment of countries and the oppression of women. Then the concepts of patriarchy and relative male dominance will be used in an attempt to explain the global oppression of women. I shall end up by posing some questions about the possibilities for change. My examples of underdevelopment will mostly be taken from Africa, since this is the continent where I now work and live. My perspective will be a feminist one. It will be the same perspective found in my 1986 study of feminist perspectives in peace education.[2] In this work, I distinguish between six feminist perspectives and choose one which comes close to what I have termed "a radical feminist perspective." In feminist scholarship, "a feminist perspective" often means a "radical feminist perspective" which it will also mean here.[3]

Two Points of Caution

Before I go into the questions I am going to raise and develop my arguments, I want to comfort my listeners on two points:

The Dangers of Analogies

Though I shall be jumping from women and men as groups of people to countries, the industrialized and the developing, I am aware of the dangers of making analogies between analytical levels. Nations are not small groups and do not have the same social dynamics. Yet I see analogies, even between different analytical levels, as useful pedagogical tools which may aid our thinking and provide glimpses of novel insight. And secondly:

Social Mechanisms

Here, I am concerned with social mechanisms which among nations work to the detriment of the Third World and within nations work to the detriment of women. For instance, Hakan Wiberg has pointed out that many effects of social mechanisms do not presuppose a conspiracy or evil individual or collective intentions. They may rather, as he asserts, depend on professional socialization, bureaucratic inertia, bargaining procedures, selective perception mechanisms, collective historical experience or tradition built up over long time, market mechanisms etc.[4]

I happen to think that attempts to understand social mechanisms at work are more fruitful than distributing blame among actors, whether individual or collective. An excellent example of attempting to understand the social mechanisms at work during professional socialization has been given by Carol Cohn in her participant observation of men working with strategic studies and military analysis. She first entered the Center on Defense Technology and Arms Control wondering how men could engage in dispassionate discussion of nuclear war; how they could use the concept of deterrence to explain why it is safe to have weapons of any kind and number, but how it is not safe to use them. She spent a whole year attending lectures, conversing with defense analysts and learning their specialized language, trying to understand what they thought and how they thought. She discovered that the men were not cold-blooded and unconcerned, rather they were endowed with charm, humor, intelligence, concern, decency and she liked many of them. She also discovered that her own thinking was slowly changing. She now had to ask a new question: How can I think this way? How can any of us? She discovered that the longer she stayed in the Center and the better she learned to speak the language of the defense intellectuals, the less frightened she became of nuclear war. She says that the professional socialization which goes on when you learn to speak the language of the defense intellectuals is not a conscious, cold-blooded decision to ignore the effects of nuclear weapons on real live human beings. "It is simply meeting the challenge of learning a new language, but by the time you're through, the content of what you can talk about is monumentally different, as is the perspective from which you speak."[5]

Some Similarities Between the Underdevelopment of Countries and the Oppression of Women Seen from a Feminist Perspective

Although analogies can be misleading, it is nevertheless valuable to compare the relationship of women vis-a-vis men on the one hand, with the relationship of developing countries vis-a-vis the "advanced" industrial world.[6] Both are struggling for liberation from subordinate positions in a hierarchical structure, whilst attempting to throw off the very ideology of their oppressors which they are taught by their "masters" and often even internalize themselves.

A Perspective

The word "perspective" comes from the Latin word *perspectus*, which again derives from *perspicere* meaning "look into, see thoroughly, try out, investigate." The Swedish researcher, Stig Lindholm, defines a perspective as that which helps him to see aspects of reality.[7] We all apply various perspectives when we interpret reality around us. The perspectives help us make sense out of what we see and give direction and guidance for our focusing. They will also limit what we see, since when we are focusing on one part of reality, we have trouble seeing another. Our perspectives are built up of values, beliefs and assumptions which may be more or less substantiated and well founded. Researchers within any field, view the world and their own research from a certain perspective which they very often do not bother to make explicit and even may not be aware of. It is seldom that researchers are aware, as Carol Cohn was, that their perspective is changing and are able to describe the change.

The Radical Feminist Perspective

Of all the feminist perspectives used by feminist researchers to analyze social phenomena, the radical perspective is the most fundamental. Metaphorically, we may say that analysis from this perspective will be less concerned with the rights of women to a bigger share of the pie or with the necessity of state rather than private ownership of the pie, as with changing the basic recipe of the pie.

The most thorough outline and discussion of the theory of radical feminism which has been written thus far is the voluminous book (740 pages) by Marilyn French called "Beyond Power."[8] In this book, she writes about those who believe they consider women equal to men, but see women as fettered by their traditional socialization. These people, she believes, see women as large children who have talent and energy, but who need training in male modes, male language, and an area of expertise in order to "fit in" in the male world. She refers to a philosopher who has commented that women are "not yet ready" for top government posts. This she sees not only as patronizing, but also as a lack of comprehension of feminism. I quote her here: "For although feminists do indeed want women to become part of the structure, participants in public institutions, although they want access for women to decision-making posts, and a voice in how society is managed, they do not want women to assimilate to society as it presently exists, but to change it. Feminism is not yet one more of a series of political movements demanding for their adherents, access to existing structures and their rewards...Feminism is a revolutionary moral movement, intending to use political power to transform society, to "feminize" it. For such a movement assimilation is death."[9] French has here pointed to:

-   the paternalistic attitude of men claiming that women need training in male mode thinking to be ready for top government positions and
-   the lack of understanding for radical feminism wanting to change society and not assimilate to it as it exists.

The Paternalistic Attitude

Both of these aspects can also be found in the attitude of the industrialized countries toward what was long termed the "underdeveloped" countries. I do not see these attitudes as stemming from a male conspiracy, but rather as a result of an attempt to integrate both women and colonized, or neo-colonized people, into certain economic structures. According to David Livingstone, who first came to Africa as a missionary sent out by the London Missionary Society, the most important duty of the European Christian Missionary in Africa was to integrate the African into European economic structures.[10] Christian missionaries worked closely with the colonial governments, which also helped them erect schools, an essential component of any mission station. These schools were used to change the culture, beliefs and value system of the Africans to a form that was more acceptable and supportive of European socio-economic structures.[11] According to Walter Rodney, the main purpose of the colonial school system was to train Africans to man the local administration at the lowest jobs in the private capitalist firms owned by Europeans. It was not an educational system designed to give young people confidence and pride as members of African societies, but one "which sought to instill a sense of deference towards all that was European and capitalist." European racism and contempt was expressed not only by hostility to African ways of living, but also by paternalism and by praise of negative and static social features.[12]

In colonial times, the argument that the colonized people were not yet ready to take over the leading government positions has been heard over and over again from white rulers wanting to hold on to their power. The colonized people had to be trained in the colonizers modes of thinking in order to take over. The same type of argument, though in a different coating and in a more

modernized version, can now be found in the policies of the IMF, the World
Bank and various donor agencies towards the Third World. For instance in a
recent World Bank report on the economic reforms and development prospects
of Zambia, the country is told what it should do and how it should develop.[13]
It is told not to make any further public investments, even in the designated
growth industries. Furthermore, such investments "should not be required as
the new policies create an economic environment conducive to the private
sector playing an increasing role in the development of manufacturing."[14]
Another recent World Bank report which deals with the educational policies for
Sub-Saharan Africa provides another example of the same paternalistic attitude
of "we know what is best for you."[15] In an analysis of the report, I have shown
how the authors behind it want Euro-American culture to be adopted as
"academic standards" and have examination systems, developed in the West,
determine the "quality" of African students.[16] The group of authors further
suggest "expert" assistance to Africa to work out educational plans in line with
the recommendations of the group and insist that studies in overseas countries
undertaken by African students, be continued. This insistence is coupled with
the reluctance to build up institutions of higher learning in Africa, institutions
that could enable Africans to become producers of technology and knowledge
instead of merely users of knowledge produced in the west.

The Necessity of Changing Society

Both feminist thinkers and leaders in developing countries have pointed out
the dangers of assimilation to the society, as it is, and the necessity of changing
it, very much in the same direction. The feminist scholar Joan Rothschild sees
a feminist perspective as a certain set of values. I quote her here : "Feminism,
in seeking to have women realize themselves as independent, autonomous
human beings, must necessarily reject social systems and their ideologies that
exploit and dominate. Feminism means creating a society in which a set of
values can be brought to prevail that can end such systems of dominance."[17]

When the African leaders mobilized their societies to fight against colonial-
isation, the main purpose was not to change administrative hands.[18] It was not
just to substitute white people, the expatriates, with black people. African
leaders like Nkrumah, Kaunda, and Nyerere stressed that what they wanted was
a new society; a society where people should be equal and no one be exploited.
Like radical feminists, they wanted to change the basic recipe of the pie and not
just take it over from the white people. Nyerere in his essay: "Socialism is not
Racialism" stressed that socialism, or *ujamaa*, is an attitude of mind based on
the principle of human equality.[19] In the Arusha Declaration, it is further
stressed that socialism is a way of life, a new way of relating to each other.[20]
In this declaration, it is stressed that the first duty of a member of the new socialist party of Tanzania is to live his own life in accordance with the socialist

principles he preaches. This is very similar thinking to the feminist insistence that the personal is political. Marilyn French puts it this way: "Such a split between pronounced value and actual value, between what is said and what is done, is not acceptable to feminists."[21] The values, which the progressive African leaders and radical feminists would like to see govern both public and private life, are not very different. Nyerere outlines in his policy booklet "Education for Self-Reliance" that the educational system of Tanzania must emphasize co-operative endeavor, not individual advancement. It must stress concepts of equality and the responsibilities to give service.[22] These values are very different from the ones transmitted through the colonial school system and which also underlie the educational policies to which the World Bank adheres.[23]

The Fallacy of Unilinear Mechanistic Thought

As Third World psychologist Carmen Barroso points out, theories of development and theories on the subjection of women, present common problems.[24] She refers to Sachs who has pointed out that after the Second World War "narrow economism made people think that the rapid growth of productive forces would set in motion the whole development process which would expand more or less spontaneously to take in all branches of human activity."[25] He charged both orthodox Marxists and their adversaries with this grossly simplified mechanistic materialism. Today we may both question the validity of the unilinear mechanistic thought concerning development and we may question the assumption that rapid growth is a necessary or sufficient condition for a better quality of life. Environmentalists point to the detrimental effects rapid economic growth have on the soil, forests, oceans and air.[26]

With regard to the liberation of women, we still find different versions of unilinear mechanistic thought. Entering the paid labour force, a probably necessary precondition of women's liberation, is at the same time regarded as somehow being a sufficient precondition. But in the past years, feminist research has shown how women who enter the labour force also take on a double shift if they marry and have children.[27] Full-time career women with families are, for instance, much less politically active than married men or women who are just part time employed in the wage sector.[28] The same type of unilinear mechanistic thought has been applied to the field of women and education. When discussing women in development, Anita Anand states: "Education, along with income generating capacity, has been perceived as the golden door of success and equal participation of women in the development process. It is true that women need education to be able to participate in society, but the nature of this education has not been sufficiently questioned."[29] In an analysis of the effects of the Norwegian educational system on the training of girls and women, Runa Haukaa and myself have pointed out that getting access to and participating in men's education may not mean liberation of women.[30] We have also pointed to the fact that formal equality does not necessarily mean real equality. In a further analysis, I have challenged the assumption that education will automatically provide a key to equal participation of women in the development process.[31]

Some researchers have also started to analyze what economic growth can do to the lives of women. Some have shown how economic growth may mean a change of the load of work done by women from paid to unpaid labour.[32]

More Analogies

Many more analogies could be made. For instance both feminist researchers and researchers in the Third World have found that general theories have been developed from a very limited perspective, that of a small white male elite.[33] The economist Gunnar Myrdal has described why Western economic models are unsuited to explain economic behavior in South East Asia. This sub-continent must develop theories on the basis of their own reality. So also, feminist researchers have repeatedly denounced the limited applicability of the social sciences based on investigation of the male half of humanity. It would be easy to cite 20 to 30 topics which have been inadequately conceptualized as far as women are concerned.[34]

Both women and colonialized people have found that their own history and past achievements have been made invisible in the history books, normally written by white males descending from the colonizers.[35]

The Concept of Patriarchy

"Patriarchy can be defined as a set of social relations between men, which have a material base and which, though hierarchical, establish or create interdependence and solidarity among men that enable them to dominate women."[36]

Though patriarchy is hierarchical and men of different classes, races or ethnic groups have different places in the patriarchy, they are also united in their shared relationship of dominance over their women. They are dependent on each other to maintain that domination. It is important to note that patriarchy has to do both with hierarchical structure, where some men rule over other men and also women, children and nature, and with solidarity between men in their domination of women.[37] The theory of patriarchy builds on the assumption that the material base, upon which patriarchy rests, lies most fundamentally in men's control over women's labour power. The system functions in such a way that men limit the access of women to essential productive resources and instill in women the belief that it is "natural" for women to do unpaid house-work and they should do this "for love." Also women instill this belief in themselves and in their children.

Men also keep their control by restricting women's sexuality. The particular ways in which men control women's access to important economic resources and restrict their sexuality vary enormously both from society to society, from subgroup to subgroup and across time.

The concept of patriarchy can be used to explain the domination of women by men almost everywhere. Used together with the concept of relative male dominance, it also adds to our understanding of how the oppression works and how women themselves cooperate in it. Many Africans argue, for instance, that it is natural for women to do housework, cooking, cleaning, washing, to do most of the heavy work of carrying--fetching firewood and water--and to do subsistence farming. They do not see this division of labour as exploitation. They rather argue that it is natural and part of African tradition.[38]

In 1971, the TANU Party of Tanzania clarified its definition of development in published guidelines, declaring:

"Any action which gives people more power of decision and domination over their own lives is an act of development, even if it does not increase health or food. Any action which decreases the power of decision and domination over their own lives is against development, even if it adds to their health and food. For us, significant development is the kind which removes contempt and exploitation."[39]

The development researcher Marja Liisa Swantz comments: "It has been disquieting for many men to discover that these words did not only apply to German or British colonialism, under which the country has suffered consecutively for almost eighty years, but also to male colonialism over the female citizens. The new socialist policies of Tanzania were offering women opportunities which they had never previously had."[40]

The male colonialism she describes to me seems to be built more on traditions than on evil, collective intentions. It builds on traditions, which before the introduction of monetary economy and private ownership of land, did not in the same way as today work to the detriment of women. The effects of the traditional division of labour today is that women, in relation to men, get less time for themselves and fewer possibilities to decide over their own lives. The African poet Kwanele Ona Jirira has put this beautifully in her poem to her housekeeper mother from which I shall read you the first verse :

Just when the rooster had sung its morning song
In the early dawn
You rose up from your mat, Mother,
To fetch water from the village well
Down near the river bend
In the early dawn
You came back home your feet wet from the morning dew
You boiled the water on the coal fires
Of our kitchen-hut
The water that we and Baba used for our morning baths
The water that you used to make our morning porridge
And after all our needs were met
You would leave home for work
But .... you never had time for yourself[41]

The concept of so called natural division of labour has also been used by elites, in the Industrialized world, to exploit the workers in their own countries and the Third World populations. Those populations are looked at as cheap labour, fit to produce raw materials or to staff the lowest jobs in the firms owned by the elites from Industrialized countries. The processing of the raw material, the production of new knowledge and technology is looked at as naturally belonging to the Industrialized world. This is also division of labour, but in whose interest?

The concept of patriarchy seems to be an important tool to help our understanding of how the exploitation of women's labour power in the Industrialized world is connected to the exploitation of women's labour in the Third World. Cynthia Enloe has shown how the multinational companies in the micro-electronics and garment industries shop around the world for the cheapest and most obedient and docile female labour power.[42] Whole industries are built on the exploitation of young girls, mostly in South-East Asia, who work long hours, in extremely unhealthy conditions for a minimal wage. Feminist researchers have been able to show that even in these conditions of exploitation in industrial work places, women have been able to build a counter-culture and develop what the Norwegian feminist researcher, Bjorg Ase Sorensen, calls "caring rationality" (ansvarsrasjonalitet).[43] Cynthia Enloe sees hope in the women working in the new textile factories in the Philippines and Indonesia and their protests against poor air ventilation. She holds that to what extent these workers succeed in organizing will, in turn, affect the international sexual division of labour. Today the competition between capitalist states is a critical dynamic in the international system. Textiles is one of the most visible arenas in which that competition is occurring. Enloe sees it as a test of women's international solidarity, to resist allying with patriarchal states in that competition and, instead, to create bonds of support among women textile workers worldwide.[44]

The Concept of Relative Male Dominance

The concept of relative male dominance has been used by feminist researchers to explain how marriage functions as an institution for distributing power between the sexes.[45] Though each monogamous marriage is only between two people, a woman and a man, the effect of the power struggle, if it is rather similar in most marriages, will aggregate to a social system which organizes production and reproduction. The concept of male dominance points to a situation where a man dominates a woman, but says nothing about his intentions to do so. In fact, it is important in an oppressive relation which is also coupled with intimacy like marriage that the dominance and power exerted are unintended. As the Norwegian feminist researcher Hanne Haavind has pointed out in marriage, male dominance may be interpreted as an aspect of love. She defines sexual love as an emotional state in which male dominance and female subordinance will be valued positively by both men and women.[46]

The concept of relative male dominance to me seems fruitful when one wants to understand the oppression of women. It does not imply that all men dominate all women, but the relative dominance of males is systematized in the institution of marriage. It also seems fruitful to look at masculinity and femininity as relational concepts. This means describing the way a person relates to another person of the opposite sex, more than the specific qualities or character traits he or she possesses. Now it does not seem to be so negative for women to be active and assertive as long as they do not dominate men. Hanne Haavind claims that what today is regarded as positive female behavior is a type of subordination, which does not appear as such, but rather as something the woman herself has chosen.[47] The same goes for masculine behavior. Women can do anything as long as they do this in a position of relative subordination to (their) men. The concept of relative masculine dominance takes on a personal meaning for both men and women. The relationship of dominance and subordination is kept through mutual agreement. In a way, one can say that women collaborate with men in their own oppression.

The concept of underdevelopment also has to do with relations. Underdeveloped in relation to whom? In relation to which criteria? Walter Rodney says in his widely read book: *How Europe Underdeveloped Africa* - "Underdevelopment makes sense only as a means of comparing levels of development...At all times, one of the ideas behind underdevelopment is a comparative one....A second and even more indispensable component of modern underdevelopment is that it expresses a particular relationship of exploitation: namely, the exploitation of one country by another."[48]

James Robertson argues that the HE (hyper-expansionist) approach to the future is based on essentially masculine assumptions of elitism and domination.[49] It implies that by becoming super industrialized, as the less developed countries become industrialized, today's industrialized countries will maintain their relative economic superiority. The concept of underdevelopment has also to do with the distribution of power between actors, not on the micro, but at the macro levels. It may, however, also be more fruitful to look at the relation between countries than merely at mechanisms in one of the blocs concerned. Blaming either the Industrialized countries or the Third World countries for the exploitative world order, may be missing the point. It may be that the key to understanding here, as in the above-mentioned feminist analysis, will lie in studying the relationship itself. Can it be said about Third World countries, as it is being said about women, that they collaborate with their oppressors in their own oppression? Do they do this because they adhere to the same values as their oppressors? A solution for an oppressed country could be to break the relationship with the oppressor, to become self-reliant. A parallel here can be drawn to economically independent women.

Underdevelopment has to do with a relationship of oppression, a relationship where the ruling elites have the power to decide who is underdeveloped and to decide on the criteria for underdevelopment. These elites rule through the multinationals and through money-lending and policy-making institutions like the IMF and the World Bank. In the top positions of the fifty largest multinationals in the world there are no women. There are no black men either. There are 42 white men, half Europeans, half Americans, six from Japan, one from Kuwait, one from Brazil and one from South Korea. (One of the companies, Unilever, has two bosses, one from Britain and one from Holland.)[50]

Through institutions like IMF and the World Bank, these elites define what they see as positive behavior on the part of the Developing countries.[51] Those countries are valued most which follow the IMF/World Bank recipe but appear as if they are doing this from their own choice. Such countries are praised as oppressed women are praised. They are being promised rewards like this in a recent World Bank report:

> Countries which have demonstrated their willingness to address policy issues should have access to increased, longer term and more flexibly offered international aid.[52]

What Are the Possibilities for Change?

Third world countries are today trying to rid themselves of their oppression in order to be able to follow their own path to, and definition of, development.

Likewise, feminists are striving to liberate themselves from patriarchal structures in order to build a female culture. I must admit that the prospects for success right now look grim. Today it is the larger industrialized capitalist countries, especially the USA, which decide the quantity of financial resources to be made available to the crises-ridden Third World through the multilateral institutions. It is they who also decide the financial terms of and the conditionality attached to such assistance.[53]

These countries have the power to apply their definitions of "development," or in the educational sector, "the quality of education" accepted.[54]

In her recent book, *A Fate Worse than Debt*, Susan George shows that creating dependency through financial debt may be a more effective way of controlling and changing the social system and value structure of a society than by waging war against it.[55] I am not saying here that it is the intention of the ruling elites, or of money lending institutions like the IMF and the World Bank, to change the policies that the new African states want to follow. I am merely saying that this is the effect their adherence to certain market economic principles have on the development of the debtors.

As I pointed out earlier in this lecture, neither feminists nor the named leaders of developing countries want to assimilate to society as it is. They want power to be able to change society. The danger in both cases is that on the road to power both women and Third World countries may be forced to model themselves after the ruling male elites. This may also be done in a fashion where it does not seem as something they are forced to do, but something they want to do. They copy the ways of their oppressors and start adhering to the same value system.

It is easy for a Westerner critical of the development of the Industrialized world, coming to a socialist developing country, to be disappointed when she sees that what the elites here want for themselves are the same things she feels destroys the Western countries: more cars, more advanced technology, soap operas, programs created by commercialized television, and heavier industries that may pollute the air and destroy people's health. It is easy for her to talk about the detrimental effects of rapid economic growth, of pollution, alienation and stress, of the dangers of copying our ways--and to advocate the use of small and intermediate technology. It is easy when you have all the material things to see that you do not want them. Likewise, it is easy for men to tell women that they should not copy their ways; that the work women do in reality is so much more valuable than the work men do, even though it has been unpaid. For men to tell women that they regret that they have had so little contact with their own children; had no time and ability to build up friendships; that they are stressed and feel their lives as shallow and wasted--they may then warn women against adopting this lifestyle.

Maybe my analysis here, built on feminist concepts like patriarchy and relative male dominance and feminist understandings of the personal as political, may have helped us to see how we are all interwoven in the same web and that change has to come from several places simultaneously. Rather than telling the developing countries what they should do even to the extent of warning them against copying us, we in the Industrialized world might start changing our own priorities. The developing countries have to unite to strengthen their struggle against oppression and exploitation and have to work out their own practices. But since we in the Industrialized world constitute part of their problem, we also have to change our own practices. Likewise, women also have to unite to strengthen their struggle against patriarchy. But, males can also help in the liberation of women, by changing their own male role, both by doing away with oppressive practices and traditions and by attempting to lead the type of life they have prescribed as ideal for women.

Notes

1.   Virginia Wolf, *Three Guineas* (London: The Hogarth Press, 1938; re-published in Penguin Books, 1977), p. 205.

2.   Birgit Brock-Utne, *Feminist Perspectives on Peace and Peace Education* (Pergamon Press, 1989).

3.   Marilyn French, *Beyond Power: On Women, Men & Morals* (London: Abacus, 1986), p. 738; and Joan Rothschild, "A feminist perspective on technology and the future," in *Women's Studies International Quarterly* (1981), Vol. 4, No. 1, pp. 65-74.

4.   Hakan Wiberg, "Dilemmas in Disarmament Education," in Magnus Haavelsrud (ed.), *Approaching Disarmament Education* (Guilford: Westbury House, 1982).

5.   Carol Cohn, "Sex and Death in the Rational World of Defense Intellectuals," *Signs* (Summer, 1987), Vol. 12, No. 4.

6.   Carmen Barroso, "Psychology, Development and Women: Do They Have Anything in Common?," *Women's Studies International Quarterly* (1981), Vol. 4, No. 2, pp. 163-167.

7.   Stig Lindholm, *Paradigms, Science and Reality. On Dialectics, Hermeneutics and Positivism in the Social Sciences*. Research Bulletins from the University of Stockholm, IX.

8.   See French, *op. cit.*

9. *Ibid.*

10. Roland Oliver, *The Missionary Factor in East Africa* (London: Longman Green and Co., 1965), p. 11.

11. Z.E. Lawuo, "The Beginnings and Development of Western Education in Tanganyika: The German Period," in Abel Ishumi and G.R.V. Mmari (eds.), *The Educational Process. Theory and Practice with a Focus on Tanzania and Other Countries* (Department of Education: University of Dar es Salaam, 1978), p. 46.

12. Birgit Brock-Utne, *Learning to Lose - Education for Underdevelopment*, Paper presented to the staff seminar (Dar es Salaam: Department of Education, 1988a), p. 22.

13. World Bank, *Zambia: Country Economic Memorandum Economic Reforms and Development Prospects, Report No. 6355 ZA: Document of the World Bank* (November 19, 1986), p. 140.

14. *Ibid.*

15. World Bank, *Education Policies for Sub-Saharan Africa: Adjustment, Revitalization and Expansion, Report No. 6934: Document of the World Bank,* (September 15, 1987), p. 277.

16. Birgit Brock-Utne, *A Critical Analysis of World Bank Report No. 6934: Education Policies for Sub-Saharan Africa: Adjustment, Revitalization, and Expansion,* Paper requested by the Bureau of Education and Scholarships for Overseas Studies, NORAD (Dar es Salaam: Department of Education, 1988b), p. 34.

17. Joan Rothschild, "A Feminist Perspective on Technology and the Future," *Women's Studies International Quarterly* (1981), Vol. 4, No. 1, p. 88.

18. T. Luta Maliyamkono, *Comments on the World Bank Document on "Financing Education in Developing Countries,"* a World Bank Publication (University of Dar es Salaam, 1987), stenciled, p. 1.

19. Julius Nyerere, "Socialism is not Racialism," *The Nationalist* (1967). Also reprinted in Julius Nyerere, *Ujamaa, Essays on Socialism* (Dar es Salaam: Oxford University Press, 1968), pp. 38-41.

20. See Nyerere, 1968, *op. cit.*, p. 17.

21. See French, *op. cit.*, p. 477.

22. Julius Nyerere, *Education for Self-Reliance: Policy Booklet* (March, 1967). Also reprinted in Nyerere, 1968, *op. cit.*, p. 52.

23. See Brock-Utne, 1988b, *op. cit.*

24. See Barroso, *op. cit.*, p. 164.

25. Ignacy Sachs, "The Logic of Development," *International Social Science Journal*, 1972, Vol. 24, No.1, pp. 37-43.

26. Birgit Brock-Utne, "Formal Education as a Force in Shaping Cultural Norms Relating to War and the Environment," in Arthur Westing (ed.), *Cultural Norms, War and the Environment* (Oxford, New York: Oxford University Press, 1988).

27. Maria Bergom Larsson, "Women and Technology in Industrialized countries," *Science and Technology Working Paper Series* (New York: UNITAR, 1979).

28. Beatrice Halsaa Albrektsen, *Kvinner og Politisk Deltagelse* (Women and political participation) (Oslo: Pax, 1977).

29. Anita Anand, "Rethinking Women and Development," in *Women in Development. A Resource Guide for Organization and Action*, ISIS, The Women's International Information and Communication Service, 1983.

30. Birgit Brock-Utne and Runa Haukaa, *Kunnskap uten makt. Kvinner som laerere og elever* (Knowledge without power. Women as teachers and pupils) (Oslo/Bergen/Tromso: Universitets forlaget, 1980), p. 222. Reprinted in 1981 and 1984. German edition: *Wissen ohne Macht* (Frankfurt am Main: Focus Verlag, 1986).

31. Birgit Brock-Utne, "Education as the Key to Equal Participation of Women in the Development Process," in Margaretha von Troil, "Exchange of knowledge in technology transfer from Finland to Tanzania," Report 11, TECO Publication No.12 (University of Helsinki: Institute of Development Studies, 1986), p. 290.

32. See Bergom Larsson, *op. cit.*

33. Georges Balandier, "Sociology," *International Social Science Journal* (1972), 24 (1), pp. 37-43; Carmen Barroso, "Psychology, Development and Women--Do They Have Anything in Common?," *Women's Studies International Quarterly* (1981), Vol. 4, No. 2, pp. 163-167; and Gunnar Myrdal, *An Asian Drama. The Poverty of Nations* (New York: Allan Lane, 1968).

34. See Barroso, *op. cit.*

35. Julius Nyerere, *Freedom and Unity. Uhuru na Umoja* (Dar es Salaam: Oxford University Press, 1966), p. 186; G.R.V. Mmari, "The Role of Formal Education in Developing Countries: The Tanzania Case," in Ishumi and Mmari (eds.), *The Educational Process. Theory and Practice with a Focus on Tanzania and Other Countries* (Department of Education: University of Dar es Salaam, 1978); S. Ndunguru, *Educational Essays for Teachers* (Arusha: Eastern African Publications Limited, 1976), p. 150; Elise Boulding, *The Underside of History. A View of Women Through Time* (Boulder, Colorado: Westview Press, 1976), p. 830; Dale Spender, *Women of Ideas and What Men Have Done to Them* (London/Boston/Melbourne and Henley: Routledge & Kegan Paul, 1983), p. 586; Sheila Rowbotham, *Hidden from History: 300 Years of Wom-*

en's Oppression and the Fight Against It (London: Pluto Press, 1973), p. 182; and Birgit Brock-Utne, *Learning to Lose--Education for Underdevelopment*, op. cit, p. 22.

36. Heidi Hartmann, "The Unhappy Marriage of Marxism and Feminism. Toward a More Progressive Union," in Alison Jaggar and Paula Rothenberg, *Feminist Frameworks: Alternative Theoretical Accounts of the Relations between Women and Men* (New York: McGraw Hill Book Company, 1984), p. 446.

37. See Brock-Utne, 1987, *op. cit.*, p. 41.

38. Kihumbu Thairu, *The African Civilization. Utamanduni wa Kiafrika* (Nairobi: Kenya Literature Bureau, 1985), p. 234.

39. TANU (Tanganyika African National Union), *Guidelines*, 1971.

40. Marja Liisa Swantz, *Women in Development: A Creative Role Denied? The Case of Tanzania* (London: C. Hurst & Company and New York: St. Martin's Press, 1985).

41. Kwanele Ona Jirira, "A Poem for my Housekeeper Mother" (London: African Women, Quarterly Development Journal, 1988), Issue No. 1, p. 26.

42. Cynthia Enloe, *Women Textile Workers in the Militarization of Southeast Asia*, Paper presented at the Conference on Perspective on Power: Women in Asia, Africa and Latin America (Duke University, Durhan N.C., 1981), p. 22; and Cynthia Enloe, *Sex and Levi's: The International Sexual Division of Labour*, Pamphlet: Worcester, MA: Clark University (1981), p. 4.

43. Bjorg Ase Sorensen, "Ansvarsrasjonalitet: Om malmiddeltenkning blant kvinner" (The rationality of caring: About aims and means among women), in Harriet Holter (ed.), *Kvinner i fellesskap* (The collectivity of women) (Oslo/Bergen/Tromso: Universitets-forlaget, 1982), p. 444.

44. See Enloe, *op. cit.*

45. Hanne Haavind, "Makt og kjaerlighet i ekteskapet" (Power and love in marriage), in Runa Haukaa, Marit Hoel and Hanne Haavind (eds.), *Kvinneforskning: Bidrag til samfunnsteori* (Women Studies: A contribution to social science theory) (Oslo/Bergen/Tromso: Universitetsforlaget, 1982), pp. 138-172.

46. See Haavind, *op. cit.*, p. 148.

47. *Ibid.*, p. 151.

48. Walter Rodney, *How Europe Underdeveloped Africa* (Dar es Salaam: Tanzania Publishing Company, 1980), pp. 21-22. (First published in 1972).

49. James Robertson, "The future of work: Some thoughts about the roles of men and women in the transition to a SHE future," *Women's Studies International Quarterly* (1981), Vol. 4 (1), pp. 83-95.

50. Odd Iglebaek, "Gigantiske profitter hentes i u-landene" (Gigantic profits are drawn from the Developing countries), *Sor-Nord Utvikling* (NORAD, Oslo, 1987), No. 7., p. 27.

51. See Brock-Utne, 1988b, *op. cit.*

52. See World Bank, *Education Policies for Sub-Saharan Africa: Adjustment, Revitalization and Expansion*, p. xii and p. 153, under the point dealing with organizing support for programme implementation.

53. John Loxley, "The IMF, the World Bank, and Sub-Saharan Africa: Policies and Politics," in Kjell Havnevik, ed., *The IMF and the World Bank in Africa, Conditionality, Impact and Alternatives*, Seminar Proceedings No. 18 (Uppsala: Scandinavian Institute of African Studies, 1987), pp. 47-65.

54. See Brock-Utne, 1988b, *op. cit.*

55. Susan George, *A Fate Worse than Debt* (London: Pelican, 1988).

19

Women Under Dictatorship and Military Regime: The Case of Chile

Maria Elena Valenzuela

Introduction

The militarization of Chilean society, during sixteen years of dictatorship, has deeply affected women. Government policies and discourse furthered their oppression by appealing to the logic of patriarchal domination. In response to these policies, through actions that redefined political spaces and widened the form and content of politics, women mobilized to defend life, to promote gender-specific demands and political activity. The authoritarian government was thus confronted with resistance from women, whose new organizations and activities became the means for changing their condition of subordination, and redemocratizing society at large.

Military Rule and Women

Policies developed by the military regime towards women were based on women's traditional societal roles. The government promoted women's return to family life and discouraged their participation in labor and political fields. This attempt to return to the past surfaced amid policies that had, under the previous democratic government, opened doors and even encouraged women to assume new roles both in government and in labor. Thus, female participation in the labor market had increased from 25 per cent in the seventies to 30 per cent in the eighties.

Women were granted entrance to the university in 1877, 35 years after the founding of the University of Chile. Today, 40 per cent of the university's student body is composed of women. While male exceeds female enrollment by 2.6 per cent at the primary level, female participation in secondary schools exceeds the male by 5 per cent.[1] At the same time, the percentage of women with higher education in the work force increased from 2.6 per cent in 1960 to 15 per cent in 1982, while male participation increased from 2/3 per cent to 7.9 per cent during the same period.

In spite of these changes in women's roles, the military government was reluctant to address these issues in legal, labor and political fields. In legal affairs, this was evident in the maintenance of the *potestad marital*, which gave the husband rights over his wife and her property. According to the marriage law, the husband owed protection to the wife in exchange for her obedience.

In the labor force, the government promoted a policy of diminishing the role of women. Women employed outside the home were treated as a secondary force and were discriminated in favor of men. Government programs for unemployment aid established various barriers to women's income, and labor legislation developed by the government eliminated some protective clauses for working mothers. Discrepancies in salaries continue, and even though the proportion of domestic workers has decreased, it still represents 25 per cent of the female work force. Between 1960 and 1985, women's median incomes were between 68 and 38 per cent of the income of males, with identical educational backgrounds. The labor market also continued to be highly segmented, with high levels of work force polarization between male and female jobs that remained relatively constant between 1960 and 1982.

In political affairs, the government assigned to women the role of educating children for the nation, thus assuring the ideological continuity of the regime. Women were also given a leading role in maintaining social order, but were excluded from the exercise of power--their participation in important public offices has been limited.

Moreover, women could not be members of the legislative body; an important reversal, since in the last democratic parliament there were 15 women among the senators and deputies. However, since the 1973 coup, the military regime has actively sought the political *support* of women, considering them natural allies of the government. This alliance was based upon their supposedly shared values and ideals--a dualist concept of social relations--in which the principals are God, expressed as virtue; and human beings expressed as sin and flesh. Women with their inherent values of dedication, sacrifice, and selflessness to their family and children are naturally close to God. Men, by dedicating their lives in service to God or the nation, also manifest virtue and are close to God.[2] Stemming from this concept are constant references to the divine mission of the armed forces in their defense of patriotic values and their images as saviors. Thus, the alliance that the regime sought to establish between mothers and soldiers is based on their shared capacity to defend and transmit superior values.

In this context, the opposite of spiritual is political. Politics is defined as a greedy, manipulative activity in which people seek earthly power. The armed forces, therefore, distanced themselves symbolically from politics. They assumed control of the state for the "common good" and to unify the interests of the nation. Politics were symbolically associated with the masculine-instinctive, while women were "rewarded" for the apolitical character to which their sex entitled them, through the invitation to join together with the armed forces as the pillars of the new society.[3]

The government strongly encouraged the organization of women in charity groups. Considering the interests of women as those linked to motherhood or the prolongation of their maternal roles, the government promoted the creation of "volunteer armies." For this purpose, it restructured preexisting women's organizations; created organizations through the different branches of the armed forces; and developed a parallel institutional structure to the political-administrative structure, which is controlled by the wives of national, regional local authorities.

The diverse organizations gathered around this official volunteerism, were shaped as much by the characteristics of their participants as by the nature of the work they developed. Thus, there were organizations with social content and others with a stronger link to government activities. Among the latter was CEMA-Chile: volunteer members of this organization were primarily the wives of army officials, organized according to military parameters and the military ranks of their husbands. CEMA-Chile administered approximately 10,000 mothers' centers throughout the country. The Women's National Secretariat channeled civilian female support for the regime in order to promote government programs aimed at the poorest sectors; they trained nearly three million women between 1975 and 1983.

The political role of these organizations was not obvious, but was effective. Through these groups the regime established a standard for women's legitimate action that reinforced traditional female identities and social spaces.[4] Regime actions were not designed to improve the living conditions of poor women, but rather to promote their adaptation to these conditions. Women were taught to be good wives, mothers, and homemakers through training programs that enabled them to improve their domestic performance.

The activities of "volunteer organizations" have been fundamental in the implementation of the dictatorial scheme. On one hand, they have fulfilled the clientelistic function of working with bases in the civil society, which the armed forces are unwilling and unable to do because this would bring a discussion of social issues into the barracks. Monolithic control of the armed forces implies keeping military personnel away from direct contact with civil society. Volunteers' institutions were, therefore, established as channels of communication between the authorities and their bases of support.

On the other hand, "volunteerism" served to counteract the negative effects of the free-market economy and helped to palliate the negative consequences of the neo-liberal economic model for the poorest social sectors.[5] Through training courses and social assistance programs, CEMA-Chile not only helped the members of the mothers' centers to overcome the effects of the economic crisis within their families, but also reinforced the regime's economic model and diminished the conflictive potential of reversing the redistributive tendencies of the previous democratic period.

Women Confront the Dictatorship

Paradoxically, the end of more than 20 years of "feminist silence" came during the military dictatorship. The new organization of women under the regime was both a response to economic and political crises and a manifestation of opposition to authoritarianism.

In an attempt to depoliticize Chilean society, the military government repressed and sought to impede the development of social organizations. The prohibition of partisan politics forced traditionally private arenas into politics, attracting public interest and thus becoming arenas of conflict between the dictatorship and democracy. This unintended politicization of the private sphere created a favorable climate for publicizing conflicts derived from gender inequalities. These conflicts had previously been displaced by partisan politics during the democratic period. The dividing line between public and private became diffused and the latter, considered the exclusive domain of women, increasingly became one of the principle areas of confrontation.

The women's movement expressed itself in different forms. Women organized themselves for the defense of human rights and developed ingenious survival strategies to endure the economic crisis and the effects of regime policies on the poor. Women mobilized themselves for the end of the dictatorship, and began to redefine their relationship to politics. This led them to question authoritarian relations in all areas of society, which later resulted in a reconceptualization of democracy.[6] While not all groups assumed gender demands as one of their immediate priorities, their actions played an important role in the reappraisal of women's contributions to politics. A virtual explosion of women's organizations, contextualized within both the social and political fabric of the society, highlighted the existence of women's issues and encouraged the development of practices responding to women's concerns, while seeking to avoid patterns of subordination.

Women and Human Rights

Ironically, the traditional separation between public and private spheres helped women assume leading roles in the period immediately following the coup. The regime, which claimed to be defending the most traditional of institutions, the family, had to confront the denunciations of women who mobilized to defend their homes from repression. These denunciations broke the repressive logic of the state, because they were presented, despite their strong political character, as an emotional defense of the family, not a threat to military rule.

Organizations predominantly composed of women, such as the Families of the Detained and Disappeared and the Families of Political Prisoners were the first to develop public activities denouncing and opposing the regime after the coup.[7] Other predominantly female groups followed. Despite high levels of female participation, human rights organizations did not identify themselves according to gender. Instead, they stayed within the limits of the traditional definition of politics, by focusing on assistance to the victims of repression. The close links of these groups to the proscribed political parties, out of whose ranks came most of the victims of the repression, led the organizations to give higher priority to partisan activities. This meant less autonomy for the groups and further inhibited their identity as women's organizations.

Women and the Economic Crisis

The military-patriarchal logic facing the economic crisis prevented the regime from recognizing the problem of women's survival. In the economic crisis, women increasingly assumed the role of head of household and this contributed to the growing feminization of poverty.

The structural economic transformations, promoted by the government since 1973, led to high levels of unemployment which in turn caused a strong regression in the distribution of income and a fall in the population's living standards.[8] The poorest Chileans made up 40 per cent of the population and their share of income decreased from 12 per cent in 1970-1973 to 9.3 per cent in 1984. At the same time, the wealthiest portion of the population increased their share from 50.5 per cent of total income in 1970-1973 to 60.9 in 1984.

Between 1970 and 1982, the proportion of female heads of household increased by 4 per cent of the total number of women in the work force.[9] The 1982 census showed that only 22 per cent of homes were run by women; in the poorest areas, this percentage easily reached 40 percent. As recent studies have shown, these changes brought on marital conflicts and women undertook an extra work load in order to avoid this additional strain.[10] A study carried out by Lucia Pardo showed that women working at home spend 56 hours weekly in domestic labor; that is 16 percent more than legal full-time work. Moreover, women who work full time outside the home, spend an additional 33 hours weekly on domestic tasks.[11] They therefore work 81 hours a week, which is 69 percent above the legal level.

The deteriorating economic situation led large contingents of poor urban women to initiate several collective strategies for survival, to satisfy basic needs of their families. Women formed more than a thousand popular economic organizations in Santiago alone, including subsistence and craft workshops, soup kitchens, and such programs as "collective shopping." These groups consisted mostly of housewives who were trying to meet their families' basic food and survival needs, in a state that had forsaken its benefactor character.

Additionally, the economic crisis had serious repercussions on the personal lives of these women. In the poorest homes, the incorporation of women into the labor force often necessitated removing daughters from school to do domestic chores, while sons continued their studies. At the same time, the number of homes with female heads increased, in part as a result of the migration of men in search of work opportunities, and in part because of the difficulty of unemployed men adjusting to the new balance of power in the home.

Even though the new economic organizations created by women had the problems of survival as a principal objective, they rapidly became promising centers for political organization and the development of a women's social movement. They maintained an important degree of autonomy; most did not establish direct relations with political parties. They questioned "class contradictions" and focussed attention on social conflicts previously ignored. In response, the most orthodox sectors of the Chilean left maintained that women's issues would be resolved with the coming of socialism. For these groups, recognizing the existence of gender--demands admitting implied differences, even disagreements--within the working class, which could detract from the principal struggle against the dictatorship. The orthodox left thus opposed gender-specific demands, insisting on the necessity of keeping the family united and directing all efforts toward this struggle.

While these women's organizations did not propose the end of gender discrimination--as in the middle-class based feminist movement--the changes in women's lives caused by the economic crisis led to a greater sense of personal worth, and created a sense of gender identity. As Maria de la Luz Silva states: "Women's experience of leaving their homes, making contact with other women suffering the same problems and discovering their own unsuspected capacities and abilities, had an important impact on their lives. For example, women had a greater sense of self-worth, questioned their gender roles, reevaluated the marital relationship, and assumed their identities as women and as social actors."[12] This perspective also emerges from a study by Claudia Serrano, who interviewed women who had joined the labor market in the midst of the economic crisis. She states: "We observe in none of the cases a return to the initial position: women in the home, men at work."[13]

Women and Politics: Opposition Groups

Under military rule, the organizations of civil society became a substitute political arena that contributed to the politicization of the private and social spheres; thus facilitating specific demands over and above ideological alignments, previously subsumed by other national priorities. Furthermore, the influence of the international women's movement clearly contributed to the generation of gender identity in the struggle for democracy.[14]

The first mobilization and organizing of women began in the 1970's. In 1976, a Women's Department was created within the Coordinadora Nacional Sindical (CNS), which tried to organize female workers and the wives of male workers, and encouraged their participation in union activity. The creation of the Women's Department is most significant, as it advanced gender-specific demands, breaking the mythic solidarity of the working class.

In 1977, middle-class professional women formed a group that became the Circle for the Study of Women, which established the basis of the local feminist movement. Most of the women had been politically active previously in peripheral roles in leftist political parties, and they recognized the authoritarian framework that characterized the entire society.

It was not, however, until the period of political opening, ten years after the military coup, that women's mobilization took a wider significance. They had originally mobilized for the anti-dictatorial struggle more than for gender demands, but the majority of these demands evolved toward the incorporation of a feminist perspective. After the creation of the Feminist Movement in 1983, feminism spread rapidly to the popular sectors, destroying the myth that feminist concerns only reflect the interests of middle-class women. Shantytown groups, with a clear feminist bent, were created--such as the Women's Liberation Front, the "Domitilas," and the "Siemprevivas"--and defined themselves in terms of their domestic roles. They were primarily interested in the struggle for survival.

Given the diversity of women's organizations and their shared confrontational nature, an umbrella group was created--the Movement for the Emancipation of Women 1983 (MEMCH-83)--which took its name from the suffragist movement that led the struggle between 1935 and 1953 for women's right to vote. MEMCH-83 originally gathered 24 women's groups and organized several demonstrations repudiating the regime.[15] The objective of the movement was to promote opposition activities among the diverse women's groups and facilitate their coordination. Even though these organizations did not actually mobilize a majority of women, they gave important visibility to women's demands.

The increasing partisanship among women's organizations led these groups to develop different concepts of politics and the role of women therein. While the most orthodox sectors of the left argued that gender demands distracted people from the principle objective of ousting the dictatorship, feminist groups refused to prioritize objectives. They pointed out that women's oppression was a departure point for women's political participation. While some women get involved in politics because of their needs and sense of isolation, other women join a political cause first and assume that their needs and demands will be addressed later.[16]

In their approach to politics, feminist groups argued that it was necessary to redefine the concept of democracy, since in their view democracy had never existed for women. As Kirkwood states, the struggle for democracy should include the struggle for women's liberation; otherwise patriarchal structures will not be eliminated.[17] The argument implies that there is an authoritarian pattern behind political and personal relations, both structures must therefore be democratized. It is in this context that the Feminist Movement coined its slogan, "Democracy in the Country and in the House;" seeking not only more equality for women, but also a transformation of political and day-to-day relations. Without ignoring the problem of social inequality, feminist demands identify expressions of inequality in a broader context, focusing their attention on those social institutions that reproduce discrimination: the family, the educational system, the political parties of all ideologies, the state apparatus and the legal system.

Conclusion

The militarization of Chilean society since the coup of 1973 affected all the population and, in a special way, women. The military is an important symbol in a male-dominated culture. The effects of militarization on women operated both directly and through changes in cultural norms. Increasing military expenditures produced cutbacks in social spending, increasing the feminization of poverty. Women political prisoners were victims of sexual abuse. The government endorsed a "macho" ideology defining women's proper place, at home.

Confronting the military regime, women organized for peace and democracy. The women's movement played an important role in the struggle against the military dictatorship, becoming an emerging political actor.

The political importance of the women's movement during this period does not lie so much in its capacity to mobilize large numbers of people, but rather in that women have reinforced the pro-democracy movement and brought greater participation of sectors that would otherwise have remained excluded from the political system.

Notes

1. Joefina Rosetti, "La educacion de las mujeres en el Chile contemporaneo," in *Mundo de mujer, Continuidad y cambio* (Santiago, 1988):97-181.

2. Peter Brown, *The Devil and the Flesh* (New York: Columbia University Press, 1988).

3. Giselle Munizaga, *El discurso publico de Pinochet* (Buenos Aires, 1985).

4. Ana Maria Arteaga, "Politizacion de lo privado y subversion de lo cotidiano," in *Mundo de mujer. Continuidad y cambio* (Santiago, 1988):565-592.

5. Norbert Lechner and Susana Levy, "Notas sobre la vida cotidiana III: El disciplinamiento de la mujer," *Material de Discusion*, FLACSO (Santiago, 1984).

6. Patricia Chuchryck, "Protest, Politics and Personal Life: The Emergence of Feminism in a Military Dictatorship, Chile, 1973-1983" (Doctoral Dissertation, University of York, 1984).

7. Hugo Frohling, "Reproduccion y socializacion de nucleos de resistencia: La experiencia de la Vicaria de la Solidaridad en Chile," Paper presented at the Seminar on "La cultura del miedo bajo regimenes militares" (Buenos Aires, June, 1985).

8. Jose Pablo Arellano, "La situacion social en Chile," *Notas Tecnicas CIEPLAN*, No. 94 (Santiago, 1987), 34 pages. (This is a working paper.)

9. Adriana Munoz, "Fuerza de trabajo femenina: Evolucion y tendencias," in *Mundo de mujer. Continuidad y cambio* (Santiago 1988):185-277.

10. Eugenia Hola, "Mujer, dominacion y crisis," and Ximena Diaz and Eugenia Hola, "La mujer en el trabajo informal urbano," both in *Mundo de mujer. Continuidad y cambio* (Santiago, 1988):13-50 and 323-385.

11. Lucia Pardo, "El impacto socioeconomico de la labor de la mujer," *Revista Politica*, No. 7 (1985):14-37.

12. Maria de la Luz Silva, "La participacion de la mujer en Chile: Las organizaciones de mujeres." Paper presented at the international conference on "La participacion politica de la mujer en el cono sur," (Montevideo, June, 1986).

13. Maria de la Luz Silva, "La participacion de la mujer en Chile: Las organizaciones de mujeres." Paper presented at the international conference on "La participacion politica de la mujer en el cono sur," Montevideo, June, 1986.

14. Claudia Serrano, "Pobladoras en Santiago: Algo mas que la crisis, " in *Mujeres, crisis y movimiento*, ISIS-MUDAR (Santiago, 1988). This influence came about indirectly because of the ease of communication and directly through the great numbers of Chilean women who had left the country after 1973 for political reasons, and returned to introduce the European and North American strains of feminism in Chile.

15. Natacha Molina, *Lo femenino y lo democratico en el o7 3 Chile de hoy* (Santiago, 1986).

16. Julieta Kirkwood, *Ser politica en Chile: Las feministas y los partidos* (Santiago, 1986).

17. Julieta Kirkwood, "Los nudos de la sabiduria feminista," *Documentos de Trabajo*, FLACSO (Santiago, 1984).

PART FOUR

THE AGENTS OF PEACE CULTURES

Introduction to Part Four

Elise Boulding

We have looked at the development of peace cultures in terms of concepts and strategies for common security; in terms of how human behaviors and the institutional structures that pattern them can, under certain conditions of social learning, move from violence to nonviolence; and in terms of how the marginalized and the oppressed of the world's peripheries can bring their own knowledge and wisdom to bear on the problems of the societies of which they are a part. Now we will look at some specific agents of peace culture--peace movements, communications media and churches.

Peace researchers have been studying peace movements for decades. Alger, by putting peace movements in the context of social change movements generally, challenges peace researchers on two counts: to find the specificity of peace movements as contrasted with other social change movements; and to develop relationships with the groups they study at the grassroots level or risk missing precisely the specificities of the knowledge and skill of these groups. Alger quotes a warning given by Mushakoji that peace researchers have been guilty of ignoring the center-periphery paradigm and settling for "center-type" knowledge of what is actually happening at the peripheries, where the grassroots social movements are to be found. Both scholars see peace movements as moving ahead of peace researchers in terms of awareness of the interconnectedness of problems, and scope of vision about the new society. The kind of "knowing" that Alger and Mushakoji are calling peace researchers to is the kind of knowing that Mische referred to in her eloquent plea (Part Three) that we take the earth as teacher.

Kodama, focussing on European peace activists, discovers that they are indeed the peripheries of their own societies. High-status men are noticeably absent, women and students noticeably present. These peripheries are part of that same broader set of social movements identified by Alger, rejecting the common foe of the old patriarchal, competitive, anti-environmental order and defining themselves as citizens of a world to come--feminist, localist, green, participation-oriented.

If peace activists are to be considered as agents of a coming peaceable order, the media tend to be thought of as counter-agents, blocking change by casting a blanket of silence over peace activities. Singh, a communications researcher, surprises us with what is again a center-periphery analysis: the center (the media powers) are in fact not so powerful. They are not in touch with what is going on and they do not arouse public thinking and feeling. It is the face-to-face and door-to-door local contact work at the periphery that generates human energy and responsiveness, not the media stories. Singh castigates peace researchers for looking only at the conventional media, and suggests that all forms of human communication need to be studied in order to understand the social dynamics of peace processes.

Finally, we come to that most controversial agent of peace, the "Warrior Church." Williamson's piece on the Churches as Agents of Peace and Development (excerpted from a longer document) is in fact an action piece, prepared for a new global network of peace activists in communities of faith, sponsored by IPRA's Religion and Conflict Network. The peace leaders from churches in a number of Latin American countries, who gathered in Rio for the IPRA Conference, based their dialogue on this document. The development of a common research and action agenda which began in Rio has already been followed by two international workshops and a further planning meeting at the 25th Anniversary Conference of IPRA held in Groningen, the Netherlands, in July 1990. Church activists, using the base community approach at the local level, have understood the power of the periphery perhaps sooner than any other major international set of actors. Their new partnership with peace researchers should help document this vital process.

20

Creating Global Visions for Peace Movements

Chadwick F. Alger

Peace movements are in a state of flux that is on the one hand presenting new opportunities for increased grassroots participation and impact, but on the other hand, creating difficulties in the self-identity of these groups and of individuals affiliated with them. Many participants in peace movements thought that they understood with certainty the meaning of peace, only to be perplexed by debate about positive peace versus negative peace and direct violence versus structural violence. They are challenged and encouraged by increasing emphasis on the significance of grassroots initiatives; but at times they are puzzled by simultaneous emphasis on the importance of transnational movements. They saw distinctions between peace movements and movements focused on other issues such as development, human rights and ecology; but increasingly they hear those involved in these movements declare that they too are workers for peace--as when the Pope declared: "Development is another word for peace." What should be the self-identity of groups and individuals working for peace? What should be their global vision of a movement toward peace in which they fit their own efforts?

There are those who perceive the growing "lack of focus" of "the peace movement" as a sign of weakness; but it may also be interpreted as a sign of intellectual vitality, of openness to broader visions and new ideas, and as a sign of willingness to acknowledge the reality of growing interconnections between scattered arenas of peacelessness that were once perceived to be separate and independent of each other. We tend to accept this latter view, sensing that the present state of flux is provoking a global dialogue of contending and complementary views out of which will emerge new visions of peace potential from a global perspective. It is the purpose of this paper to pose some of the difficult challenges and opportunities that the present state of flux now offers to those endeavoring to understand where their particular peace efforts fit into the global peace movement.

Where does the peace movement fit in the larger constellation of organizations working for human betterment? It will be useful at the onset to pose the question in terms of three clearly differentiated possibilities. First, does the broadening definition of peace, that is emerging out of global practice and dialogue, suggest that peace is *the* goal toward which humanity is striving? This approach would say that the pursuit of nonviolence, economic justice, human rights and ecological balance would be best perceived as facets of the struggle for peace. Second, is peace *one* of the prime goals for achieving human betterment, along with economic justice, human rights and ecological balance? From this perspective, peace overlaps with each of the other goals, producing the need for coordination, but each goal is seen to require its own distinctive movement. Third, do the separate struggles for peace, economic justice, human rights and ecological balance suggest that all confront a common foe, such as Milbrath's notion of a Dominant Social Paradigm?[1] Does contemporary experience point toward the need for an integrated assault on this common foe that could require reconceptualization and reorganization of the array of social movements that arose before it was realized that all were facing a common foe?

Three Transformations in Peace Thinking

A fundamental factor in the challenges now confronted by peace movements is the global dialectic in peace thinking in the Twentieth Century. This has produced three fundamental transformations. The first transformation was from a definition of peace limited to 'stopping the violence,' to a much broader notion of peace as reflected in the UN Declaration of the Preparation of Societies for Life in Peace. This definition has been aptly summarized by the United Nations University as:

> "The removal of institutional obstacles and the promotion of structural conditions facilitating the growth of socio-cultural, economic and political trends, aiming at and leading to Life in Peace understood as both subjective life styles and objective living conditions congruent with basic peace values such as security, nonviolence, identity, equity and well-being as opposed to insecurity, violence, alienation, inequity and deprivation."[2]

This broader definition of peace has emerged out of a great global dialogue--in the UN system, non-governmental organizations and scholarly debate--that has demonstrated that people in different circumstances experience peacelessness as a result of a variety of conditions, such as sickness, poverty, oppression, war or threat of war, threat to cultural survival, and pollution of water, air and food. This great global dialogue suggests that progress toward peace from a global perspective requires overcoming simultaneously a diversity of causes of peacelessness. This is partly necessary because there are causal connections between war, injustice, oppression and pollution. But equally important is the fact that peace strategies can only gain global acceptance if they simultaneously attempt to overcome the primary causes of peacelessness worldwide.

The second transformation in peace thinking is closely intertwined with the first. The broadening definition of peace now makes it increasingly apparent that peace is not a condition that a few leaders alone can attain for the people of the world. As long as peace was believed to be attainable 'simply' by stopping aggression and violence (i.e. negative peace), it was plausible, although I believe this too was an illusion, that a few leaders could secure peace for the masses. But the broadened notion of peace (including also positive peace) clearly reveals that a diversity of sectors of any society and a diversity of sectors of relationships between societies, contribute to peacelessness and thus must be involved in peace making. This does not mean that governmental leaders, and a variety of non-governmental institutions and leaders, no longer have important roles to play in peacebuilding. But it does mean that they cannot attain a strong and lasting peace alone without widespread knowledge, participation and support from the people of the world.

A third transformation in peace thinking largely follows from the first two and is perhaps still more implicit than explicit. This transformation sees peace as an unfolding potential that grows out of the pursuit of peace. This suggests that the further we move toward the attainment of our present notion of peace, the more highly developed our future image of peace will be and the possibility of achieving this new image. This is dramatically different from the perspective that looks on peace as a return to conditions before war broke out, or that looks upon peace as a resolution or settlement of certain conflicts so that people can return to other pursuits, assured that the settlement will guarantee the peace. Instead, the broader definition of peace reveals a diversity of human activities through which peace can be pursued, implying that all occupations have peacemaking potential. Only now is this potential beginning to be discovered.

Naturally, there are those who feel uncomfortable with this multifaceted transformation in peace thinking. They still cling to the notion that "stopping the violence" or "banning the bomb" must be achieved first, as a prerequisite for achieving other goals which they like to refer to by terms such as social justice, economic well-being and ecological balance. This is not surprising because there is indeed much violence in the world and fear of widespread destruction by nuclear weapons, even destruction of the planet's ecosystem, is a conscious concern of people all over the world. Efforts to limit, and even abolish, the production and deployment of these weapons must be intensified. But for millions of people, other forms of peacelessness--malnutrition, disease, poverty, racial discrimination, sexual discrimination, and destruction of culture--are even more tangible parts of everyday life. It would seem obvious that a sound foundation for worldwide peace can be constructed only by simultaneous responsiveness to pleas for relief from people whose lives are made miserable by a diversity of causes of peacelessness.

This broad approach is supported by experience in humankind's great peace laboratories, the League of Nations and the United Nations system. When viewed from a seventy year perspective, these laboratories have demonstrated that so-called negative peace strategies (stopping the violence) such as collective security, peaceful settlement, peacekeeping and disarmament have repeatedly had very limited success. Workers in both the League and the UN laboratory have found it necessary to broaden the agenda to include other causes of peacelessness. Thus, we see a dramatic long-term growth in concern for economic well-being, self-determination and human rights, and more recently, attention to ecological issues. Some have mistakenly concluded that these global organizations, failing to keep the peace, decided instead to deal with more tractable issues in a strategy of avoidance. Instead, I believe that feedback from these laboratories has demonstrated that the agenda had to be broadened because negative peace strategies cannot be successful without simultaneously achieving a certain degree of success on positive peace issues. At the same time, it has been learned that positive peace strategies may at times be more effective and make the need for using negative peace strategies unnecessary.[3]

The "Common Foe" Approach to Contemporary Social Movements

A number of scholars perceive an array of social movements, including the peace movement, to be struggling against a common foe. Milbrath sees close linkage between "the struggle for peace, the struggle for partnership between the sexes, and the struggle for protection of the integrity of the environment." He notes that all three problems "have their roots in the same social malady--the Dominant Social Paradigm (DSP) that dominates modern Western thinking." The DSP has the following belief elements:

1. Humans should dominate nature.
2. It is natural for men to dominate women.
3. Power is the key to control and security.
4. Economic strength, science, and technology should be stressed in order to increase power.
5. Competition, and markets, should be stressed in order to maximize achievement and power.
6. We must take large risks in order to maximize achievement and power.
7. We do not need government foresight and planning; the market will take care of the future.
8. There are no limits to growth.
9. Human progress (in the sense of DSP) need never cease.

Milbrath sees a deeper belief hidden behind the nine listed: "Most 'other' creatures, human and non-human, are our competitors and/or enemies they--must be dominated and controlled in order for us to feel secure."[4] He believes that we must recognize "the common roots" of environmental, feminist and peace problems and create a "new belief paradigm that will enable humans to live harmoniously with each other and with all the other creatures in nature."[5]

Other scholars are reaching strikingly similar conclusions. John J. De-Deken, in a study of the current peace movement in Flanders, asserts that the "new" social movements such as the green movement and the peace movement "try to defend the integrity of the life-world as such, against the one-sided process of purposive-oriented rationalization. In a way, they form an oppositional power against the *colonization* of the life-world."[6] Karl Werner Brand claims that the peace movement is only the top of an iceberg of the post-materialistic, anti-technocratic opposition.[7] Claus Offe has observed that contemporary social movements:

> "...converge on the idea that life itself--and the minimal standards of 'good life' as defined and sanctioned by modern values--is threatened by the bland dynamic of military, economic, technological and political rationalization; and that there are no sufficient and sufficiently reliable barriers within dominant political and economic institutions that could prevent them from passing the threshold to disaster."[8]

Brian Tokar's study of *The Green Alternative* has a quite similar ring when he notes that the "Greens are not a single issue movement...As ecology describes the interconnections among all living things, an ecological politics needs to embrace the interconnectedness of all aspects of our social and political lives and institutions. ...The Domination of human by human is an ecological problem."[9] He lists the "four pillars" of the West German Greens: ecology, social justice and responsibility, democracy in politics and in the economy, and nonviolence. This treatise of the Greens takes up the "four pillars" in this order, progressing from ecology to nonviolence, and concluding that "war has always been an ecological problem." In contrast, Western peace movements would tend to begin with nonviolence, perhaps moving on to economic well-being, then social justice, and ending with ecology.

Rajni Kothari also perceives the emergence of an array of social movements responsive to a common foe. He observes that "an unprecedented convergence is taking place between the environment and feminist movements, between these two and the human rights movement (the latter is becoming wholly redefined), and between all of them and the peace movement."[10] Kothari describes Indian movements that have arisen in opposition to the "development" strategies of the state. He observes that the state is now perceived as an agent of technological modernization, with a view more to catching up with the developed world and emerging on the world and regional scenes as a strong state (hence the vast sums spent on armaments) than coping with the pressing, often desperate, needs and demands of the poor.[11] He perceives tendencies:

> "... that seek, on the one hand, to integrate the organized economy into the world market and, on the other hand, remove millions of people from the economy by throwing them in the dustbin of history--impoverished, destitute, drained of their own resources and deprived of minimum requirements of health and nutrition, denied 'entitlement' to food and water and shelter--in short, an unwanted and dispensable lot whose fate seems to be 'doomed.'"

Kothari sees "grass-roots movements and non-party formations" as springing "from a deep stirring of consciousness and an intuitive awareness of a crisis that could conceivably be turned into a catalyst of new opportunities." These new movements are attempting to "open alternative political spaces" outside the traditional arenas of party and government.[12]

Kothari observes that the very content of politics has been redefined. Issues that "were not so far seen as amenable to political action...now fall within the purview of political struggle."[13] These include people's health, rights over forests and other community resources, and women's rights. Not limited to economic and political demands, the struggle extends to ecological, cultural and educational issues. Examples include people's movements to prevent the felling of trees in the foothills of the Himalayas, the miners' struggle in Chattisgarh (a predominantly tribal belt in Madhya Pradesh), an organization of landless activists in Andhra Pradesh, a peasant's organization in Kanakpura in Karnataka against the mining and export of granite and a movement for regional autonomy in the tribal belt of Bihar and Orissa. While basing his analysis on Indian experience, Kothari sees these movements as part of a "phenomenon (that) has more general relevance."[14] They are, in his view, responsive to:

> "...a new...phase in the structure of world dominance, a change of the role of the state in national and sub-national settings, and a drastically altered relationship between the people and what we (half in jest and half in deception) call 'development'"[15]

It is obvious that the Greens, and those opposing the "colonialization" of the life-world, "the one-sided process of purposive-oriented rationalization," the Dominant Social Paradigm and "the structure of world dominance," share some goals with all peace movements. But Europeans cited tend to commence their analysis with ecology and Third World scholars tend to use poverty as the point of origin. On the other hand, peace paradigms and peace movements, tend to begin with nonviolence, with poverty coming next and ecology last. How should the increase in overlapping agendas of peace, ecological and anti-poverty movements be taken into account? (1) Should the peace movement insist that overcoming violence, poverty and destruction of the environment--and other peace issues--all be treated as part of an expanding peace movement? (2) Should these various movements maintain their separate identities while cooperating on common agenda items? (3) Should a new generation of movements be developed that provide an integrated strategy against an increasingly visible common foe?

Kothari does not answer these difficult questions but gropes toward one in pointing out that "the important point is...the interrelationship of dimensions and movements, of a holistic approach to life, which goes against the grain of modern scientific culture and its emphasis on specialization and fragmentation."[16] He has a vision in which:

> "...as the feminist values become more generalized, a holistic approach will develop. It will be an approach that is also plural and based on complementarities. This is more likely to happen in the non-Western world than in the West because of the former's traditions of plurality and androgyny."[17]

Social Movements in Global Perspective

There is a growing literature illuminating the dynamic response by social movements in all parts of the world to a pressing array of social problems. If these movements are to cope with powerful transnational production, marketing, communications and military organizations that are intruding on local space, they will require, at the very least, some kind of shared global vision of their common enterprise. Kothari says: "The basic question is: can this activism, all these 'movements,' produce a macro challenge, a general transformation (whether one calls it a revolution or not)?"[18]

Writing out of experience with the Lokayan movement in India, D.L. Sheth perceives a new mode of politics arising across regional, linguistic, cultural and national boundaries. It encompasses peace and anti-nuclear movements, environmental movements, women's movements, movements for self-determination of cultural groups, minorities and tribes, and a movement championing non-Western cultures, techno-sciences and languages. Importantly, this new politics is "not constricted by the narrow logic of capturing state power." Rather, Sheth discerns the need for new insights on micro-macro linkage. He concludes:

> "It is the dialectic between micro-practice and macro-thinking that will actualize a new politics of the future...In brief, a macro-vision is the prime need of these groups and movements, and this can be satisfied only by a growing partnership between activists and intellectuals in the process of social transformation."[19]

Sheth notes that one of the three principles on which a "new politics" is based, is "an awareness that the local power structures against which (local) people are fighting derive their power from macro structures of the present national and international order."[20] In response, he notes that "a macro theory of transformative political action is required which is based on the values and practice of democracy and which has synthesizing potentials for integrating the perspectives and actions of various issue-based movements in a larger framework of transformation."[21] But Sheth insists that "it is necessary that a theory of alternative action emerge through the process of grassroots movements making their impact on the global thinking, rather than the other way round."[22]

Swedish economists Mats Friberg and Bjorn Hettne describe a challenging vision of an emerging worldwide "Green" movement that offers an alternative to the "Blue" (market, liberal, capitalist) and the "Red" (state, socialism, planning). They reject "mainstream development thinking" in which "the state is always seen as the social subject of the development process." Instead, from the Green perspective, they see that "the human being or small communities of human beings are the ultimate actors. The state can, at most, be an instrument for this ultimate actor."[23] In other words, Friberg and Hettne consider that "the tribes and nations of the world are much more basic units of development" than states. They use human needs as a starting point from which the following are derived:

* CULTURAL IDENTITY - the social unit of development is a culturally defined community and the development of this community is rooted in the specific values and institutions of this culture.
* SELF-RELIANCE - each community relies primarily on its own strength and resources.
* SOCIAL JUSTICE - development programs should give priority to those most in need.
* ECOLOGICAL BALANCE - the resources of the biosphere are utilized in full awareness of the potential of local ecosystems as well as the global and local limits imposed on present and future generations.[24]

The Green approach sees the capitalist societies of the West and the state socialist societies of the West as "two variants of a common corporate industrial culture based on the values of competitive individualism, rationality, growth, efficiency, specialization, centralization and big scale." According to Friberg and Hettne, how these values came about can only be partly explained by economic factors. Rather, "their roots have to be sought, ultimately, in the cultural projects of Western civilization."[25] Thus, for the Greens, the "unbalance between the modern large-scale rationalized sector and the non-modern small-scale personalistic sector" would be an essential element of the predicament of Third World people in all regions of the world. More generally, their problems would not be simply those arising from capitalism or socialism, but have to do also with "the nation-state, bureaucratic forms of organization, positive science, the patriarchate and the urban way of life."[26] Friberg and Hettne do not wish to eliminate states, only to make them serve the human needs desired by (local) communities better. They see the "Green project" requiring "stronger institutions on the local level," as well as the de-emphasis of the state. But, they do not present concrete ideas for global institutions which fit the Green approach, nor do they indicate whether these institutions should be linked directly to local peoples.

Friberg and Hettne's Green movement transcends single countries and regions. Their "main hypothesis is that the Green movement derives its strength from three rather different sources:"

1. THE TRADITIONALISTS who resist modern penetration in the form of commercialization, industrialization, state-building and professionalization. They derive their strength from "non-western civilizations and religions, old nations and tribes, local communities, kinship groups, peasants and self-employed people, informal economies, women, culture, etc.

2. MARGINALIZED PEOPLE who cannot find a place within the modern sector, "the unemployed, temporary workers, women, youth, the uneducated, workers with soulless jobs, etc."

3. POST-MATERIALISTS who experience some sort of "self-emancipation," often through "opportunities provided by an affluent modern society. ...They are young, well-educated and committed to non-material values. Their occupations are person-oriented rather than thing-oriented."[27]

Friberg and Hettne perceive these three groups to be at different places in the "center-periphery structure of the world." The traditionalists are to be found primarily in peripheries, the marginalized at the middle level, and the post-materialists near the centers. They are now not part of a single Green movement. Rather, Friberg and Hettne see all three as potential elements of a worldwide movement.

It is very significant that each of these Indian and Swedish scholars perceive a related set of movements against dominant global and national structures to be a worldwide phenomenon. While focusing on the Indian context, Kothari notes "a more general relevance" and discusses the various dimensions of "new grassroots politics" from a global perspective.[28] Sheth perceives a new mode of politics arising across regional, linguistic, cultural and national boundaries. Challenging is the "main hypothesis" of Friberg and Hettne that asserts that the Green movement derives its strength from "traditionalists" in the world periphery, "marginalized" people in what might be called the "semi-periphery" and "post-materialists" near the world centers.

Another common thesis of these Indian and Swedish scholars is a strong local emphasis. For Friberg and Hettne, "the human being or small communities of human beings are the ultimate actors." They emphasize self-reliance and cultural autonomy for local communities. Kothari underlines the importance of a diversity of local peoples movements which are attempting to "open alternative political space." Sheth emphasizes local self-determination and the fact that movements are based on a new perspective that "is based, to a large extent, on the day-to-day experience of ordinary people." But both Kothari and Sheth emphasize that "micro practice" must be guided by "macro thinking" that is significantly shaped by grassroots movements themselves.

Three Elements of a Global Vision for Peace Movements

It is not our intent to imagine a holistic global vision for peace movements. Instead, we are attempting to gain insight on necessary elements of a vision by examination of works on social movements by scholars from a number of countries. Three elements seem to be particularly important. First, the vision must be inclusive of the diversity of themes through which people in various parts of the world are attempting to overcome peacelessness. It is obvious that the list of themes must include those such as nonviolence economic well-being, social justice, feminism and ecological balance. But there is danger that lists constructed in one part of the world may be inadequate in conveying the perspective of people in other parts of the world. For example, cultural identity and self-determination may be presumed to be included in a theme such as social justice or human rights, but may receive secondary consideration in the context of these themes. Thus, the list of themes should be open, and inevitably overlapping and messy, in an effort to validly reflect the central concerns of people in all parts of the world.

Second, the vision must expect strong and sustained participation at the grassroots. It is not difficult to reach the conclusion that most of the peacelessness in the world is associated with lack of grassroots participation. The peacelessness that has been generated by "security states" and their arms races and militarization is strongly associated with lack of participation by people at the grassroots in the attainment of their own security. At the same time, the peacelessness that has been fomented by state "development" plans is rooted in the lack of grassroots participation in formulation of strategies for satisfying basic human needs. But there is still a tendency in much peace research to presume that states must be the prime agents in peace strategies, and to assume that people at the grassroots are incompetent to formulate and implement their own peace strategies. Relevant here is Kothari's call "for a review of ideological positions that continue to locate 'vested interests' in local situations and liberation from them in distant processes--the state, technology, revolutionary vanguards."[29]

Third, visions are required that specify possibilities for local control over powerful entities, such as states and transnational production, financial, marketing and communications corporations that intrude on local space. Also, what kinds of relationships would there be between local communities in distant parts of the world? New visions of what some would call micro-macro relations are an indispensable part of any useful global vision for peace movements. But at the same time it must be recognized that, for most of us, the possibility of significant impact of local people on macro institutions is "unthinkable."

This is because of the way education and specialization have shaped our present perceptions of, and expectations of, micro-macro relations. For this reason, this third topic merits somewhat greater attention.

An integral part of disempowerment of the grassroots is the mythology of the state system that legitimizes activities through which economic-political-military bureaucracies of states dominate the external relations of societies in pursuit of the "national interest." Evidence of the power of the myth is to be found in the fact that virtually all states depend on a small elite to define the "national interest." Products of these "national interest" policies have been arms races, militarized societies and "development" that does not fulfill human needs but does destroy the environment. How might visions that replace the mythology of the state system provide for local control of the necessary functions of states?

At the same time, a significant contributor to peacelessness is the overwhelming presence of transnational production, financial, marketing, communication and service corporations in virtually every city and town in the world--as employer, entertainer, and provider of consumer goods, health care, insurance, news and housing. Literature on world capitalism and dependency has usefully illuminated the multitude of ways in which the lives of local people are dominated by these macro institutions. But there is now increasing concern that the expansion of scholarly attention to the impact of global intrusions on local space has not been accompanied by adequate attentiveness to local response.

Some scholars are now criticizing their colleagues for not contributing knowledge that would be useful in creating political movements for overcoming local dependency. Richard Child Hill, in an overview of the "emergence, consolidation and development" of research on urban political economy, makes this parting declaration:

> "If, as some scholars imply, the city has become the 'weak link' in the world capitalist system, then the most pressing urban research issues today center upon investigation of the conditions under which global-local contradictions...give rise to political movements and public policies directed toward changing the structure and dynamics of the trans-local system."[30]

Craig Murphy makes a similar criticism of world systems research in "a plea for including studies of social mobilization in the world system research program," by asking for "a theory of the role of political consciousness and social mobilization in the dynamics of world capitalism."[31] Murphy asserts that Stavrianos' popular history of the Third World, *Global Rift* points the way because he "tells the story of the Third World by constantly focusing on mobilization against capitalism...But the broad strokes of Stavriano's history need to be filled in by detailed studies of individual political movements, unique and repeated cases of people becoming convinced to act against capitalism...the stuff of actual social mobilization."[32]

A few scholars are now creating a new literature on local response to macro intrusions. Their research offers insights significant to those who would wish to create useful visions of stronger grassroots peace movements. We will cite only a few examples.[33]

Sensitive to this issue are two anthropologists working in Central America. Asking that local history in Guatemala be put in global context, Carol A. Smith criticizes anthropologists for recognizing global forces while neglecting "the way in which local systems affect the regional structures, economic and political, on which global forces play." At the same time, she observes that scholars in the other social sciences "are even more likely to view local systems as the passive recipients of global processes."[34] Based on his work in Nicaragua, Richard Adams acknowledges the impacts of global capitalist expansion. Yet he observes that it is necessary to recognize that local "life and culture continue to yield new emergent social entities, new adaptive forms brought into being in order to pursue survival and reproduction both through and in spite of the specific work of capitalism."[35] Yet another anthropologist, John W. Bennett, writing in the context of "microcosm-macrocosm relationships" in North American agrarian society, has warned against unfounded assumptions about the domination of the local community by external influences and directs attention to the ways "the local spatial system retains many of its 'traditional' institutions and utilizes these to manipulate and control the external forces."[36]

Wallerstein notes that "the household as an income-pooling unit can be seen as a fortress both of accommodation to and resistance to the patterns of labor-force allocation favored by accumulators."[37] His conclusion is supported by illuminating studies of households in Oaxaca, Mexico and Davao City, Philippines, that offer insight on the capacity of households to resist efforts by the state to "help" marginal and poor workers to cope with the intrusion of worldwide economic processes into their daily lives. In this study, Hackenberg, Murphy and Selby criticize dependency theorists, and implicitly most world systems theorists, by noting that their kind of theory is "less interested in the reactions and strivings of the exploited than it is in delineating the historical, sociological, cultural and economic forces that coadjust to exploit them." Because dependency theory portrays the urban household as "fairly helpless," the authors "take leave of dependency theory" and depict the household as a vital institution that endeavors to protect its interests by doing battle with state programs that would undermine the integrity of the household by "opportunities generated by development" that would exploit "the desires of some household members to better themselves economically at the expense of other members."[38]

Insight on visions that explicate local control over intrusive macro processes can also be gained by closer observation of increasingly creative efforts of
local people to "Think Globally and Act Locally." Relevant here are local
campaigns too numerous to mention.[39] They include local government actions
to establish nuclear free zones, to disinvest in corporations doing business in
South Africa and to offer sanctuary to immigrants that the national immigration
service wishes to deport. This new paradigm is also reflected in the European-
centered "Towns and Development" program in which European towns and
cities have established programs for offering development assistance to Third
World towns and cities.[40] In some cases, as in Bruges, Belgium, this involves
the appointment of an Alderman for Development. Evidence of the growth in
these kinds of activities can be found in the new *Bulletin of Municipal Foreign
Policies*. Still missing is a more holistic vision of the implications of fragmentary efforts to identify and act on the local policy implications of growing
worldwide involvements manifest in the daily lives of people in local settlements.

Implications for Peace Research

Finally, what are the implications of these conclusions for peace research?
This is another way of saying: Where do peace researchers fit in our global
visions for peace movements? This is a fourth necessary element in global
visions for peace movements. Sheth, in an already quoted passage, aptly describes the challenge that confronts peace researchers:

> "It is the dialectic between micro-practice and macro-thinking that will
> actualize a new politics of the future...In brief a macro-vision is the
> prime need of these groups and movements, and this can be satisfied
> only by a growing partnership between activists and intellectuals in the
> process of social transformation."[41]

Other researchers too are saying that we must employ new methodologies
in the creation of knowledge of value to the grassroots. Catalin Mamali has
succinctly described the connection between research and participation by
observing that "the conscious participation of the members of a social community in its evolution process, *also depends upon the level and quality of participation of its members (specialists and laymen) in knowing the reality they live
in.*" Pointing out that each member of a community has a double cognitive
status, that of observed and that of observer, he notes that prevalent research

practice inhibits "'the subjects' natural observer status." Thus he concludes that a "just distribution of social knowledge cannot be reached unless its process of production is democratized."[42]

Grassroots peace movements are a serious challenge to present research agendas throughout the world. While necessary evidence is not available for making an authoritative worldwide assessment, it appears that grassroots movements in all continents have grown more rapidly than the capacity of researchers to observe and interpret their activities. Kinhide Mushakoji has observed that "peace research at the 'grass-roots' level should make special efforts to create new paradigms because it has been one of the weakest points of conventional peace research." Mushakoji advocates research based on the center-periphery paradigm, criticizing traditional peace researchers for having a "tendency to focus on the danger of potential war between the superpowers."[43] In other words, Mushakoji is asking that grassroots peace movements be put in the paradigm so that the impact of centers on the grassroots are made transparent, enabling individuals and groups at the grassroots to perceive the concrete activities through which this influence is transmitted. At the same time the efforts of grassroots movements to overcome peacelessness must be a part of the paradigm so that grassroots movements can use this knowledge for enhancing their potential.

Mushakoji also stresses the importance of basing grassroots peace research on the values of people living in grassroots communities, overcoming the tendency to import values in research paradigms developed in the centers. He further advocates that peace researchers should seek out the problems of local peace activists and address these problems in their research, feeding back the results to local activists, receiving feedback again and advancing with another round of research.

Mushakoji pushes even further in urging departure from the traditional research methodologies of academic centers, advocating that peace research at the grassroots level should approach local values through an organized effort of endogenous peace-learning. This conscientization process, he says, "must be developed in such a way that it deepens the awareness of 'peacelessness.'" In envisaging peace researchers as working with activists in the building of a peaceful grassroots community, he joins Paulo Freire in advocating that researchers and the people become co-investigators.[44] Mushakoji cites as an example of the kind of feedback process he is advocating research in India on the practice of nonviolent resistance.[45]

Notes

A version of this chapter was published in *The Future of the Peace Movements*, edited by Katsuya Kodama (Lund, Sweden: Lund University Press Research Insitute, 1989). It is reprinted here with permission of the author.

1.   Lester Milbrath, "Making Connections: The Common Roots Giving Rise to the Environmental, Feminist and Peace Movements," Annual Meeting of the International Society for Political Psychology, July, 1988.

2.   United Nations University, Memo for Panel of UN Experts, 'Life in Peace-3,' January, 1986.

3.   This section was extracted from Chadwick F. Alger, "A Grassroots Approach to Life in Peace: Self-Determination in Overcoming Peacelessness," *Bulletin of Peace Proposals* (1987), Vol. 18, No. 3, pp. 375-392.

4.   See Milbrath, "Making Connections: The Common Roots Giving Rise to the Environmental, Feminist and Peace Movements," p. 16.

5.   Ibid.

6.   Johan J. De Deken, "A Socio-Political Profile of the Current Peace Movement in Flanders," *Vredesonderzoek*, Interfacultari Overlegorggan Voor Vredesonderzoek van de Vrije Universiteit, Brussels (1988), No. 1.

7.   Karo Werner Brand, D. Busser and D. Rucht, *Aubruch Eine Andere Gessellschaft, Neue Soziale Bewegungen in der Bundersrepublik* (Frankfurt: Campus, 1983), as cited by De Deken, Ibid., pp. 8-9.

8.   Claus Offe, "New Social Movements: Challenging the Boundaries of Institutional Politics," *Social Research* (Winter, 1985), Vol. 52, No. 4; as cited by Saul H. Mendlovitz and R.B.J. Walker, eds., *Towards a Just World Peace: Perspectives from Social Movements* (London: Butterworths, 1987).

9.   Brian Tokar, *The Green Alternative* (San Pedro, CA: R & E Miles, 1987), pp. 55-56.

10. Rajni Kothari, "Mass, Classes and the State," in Mendlovitz and Walder, eds., *Towards a Just World Peace* (Boston: Butterworths, 1987), p. 400.

11. Rajni Kothari, "Party and State in Our Times: The Rise of Non-Party Political Formations," *Alternatives* (Spring 1984), IX, No. 4, p. 544.

12. *Ibid.*, pp.550-551.

13. *Ibid.*, p. 552.

14. *Ibid.*, p. 559.

15. *Ibid.*, p. 559.

16. See Kothari, 1987, p. 401.

17. Ibid., p. 401.

18. Ibid., p 401.

19. D.L. Sheth, "Grass-Roots Stirrings and the Future of Politics," *Alternative*, IX (1983), p. 23.

20. Ibid., p. 7.

21. See Kothari, 1987, p. 249

22. See Sheth, 1983, p. 7.

23. Mats Friberg and Bjorn Hettne, "The Greening of the World: Towards a Non-Deterministic Model of Global Processes," University of Gothenburg, Sweden (xerox), 1982, p. 23.

24. Ibid., p. 22.

25. Ibid., p. 36.

26. Ibid., p. 35.

27. Ibid., p. 42.

28. Rajni Kothari,

29. See Kothari, 1987, pp. 399-401.

30. Richard Child Hill, "Urban Political Economy: Emergency, Consolidation and Development," in Peter Smith, ed., *Cities in Transformation: Class, Capital, State* (Beverly Hills: Sage, 1984), p. 135.

31. Craig Murphy, "Understanding the World Economy in Order to Change It: A Plea for Including Studies of Social Mobilization in the World System Research Program," International Studies Association Convention, 1982, p. 1.

32. Ibid., p. 17.

33. For others, see Chadwick F. Alger, "Perceiving, Analyzing and Coping with the Local-Global Nexus," *International Social Science Journal* (August, 1988) 117, pp. 321-340.

34. Carol A. Smith, "Local History in Global Context: Social and Economic Transitions in Western Guatemala," in DeWalt and Pelto, eds., 1985, pp. 109-110.

35. Richard N. Adams, "The Dynamics of Societal Diversity: Notes from Nicaragua for a Sociology of Survival," *American Enthnologist* (1981), Vol. 8, No. 1, p. 2.

36. John W. Bennett, "Microcosm-Macrocosm Relationships in North American Agrarian Society," *American Anthropologist* (1967), Vol. 69, No. 1, p. 442.

37. Immanuel Wallerstein, "Household Structures and Labor-Force Formation in the Capitalist World-Economy," in Joan Smith, Immanuel Wallerstein and Hans-Dieter Evers, eds., *Households and the World Economy* (Beverly Hills: Sage, 1984), p. 21.

38. Robert Hackenberg, Arthur D. Murphy and Henry A. Selby, "The Urban Household in Dependent Development," in Robert McC. Netting, Richard R. Welk and Eric J. Arnould, eds., *Households: Comparative and Historical Studies of the Domestic Group* (Berkeley: University of California Press, 1984).

39. For more detailed treatment see Chadwick F. Alger and Saul H. Mendlovitz, "Grassroots Initiatives: The Challenge of Linkages," in Mendlovitz and Walker, eds., *Towards a Just World Peace: Perspectives from Social Movements* (London: Butterworths, 1987). Also see Alger, "Perceiving, Analyzing and Coping with the Local-Global Nexus," op. cit.

40. Nico Kussendrager, "Towns and Development: NGO and Local Authority Joint Action for North-South Cooperation Casestudies from Belgium, Germany, the Netherlands and the United Kingdom," second edition (The Hague: Towns and Development Campaign Secretariat, 1988).

41. See Sheth, "Grass-Roots Stirrings and the Future of Politics."

42. Catalin Mamali, *Societal Learning and Democratization of the Social Research Process* (Bucharest: Research Center for Youth Problems, 1979), pp. 13-14.

43. Kinhide Mushakoji, "Peace Research as an International Learning Process," *International Studies Quarterly* (June, 1978), Vol. 22, No.2, p. 186.

44. Paulo Freire, *Pedagogy of the Oppressed* (New York: Herder and Herder, 1971), p. 97.

45. For fuller treatment, see Alger, "A Grassroots Approach to Life in Peace: Self-Determination in Overcoming Peacelessness," *Bulletin of Peace Proposals* (1987), Vol. 18, No. 3, pp. 375-392.

21

A Paradigm for the New Peace Movements in Western Europe

Katsuya Kodama

The New Wave of Peace Movements

The big swell in new peace movements at the end of the 1970s and in the beginning of the 1980s was a political event which has exerted a significant amount of impact on our way of thinking about peace and security issues. In response to NATO's double-track decision to deploy Pershing IIs and cruise missiles, large peace movements arose in many of the West European countries. The mass demonstrations and gatherings in opposition to nuclear weapons held in several large cities of Western Europe are still fresh in our memory. The wave quickly crossed the Atlantic to the United States, where the main issues in question were the Freeze resolution and funding for new weapons systems. Stimulated by these movements, Japan also experienced both the emergence of new peace movements and the revival of previously existing peace movements. The movements in Japan attempted to issue a warning to the government that it must maintain its three previously established non-nuclear policies (policies prohibiting production, possession or deployment of any nuclear weapons on Japanese soil). In addition, it is important to mention several attempts to establish new independent peace groups in some of the East European countries.

Some peace organizations and initiatives, such as the Green party in West-Germany, No to Nuclear Weapons in Denmark and Norway and Freeze campaign, were newly born. At the same time, some old peace organizations such as CND (Campaign for Nuclear Disarmament) in the United Kingdom, and Peace and Arbitration Society in Sweden, were revitalized and renewed to meet the demands of the present age. The wave of these popular movements, with some unique characteristics different from the previous ones, are called the new peace movements. Although many of these movements have been less active for the last few years, the impact of their activities should not be underestimated.

It is not easy to find completely new elements in *the new peace movements*. Most of the elements which are now considered to be new can be found in an earlier peace movement, or another social movement. There are, however, differences in degree, political orientation and the context in which they are active. However, there are actually new trends in the new peace movements, without which the massive expansion of the movements would have hardly been possible. This paper attempts to examine some specific features of the new peace movements of the West European countries from the end of the 1970s to the beginning of the 1980's. Although the new peace movements in North America and Japan share some of the characteristics of the new peace movements in Western Europe, they are not covered in this paper.

It should be kept in mind that the movements are so diversified that any generalization runs the risk of over-simplifying the matter. In fact, some researchers have noted that diversification and heterogeneity are one of the more important characteristics of the new peace movements. It appears, however, that those arguments, which in essence assert that "the peace movement has no single position but rather hundreds of distinct positions, the peace movement is nowhere since it is everywhere," are not bound to promote meaningful debate. The attempt to generalize the characteristics of new peace movements in this paper invite both commentary and critique.

Actors

Well-Educated Middle Classes with One
or Two Socially Handicapped Conditions

A few studies on the class backgrounds of peace activists are available for our discussion of the peace movements of the 1960's. Frank Parkins' study of the Campaign for Nuclear Disarmament (CND) in Great Britain showed that the members of the movement were mainly drawn from highly educated people of the middle class.[1] Herman Schmid, in his study of a Swedish peace organization, 'Swedish Peace and Arbitration Society,' also demonstrated the concentration of the well-educated middle classes among the activists.[2]

A number of scholars have also argued that the core of the new peace movements is also well-educated middle classes, though they seem to lack concrete evidence for their conclusions.[3] However, the opinion polls conducted in Britain, Italy, the Netherlands, Norway, the Federal Republic of Germany and the United States in 1982 support their arguments. These polls indicate that anxiety about nuclear weapons is most prevalent among the well-educated middle classes.[4] Although high anxiety about nuclear weapons among well-educated middle classes cannot immediately prove their frequent participation in the peace movements, the data can be used as supportive evidence for the argument.

My survey, recently carried out on Swedish peace organizations, basically confirms this argument.[5] In general terms, it may be said that Swedish peace activists are predominantly A) well-educated, B) from the employed middle-classes, C) engaged in white collar occupations and D) frequently employed in the public sector. However, it should be noted that this general validity does not apply to all the peace organizations surveyed and that the Peace Committee constitutes a significant exception. The constitution of the social backgrounds of members of the Peace Committee is different from the other organizations, because the Peace Committee is an organization which shares the traditions of 'older' social movements as well as their Marxist-Leninist ideological orientation.[6]

The argument that the core of peace movements is the well-educated of the middle classes, nevertheless, seems to have some shortcomings. It has been verified that well-educated people are more likely to be found represented among activists than those with lower levels of education. In terms of social strata, the middle classes are more frequently represented than other class groupings. However, it would be a mistake to assume that these two characteristics are the only definitive marks of a peace activist. For one thing, one might ask whether or not some third characteristic might be generally shared by peace activists. It seems correct to say, as some leaders of peace organizations noted during my interviews, that *male well-educated middle classes* are conspicuously absent in the new peace movements.

My study of the 1983 World Assembly against Atomic and Hydrogen Bombs in Hiroshima clearly shows that young males and middle aged females were the most frequent participants. Middle aged males, a social category most likely to have high economic stability, exhibited a relatively low level of participation in the assembly. Although the survey does not give any data on educational and class characteristics, the lack of middle aged men in the peace activities urges the reconsideration of the argument that the core peace activists are the well-educated middle classes.

Chart 1. Constructions of Generations of Participants in the 1983 World Assembly against Atomic & Hydrogen Bombs:

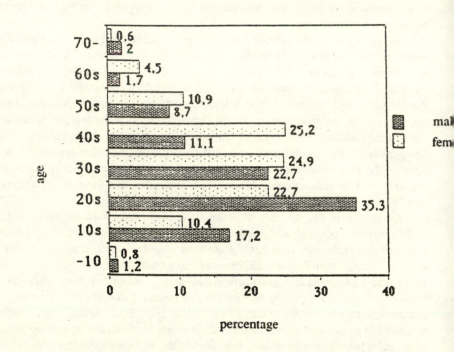

(In this survey, 702 questionnaires out of around 4,000 were answered: Return ratio was therefore around 17.5.)

Taking such observations into consideration, I suggest that the prevalent belief that the core actors are well-educated middle classes should be modified by adding *"with one or two socially handicapped conditions."* In fact, this proviso helps to explain the active involvement of women, university students, retired persons and the unemployed. If we use the Center-Periphery model, it can be said that the core of the new peace movements stands on the periphery of the center. One explanation for this is that if you are socially, economically and politically competent, you are likely to accept the status quo. This analysis reminds us of Galtung's theory of rank-disequilibrium.[7] By applying this theory, we arrive at the hypothesis that likely participants in the peace movements are in the condition of rank-disequilibrium, that is to say, Topdog in one dimension, but Underdog in another. In other words, complete Topdog and complete Underdog are not likely to be peace activists. Many female activists are, in my observation, fairly well-educated, but because of sex discrimination, their social position is lower than that of males. University students are placed high in the education category, but their income is usually very low; though it should be considered that their income bracket will likely change in the near future. The retired people who are involved in peace activities are mainly those who enjoyed relatively high economic and social positions when they were in their prime years, but have limited resources at present. The unemployed with relatively high educational background who become peace activists, are economically handicapped at the moment but their class status will probably be middle class when they are employed.

With this hypothesis in mind, we examined the correlations between A) gender dimension and age dimension, B) gender dimension and education dimension, and C) dimensions of occupation, income and income satisfaction, by using the data from my survey on the Swedish peace organizations.[8] Our multi-variate analysis showed that Galtung's theory of rank-disequilibrium is to a large extent both valid and useful. The analysis also verified our tentative hypothesis that the core actors in peace movements are drawn from the members of the middle classes who also have one or two socially handicapped conditions. This particular nuancing of the method of analysis will hopefully provide a tool for more sophisticated discussion of the social backgrounds of peace activists in the future.

Self-Identification

Concerning the new social movements, Claus Offe argues that the actors do not rely for their self-identification on either the established political categories (left/right, liberal/conservative, etc.,) nor on the partially corresponding socio-economic categories (such as working class/middle class, poor/wealthy, rural/urban population, etc.).

It seems correct to apply Offe's argument more specifically to the new peace movements, too. In previous peace movements, many of the participants--although there were important exceptions--identified themselves fairly clearly as belonging to the working classes and to the liberal-left political culture. The participants in the new peace movements, however, are less willing to find their identity in terms of socio-economic affiliation. Consequently, a crucial determinant factor would be 'what criteria they use for their self-identification.'

One of the striking features of the new peace movements is their sense of geographical-cultural identification. In European peace movements, slogans such as "Europe is one," or "Independent Nuclear Free-Europe" have repeatedly been employed. The plans to deploy American and Soviet nuclear missiles in many of the European countries have yielded a new Europeanism. The rise of new peace movements in Europe was a response of Europeans to the nuclear tyranny of the two superpowers. The successful creation of "European Nuclear Disarmament" (END) is both the result and the promoting factor for European identity among peace activists in Europe.

Gender differentiation is another important self-identifier in the new peace movements in Western Europe. The new peace movements are surprisingly dominated by women. Women's role in earlier peace movements was by no means insignificant, but it was not as important as that in the new movements. Despite the continuous existence of the Women's International for Peace and Freedom (WILPF) since 1915, the continuity of a broad women's anti-militarist tradition only became clear in the late 1970s with their independent role in the new peace movements.[9]

On 12 December 1982, some tens of thousands of women from the United Kingdom and continental Europe surrounded the air base at Greenham Common, where cruise missiles were due to be deployed. It is well-known that a small group of women have camped outside the base for years despite occasional imprisonment. In like manner, the idea of a women's peace camp has spread to other military bases in England, as well as to the Netherlands, Sicily, Canada and the United States.

Women in the Scandinavian countries have also been quite active. A group of women in Norway submitted a proposal to march from Copenhagen to Paris in 1981. Women for Peace groups, in support of the march, sprang up all over Scandinavia and 6,000 women (and 4,000 men) participated in the march. This was followed by a massive peace rally in Goteborg, Sweden in May 1982. These marches have now developed into 'The Great Peace Journey' activities.

A number of women researchers attempt to explain the dominance of women in the new peace movements in terms of specifically female characteristics.[10] They say that women, being brought up as the more peaceful gender, are more capable of solving conflicts in non-violent ways than men. They do not hesitate to say that women can and must play a crucial role in creating world peace, because these characteristics belong uniquely to women. What is important here is the strong connection between their sense of identity as women and their peace activities. It is clear that many female peace activists share this belief and have strong feelings of self-identification as the female sex.

Last but not the least, an important self-identification of actors of the new peace movements is their use of global or universal self-designations. They identify themselves as 'world citizens,' 'human beings,' or 'potential *Hibakushas* (victims of nuclear war.) This is not anything new. As the world becomes smaller and the danger of human annihilation increases, this self-identification becomes more popular and important than ever before. In this regard, one of the slogans of the peace movements, "Think globally, act locally!" seems to draw our special attention. As Alger maintains, new visions of what some would call micro-macro relations are an indispensable part of any useful global vision for peace movements. It is important to note that new self-identity as 'world citizens' is being developed through the activities at local levels.

It seems correct to say that these three self-identifications of the participants as Europeans, as women, and as world citizens are the crucial keys in the creation and increase of new peace movements in Western Europe.

Modes of Action/ Organizational Ways

Informality and Decentralization

According to Robert Michels, protest organizations survive and prosper to the degree that they adopt the systematization, centralization and bureaucratization of established institutions.[11] It seems, however, that the organizational structures of the new peace movements attempt to move in the opposite direction. Those involved in the new peace movements avoid and even hate centralization and bureaucratization, though there are significant exceptions like physicians' groups against nuclear weapons. The new peace movements are *informal, ad hoc, context-sensitive and egalitarian.*

The Freeze campaign in the United States, for example, has decentralized, informal and egalitarian characteristics. The principle of the self-determination of local groups counted heavily in this campaign. In spite of the fact that millions of American people supported the Freeze campaign, it is reported that the executive committee possessed only a fraction of the list of local activists. They had only extremely limited control over local groups.[12]

Symbolic of this point is the group of women camping outside the Greenham Common military base. In spite of their existing for a number of years, they have not developed a formal, systematized organizational structure. They have neither formal membership, nor formal leadership. Spontaneous participation of individuals is a fundamental principle of their operation.

It has been reported that other organizations in the new peace movements, (e.g., West German Green party,[13] No to Nuclear Weapons in Norway,[14] No to Nuclear Weapons in Denmark[15] and Women for Peace in Sweden),[16] are also highly informal and decentralized.

This grass-roots character of the new peace movements has no doubt encouraged spontaneity and vitality, which would be difficult under the aegis of solidly centralized and bureaucratized structures. As the new peace movements stagnate, however, the movements face a difficult dilemma between the need to create a more solid organizational basis and to retain their grass-roots character, the key source of their spontaneity and vitality.

Participation-Oriented Mobilization

The new peace movements are participation-oriented; they consist of campaigns, network formations, demonstrations, mass assemblies and voluntary helpers. Peace organizations usually have very small memberships, but they can and do mobilize the large masses for peace rallies and assemblies as their past history clearly shows. Many participants in the new wave of peace movements are not formally affiliated with any peace organization. Through information provided by mass media and/or personal networks, people spontaneously participate in mass demonstrations and mass assemblies. The peace organizations themselves, or even the campaign's own central planning committee, merely coordinate such mass mobilizations. Because of this campaign method of mass mobilization, it is very difficult for the organizers of a particular campaign to predict the number of participants beforehand.

'No to Nuclear Weapons' in Denmark, for example, has a small central office in Copenhagen which confines itself to coordination, communication and technical assistance functions. Although they successfully mobilized 60,000 to 100,000 people nationwide at the 1984 Easter march, the number of consistently active individuals working with 'No to Nuclear Weapons' is estimated to have been a mere 1,200 or so.[17] The success of a peace march or peace assembly is greatly dependent on the general atmosphere of the society in which it takes place.

One more extreme case which might be cited is 'Women for Peace' which operates in the Scandinavian countries. Women in the Scandinavian countries launched a women's movement for disarmament and peace in 1980. They successfully organized a peace march from Copenhagen to Paris in 1981; a massive rally in Goteborg in 1982; a march from Stockholm to Minsk in 1982; and 'Great Peace Journey' in 1985 and 1986 in collaboration with the Swedish section of WILPF. It merits attention, however, that, in spite of their energetic level of participation, women in the movement are skeptical of forming solid organizations. Although the Swedish group has recently begun to grant individual membership and has established a central office in Stockholm with a view to getting grants from official sources, other groups have remained distant from such practices. Instead, these other groups confine themselves to coordinating rallies, marches and petitions, without forming solid *organizational structures*. Activists in 'Women for Peace' are usually kept informed through well-developed information networks maintained by telephone, mail and personal visits.

In the new peace movements, individual participation is an essential element. The roles of organizations are, in some cases, merely to inform the public of meetings and to coordinate the activities of participants. This method of mobilization, however, has a few shortcomings. They are, among others, 1) lack of financial basis, 2) difficulty in maintaining a consistently strong program, 3) an ambiguously defined constituency and 4) difficulty in approaching divisive and/or complex issues (e.g., withdrawal from NATO). Whether this modus operandi is just a passing dream, which will be replaced again by more traditional solid systematizations, or whether it will remain an effective method of changing the political climate, is of sociological as well as political interest. Several years more must pass before we can answer this crucial question.

Political Ideology

Nuclear Pacifism Beyond the Bloc Theory
The basic ideology cherished by the past peace movements--the uprising in 1950s-60s and anti-Vietnam war movements--is a mixture of anti-imperialism and (nuclear) pacifism. Most of those involved in the movements criticized the American government and other allied powers for their imperialistic entanglement in the build-up of nuclear weapons or the Vietnam war. Many of those who protested in this manner belonged to the *'Marxist'* or *'new left'* political culture and values; although we should not neglect to mention some important exceptions such as apolitical radicals and religious pacifists. Some earlier movements even argued that the Soviet Union is a power acting on behalf of peace against American imperialism and that Soviet nuclear missiles are of a purely defensive character.

Political culture and values in the new peace movements are considerably different. The heated nuclear arms race between the two blocks cast a certain amount of doubt upon the belief in the 'peaceful character of Soviet missiles' as well as the validity of the notion of balance of power. The new peace movements do not accept the concept of defensive nuclear weapons. They argue that, *any nuclear weapons regardless of which political bloc possesses them are offensive and perilous*. The new movements make a harsh charge not only against the deployment of American nuclear missiles, but also against the deployment of Soviet nuclear missiles (e.g. the SS-20). It is not an exaggeration to say that nuclear pacifism is a key political ideology in the new peace movements.

Another important element, which is closely connected with what we have argued above, is that the actors attempt to go beyond the bloc theory. The East-West problem and how to do away with the two-bloc system are dominant topics of discussion in the new peace movements. The theory of balance of power, which is still advocated by military strategists and some politicians, is extremely unpopular among the new peace movements. It is in fact the frequent target of criticism. What the new peace movements in Europe are attempting to do is to create a unified and non-nuclear "greater Europe," by transcending the bloc confrontation.

On this point, the special attention given by the West-European peace movements to the independent peace movements of Eastern Europe is worthy of note. Since the beginning of the 1980's, a few attempts to establish unofficial, or independent peace groups in the Eastern bloc have been reported. They are, for example, Moscow Trust Group in USSR, Peace Group for Dialogue in Hungary, and Church Peace Movements in GDR. These movements have been heartily received by many of the Western peace movements. In fact, these attempts have been well covered by the magazines of West-European peace movements (e.g., *Journal of European Nuclear Disarmament*).

The question which must be asked is "Why are peace groups in the west paying so much attention to the small groups in the Eastern bloc when doing so might risk jeopardizing relations with the much bigger official peace movements there?" The answer is to be found in their belief in bringing about denuclearization *by transcending the bloc system*. What the new peace movements are seeking is not merely detente between the two blocs, but a new world order without antagonism between the two blocs. Their belief is that a dialogue with official movements, which are tied with the government in Moscow, will not contribute to transcending the bloc system and might even consolidate it, even though it has some potential to promote detente between the two divided blocs. The existence of independent peace movements is considered to be crucial by the West European movements. Without such movements, they believe it is not possible to move beyond bloc theory and its model of the world. They seek--and, if there is no group to be found to persuade people to establish--unofficial groups in the opposite political bloc which will not only call for de-nuclearization but also question the authoritative control by Moscow. The new peace movements are so passionately concerned about independent peace movements in the Eastern bloc, because the issue touches upon their central belief that the world order itself must be changed before their goals have a chance of being fully realized.

My questionnaire survey on Swedish peace activists contained a few questions to tap Soviet-U.S. orientation.[18] The following table shows the result from one of the questions.

Table 1. Responsibility for Political Tension
Question A: Which country do you think has the main responsibility for the political tension in the world today?

Groups/Answer	U.S.A.	Soviet Union	More or Less Same	N.A.
Christian Peace M.	13% (33)	0% (1)	84% (215)	3% (8)
Peace Committee	82% (110)	0% (0)	14% (19)	4% (5)
SPAS	24% (62)	1% (2)	75% (197)	1% (3)
WILPF	15% (37)	1% (3)	83% (208)	2% (4)
Women for Peace	25% (57)	0% (1)	73% (163)	1% (3)
General Public	4% (7)	11% (19)	82% (139)	2% (4)

If we compare the general public with the peace organizations, the general public places more responsibility on the Soviet Union (11%) than on the U.S.A. (4%), while respondents of the peace organizations place more responsibility on the U.S.A. (82% for the Peace Committee; 13-25% for the other organizations) than on the Soviet Union (0-1%). There are clear differences between the peace organizations and the general public in this respect. However, it also seems important to note that the high majority of both the general public and peace activists of the four peace organizations, with an exception of the Peace Committee, answered that U.S.A. and the Soviet Union are both responsible for the world tension in the similar degree. This finding confirms the argument that the new movements make a harsh charge not only against the deployment of American nuclear missiles, but also against the deployment of Soviet nuclear missiles (e.g., the SS-20).

But it is important to note that this argument is not valid for all the peace organizations. There is a clear cut between the Peace Committee which is much more critical of the U.S.A., and the other organizations in this respect. The anti-U.S.A. attitude of the Peace Committee is not so surprising, because 'the Peace Committee is an anti-imperialistic front organization for peace, for support of liberation movements against fascism and oppression,' as the program of the organization states.[19] To criticize imperialistic militarism of the United States is a natural consequence of this logic.

Values

Post-Material Values

Ronald Inglehart ascertained that there had been a *"silent revolution"* in values and attitudes affecting the entire population of some European countries.[20] He discovered that the aged cohorts, who had experienced the wars and scarcities of the era preceding the West European economic miracle, accord a relatively high priority to economic security and security needs, while among the younger cohorts, a set of "post-bourgeois" values, relating to the need for belonging, and to esthetic and intellectual issues, take higher priorities.

A number of scholars have mentioned the changes in values and attitudes among the participants in social movements. Jurgen Habermas, for example, mentions that the new conflicts in the last ten to twenty years no longer arise in areas of material reproduction but in areas of cultural reproduction, social integration, and socialization. The new conflicts are, he says, not sparked by *problems of distribution*, but concern the *grammar of forms of life*.[21] Similarly, Claus Offe describes the key values of new social movements as autonomy and identity (with their organizational correlates such as decentralization, self-government, and self-help) and opposition to manipulation, control, dependence, bureaucratization, regulation, etc., while key issues of old movements are considered to be economic growth, distribution and security.[22]

It is not difficult to find such "alternative,""post-material" values in the new peace movements, which clearly have some affinities with new social movements generally considered. Kim Salomon, for example, argues that the peace movements are essentially anti-establishment movements with post-material values whose central concepts are participation, solidarity and self-determination.[23] The new peace movements are not merely opposed to nuclear weapons and the political systems which produce nuclear confrontation, but also to entire cultures and value systems which exhibit strong links with nuclear weapons. In the new peace movements, nuclear weapons are considered symbolic of authoritarian, materialistic, bureaucratic, male-dominated culture.

In this regard, women's peace movements and ecologists' peace movements merit special attention. According to the perspective of women's movements, nuclear weapons and war systems are the products of authoritarian male culture, and therefore, the whole value system must be changed in order to eliminate nuclear weapons. They go so far as to say that we should stop discussing national security issues in terms of numbers of guns, because such a discussion reinforces the militaristic-materialistic culture, without questioning its fatal assumptions. Ecologists' peace movements and the Green party in West Germany, for example, are also strong critics of 'industrial' values. They do not accept the traditional concept of progress and criticize the established authorities. The fact that 'Green' representatives wear T-shirts at their Congress has a symbolic implication.

My questionnaire survey on Swedish peace activists attempted to measure the degree of post-materialist orientation of peace activists.[24] One important problem that faces us at the outset is what method to use to measure adherence to post-materialist values. In 1970 and in 1971, the European Community carried out public opinion surveys in France, West Germany, Belgium, The Netherlands and Italy. Data for 1970 are also available from Great Britain. These surveys included a series of questions designed to indicate which values an individual would rank highest. Ronald Inglehart utilized the results of this question to identify the extent of adherence to post-materialist, or post-industrial values. The question was formulated as follows:

> If you had to choose among the following things, which are the two that
>   seem most desirable to you?
> - Maintaining order in the nation.
> - Giving the people more say in important political decisions.
> - Fighting rising prices.
> - Protecting freedom of speech.[25]

According to Inglehart, views with an emphasis on order (first option) and economic stability (third option) can be said to contain materialist value priorities, while the choice of the items concerning political participation (second option) or free speech (fourth option) reflects an emphasis on post-materialist values. On the basis of the responses given on these four items, Inglehart classified the respondents into basically three value-priority types, namely a pure materialist type (order and economic stability), a pure post-materialist type (political participation and free speech) and an in-between type (a mixture of choices).

My survey on the Swedish peace activists followed Inglehart and used the same question for our analysis.[26] Table 2 shows the data on post-Materialist orientation of peace activists from the survey.

The contrast between peace activists and the general public is quite striking. Approximately two-thirds of peace activists from all five organizations have a post-material orientation, while the figure for the general public is a mere one fifth. Obviously, there is a much larger proportion of post-materialists in the peace movements than in the general public. The differences among the five peace organizations are very small. We note, however, that Women for Peace has slightly more post-materialists than other peace organizations, but the difference is not so salient. It seems quite possible and sufficient here to say that peace activists possess post-materialist values more strongly than the general public. Findings from our survey seem to be in agreement with the

Table 2. Post-Materialist Orientation of Peace Organizations

Groups	Materialist	In-Between	Post-Mater.	N.A.	Average V.
Christian Peace M.	1 (0%)	91 (35%)	163 (63%)	2 (1%)	1.64
Peace Committee	1 (1%)	41 (31%)	91 (68%)	1 (1%)	1.68
SPAS	3 (1%)	83 (31%)	176 (67%)	2 (1%)	1.66
WILPF	6 (2%)	91 (36%)	151 (60%)	4 (2%)	1.58
Women for Peace	2 (1%)	52 (23%)	169 (75%)	1 (0%)	1.75
General Public	20 (12%)	112 (66%)	34 (20%)	3 (2%)	1.08

arguments by some scholars that the new peace movements are not merely opposed to nuclear weapons and the political systems which produce nuclear confrontation, but also to entire cultures and value systems which exhibit strong links with nuclear weapons.

Concluding Remarks

A few years have already passed since the surprisingly massive and vigorous wave of peace movements in the beginning of the 1980s. Now that the dust from this whirlwind of activity is beginning to settle, a number of peace researchers, political scientists and sociologists have begun to direct their critical attention to an evaluation of this most recent wave of peace movements and to analyze their potential for realizing the social changes that they have been trying to bring about.

What we have attempted to show in this article is that peace movements are more than mere political pressure groups which simply demand policy changes on military issues. New peace movements challenge not only a government's policy on military issues but also call into question social structures, ways of thinking, life styles, values, etc. The society they are pursuing might be called the post-materialist society, civil society, green society, post-industrial society, alternative society or feminist society. Although their visions may not be clearly formulated yet, it can safely be said that they are struggling to establish a future society in which equality, environmentalism, solidarity, self-determination and peace are the basic principles. We do hope that this short article will be taken as a challenge to acknowledge the rich potentiality of new peace movements and an encouragement to further our understanding of this complex reality through further research.[27]

Notes

1. Frank Parkin, *Middle Class Radicalism; The Social Bases of the British Campaign for Nuclear Disarmament* (Manchester: Manchester University, 1968).

2. Herman Schmid, "On a Study of a Swedish Peace Organization," a paper presented at the Second Nordic Conference on Peace Research (Hillerod, Denmark, 1966).

3. For example, Kim Salomon, "The Peace Movement an Anti-Establishment Movement," in *Journal of Peace Research*, 1986, Vol. 23, No. 2.

4. International Herald Tribune (October 10, 1982).

5. November 1988 to February 1989 Survey. An extensive questionnaire survey was undertaken from November 1988 to February 1989. 300 members out of the total membership were selected completely randomly from each of the five Swedish peace organizations. In addition to the first questionnaire, two reminders were sent to the sampled members, except the members of the Peace Committee. Given the nature of the cooperation from peace organizations, the number of answers from our samples of peace organizations is higher than we expected. Final return ratio is 87% from the Christian Peace Movement, 45% from the Peace Committee, 89% from the Swedish Peace and Arbitration Society, 85% from the Swedish section of WILPF, 76% from Women for Peace and 63% from the general public. The return ratio from the samples of the Peace Committee is low because reminders were not sent to them because of technical difficulties. I would like to express my sincere gratitude for the kind cooperation of many peace activists and the Swedish peace organizations to the questionnaire survey. I do hope that findings from the survey will, in one way or another, be useful for peace activists who participated in the project.

6.   Katsuya Kodama, "Bibliography: Literature Survey on Peace Movement Studies," in K. Kodama, ed., *The Future of the Peace Movements* (Lund University Press, 1989).

7.   Johan Galtung, "A Structural Theory of Aggression," in *Journal of Peace Research*, 1964b, No. 2.

8.   See Kodama, "Bibliography: Literature Survey on Peace Movements Studies"; and November 1988 to February 1989 Survey.

9.   Nigel Young, "The Contemporary European Anti-Nuclear Movement," as *PRIO Working Paper 3/83*, 1983.

10.   Birgit Brock-Utne, "Feminism, Peace and Peace Education," in *Bulletin of Peace Proposals*, 1984, Vol. 15, No. 2; and Hilka Pietila, "Women's Peace Movement as an Innovative Proponent of the Peace Movement as a Whole," in *IFDA Dossier*, No. 43, September, 1984.

11.   Robert Michels, *Political Party* (Free Press, New York, 1908).

12.   David Lewis, "Tougher Choices for the Freeze," in *Not Man Apart*, October, 1984.

13.   Paul Wehr, "Disarmament Movements in the United States," in *Journal of Peace Research*, 1986, Vol. 23, No. 2.

14.   Lon Grepstad, "Norway and the Struggle for Nuclear Disarmament," a paper prepared for the 1981 World Conference Against Atomic and Hydrogen Bombs. Tokyo, Hiroshima and Nagasaki, 1981.

15.   M. Krasner & N. Petersen, "Peace and Politics: Danish Peace Movement and Its Impact on National Security Policy," in *Journal of Peace Research*, 1986, Vol. 23, No. 2.

16.   Jan Andersson & Kent Lindkvist, "The Peace Movement in Sweden," in Werner Kalterfleiter & Robert L. Pfaltzfraff, eds., *The Peace Movements in Europe and the United States*, (Croom Helm, London & Sydney, 1985).

17.   See Krasner & Peterson, "Peace and Politics: Danish Peace Movement and Its Impact on National Security Policy."

18.   See November, 1988 to February, 1989 Survey.

19.   See Andersson & Lindkvist, "The Peace Movement in Sweden."

20.   Ronald Ingelhart, "The Silent Revolution in Europe: Intergenerational Change in Post-Industrial Society," in *The American Political Science Review*, 1971, Vol. 65.

21.   Jurgen Habermas, "New Social Movement," in *Telos, 49*, Fall, 1981.

22.   Claus Offe, "New Social Movements: Challenging the Boundaries of Institutional Politics," in *Social Research*, Winter, 1985.

23.   See Kim Salomon, "The Peace Movement an Anti-Establishment Movement."

24.   See November, 1988 to February, 1989 Survey.

25.   See Inglehart, "The Silent Revolution in Europe: Intergenerational Change in Post-Industrial Society."

26. See November, 1988 to February, 1989 Survey.

27. Some of the findings in this article are included in my article "The Peace Movements for the Future--From a Survey on Swedish Peace Movements," in K. Kodama (ed)., *The Future of the Peace Movements* (Lund University Press, 1989).

22

Mass Communicators for Peace: Another Way

Kusum Singh

Can Peace Messages Win Mass Communication?

Is "Peace through strength" an effective peace message? Do scholars and teachers have a role in "communicating for peace?" To all these questions the answer is yes. But as spelled out in the following pages, this affirmation may depend, among other things, on rejecting reliance on mass media; transcending *machismo* definition of strength and broadening research and teaching to cope with the emerging role of mass movements in achieving mass communication.

In many countries peace activists are increasingly frustrated in efforts to communicate with enough people through the media. Indeed, many of them have learned that concentration on efforts to break into the media invites failure. It serves to convey the idea, which I contest, that the mass media--whether controlled by profit-seeking conglomerates or by the state--is invincible.

Media is a very effective tool; however, it serves no worthwhile purpose to try to get attention by merely hiring a public relations firm, or buying TV ads, trying to be media stars. The public relations firms are not only expensive, but happen to be more interested in selling advertisers access to the minds and ears of the audiences. The peace activists, on the other hand, are interested in organizing a mass movement to win the hearts and the minds of the people. In so doing, they might even succeed in circumventing the so-called powerful mass media.

Take the example of Mohandas Gandhi and his followers in India who had almost no access to all the then-available media of communication: the press, the radio, the schools, and the major bureaucratic organizations. Indeed, many observers in the early 1940s believed that British colonial control of India was an immutable fact and the British themselves believed in their own invincibility. Yet, Gandhi and his followers were able to overcome enormous obstacles in communicating highly controversial messages to huge masses of the people dispersed over vast areas (as did other successful leaders before mass media were invented).[1] But while Gandhi became one of the biggest media stars in history, he achieved this status of "great communicator" *without aiming at the media primarily*. Interestingly enough, the former Prime Minister Rajiv Gandhi's recent reenactment of Mahatma Gandhi's historic Salt March of 1930 did not achieve the same result. The Indian people perceived it as a government publicity stunt to distract their attention from domestic problems. The *Indian Express* called it "the dandy's march to the 21st century."

In an overly technological age, it is easy for politicians and communication professionals to fall prey to the mass media's sensational "photo opportunities" of gimmickry and of overreporting violence whenever and wherever it occurs. Unfortunately, this serves to convey the idea that form is more important than content and that the struggling people around the world better resort to violence if they want media attention.

Peace activists have nevertheless been successful in achieving mass communication in various parts of the United States. Mitch Snyder's Center for Creative Non-Violence has drawn attention to the plight of the homeless and the Beyond War Organization has succeeded in suggesting real peace alternatives to war. Certain fundamental social change is slowly taking place in the direction of a more egalitarian, less racist and less sexist society.

The United States is a country where the normal channels of public activism are more widely used than in any other large country of constitutional capitalism.[2] These channels include voter registration, candidate selection, electioneering, and efforts to influence elected and appointed officials through lobbies, petitions and consultation. Yet popular interests can often best be served when activists also engage in marches, demonstrations, strikes or, in some cases, open civil disobedience. To produce national changes, the local activists need to communicate through nonmedia and small media channels, instead of relying on the major mass media.

Jesse Jackson's presidential campaign is a very good example of how working through face-to-face contacts, small organizations and networking can slowly succeed in mobilizing people for militant and effective action without over-reliance on CBS or NBC or ABC. *The New York Times* called his campaign "one of the most cost-effective campaigns of modern politics. Mr. Jackson has been gathering delegates at a cost of about $10,000 each, as against about $25,000 a delegate for Governor Dukakis, the biggest spender on the Democratic side."[3] According to *The Nation*, Jackson is not only a media star but is able to speak such "unspeakable words" as race, class, equality on behalf of the most "dispossessed" and disaffected" Americans of all. The Nation editorial goes on to say that "Despite the contempt and condescension of the media--or perhaps because of it--Jackson went to the most remote and isolated grass roots in the American social landscape to find the strength for a campaign that has already begun to transform politics."[4]

Despite media inattention, nonviolence as a force for social struggle was effectively demonstrated by the Druze of the Golan in the face of overwhelming Israeli police and military force. For many people, first awareness of the Druze came as the result of the fighting in Lebanon in the wake of Israel's invasion of that country in June 1982.[5] Much less publicized were the Druze villagers in the Syrian Golan Heights, who waged a courageous nonviolent campaign against the Israeli occupation in 1982. The initial cause for the uprising was the final passage of legislation formally annexing the Golan to Israel in 1981. The Druze were then to be forced into accepting Israeli citizenship and giving up their own identity. They appealed and petitioned for a reversal of the decision, without success. Then, finally they publicly pronounced their intent not to cooperate with any attempt to coerce the Druze into Israeli citizenship.

The Israelis conducted a campaign of disinformation and fabricated press reports to the effect that the Druze resistance had been abandoned. Instead, their struggle became even more well known through "walking newspapers." Despite the fact that the villages were cut off from one another by armed soldiers, they knew which village was running short of food through interpersonal channels of communication. The villagers would walk en masse to that neighboring village, overwhelm the Israeli soldiers, not merely by sheer numbers, but more so by their entry. Groups of women would surround Israeli soldiers and sometimes succeed in wresting at least some weapons from their hands. They would then hand the guns over to Israeli army officers, requesting the removal of the forces. Once, several Israeli soldiers were locked inside a stable. Villagers took the keys to the commanding officer, told him where they were locked, and suggested he let them out and send them home.

Nonviolence is based on the belief that all human beings have a conscience to which it is possible to appeal, no matter how brutal they may appear. Moreover, the power of love against an opponent can be the most revolutionary weapon in rendering the weapons of an adversary impotent. The so-called "weak" invite suffering on themselves rather than inflict it on their opponents. This in turn may result in a sense of guilt, or at least some conflict, in the mind of the oppressor, if not complete conversion.

I suggest that, *subject to many conditions and adaptations*, nonviolence as practiced by Gandhi might become relevant in various parts of the world. With enough understanding of his communication ideas and techniques, some people may be able to invent more human approaches to communication and leadership. We know that nonviolent struggle empowers every man, woman, child, and elderly to take an active part in shaping her/his destiny. That struggle may arouse not only sympathy and support from people around the world, but also help split the opponents by appealing to their conscience. Johan Galtung reports, "Personally I have experienced both in Rhodesia, before it became Zimbabwe, and in India in its fight with the Sikh community, top police officers telling me that they would have relatively little difficulty handling violence but no idea of what to do if '100,000 Africans should march nonviolently on Salisbury' or 'the Sikhs should turn themselves into a massive civil disobedience campaign with millions of participants.'"[6]

Although casualties cannot be avoided in any struggle challenging an oppressive system, violence undoubtedly causes more deaths. For instance, eight thousand out of a population of 200 million in India were killed in a nonviolent struggle against the British; while one million Algerians, out of a population of between nine to ten million, died in a violent war in the independence struggle against the French.

Noncooperation, that is withdrawal or withholding of one's cooperation can go a long way in overcoming an unjust system, whether it be social, political or moral. In the Greek play, *Lysistrata*, women refused to have sex with their husbands "unless you men negotiate a truce and make an end of war." Recently Brazilian women used the same method against the military regime to prod their men to return to civilian rule. In the Philippines, the military power of Marcos was rendered inoperative by ordinary people, including nuns and priests, who confronted his soldiers upon finding out that elections had been a fraud.

Peace Through Strength, Yes!

By strength, I do not mean an overkill capacity that conjures up an image of machismo. Behind any image of strength may in fact lie the reality of weakness. The men in neither the White House nor the Kremlin could *use* their "superpower" strength without destroying themselves along with more civilized parts of humanity.

I am talking, rather, of the strength that flows less from fire power and more from the courage to organize nonviolent resistance to militarism and aggression. In the largest nonviolent mass movement in history, Mohandas Gandhi and his followers succeeded in uniting the Indian people divided by religion, caste, language, gender and social role. They miraculously transformed an elite struggle into an open popular movement against the military might of the British.

The civil disobedience movement led by Martin Luther King Jr. and his followers in the United States was also a moral crusade instead of an armed rebellion. They too succeeded in awakening thousands from decades of apathy and hopelessness. Their strength flowed from their personal courage in risking their own lives in nonviolent combat against police brutality and machine-gun fire.[7] Indeed, as with Gandhi's mass movement, they too made news by being willing to die on behalf of freedom from oppression. In so doing, they stirred the conscience of the world.

Kenneth Boulding points out that historians have been singularly insensitive to the kind of innovation that Gandhi's nonviolent struggle made toward combining defiance with disarming behavior which helped turn the threatener and the threatened into a "we" group.[8] Gandhi was an innovator in the sense that he did not play according to the rules expected by the British regime. He confronted his powerful adversary with a new political instrument based on "soul-force" rather than "physical force." The transformation was possible because the substance of the messages was based on widespread popular needs and sentiments.

But can a nonviolent struggle within one nation be successfully developed into a larger international movement toward a more peaceful world? Can nations with different systems and ideologies sit down and talk instead of throwing around accusations? Overcoming communication barriers between nations, however, does not necessarily mean that the genuine needs of the people of the world will be met. A more perfect two-way horizontal communication between the top elites of the world may merely open up a more efficient system of manipulation of the people at large.[9] In other words, "Persons, families, neighborhood or village groups and even university departments, labor unions, and ordinary legislators are but pygmies in comparison with the huge private and public bureaucracies and globe-spanning clusters, constellations, complexes and establishments that dominate most of the planet. People are increasingly objects to be studied, polled, influenced, encouraged to quarrel among themselves and, in some cases, co-opted or drawn into ritualistic dramas of fraudulent participation."[10]

According to Riane Eisler, it is impossible to build a just and peaceful world on a "dominator" system made up of global corporate, military and political leaders. Instead, she calls for a "partnership" system that includes the great majority of middle- and low-income people at the bottom of the 'Eiffel Tower' pyramid of wealth and power. More important, their activity is oriented toward developing common purposefulness rather than exploitation.[11]

Serious study of progressive mass movements of the past and of today's struggles toward structural reforms in the interest of just peace can be enormously rewarding for communications scholars. The rich heritage of nonviolent struggle needs to be retrieved as part of our history. This is very important because what we see as happening in the past, helps to determine what we see as our present and future options. If we see history as predominantly characterized by violence, even though in fact it was not, we will assume that our only realistic choices are "wars to end war." In other words, "A very important question in the interpretation of history is how we see war: as an interruption in the evolution of peaceful behavior, or as the essential dynamic of history, where peace is just an interval between wars."[12]

Nonviolent movements have wielded great power in the past and they were extremely important in the shaping of history. According to Professor Gene Sharp of Harvard's Center for International Affairs, "Societies that have had a major part of their history formed by nonviolent struggle often have not themselves recorded that history for posterity."[13] He gives the example of the Hungarian nonviolent struggle against Austria in the mid-nineteenth century which forced the Austrian empire to recognize the Hungarian constitution and helped form the boundaries in Central Europe. Yet even in the Hungarian language, that struggle, as pointed out by Gene Sharp, does not have a good historical account.

There were nonviolent struggles even against the Nazis about which we know very little. One of these occurred in Berlin, forcing the release of at least 1500 Jewish men in 1943. That case has only recently been researched.

Even the American War of Independence (1776-1783) needs a fresh analysis by researchers who are not afraid of questioning some of the premises that have been accepted for so many centuries as "given." For instance, a recent study reports that while on occasion impatience led to violence, the colonists employed nonviolent practical methods of persuasion to demonstrate their willingness to sacrifice for their beliefs. The women went to their spinning wheel and undertook the responsibility of producing homespun cloth that resulted in a drastic drop in the English imports to the American colonies from 2.5 million pounds sterling to 2.0 million in 1765. "The colonists united against the British through nonviolent economic pressures. They boycotted English cloth, gave up their 'mourning rituals' which required a great deal of British lace, reduced their consumption of British tea and organized regional boycotts of other English goods."[14] The power of their resolve was evident in the British reaction to these boycotts. Within a short time, the English government repealed several of the acts that the colonists were opposing. In other words, the Americans had initiated what Gandhi would more than a century later use successfully in South Africa and India.

No doubt, there are many more cases of nonviolent struggles which seemed to have slid into some deep "memory hole" of history. How many of us, for instance, know of the Muslim nonviolent uprising in the Northwest Frontier Province of British India led by the Muslim Khan Abdul Ghaffar Khan (known as the Frontier Gandhi). Gandhi was particularly impressed by their struggle since Afghans are better known for their martial confrontation rather than submitting themselves to the discipline of nonviolence in fighting an oppressive regime.

A more glaring example is the way "history" has ignored "herstory." Jean Baker Miller documents the manner in which most of the members of the professional and academic world still do not consider the study of women to be serious work: "There were always some slaves who revolted; there were some women who sought greater development of self-determination. Most records of these actions are not preserved by the dominant culture, making it difficult for the subordinate group to find a supporting tradition and history."[15] For Riane Eisler "The problem begins with the fact that the information gathered by most experts chronically leaves out women. Thus, most policymakers work with only half a data base. But even if the data is before their eyes, policymakers still cannot take appropriate action if the present system is maintained."[16]

Needless to say that to change political, economic, social, cultural and religious institutions demands a great deal of energy and courage. Each new step reveals the necessity of analyzing more deeply the cultural and psychological forces impinging on us all. For instance, there are a great many people who believe nonviolence to be powerless against military power. Could it be that it is in the interest of those in power to teach us that only violence is successful because they themselves have military superiority? They therefore have a greater chance to maintain oppression if the oppressed also believe in violence.

Israel, for instance, would feel far more threatened if the Palestinians were to organize a totally nonviolent struggle in the occupied West Bank and Gaza. Mubarak Awad, an Arab, who tells his fellow Palestinians that nonviolent methods offer the best hope of ending Israel's 20-year occupation of the West Bank, has been expelled by the Israeli government. Logically, one would think that Awad's Palestinian Center for the Study of Nonviolence in Jerusalem would be welcomed by Israel for its peaceful means of expressing Palestinian nationalism. Instead, the Israeli government is actively developing means to reduce the potential impact of a nonviolent struggle.[17] This is being done both through legal strictures drastically curtailing the ability to organize and through harsh repression of any militant nonviolent action. The nonviolent activists know that their success depends on using superior moral means, "When you are able, competent and generous, you don't need arms."[18]

What Can Communication Scholars Do?

What we can offer toward peace depends on a number of factors, of which perhaps none is more important than helping to bring about a worldwide change of attitudes of people toward war and peace. "Since wars are born in the minds of men (women and children)," states the Preamble of the UNESCO Charter, "it is the minds of men where we have to erect the ramparts of peace."[19]

Can communication scholars help bring about this miracle? In part, without doubt. Many communication experts have already shown remarkable strength--both intellectual and moral--in exposing the myriad misuses of the media. On the other hand, there are obvious difficulties. The best work of those well-known and hundreds of less well-known researchers has been "against the stream," underfunded and (as one might well expect) either ignored or distorted by the mass media. Moreover, it is not easy for any researcher to escape the dead hand of value-free positivism and face up openly to the value premises that guide all research.

Communication is a young science in relation to the depth and richness of the human experience. Younger still is serious research on holistic approaches to war and peace. The combined power of several approaches, properly synthesized and applied, can add up in a reasonable time to progress of breakthrough proportions. The full power of what mass communication can offer can only be appreciated if the various strands of human communication are grasped as a whole. Perhaps it is far easier to be a specialist and document effects of violence and aggression than to approach human behavior holistically and look for more positive trends.

Indeed, this is a difficult challenge for mass communication researchers, as well as for activists, to understand how diverse and conflicting strands came together as they did, in the many mass movements of the past and succeeded through moral and economic strength rather than military force. As Loren Eiseley points out, "...science is not natural to man at all. It has to be learned, consciously practiced, stripped out of the sea of emotions, prejudices and wishes in which our daily lives are steeped. No man can long endure such rarefied heights without descending to common earth. Even the professional scientist frequently confines such activity to a specific discipline and outside of it indulges his illogical prejudices."[20]

Truly constructive research would recognize that the fate of any apparently progressive movement may depend on whether communication scholars can escape the "media trap" by recognizing the vital roles of interpersonal, organizational and political communication--roles underestimated when professionals overemphasize mass media. We also need to examine, in more depth, the power of moral values as expressed through personal example and cooperative action. Gandhi's liberation movement, like many mass movements around the world, was national and not international in its scope. Can the United Nations as a peace-keeping force be strengthened through trade, travel and even intermarriages across the international borders?

The insights especially relevant to peace come from research on perception and attribution, and creation of images and myths about power and leadership. The constant bombardment of violence in TV, cinema and popular novels would suggest that war dominates our perceptions of the world and our relations to it. In fact, Boulding maintains that peaceful pursuits like, "plowing, sowing, reaping, producing, falling in love, having children, dancing, singing, having fun, learning, studying--represent somewhere between 85 to 95 percent of human activity and that over the years war has rarely been more than 5 to 15 percent."[21]

As for leadership ability, most discussions bow to the old-fashioned idea of charisma--the kind of autocratic charisma that encourages dependency rather than motivates people to work together on their own initiative. According to Max Weber, charisma is a "certain quality of an individual personality by virtue of which he is set apart from ordinary men and treated as endowed with super-natural, superhuman qualities and regarded as of divine origin."[22] Still earlier, in his "Great Man" theory of history, Carlyle had noted the importance of extraordinary personal characteristics. Nietzsche went still further with his concept of "uber mensch," literally "over-man" or "superman." But all these terms, charisma, the Great Man, superman, express an underlying ancient theme that autocratic leaders with extraordinary superhuman characteristics are needed to lead the "ignorant masses" into the age of enlightenment.

My research on Gandhi suggests that there can be another kind of charis-ma--a democratic charisma.[23] This is the kind of charisma that mobilizes people for self-activation rather than pacifying them by encouraging dependen-cy. As Nehru pointed out, Gandhi "did not descend from the top but rather seemed to emerge from the millions of India, speaking their language and incessantly drawing attention to them and their appalling condition."[24] In other words, Gandhi was very much a part of the ordinary men and women and endowed with not divine but rather superordinary qualities of common touch. His leadership was based on simplicity and humility, not quite in keeping with the traditions of Indian elites. His charismatic tie to the Indian people was based more on reality, than on an ingenious concoction of superhuman power. And yet, Gandhi could not escape the onslaught of deification. In India, after the British were thrown out and Gandhi was assassinated in 1948, he was bestowed with an awe-inspiring charismatic status by the new elites of modern India.

The idea of a leader's self-identification with followers, of course, was not an invention of Gandhi or Martin Luther King or even Jesse Jackson. For centuries peasant leaders have done this. A little earlier, during the period leading to the 1917 Russian revolution, Lenin had also done this. Although very much of an elitist, Lenin nonetheless went much further than most of the other Bolsheviks of his day in living a simple life, identifying himself with the workers and peasants he hoped to win to the Bolshevik cause, and opening his mind to their complaints and ideas. More recently, one can find the same quali-ty--in varying proportions--in those many Third World leaders who have been successful in leading "Marxist-Leninist" rebellions or revolutions: Castro,

Neto, Cabral, Mondlaine and above all the many lesser known or unknown Sandinistas in Nicaragua and their counterparts in El Salvador, Honduras and Guatemala. Then in Iran, there is the fascinating phenomenon of Ayatollah Khomeini, who speaks autocratically in the name of Allah but in all his modes of life symbolises personal austerity. There are the even more interesting examples of Lech Walesa, the leader of the Solidarity Movement in Poland, and Vaclav Havel of Czechoslovakia, pointing to new Eastern European movements dedicated toward the building of genuine socialism.

Entrenched perceptions of unique charismatic leaders capable of leading humankind out of the wilderness of alienation, inflation and the arms race become so interwoven with the-way-things-are that they become very difficult to change.[25] Take for example, the experience of the Soviet Union and the United States. Even after the Stalin era of terror and the experience of Vietnam, Cambodia, Watergate and Irangate when the Soviets and the Americans began to learn the lessons of power and its limitations, many in these countries are still eager to follow a leader who promises charismatic and technocratic solutions to democratic problems. Ronald Reagan, after all, was acclaimed as the "Super-American" by the *New York Times*.[26]

Indeed, political observers are still puzzled by Reagan's personal popularity (even after Iran-Contra and other sleazy affairs) among large numbers of people who rejected most of his policies. They would have us believe that technical mastery of television is the secret of Reagan's success. They ignore the creativeness of a new breed of experts, who specialize in manufacturing images that appeal to the subconscious aspirations, deep emotions and latent values of target audiences. One possible explanation for Reagan's "mastery of television" perhaps is the enormous appeal of a few deeply held values, simply presented, as contrasted with the confusing complexity of such basic issues as war, racism, sexism, poverty, unemployment, environmental degradation, hunger and homelessness.

"What are the values projected by the political image makers?" This question can best be answered by applying to political campaigns, the same powerful tools of analysis pioneered by George Gerbner and his associates in probing imagery and violence in American TV entertainment. As founders of the 'cultural indicators' school, they have sought to arrive at the 'meaning' structure of dominant forms of television output by way of systematic quantitative analysis of overt elements of television representation.[27] These sensitive practitioners of content analysis are increasingly concerned with a more critical, qualitative analysis which may be perceived by the traditionalists as "low in objectivity." No matter how ambiguous such an attempt may seem, it is nevertheless of value in interpreting and capturing the functional importance of these images.

Such analysis can, moreover, help demystify politics by unmasking the content hidden by the politics of form: "It is not the ability of President Reagan to communicate that brought him his enormous popularity; rather, it was the decline in inflation and the leveling off of unemployment that made Reagan's form persuasive."[28] Other scholars point out that "there is a strength in Reagan's presidency that recent politicians have forgotten, namely that presidents are teachers and invokers of memory. The president is the ceremonial leader, the keeper of the myth."[29]

Fundamentally then, the question that needs to be addressed is: How to distinguish between reality and imagery? More importantly, how to replace false imagery with genuine commitments tested in action? How do we identify leaders that encourage dependency of their followers by projecting charismatic images of themselves as capable of solving all problems? And can we identify other kinds of charismatic characteristics in a leader that encourages self-reliance and self-confidence of their followers in doing things in cooperation with other people?

Eric Fromm points out that when peoples' efforts to act responsibly and creatively are frustrated, they attempt to identify themselves with those who do have power and prestige in real life or in fantasy. Instead of accepting their own powerlessness, they find escape in identifying themselves with charismatic leaders and celebrities extolled by the media.[30] Thus, in West and East, North and South, leaders may easily mislead their people into justifying their imperial ventures as national interests and distract peoples' attention from domestic failures.

Genuine development of peace and democracy in any country requires enormous and continuing participation by the majority of the people at all times and not merely during the elections. And the emergence of such participation depends not only on spontaneous actions by large numbers of people but also on the nature of leadership and the kinds of actions led. Special attention is, therefore, needed to project the imagery used by progressives in trying to promote the widespread participation in decision-making that is the essence of genuine, rather than nominal or formalistic, democracy.

Neither do we know very much yet about a possibility even more intriguing for world peace: What are the effects when the same image is affirmed by vast numbers of people? Today's widespread fear of nuclear holocaust or collective resignation over the impossibility of real peace, may be having a far more profound negative effect in world affairs than has yet been appreciated.

Similarly, a spreading belief in the achievability of peace might have positive effects that would go far beyond the obvious generation of hope and motivation. Professor Richard Smoke and Willis Harman in their very impressive book, *Paths to Peace*, maintain that "some psychological conditions that hinder peace--hostile expectations, unconscious attractions to conflict, and so on--may be overcome more readily by techniques for the affirmation and imaging of peace than perhaps by rational discussion."[31] It is useful to have an image of a possible future, according to these authors, particularly an image that is consistent with present knowledge and realistically consistent with what one wants the future to be. It may be especially helpful to contemplate images of the future that differ from the present in fairly fundamental ways--ways as fundamental as the contemporary "paradigm shift" appears to be.[32] In other words, social change means "delegitimizing of war" in a more fundamental and comprehensive way, so that we come to believe that war is obsolete.

Has not the necessary attention of communication scholars to the mass media often resulted in the fatal error of confusing the part with the whole? Has it not too often diverted attention from other aspects of communication in the sense of "the way in which people come to accept things in common."[33]

A mass movement is one way in which people come to accept things in common. As I have already indicated, it is not only based on inter-personal and organizational communication, it is also a way in which ordinary people can get around--or into--the mass media without too much reliance on mass media. Other modes of communication are exemplified by the work of the United Nations, its General Assembly, its Security Council and the many UN subsidiary organizations in which people come together to debate problems that transcend national boundaries. Strangely, these forms of global communication are rarely reported in the U.S. media. Thus, how many people ever heard that in November 1984, the General Assembly adopted a resolution proclaiming that all people have "a sacred right to peace?" Should not both mass movements and UN activities--including coverage of both by the small media and the mass media--be added to our agenda on communication research and education?

Transnational communication should also include lateral or horizontal communication at all levels of a society. My term for this, "bottom sideways" communication refers to a circular process that has the merit of leading to bottom-up as well as top-down decision making.[34] Many groups of Soviet and U.S. people have been visiting each other to learn more about their common interests and the possibilities of a peaceful future. These activities will be increasingly helped by the long-range program "Human Rights in the Future," sponsored by the American Council of Learned Societies and the Soviet Union's Institute of State and Law. This program is aimed at getting both researchers and activists to undertake the many necessary steps needed to make it possible for the year 2000 to be legitimately seen as a slow dawn of the first "Human Rights Century."

Notes

1.   Kusum Singh, "Mass Line Communication: Liberation movements in China and India" in G. Gerbner and M. Siefert, eds., *World Communication: A Handbook* (New York: Longman, 1984), pp. 302-308. For a more detailed documentation, see "Gandhi and Mao as Communicators: A Comparative Study of Practice and Theory," Doctoral Dissertation (University Microfilms International, 48106, University of Pennsylvania, 1978).

2.   G. Gross and Kusum Singh, "Democratic Planning: The Bottom-Sideways Approach" in Gartner, et al., ed., *Beyond Reagan* (New York: Harper & Row, 1984), pp. 286-305.

3.   *The New York Times* (March 27, 1988).

4.   *The Nation* (April 16, 1988).

5.   S.R. Kennedy, "The Druze of the Golan: A Case of Nonviolent Resistance," *Journal of Palestine Studies*, 1987, pp.48-64.

6.   Johan Galtung, "On the Causes of Terrorism and Their Removal," *IFDA Dossier* (July/August, 1988), pp. 29-42.

7.   In the United States, Martin Luther King, Jr. embraced satyagraha as the only moral and practical way for oppressed people to struggle against social injustice. See Stephen B. Oates, *Let the Trumpet Sound: The Life of Martin Luther King, Jr.* (New York: Harper & Row, 1982).

8.   Kenneth Boulding, "Moving From Unstable to Stable Peace," in A. Gromyko and M. Hellman (ed.), *Breakthrough: Emerging New Thinking* (New York: Walker and Company, 1988), pp. 163. Published simultaneously in the Soviet Union by Progress Publishing Company, Moscow.

9.   Kusum Singh, "Elite Control and Challenge in Changing India," in G. Gerbner (ed.), *Mass Media Policies in Changing Cultures* (New York: John Wiley & Sons, 1977), pp. 147-158.

10. G. Gross and Kusum Singh, "The Golden International: Communication Triumph and Breakdown," in H. Didsbury (ed.), *Communications and The Future: Prospects, Promises, and Problems* (Bethesda, Maryland: World Future Society, 1982), pp. 32-38.

11. Riane Eisler, *The Chalice and the Blade* (San Francisco: Harper & Row, 1987).

12. See Boulding, *op. cit.*, p.162.

13. Gene Sharp, *Nonviolent Struggle* (Philadelphia: New Society Publishers, 1983).

14. W.A. Smith, "From Nonviolence to War: The American Justification," paper presented to Peace and Conflict Studies, University of California, Berkeley, Spring, 1988.

15. Jean Baker Miller, *Toward a New Psychology of Women* (Boston: Beacon Press, 1986).

16. See Eisler, *op. cit.*, chapter 12.

17. See Kennedy, op. cit.

18. Comment by Yeshya'ahu Toma Sik, of the World Service Authority and War Resisters International/Israel Section, Tel Aviv, during the February 5, 1983, visit to Majdal Shams in the Golan Heights. Cited by S.R. Kennedy, Ibid.

19. United Nations, UNESCO Charter.

20. Loren Eiseley, *The Man Who Saw Through Time* (New York: Charles Scribner's & Sons, 1973).

21. See Boulding, op. cit.

22. Max Weber, *The Theory of Social and Economic Organizations* (New York: Free Press, 1947).

23. Kusum Singh, "People against Charisma," *Communicator*, pp. 20-25. This was further discussed in my January, 1987 interdisciplinary course on "Two Faces of Charisma" at Saint Mary's College of California. Then again in the Fall semester, Communication Department senior students analyzed it in "Image and Charisma" seminar.

24. Jarva Nehru, *Nehru on Gandhi* (New York: The John Day Company, 1948).

25. Kenneth Boulding, *The Image* (Ann Arbor: The University of Michigan Press, 1956). Boulding's concept of "image" relates basically to anything that is perceived, as distinguished from Boorstein's concept, which relates only to those images defined by him as "pseudo events" in his book by the same name.

26. *The New York Times* (April 5, 1981).

27. G. Gerbner and L. Gross, "Living with Television: The Violence Profile," *Journal of Communication* (26:2, 1976), pp. 172-199. Also see Gerbner (1986) "Television imagery and the populism," paper presented at the International Association for Mass Communication Research, New Delhi.

28. A. Sanders and K. Wagner, "The Myth of Charisma in American Politics," *Social Policy* (Winter, 1988), pp. 57-60.

29. J. Carey, "Reagan and the Mythology of the American Childhood," *In These Times* (August 19-Sept. 1, 1987).

30. Erich Fromm, *The Heart of Man* (New York: Free Press, 1966).

31. Richard Smoke and Willis Harman, *Paths to Peace: Exploring the Feasibility of Sustainable Peace* (Boulder: Westview Press, 1987).

32. *Ibid.*, chapter 5.

33. This is the definition used by John Dewey after his assertion that "There is more than a verbal tie between the words common, community, and communication. Men live in a community by virtue of the things they have in

common." Quoted by Ashley Montague (1979) in *The Human Connection*. (McGraw Hill), p. ix. Building on Dewey, Montague begins his book this way: "Communication is the name we give to the countless ways that humans have of keeping in touch--not just to words and music, to pictures and print, but also to cries and whispers, nods and becks, postures and plumages: to every move that catches someone's eye and every sound that resonates upon another ear. Human communication, as the saying goes, is a clash of symbols; and it covers a multitude of signs" (*Ibid.*). Almost everything said above is included tacitly in such brief and formal definitions as "the interchange of information by any means" (*The American Heritage Dictionary*) or "the exchange of meanings between individuals through a common system of symbols" (*The Encyclopedia Britannica*).

34. Kusum Singh and G. Gross, "Alternative Communication Strategies in Third World Countries," *Economic and Political Weekly* (Bombay, February 21, 1981).

23

Research Network on the Churches' Role in Peace and Development Project Outline

Roger Williamson

Overall Conception

The Life and Peace Institute, the Christian Peace Research Institute based in Uppsala, Sweden has launched a Research Network on the Churches' Role in Peace and Development. The work is an attempt to deepen and intensify the work already being done by churches on these issues. In this regard, analysis and worldwide networking are a priority. At the international level, the churches can be considered as an NGO network of a relatively high degree of organisation. The network proposed by the Life & Peace Institute should be seen as a contribution to the need for networking and research around issues of disarmament and development. Charles Elliott has focussed this issue in a hard-hitting way by saying that we cannot "continue to act as though the poverty of nearly a billion people can be eliminated by aided projects."[1]

In particular, three current worldwide emphases could be mentioned to which this project would make a significant contribution:

The United Nations' Work on Disarmament and Development
The final document from the recent UN Conference, including the Programme of Action, stressed the importance of the work of NGOs on these issues.[2] In a passage quoted by Inga Thorsson, Professor Bjorn Hettne writes:

> The conventional pattern of development ("growth and modernisation") actually seems to create internal and external conflicts that breed the arms race but ... there may be (an)other, more "peace intensive" development option ("another development") with a con-

trary effect. If this is correct, then the causational chain between disarmament and development must be reversed. Rather than conceiving disarmament as a condition for development, one could argue that development--development of a certain kind--is a condition for disarmament.[3]

The World Council of Churches' Conciliar Process on Justice, Peace and the Integrity of Creation

This council is seeking to make churches more aware of the links between economic injustice, threats to peace and the destruction of the environment. As early as its 1975 Nairobi Assembly, the World Council of Churches had given this committed definition of development:

> The development process should be understood as a liberating process aimed at justice, self-reliance and economic growth. It is essentially a people's struggle in which the poor and the oppressed are, and should be, the active agents and immediate beneficiaries.

The World Council of Churches' Emphasis on Ecumenical Sharing of Resources

This proposed network, if adequately funded, promises to channel additional resources for research to Institutes in countries of the South. The network has the following main elements:

1. *Network Meetings.* This involves formation of a core group of one representative per Institute. The group will meet at least once per year. Representation will consist mainly of Institutes from the South.
2. *Analysis and Publications.* The Institutes, through consultation in the network meetings, will provide studies on the churches' contribution to peace and development. Together, the Institutes will decide on a joint agenda for the network and assess the studies produced. It will be the network itself which decides the precise priority of research areas and determines which studies should be published.
3. *Documentation: Collection and Exchange.* The partners in the network are to be organisations involved in research and the development of the research infrastructure of their respective countries. An important element of the project will, therefore, be collection and exchange of documentation. Research bodies in North and South often lack full documentation of the areas they are studying. Institutes in the South may, for example, not have access to all the U.S. and European materi-

al and Institutes in the North may not have direct access to material produced in the South. The network will thus be a mechanism for developing the library and documentation base of each participating Institute. The focus will be on relevant material concerning the churches' role in peace and development, thereby covering economic, social, political and theological analyses.

4. *A Note on the Process.* This project outline was understood as a point of departure for discussion--not binding in any way to the organisations and persons mentioned, unless and until they committed themselves to the process. On the other hand, full consultation and face-to-face discussion of priorities could only occur once the first network meeting was agreed and funded--otherwise, at the most basic level, there would have been no way of discussing together the viability and correct emphases of the project. The approach to funding agencies requires specific proposals. The consultative nature of the process precludes laying down a definite agenda. Institutes and funding agencies must, therefore, both be clear about the nature of the process as one in which the participating agencies decide the priorities and schedule of meetings. As it turned out, partners from the Philippines and Korea who had hoped to attend the meeting were unable to do so.

Areas to Be Covered by Partner Institutes

Central America

The Central American crisis has been taken up as a priority area by the Latin American Council of Churches (CLAI), the World Council of Churches and the churches in the USA. The area shows many dimensions of the problems of militarisation and underdevelopment. The most dramatic illustrations are the situations in El Salvador, Guatemala and Nicaragua.

Guatemala, it has been said, has been turned into a nation of orphans and widows. There has been a huge displacement of population internally.

The situation in *El Salvador* came most dramatically to the world's attention with the murder of Archbishop Romero.

In *Nicaragua*, the civil-war, which finally displaced the Somoza dictatorship, was immensely costly in terms of human life. The country has continued to suffer as a result of the U.S.-backed Contra war.

Latin America: Brazil and the Southern Cone

In Brazil and the Southern Cone of Latin America, the doctrine of the "national security state" was combined with a military-led economic project which combined an allegedly "modernizing" approach with massive human rights violations. With the return to civilian rule in Brazil, Argentina and Uruguay, it seems that a turning point has been reached with respect to civil society, but the massive economic problems remain. In this context, it is of particular importance to receive detailed analysis of church response to these situations.

The Roman Catholic Bishops' Conference in Brazil (CNBB), perhaps more than any other national hierarchy, played an important and courageous role in forming a new pastoral practice to respond to conditions of military rule. Prominent individuals such as Archbishop Helder Camara and Cardinal Paulo Evaristo Arns are widely known. What is less well-known outside the country is the impressive commitment of work by the Brazilian churches in issues as wide-ranging as land-rights, independent trade unions, criticism of the economic approach of the Brazilian military, human rights, including the rights of the indigenous people.

In *Chile*, the Allende experiment was stopped short. The Catholic Church, and to a certain extent non-Catholic Churches, have spoken as advocates of human rights and acted as a "voice for the voiceless" (e.g., the work of the Vicaria de la Solidaridad).

Africa: The Front-Line States

The focus for Africa will be put on the *Front-Line States of Southern Africa*. The recent February 1988 Conference on Co-operation between SADCC Member States and the Nordic Countries, Granavolden, Norway, February 4th-7th made the following commitment:

> "The Nordic churches and their institutions will develop a partnership with the Ecumenical Documentation and Information Centre for Eastern and Southern Africa (EDICESA) and use their documentation material."

The Life & Peace Institute, whilst strictly speaking not a Nordic church institution, fully supports this resolution and welcomes the initiative taken by National Councils of Churches in Southern and Eastern Africa to establish EDICESA, as an ecumenical documentation and information centre. In the brochure introducing its work, the following is the first point under the heading "EDICESA Functions:"

"Collect, catalogue and store publications from countries in Eastern and Southern Africa which document South Africa's policies of destabilisation of the region."

The Front Line States are chosen as the priority emphasis for many reasons. In particular, the All Africa Conference of Churches sees this as a priority region. The Granavolden Conference stated:

"The churches' rejection of apartheid requires dedication
- to the liberation of South Africa
- to the independence of Namibia
- to an end to the apartheid-backed war in Angola and Mozambique
- to an end to the aggression against the Front Line States."

As EDICESA is primarily a documentation centre, it was suggested that research capacity should be sought through the University of Zimbabwe.

Asia

In Asia, two nations where the churches have been active in the struggle for human rights and democratisation have been chosen: South Korea and the Philippines. The Philippines was, for the long years of the Marcos dictatorship, a country where the churches were deeply involved in the struggle for justice and peace. The assessment of church activity in that period and the churches evaluation of the extent to which the hopes placed in the Aquino government have been fulfilled, makes the basis for an important case study. The role of the military in Philippine society, the economic development (or lack of it), the U.S. presence, the issue of full respect for human rights and "low intensity conflict" are all dimensions requiring further analysis.

In Korea, the combination of "economic miracle" and human rights violations has confronted the churches with a challenge. Democratization, the division of the country and human rights work have been the themes for ecumenical Christianity. Here, too, the strategic dimensions of superpower diplomacy play an important role. A Korean partner therefore is of great value.

The North

In addition to the national case studies, it is important to stress the North-South dimensions of the issues of armaments and injustice. Appropriate ways must be found of studying the role of the churches in the rich North in relation to the world economic and military systems.

Steps Taken

Planning Meeting, Uppsala, April 15th, 1988

In connection with the Board meeting of the Life & Peace Institute, a planning meeting was held, involving Board members and invited consultants. Professor Peter Wallensteen, Professor of Peace and Conflict Research, Uppsala, and Dr. Kaire Mbuenda (Namibia--currently Institute for Future Studies, Stockhom) agreed to act as consultants on that occasion.

First Network Meeting and Input to the International Peace Research
Association General Conference, (Rio, August, 1988)

The research institute IBASE was approached (a) with a view to participation in the network and (b) also for advice on the possibility of holding the first network meeting in Rio de Janeiro in connection with the Conference of the International Peace Research Association in August 1988.

This enabled participants in the first network meeting to attend the IPRA Conference, thereby further strengthening Third World representation in that body. It also proved possible to present the thinking behind the network during the IPRA meeting. It was agreed, prior to the IPRA meeting, that the network would be of interest to IPRA as an example of research on NGO activity for peace and justice on a world-wide basis. It was on that basis that the Life and Peace Institute was invited to conduct an informal meeting during the IPRA Conference.

Second Network Meeting 1989

The second network meeting was held and the third will be held at the IPRA conference in Groningen, Netherlands, July 3-7, 1990.

Peace and Development:
A Theory of Church Action Against Militarism and Poverty

Table 1 has been formulated as an initial attempt to conceptualize the relationship between different elements of church work for peace and development.

The churches, both as bodies within their national setting and as an international NGO network, influence, and are influenced by their socio-political environment. Beginning in the top left of the diagram, three overlapping boxes are seen. These represent the world military order, the world economic order and the church as an international network within the international system.

Interpretations of the world economic system can be divided simply into two "families" of models: the "growth" models and the "dependency" models. The former tend to stress the need to overcome certain obstacles to growth, often endogenous or internal factors. The dependency models, on the other hand, stress that poverty is a condition created by unequal exchange relationships with more powerful partners. Poverty is thus a result of dependency. According to such analytical accounts, countries are underdeveloped as an active process, not as an accident and they are then kept underdeveloped.

In the overlapping box *world military order*, there have broadly been two schools of thought on the role of the military in Third World development. There are those who see the military as a modernizing institution and those who argue the opposite case--namely that the military are the beneficiaries of, and the defenders of, an unjust status quo.

This project will give more information on the way in which the churches have responded to the place assigned to various countries within the economic and military pecking order, the rationalisations for this "division of labour" and most importantly, how the churches have reacted in their own domestic context to the military and economic profile of their nation. The emphasis will be on costs and benefits--the critical question being who benefits from the military and economic distribution of power and resources, and at whose expense do they benefit?

To a certain extent, in situations of economic underdevelopment, the church policy-makers face similar choices to those faced by representatives of other social institutions, universities, trade unions, political parties, the press. Broadly speaking, they can (a) act in a *conformist* way, without challenging the system; (b) act as an interest group, trying to protect their own social institution, position, staff, members and buildings; or (c) they can engage in risky and potentially costly acts of *solidarity* by challenging government. At the international level, since the churches are in an international network, they will look for support from partners in the choices which they make. Moving to the *top right* in the diagram, we can see that the world's churches have different, even competing, understandings of their role in national and international society. Depending upon the choices made, the partners adopted and the social projects embraced, the churches have different kinds of implicit theologies. It is now time to make this more explicit. Theology will be understood as the theory of church action. It is a systematic explanation and legitimation of the relationship between church and world, explaining why the churches have chosen to act as they do. To quote (a slightly expanded version) from the diagram:

> "An adequate *theory/theology of church action* will involve a systematic explanation of the relation between the world as perceived and the sources of theory (e.g., the Bible, tradition). It must explain church

response at the national level and at the international level to the world military order, to the world economic order both as systems and in their local form. The theory must take note of the churches both as 'acted upon' by society and as 'acting on/within' society. The churches need to survive and they claim to act for others. They can be rendered ineffective by destruction or irrelevance."

Notes

1. C. Elliott, *Comfortable Compassion: Poverty, Power and the Church* (London: Hodder and Stoughton, 1987) p. 179.

2. *International Conference on the Relationship between Disarmament and Development* (New York: Document A/Conf., 24 August-11 September 1987), 130/21.

3. Bjorn Hettne, *Approaches to the Study of Peace and Development,* quoted in I. Thorsson, "Overview of Events in the Disarmament Development Relationship Field Since 1981," UN General Assembly Paper A/Conf. 130/pc/INF/9, March 1986, p. 12. also, Bjorn Hettne, *Development Theory and the Third World,* SAREC Report R 2: Stockholm, Swedish Agency for Research Cooperation with Developing Countries, 1982.

4. The following books are cited in the longer document from which this Introduction to the Research Network is taken:

Richard Barnet, *The Lean Years* (New York: Simon & Schuster, 1980).

A.M.N. Hoogvelt, *The Third World in Global Development* (London: Macmillan, 1982).

E. Dussel, "Church-State Relations in Peripheral Latin American Societies" (in World Council of Churches, eds.), *Church & State*, WEC, Geneva, 1978, pp 62-74).

J. Pearce, *Under the Eagle: U.S. Intervention in Central America and the Caribbean* (London: Latin American Bureau, 1981).

W. Rodney, *How Europe Underdeveloped Africa* (Dar-es-Salamm: Bogle-L'ouverture Publications, London & Tanzania Publishing House, 1973).

O. Romero, *Romero: Martyr for Liberation* (London: Catholic Institute for International Relations, CIIR, 1982).

302

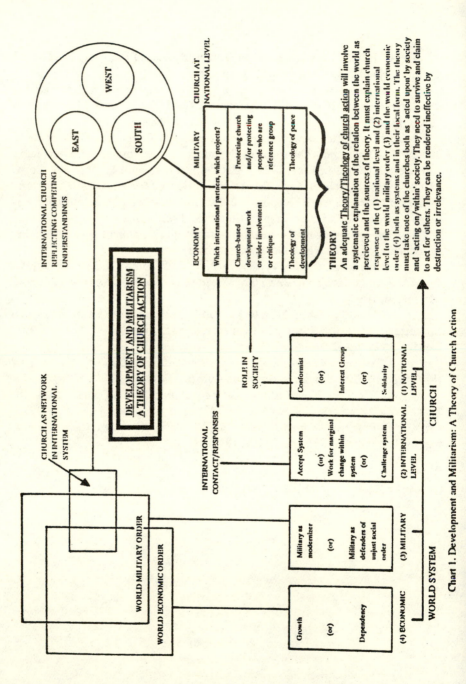

Chart 1. Development and Militarism: A Theory of Church Action

INTERNATIONAL CHURCH REFLECTING COMPETING UNDERSTANDINGS

WEST

EAST

SOUTH

CHURCH AS NETWORK IN INTERNATIONAL SYSTEM

DEVELOPMENT AND MILITARISM
A THEORY OF CHURCH ACTION

CHURCH AT NATIONAL LEVEL

ECONOMY	MILITARY
Which international partners, which projects?	Protecting church and/or protecting people who are reference group
Church-based development work or wider involvement or critique	
Theology of development	Theology of peace

THEORY

An adequate Theory/Theology of church action will involve a systematic explanation of the relation between the world as perceived and the sources of theory. It must explain church response at the (1) national level and (2) international level to the world military order (3) and the world economic order (4) both as systems and in their local form. The theory must take note of the churches both as 'acted upon' by society and 'acting on/within' society. They need to survive and claim to act for others. They can be rendered ineffective by destruction or irrelevance.

ROLE IN SOCIETY

Conformist

(or)

Interest Group

(or)

Solidarity

INTERNATIONAL CONTACT/RESPONSES

Accept System

(or)

Work for marginal change within system

(or)

Challenge system

(2) INTERNATIONAL LEVEL

(1) NATIONAL LEVEL

CHURCH

WORLD MILITARY ORDER

WORLD ECONOMIC ORDER

Military as modernizer

(or)

Military as defenders of unjust social order

(3) MILITARY

Growth

(or)

Dependency

(4) ECONOMIC

WORLD SYSTEM

Appendix on the International Peace Research Association

List of Study Groups represented as Commissions at the XII Conference of the International Peace Research Association held in Rio de Janeiro, Brazil, 14-19 August 1988:

- Peace Education Commission (PEC)
- Communications
- Women, Militarization & Disarmament
- Nonviolence
- Peace Movements
- Weapons Technology & Disarmament
- Human Rights and Development

New Study Groups Formed at Rio:

- Internal Conflict
- International Conflict Resolution
- Ecological Security
- Religion and Conflict.

Current IPRA Study Groups and their Conveners, as of September, 1990:

- Communications: Omar Souki Oliveira
- Ecological Security: Clovis Brigagao and Maurico Andres Ribeiro
- Human Rights & Development: Michael Stohl
- Internal Conflicts & Their Resolution: Kumar Rupesinghe
- International Conflict Resolution: Louis Kriesberg and K. Matthews
- Nonviolence: Glenn Paige and Chaiwat Satha-Anand
- Peace Movements: Katsuya Kodama
- Religion & Conflict: Roger Williamson
- Defense & Disarmament: Hans Gunter Brauch
- Women & Peace: Maria Elena Valenzuela
- Peace Education Commission (PEC): Ake Bjerstedt

About the Editors and Contributors

Chadwick F. Alger is Mershon Professor of Political Science and Public Policy, Ohio State University, Columbus, Ohio. He has published widely on decision-making, communication and socialization in the United Nations and on the participation of local people in world affairs. He is past president of the International Studies Association (1978-79) and former Secretary General of the International Peace Research Association (1982-86).

Vicenc Fisas Armengol is associated with the Centro de Investigacion Para la Paz, Centro UNESCO de Catalunya Barcelona. Spain. He writes on democracy and defense, the militarization of science, and has most recently published a book on non-offensive defense for Spain in 2001.

Elise Boulding, current Secretary General of IPRA, is Professor Emerita of Sociology, Dartmouth College. A futurist, she writes on local-global peace-building, development, family life and women. A founding member of IPRA, she served on the Commission to recommend the establishment of the U.S. Institute of Peace, has been a member of the UN University Council (1980-85) and served on the UNESCO Peace Prize jury (1982-87).

Kenneth E. Boulding is Distinguished Professor Emeritus of Economics, University of Colorado and Project Director at the Institute of Behavioral Science. The author of leading books in the field of peace research who also writes widely in the social sciences, he is past president of the International Studies Association, the American Economic Association and the American Association for the Advancement of Science. He was one of the founders of the *Journal of Conflict Resolution* and of the Center for Conflict Resolution at the University of Michigan.

Lothar Brock is Professor of Political Science and International Relations at the Johann Wolfgang Goethe University, Frankfurt am Main, and senior fellow of the Frankfurt Peace Research Institute. A former member of the IPRA Council, he writes on security, development and ecology.

Birgit Brock-Utne is a Norwegian social scientist with a doctorate in peace studies, on leave from a tenured position at the University of Oslo to hold a professorship at the University of Dar es Salaam, Tanzania. She is internationally best known for her analysis of peace studies from a feminist perspective. Her most recent book is *Feminist Perspectives on Peace and Peace Education* (1989).

Clovis Brigagao, a political scientist, is currently Chief of Cabinet of the State Government of Rio de Janeiro. He was Secretary General of IPRA during 1986-88, and is also a research associate at the University of Brasilia and on the Advisory Board of the Commission Sudamericana de Paz, Santiago. He has written in the fields of international relations, peace studies and ecology, and is the founder of IPRA's Study Group on Ecological Security.

Ranjit Chaudhuri is a Director of the Institute for Development of Educational Alternatives in Calcutta, India. He has studied conflict and the development of democratic process in rural India among caste, tribal and political groups.

Kevin Clements is Senior Lecturer in sociology, University of Canterbury, Christchurch, New Zealand. He writes on development, defense and security issues, and the problems of multilateral disarmament. He is the new Secretary General of the Asian Peace Research Association as of fall, 1990, and will be one of the organizers of the second Pugwash Symposium on Peace and Security in the Asia-Pacific Region in 1991.

Adolfo Perez Esquivel was the recipient of the 1980 Nobel Prize for Peace for his work to promote human rights through nonviolent action in Latin America. A sculptor and teacher by profession, he was born in Buenos Aires, Argentina in 1931. He is one of the founders of the Peace and Justice Service in Latin America. He presently serves as honorary president of both the Service's Latin American Coordination and its Argentine section. He is also president of the International League for the Rights and Liberation of the Peoples.

Ian M. Harris is chair of the Department of Educational Policy and Community Studies at the University of Wisconsin-Milwaukee. He serves as co-chair of the University Peace Studies Section of the Consortium on Peace Research Education and Development (COPRED). Writing on peace, community development and changing men's roles, he is the author of *Peace Education and Experiential Education for Community Development.*

Katsuya Kodama, born in Hiroshima, studied peace movements in Sweden as a guest researcher at Lund University Peace Research Institute from 1984 to 1990. He is currently lecturer in Sociology at Mie University, Japan, and convener of the IPRA Study Group on Peace Movements. The author of *Life Histories of Atomic Bomb Orphans* (in Japanese), he has edited two books on the comparative analysis and future of peace movements in 1989 and 1990.

Patricia M. Mische, co-founder of Global Education Associates and co-editor of its journal, *Breakthrough*, has worked with teachers and community development activists in all parts of the world. An initiator and coordinator of the transnational Earth Covenant Project (A Citizen's Treaty for Ecological Security), she writes on peace education, nonviolent approaches to international security and the care of the earth.

Peter Bushel Okoh is Executive Director of the African Peace Research Institute, Lagos, Nigeria, and editor of the Institutes's Newsletter on African Peace Research. A former research fellow at the Nigerian Institute of International Affairs, Dr. Okoh is the author of *Nature and Character of Contemporary International Conflicts.*

Sanaa Osseiran, born in Lebanon, was trained in Psychology, Middle East History and Politics. A free-lance journalist with Lebanese and Arab organizations, she has worked with the *Journal of Palestinian Studies* in recent years. IPRA's representative to UNESCO in Paris, she has organized joint IPRA-UNESCO workshops on peace-building in Lebanon, and directs the IPRA World Cultural Development Decade Project on Cultural Symbiosis in Andalusia.

Peri Pamir, originally from Turkey, has a Ph.D. from the University of Geneva and degrees from the universities of Chicago and London. From 1983 to 1988 she worked as Assistant to the Secretary General of Pugwash in Geneva, and spent the academic year, 1989-90, as a Visiting Fellow at the Center of International Studies, Princeton University.

Dion Phillips is Professor of Sociology, University of Virgin Islands, St. Thomas, U.S. Virgin Islands. He is an active member of CLAIP, the Latin American Peace Research Association, and has recently formed a task force on Peace and Security for the interdisciplinary Caribbean Studies Association.

Chaiwat Satha-Anand, Associate Professor of Political Science at Thammasat University, Bangkok, Thailand, is a founder and an executive of the Peace Information Center at the Faculty of Political Science in the University. A co-convener of IPRA's Study Group on Nonviolence and an IPRA Council member, his teaching and research are in the fields of nonviolence, comparative religious studies and political leadership. He was convener of the first and second ASEAN forum for Muslim Social Scientists in 1987 and 1988. His publications appear both in English and Thai; his most recent book is entitled, *Challenging Alternatives: Violence and Nonviolence.*

Kusum Singh is Professor in the Department of Communications of Saint Mary's College of California. The author of many articles and active in the International Communications Association, she is now working on a book on Gandhi, *Message to a Violent World: Mass Communication Without Mass Media.*

Georg Sorensen is Associate Professor of International Politics, Institute of Political Science, University of Aarhus, Denmark. He writes on international development issues. His most recent book is *Democracy, Dictatorship and Development: Economic Development in Selected Regimes of the Third World* (1990).

Amechi Uchegbu is Associate Professor of International Law and head of the Faculty of Law, University of Lagos, Nigeria. His Doctorate is from the University of London (1971), and he taught International Las at the Institute of International Relations of the University of West Indies in Trinidad (1972-75) before returning to Nigeria. He has published several articles on human rights in peace and war.

Maria Elena Valenzuela, a Chilean sociologist, has focused her research on women, peace and democracy in Latin America. She is a member of the Women's Ministry created after the return to democracy in Chile. A co-founder of the Chilean Peace Research Association, she is the coordinator of IPRA's Women and Militarization Study Group, now renamed the Women and Peace Study Group.

Alfredo Wagner Berno de Almeida is an anthropologist who has been doing field work on land conflicts with Indians and peasants in Brazil's Amazon Region since 1972. He organized the Land Conflicts Office in the Ministry of Agricultural Reform during the democratic land reform period, 1985-86, at the end of the military regime. He is currently (1990) working as a professional anthropological consultant for a Tribune supported by the Lelio Basso International Foundation for the Rights and Liberation of Peoples that will judge the murder/assassination of the peasants and Indians in Amazonia.

Roger Williamson is Research Director of the Life and Peace Institute of Uppsala, Sweden, from a London base. Founder-convener of the IPRA Religion and Conflict Study Group, he is actively involved in IPRA, the Conference of European Churches and the World Council of Churches, and the academic and ecumenical networks of these organizations. His publications are mainly on church involvement in the search for peace and justice.